D1566607

Risk and Return
in Finance

Volume I

Risk and Return in Finance

in Finance

Volume I

Edited by

Irwin Friend
University of Pennsylvania

James L. Bicksler
Rutgers University

Ballinger Publishing Company • Cambridge, Massachusetts
A Subsidiary of J.B. Lippincott Company

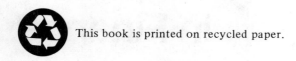

This book is printed on recycled paper.

International Standard Book Number: 0-88410-653-5-Vol. 1
0-88410-652-7-Vol. 2

Library of Congress Catalog Card Number: 76-44240

Printed in the United States of America

Library of Congress Cataloging in Publication Data

Main entry under title:

Risk and return in finance.

"Thirteen of the seventeen papers in these two volumes were originally presented at a Conference on Risk and the Rate of Return sponsored by the American Telephone and Telegraph Company and held in Vail, Colorado, during August 5-10, 1973."

Includes bibliographical references.

1. Investments—Addresses, essays, lectures. 2. Capital assets pricing model—Addresses, essays, lectures. 3. Risk—Addresses, essays, lectures. I. Friend, Irwin. II. Bicksler, James L. III. Conference on Risk and the Rate of Return, Vail, Colo., 1973. IV. American Telephone and Telegraph Company.

HG4539.R57   332.6'7   76-44240
ISBN 0-88410-653-5-Vol. 1
    0-88410-652-7-Vol. 2

Contents — Volume I

Introduction

Irwin Friend

Thirteen of the seventeen papers in these two volumes were originally presented at a Conference on Risk and the Rate of Return sponsored by the American Telephone and Telegraph Company and held in Vail, Colorado during August 5-10, 1973. The reason for the delay in publication of these papers is that several have been substantially revised in the intervening period. Eight of these papers have already been published in the academic journals,[1] but nine have not yet appeared elsewhere.

Of the four papers which were not initially presented at the Vail Conference, one by Yoram Landskroner, "The Determination of the Market Price of Risk in the Absence of a Riskless Asset," is a generalization of the Friend-Blume paper on "The Demand for Risky Assets." A second and seminal paper not presented at Vail, Robert C. Merton's "An Intertemporal Capital Asset Pricing Model," has been added as background for his Vail paper, "A Reexamination of the Capital Asset Pricing Model." A third paper by Eugene Fama and James D. Macbeth, "Tests of the Multiperiod Two-Parameter Model," has been substituted for Fama's "Short-Term Interest Rates as Predictors of Inflation" because the former is considered more relevant to the theme of the Conference and to the other papers in these volumes, including in particular the Merton contributions.

The main theme covered in these two volumes is capital asset pricing under uncertainty. Rather than discuss the contributions made by the individual papers, it may be more useful in view of the lapse of time since a number of them were written to comment briefly on the present state of the arts in this field.

There have been few if any areas of finance which have received more theoretical and empirical attention in recent years than that of capital asset pricing. The original Sharpe-Lintner market-line theory advanced to explain the variations in risk differentials on different risky assets has now been widely questioned on the basis of the empirical evidence, and a large number of modified theories have been proposed to explain the observed discrepancies between theory and observation.

The evidence points to a reasonably linear relationship on the average between return and non-diversifiable risk of outstanding common stock, or at least those listed on the New York and American Stock Exchanges. However, this same return-risk linear relationship does not explain the return consistent with any reasonable measure of the actual risk-free rates of return. Actually, there is evidence both for bonds and stocks that for very risky issues in each category, e.g., unseasoned new stock issues and bonds rated below BB, the realized returns over extended periods of time have been lower than those on less risky issues.

Moreover, while over the long run the observed linear relationship between return and risk on individual stocks yields the expected positive sign of the risk coefficient more often than not, the shorter-term relationship has been erratic and has not been explained satisfactorily by the observed difference between the market rate of return on stocks as a whole and the risk-free rate. Thus, this relationship between return and risk was negligible in 1955-59 and negative in 1960-64,[2] though in both periods the stock market was moderately strong. As a result of these and similar findings, questions have been raised about the nature of the relationship between expected and actual rates of return, i.e., about the return generating model, as well as about the theory relating expected return to risk.

It may be useful to catalogue briefly a number of the theoretical and empirical attempts made to explain the observed deficiencies in the original market-line theory, including three advanced during the past year. Very early in the game, several attempts were made to test the hypothesis that the required rate of return on a risky asset depends in part on the skewness in its probability distribution, with investors preferring positive skewness. In a more innovative approach, Black and others assumed either that there is no risk-free rate, or there is no risk-free borrowing rate or the risk-free lending rate is less than the borrowing rate, though at the same time the short-selling mechanism for risky assets functions perfectly. This modification of the traditional model as well as the development of an arbitrage model led to the introduction of a minimum-variance zero-covariance or zero-beta asset to replace or supplement the risk-free rate. It was further pointed out by a number of analysts, including Jensen and Levy and Levhari, that theory did not specify the relevant investor's planning horizon and that the empirical results would reflect differences between the assumed and the true holding period. To allow for the inadequacies of a one-period model in a multi-period world, Merton introduced a third asset, in addition to the risk-free asset and the market portfolio, which would provide protection against changes in the opportunity set. Other analysts including Fama and MacBeth tested the usefulness of adding the square of the beta coefficient and the residual standard deviation of returns in explaining the differential returns on individual assets. Mayers described how the original theory which assumed all assets to be marketable was affected by the introduction of non-marketable assets, most notably human wealth. Segmented markets, inadequacies of the return generating model, heterogeneous expectations, differential taxes on different assets, transaction costs, and non-pecuniary liquidity returns on risk-free assets are some of the other suggestions which have been proposed for at least partial explanations of the observed discrepancies between theory and observation. At the statistical level, the inadequacy of a stock market index as a measure of the return on all risky assets has been repeatedly stressed.

Since all of this work is relatively well-known and is in general readily available in the published literature, I will not describe it further. However, I want to emphasize that none of the theoretical modifications seems strongly supported by the data once it is maintained that a capital asset pricing theory should as a minimum be able to explain the returns on all marketable assets and not just a selected though important subset, listed common stock. Moreover, even for this subset, it has not been possible to distinguish among a number of alternative explanations of the approximate linearity of the risk-return trade-off for listed stocks once the intercept is no longer required to be the risk-free rate or some other theoretically determined value which can be checked directly against the empirical evidence.[3]

Though of some interest, three new attempts to explain both theoretically and empirically the rates of return on risky assets, the first two of which will be published in forthcoming issues of *The Journal of Finance*, also are far from convincing. The first, by Kraus and Litzenberger,[4] introduces a measure of co-skewness in addition to the beta measure of covariance in the original capital asset pricing model, but co-skewness does not add much to the explanation and it is not possible to differentiate between the utility of this variable versus other supplementary variables which have been proposed. More important, co-skewness would not appear to explain the lower rates of return on bonds than on stocks for comparable beta values. A second paper by two colleagues and myself introduces uncertain inflation into the original capital asset pricing model, but while unlike the case for co-skewness there is little danger that the two relevant inflation covariances are acting as proxies for other variables, the additional explanatory power of the modified theory seems rather limited.[5] A third unpublished paper by Blume[6] shows that the inability to engage in short sales might explain the substantially higher rate of return generally ascribed to a zero-beta asset in empirical analysis, as compared with the observed risk-free rate. However, while this is a promising approach, it has yet to be tested even for stocks to say nothing of bonds.

In addition to these new attempts to modify the capital asset pricing model to bring theory in closer conformity with reality, recent analyses by Blume and myself of two different bodies of data than the market information usually used for this purpose raise some fundamental questions about the usefulness of any theory which assumes that only covariance risk is relevant to investors. Thus, in a recent published analysis of the stock portfolios as well as the major classes of assets and liabilities held by different individuals,[7] it was found that portfolios and assets were highly undiversified, and it was concluded from an examination of the other alternatives that the two most plausible explanations are either, first, that investors hold heterogeneous expectations as to expected return and risk or, second, that they do not properly aggregate risks of individual assets to measure the risk of an entire portfolio. Both of these explanations conflict with important assumptions typically made in capital asset theory, but the second is obviously basic since it raises questions about the justification for sole reliance on beta or covariance with the market return rather than variance (or standard deviation) of the asset's own returns as a measure of asset risk.

The second new source of data pertaining to the relative importance of covariance versus variance risk is a survey of over 1000 stockholders in the fall of 1975 which was conducted as part of a study by Blume and myself of the changing role of individual investors in the stock market. This survey collected information on the market motivation, behavior, experience and plans of these investors, including data on the stockholders' perceptions of and attitudes towards risk and on the expected rate of return required on common stock as compared with other investments. The final analysis of these data will not be available for some months, but several preliminary results are of interest. When stockholding families were asked which measures of risk they used in their evaluation of stocks, 45% stated they used earnings volatility, 30% price volatility and 17% published betas. When asked whether they would prefer to purchase a stock whose price tends to move in the opposite direction to the stock market as a whole, or one which tends to move in the same direction, less than 10% stated they preferred the opposite direction. It will be necessary to follow up this question with in-depth interviews to ensure that the expected rate of return is kept constant before reaching more definitive conclusions. Moreover, there is reason to believe that financial institutions, the other major group in the stock market, may use beta coefficients to a greater extent than individual investors. On the other hand, I know of no direct evidence supporting the almost universal academic conclusion, based on normative models and not too impressive empirical tests, that beta is the only relevant measure of market risk.

It seems to me that apart from the segmentation assumption, which most economists would like to use only as a last resort, the most plausible explanation of the differences in return between fixed-interest-bearing obligations and stocks, which have not yet been satisfactorily explained by differences in betas, are the differences in the volatility or standard deviation of returns. The important point here, however, is that we seem to need a fresh start and perhaps a new methodology in testing capital asset pricing theory against the observed facts. One such approach is the use of survey information, which may make possible faster progress in understanding investors' behavior and expectations, whether it be reaction to risk or the expected rate and subjective probability distribution of returns which we now attempt to assess from *ex post* data.

Before concluding this summary discussion of capital asset pricing, I should like to point out that in a paper in this volume, "The Demand for Risky Assets," which was also published in the December, 1975 *American Economic Review*, Blume and I have attempted to help fill in a gap in research in capital asset pricing—i.e., the paucity of empirical work on the determinants of the market price of risk in contrast to the plethora of work on the interrelationships of the risk premiums among different risky assets. In that paper, on the basis of both detailed micro-data on the composition of household wealth and macro-market data on returns, we developed what we consider fairly convincing evidence that the assumption of constant proportional risk aversion is a reasonably good approximation of the market place and that the coefficient of risk aversion is on average well in excess of one and probably in excess of two.[8] If these results are correct, and I have as yet seen no convincing evidence to the contrary, the question may be raised whether the continued expenditure of substantial intellectual and material resources on analyses which predicate quadratic, exponential, logarithmic or generalized logarithmic utility functions can be justified.

I am not arguing, of course, against the usefulness of theoretical analyses which explain the relevant economic properties of different utility functions, as exemplified by the well-known Cass-Stiglitz paper which developed the types of utility functions for which the separation theorem is valid. A more recent but as yet unpublished paper by Ross[9] addresses the other side of this coin, viz., the types of stochastic distributions of asset returns which would also imply the validity of the separation theorem. This type of theoretical analysis is highly useful, but once there is strong evidence on the type of utility function or return distribution which characterizes the market place, it seems to me that subsequent analysis is likely to be more productive when it assumes the validity of the indicated function or distribution.

NOTES

1. Marshall E. Blume and Irwin Friend, "Risk, Investment Strategy and the Long-Run Rates of Return," *The Review of Economics and Statistics*, August 1974; Marshall E. Blume, "Betas and Their Regression Tendencies," *The Journal of Finance*, June 1975; Irwin Friend and Marshall E. Blume, "The Demand for Risky Assets," *The American Economic Review*, December 1975; Robert C. Merton, "An Intertemporal Capital Asset Pricing Model," *Econometrica*, September 1973; Robert C. Merton and Paul A. Samuelson, "Fallacy of the Log-Normal Approximation to Optimal Portfolio Decision-Making Over Many Periods," *Journal of Financial Economics*, May 1974; Nils H. Hakansson, "Comment on Merton and Samuelson," *Journal of Financial Economics*, May 1974; Marcus C. Bogue and Richard Roll, "Capital Budgeting of Risky Projects with 'Imperfect' Markets for Physical Capital," *The Journal of Finance*, May 1974; and Eugene F. Fama and James D. MacBeth, "Tests of the Multiperiod Two-Parameter Model," *Journal of Financial Economics*, May 1974.

2. Marshall Blume and Irwin Friend, "A New Look at the Capital Asset Pricing Model," *The Journal of Finance*, March 1973.

3. The basic difficulty in testing two-factor linear models of asset returns is indicated in Stephen A. Ross, "Return, Risk and Arbitrage," in this volume, and more recently in an unpublished paper by Richard Roll, "Can Two-Factor Linear Models of Asset Returns be Tested?" European Institute for Advanced Studies in Management Working Paper No. 75-30.

4. Alan Kraus and Robert H. Litzenberger, "Skewness Preference and the Valuation of Risk Assets," Mimeo, May 1975.

5. Irwin Friend, Yoram Landskroner and Etienne Losq, "The Demand for Risky Assets Under Uncertain Inflation," Rodney L. White Center for Financial Research Working Paper No. 6-75a.

6. Marshall E. Blume, "Equilibrium in the Capital Markets in the Absence of Short Position," European Institute for Advanced Studies in Management Working Paper No. 76-22.

7. Marshall E. Blume and Irwin Friend, "The Asset Structure of Individual Portfolios and Some Implications for Utility Functions," *The Journal of Finance, May 1975.*

8. A change in this conclusion would require the questionable assumption that investors regard owned homes as riskless assets, in which case it would have to be concluded that investors are characterized by moderately decreasing proportional risk aversion.

9. Stephen A. Ross, "Mutual Fund Separation in Financial Theory—The Separating Distributions," Rodney L. White Center for Financial Research Working Paper No. 1-76.

Section One

Risk, Investment Strategy and the Long-Run Rates of Return

Marshall E. Blume and Irwin Friend*

1.1 INTRODUCTION

Are long-run expected rates of return for investors who take greater risks higher than for those who don't? Are investors who hold diversified portfolios of greater risk necessarily better off in the long run? What effect do different investment strategies have upon expected returns? How do objective and subjective measures of risk compare in their ability to distinguish the underlying risks of different stocks? These and other neglected questions are the subject of this chapter.

This study begins by pointing out the need for an empirical study of the relationship of long-run expected rates of return to risk despite the existence of numerous studies of short-run expected rates.[1] In response to this need, the succeeding sections examine long-run rates of return and reach the following conclusions:

1. Expected five-year rates of return are likely to be an increasing function of risk, where risk is estimated by standard a priori measures. Nonetheless, these expected returns do not appear to increase as fast as they should with risk if the capital asset pricing model held exactly in the short run.

2. Quality ratings have an edge over betas as normally computed in measuring risk for New York Stock Exchange stocks of smaller market values, while the reverse to a lesser extent occurs for the larger issues.

*The authors wish to thank the Rodney L. White Center for Financial Research of the Wharton School and the National Science Foundation for financial support.

3. Although, over a long period, average five-year rates of returns realized by rebalancing tended to be only moderately higher than those for buy-and-hold strategies, the differences in any five-year period, while possibly not statistically significant at the five percent level, are frequently of sufficient size to be of major importance to an investor.

4. Similarly, although over a long period, average five-year returns of small issues tend to be only moderately higher than those for large issues of the same risk, the differences in any five-year period may be substantial.

5. There is no necessary euphoria in investing in high-risk stocks over the long run even though they may have higher expected rates of return. From 1928 through 1968, high-risk stocks for the market as a whole tended to yield less than low-risk stocks. In other words, there is no guarantee that high-risk stocks will yield bigger returns in any single period—no matter how long—even though their expected returns may be greater.

Under certain conditions, the results of the numerous studies of expected short-run rates of return can be used to infer the long-run relationship. The next section points out that these conditions are not met precisely, so that there is need for a direct examination of long-run rates of return. This examination begins with Section 1.3.

1.2 THE IMPLICATIONS OF SHORT-RUN STUDIES FOR THE LONG RUN

Studies of the relationship of expected short-run rates of returns on common stock to risk have generally concluded that over long periods of time this relationship is positive. In booming markets, such as 1965-1968, the relationship between the average monthly rate of return and risk is strongly positive.[2] In only moderately strong markets, the relationship may be negligible (1955-1959) or even negative (1960-1964). In weak markets, the relationship is often negative (1940-1941, 1946-1947, and 1952-1953). Virtually all these recent studies measured risk by the beta coefficient (β).

Besides these general conclusions concerning monotonicity, two studies[3] have concluded that the relationship, at least as a first approximation, can be assumed linear for common stocks.[4] Finally, the short-run returns implied by common stocks for extremely low-risk assets appear inconsistent with the returns for similarly low-risk bonds or risk-free governments, sometimes being higher and sometimes lower but on the average higher over the last forty or so years. At the present time, there is no tested theory which explains these differences.

Under certain conditions, these empirical findings about the short run can be generalized to the long run. For example, if successive monthly returns were stochastically independent of each other and transaction costs zero, the short-run relationship of expected return to risk, as measured by β, would determine the long-run relationship. More precisely, if $E(R)$ is the expected short-run return, measured as one plus the rate of gain, the assumed independence would imply that the expected long-run rate of return, composed of n short-run intervals, will be $[E(R)]^n$.

Now if empirical tests have established with probability, say 0.95, that $E(R)$ is a nonnegative function of β, $[E(R)]^n$ will also be a nonnegative function of β with the same probability. If $E(R) = f(\beta)$, such a short-run empirical finding would take the form $P(f' > 0) > 0.95$. This probability statement that the sign of the first derivative of the short-run relationship is positive implies that the first derivative of the long-run relationship is also positive with the same probability. On the assumption that $E(R)$ is positive, the inequality within this probability statement can be rewritten as $P[n(f)^{n-1}f' > 0] > .95$. The reader will recognize $n(f)^{n-1}f'$ as the derivative of $(f)^n$ which is equal to $[E(R)]^n$, the expected long-run rate of return.

Again assuming independence, the empirical finding that short-run expected rates of return are not only a nonnegative function of beta but also a linear function, say with probability 0.95, would imply that long-run expected rates of return would be a strictly convex function of beta with the same probability. In other words, long-run expected rates of return should increase at a faster rate than beta increases if returns increase with risk and the linearity assumption of the capital asset pricing model holds for short-run returns.[5]

Under the assumptions of independence and no transaction costs, it would be possible to infer the relationship between expected long-run returns and risk from the short-run relationship with the same probability that the short-run relationship is held. Yet these assumptions do not describe the market place exactly, so that there is no guarantee that any inference about long-run relationships from short-run empirical results would be valid.

First of all, the independence assumption, while theoretically appealing, appears valid only as an approximation. A number of earlier studies have found some dependence among successive rates of return, although generally not of sufficient size to use for profit after taking account of transactions costs.[6] An analysis of serial correlation coefficients of individual securities conducted as part of this study again confirms the existence of a statistically significant amount of dependence.[7] Even these small amounts of dependence could invalidate the preceding statistical arguments used in inferring the relationships between expected long-run returns and risk from the short-run relationships.

Second, the more comprehensive studies of the relationship between risk and the short-run rates of return have made no adjustments for commission expenses and taxes. As a result of such costs, the short-run and long-run relationships between risk and return may differ widely depending on the investment strategy followed. Previous studies have typically based their analyses of the short-run relationships on monthly (and sometimes even weekly) data and have implicitly assumed monthly (or weekly) rebalancing of portfolios to maintain the initial weights within each group of securities of homogenous risk. This rebalancing policy would normally require some selling of stocks with the highest rates of return over the month and some buying of those with the lowest returns. Such an investment policy would obviously incur appreciably higher commissions and probably higher tax costs than, for instance, a buy-and-hold policy. In short, the expected rates of return used in almost all short-run studies might not be obtainable.[8]

A third difficulty in generalizing short-run relationships to the long run arises if we are interested in quantifying the long-run tradeoff. Even assuming the independence of short-run returns from period to period, it would be difficult to infer the actual long-run tradeoff without a better understanding of the short-run tradeoffs than current studies have provided. Although as a first approximation short-run expected returns may increase linearly with risk (at least for stocks listed on exchanges), the degree of increase fluctuates in an erratic fashion from period to period and sometimes the tradeoff for common stocks appears inconsistent with returns on low-risk nonequity instruments. Since there is no satisfactory theory as yet to explain these phenomena, the short-run relationships probably have limited value in inferring the explicit form of the long-run relationship.

Finally, the two customary procedures for obtaining empirical estimates of long-run returns from short-run returns—the cumulation of sample arithmetic or geometric mean returns—may yield strongly biased estimates of the expected increase in value. These biases would occur even if it is assumed that the observed short-run returns are independent drawings from any stationary population for which variances are defined.[9] Multiplying the sample arithmetic mean of short-run returns by itself the appropriate number of times yields an upward biased estimate of the expected period return, while the cumulation of the geometric mean of returns yields a downward biased estimate for the usual cases of empirical interest.

1.3 FIVE-YEAR RATES OF RETURN

Covering the period from February 1926 through January 1971 and in more detail the subperiod from July 1928 through June 1968, this chapter presents the average returns for nonoverlapping five-year periods for three different portfolio strategies. For each strategy, returns are reported for up to ten different portfolios spanning the full spectrum of risk. Risk is measured by Fitch ratings[10] and also by beta coefficients. In all cases, the risk measures used were available prior to the implementation of a strategy, so that an investor could have realized the returns reported in this paper.[11]

The various five-year returns calculated for the period from July 1928 through June 1933 illustrate the different strategies used in constructing the averages in Tables 1-1 through 1-3. Using beta as a measure of risk, all New York Stock Exchange common stocks in existence on July 1928 and having such risk measures were assigned to ten portfolios. The lowest risk portfolio was made up of the stocks with the smallest beta coefficients and contained ten percent of the total number of stocks. The highest risk portfolio contained the highest beta stocks and likewise ten percent. The other eight portfolios were similarly stratified by beta values. The portfolios stratified by Fitch ratings do not contain equal numbers of securities. The low risk portfolio consists of stocks rated AAA, AA, A, and BBB, while the high risk portfolio consists of stocks rated C and below. The remaining portfolios each correspond to a single rating class.

Three investment strategies were applied to each portfolio. The first strategy assumed an equal amount invested in each security on July 1928 and that these stocks were held with no rebalancing for the five-year period. Cash dividends were reinvested in the company which paid them. Any stock delisted was assumed sold at the last available price and the proceeds reinvested in the remaining stocks according to their then existing proportions. The second strategy is one in which the investment in each security is rebalanced so as to maintain equal weights at the beginning of each month.

The third strategy is a buy-and-hold strategy like the first but with the exception that the amount initially invested in each security is proportional to the market value of the stock outstanding. The returns from this strategy are particularly important because they approximate the returns from buying a segment of the market portfolio made up of stocks of similar risks. These returns can be interpreted as the returns realized by all investors from some class of risky stocks, whereas the equally weighted portfolios cannot be so interpreted. These interpretations are only approximate because the

Table 1-1.   Percentage Increases in Portfolio Value for 60-Month Holding Periods Estimated Over 40 or More Years

Date	Risk Measure and Weighting Type	Risk Class	Rebalanced Portfolios					Buy-and-Hold Portfolios		
			Arith. Av. to 60th Power	Geom. Av. to 60th Power	Arith. Av. of Nonoverlapping 60-Month Period Return			Arith. Av. of Nonoverlapping 60-Month Period Returns		
					Unadj.	Adj. for Commissions	Adj. for Comm. and Taxes	Unadj.	Adj. for Commissions	Adj. for Comm. and Taxes
2/26-1/71	FITCH: Stocks Equally Weighted	low	77.2	55.0	59.4	55.7	32.1	55.6	54.7	31.2
		2	93.5	65.0	75.1	68.1	38.9	64.6	63.3	34.2
		3	110.8	74.7	93.9	83.2	50.3	80.7	78.7	44.7
		4	133.5	77.7	107.7	92.2	60.5	89.4	86.9	53.1
		5	177.8	96.8	142.9	114.5	83.7	101.9	98.3	66.4
		high	196.1	103.4	244.8	181.5	159.3	115.4	110.3	90.5
7/28-6/68	FITCH: Stocks Equally Weighted	low	74.4	53.0	56.9	53.6	27.7	52.7	51.7	27.4
		high	222.3	115.5	137.5	103.4	83.2	80.2	76.3	61.8
7/28-6/68	BETA: Stocks Equally Weighted	low	86.2	70.3	72.9	66.1	34.1	64.7	63.0	32.9
		2	101.1	77.5	82.0	75.5	40.9	76.3	74.4	41.7
		3	112.6	82.2	86.8	78.4	43.7	74.4	72.3	39.6
		4	113.4	79.0	83.3	75.6	40.8	75.8	73.7	41.1
		5	122.7	83.4	89.1	80.5	45.2	77.8	75.7	43.8
		6	126.4	80.6	91.3	80.7	47.0	79.5	77.1	45.7
		7	152.9	92.5	106.0	91.5	55.8	86.2	83.4	51.7
		8	146.3	86.5	97.2	84.3	51.4	77.3	74.7	45.1

7/28-6/68						BETA:		
							Stocks	Proportionally Weighted
9	191.2	100.2	114.3	96.5	63.6	90.0	87.0	57.4
high	208.9	102.3	116.9	90.2	67.1	73.3	70.0	52.5
low						58.9	58.1	30.2
2						61.7	60.5	33.2
3						73.8	72.3	43.6
4						83.3	82.1	52.8
5						71.6	70.3	41.5
6						69.3	67.7	38.5
7						69.5	67.9	38.9
8						71.7	70.0	43.5
9						86.2	83.9	52.2
high						72.5	69.7	47.3

Table 1-2.   Percentage Increases in Portfolio Value for 60-Month Holding Periods Estimated Over 20-Year Periods

Risk Measure: and Weighting Type	Risk Class	1928-1948				1938-1958				1948-1969			
		Rebalanced Portfolios		Buy-and-Hold Portfolios		Rebalanced Portfolios		Buy-and-Hold Portfolios		Rebalanced Portfolios		Buy-and-Hold Portfolios	
		Unadj.	Adj. for Commissions and Taxes	Unadj.	Adj. for Commissions and Taxes	Unadj.	Adj. for Commissions and Taxes	Unadj.	Adj. for Commissions and Taxes	Unadj.	Adj. for Commissions and Taxes	Unadj.	Adj. for Commissions and Taxes
FITCH: Stocks Equally Weighted	low	35.1	10.5	26.5	5.8	67.6	32.2	66.6	33.7	78.8	44.8	78.9	49.0
	high	140.3	77.1	36.7	21.5	136.3	82.0	75.5	53.3	134.6	89.3	123.7	102.2
BETA: Stocks Equally Weighted	low	54.7	19.8	35.6	9.4	77.6	34.2	73.5	33.7	91.0	48.4	93.8	56.5
	2	64.9	28.2	54.2	23.8	101.0	50.6	95.9	50.5	99.1	53.6	98.4	59.5
	3	71.1	31.4	45.8	15.6	112.1	56.3	99.0	51.4	102.5	56.0	102.9	63.6
	4	67.4	29.1	51.9	21.9	100.2	48.0	95.3	49.3	99.1	52.6	99.7	60.3
	5	72.4	32.1	48.7	20.4	100.5	48.0	92.3	47.0	105.8	58.3	107.0	67.1
	6	77.3	35.9	55.5	27.0	124.2	65.6	110.7	62.8	105.4	58.1	103.4	64.4
	7	87.8	39.4	49.5	20.7	131.9	67.7	105.6	56.8	124.2	72.2	122.9	82.7
	8	74.0	33.4	42.6	17.3	119.4	62.6	99.5	54.8	120.3	69.5	112.0	73.0
	9	96.0	48.4	52.3	28.5	140.8	78.2	115.0	69.1	132.6	78.8	127.8	86.4
	high	123.8	64.2	39.6	24.0	140.1	78.2	86.4	56.6	110.1	69.9	107.0	81.1
BETA: Stocks Proportionally Weighted	low			34.3	10.4			59.4	26.1			83.5	50.0
	2			21.9	1.5			82.9	46.8			101.5	64.9
	3			40.5	14.4			100.5	59.5			107.1	72.7

4	36.0	11.9	137.0	91.7	130.6	93.6
5	35.0	10.5	99.6	55.8	108.2	72.4
6	44.6	17.4	93.4	49.3	94.0	59.6
7	37.7	13.1	100.5	55.6	101.4	64.7
8	31.8	9.1	86.4	47.3	111.6	77.9
9	37.6	13.1	135.1	83.5	134.8	91.2
high	22.3	6.6	109.5	69.2	122.7	88.0

Table 1-3.   Percentage Increases in Portfolio Value for 60-Month Holding Periods Estimated Over 10-Year Periods (Buy-and-Hold Portfolios)

Beta Class	1938-48				1948-58				1958-68			
	Stocks Equally Weighted		Stocks Proportionally Weighted		Stocks Equally Weighted		Stocks Proportionally Weighted		Stocks Equally Weighted		Stocks Proportionally Weighted	
	Unadj.	Adj. for Comm. and Taxes	Unadj.	Adj. for Comm. and Taxes	Unadj.	Adj. for Comm. and Taxes	Unadj.	Adj. for Comm. and Taxes	Unadj.	Adj. for Comm. and Taxes	Unadj.	Adj. for Comm. and Taxes
low	61.9 %	25.0%	44.0%	15.1%	85.1%	42.4%	74.9%	37.1%	102.5%	70.6%	92.1%	63.0%
2	95.6	50.7	53.5	24.8	96.3	50.4	112.4	68.9	100.5	68.6	90.6	61.0
3	92.6	45.6	71.1	33.9	105.4	57.2	130.0	85.1	100.5	70.1	84.2	60.2
4	93.1	48.2	69.3	33.3	97.4	50.4	204.8	150.1	101.2	70.3	56.4	37.1
5	94.4	50.1	73.1	35.5	90.3	43.9	126.1	76.2	123.6	90.4	90.3	68.6
6	118.8	71.6	86.3	42.1	102.7	53.9	100.5	56.5	104.1	74.8	87.5	62.7
7	107.7	59.2	76.4	37.1	103.5	54.4	124.7	74.1	142.2	111.0	78.2	55.3
8	104.7	61.7	66.0	31.0	94.2	48.0	106.8	63.7	129.7	98.0	116.3	92.2
9	127.9	86.6	108.6	64.8	102.2	51.7	161.7	102.3	153.4	121.1	108.0	80.2
high	95.9	68.8	74.2	45.2	76.9	44.4	144.7	93.3	137.1	117.8	100.7	82.7

strategy only adjusted for the small value of new shares issued or old shares retired in excess of those required for splits or stock dividends every five years and included only stocks with risk measures available at the beginning of each five-year period.

For each strategy and for each portfolio, returns were calculated in three ways: first, with no allowance for commissions or taxes; second, with an adjustment for commissions; and third, with an adjustment for both commissions and taxes. The adjustment for commissions used the actual round-lot commission rate applicable at the time of any required transaction.[12] The adjustment for taxes assumed the highest marginal tax rate for dividends and the corresponding capital gain taxes appropriate to the date,[13] but of course, most investors are in a much lower bracket and many institutional investors pay no income tax at all. Such returns were calculated for sequential nonoverlapping five-year periods using both beta and Fitch measures of risk.[14] Tables 1-1 through 1-3 present the averages of these five-year returns for various time periods.

1.3.1 Monotonic Relation of Return to Risk

The average five-year rates of return calculated over the longest periods analyzed in this study—eight or nine five-year nonoverlapping periods—indicate that it is likely that long-run expected rates of return are positively related to risk (Table 1-1).

For the equally weighted Fitch portfolios from February 1926 through January 1971, the average returns from both buy-and-hold and rebalanced portfolios increase as a strictly monotonic function of risk. Over the shorter eight five-year periods from 1928 through 1968, the averages increase with risk for each of the three strategies using beta as a measure of risk. Only for the rebalanced equally weighted portfolios is this tendency strongly pronounced. The rank order correlation between risk and any measure of return for this strategy is greater than 0.90, which is significantly different from zero. For both equally weighted and proportionally weighted buy-and-hold strategies, the rank order correlations are positive but with one exception not significant. The exception is the returns adjusted for commissions and taxes for the equally weighted buy-and-hold strategy, possibly reflecting the relative importance of capital gains in the returns from high risk stocks. In view of the potentially large sampling errors in estimating expected five-year returns from only eight or nine observations and the consistently positive correlations between risk and returns, it seems safe to conclude that long-run expected rates of return are likely to increase with risk.

1.3.2. No Evidence of Convexity

Though the results do suggest the monotonicity of expected returns to risk, the realized returns give no evidence of a convex relationship between expected long-run returns and monthly betas. The previous section showed that the assumptions of the market line theory and independence of successive short-run rates of return would imply such a convex relationship.

For each of the eight five-year periods from July 1928 to June 1968, the unadjusted holding-period returns for the equally weighted portfolios were regressed on β and β^2—one regression for the rebalanced and another for the buy-and-hold strategy.[15] Thirteen out of these sixteen quadratic regressions had negative signs on β^2 when theory would point to a positive sign. Three of these thirteen β^2 coefficients were in fact significantly negative, while only one of the three positive coefficients was significant. This analysis indeed provides more evidence for concavity than for convexity. Similar regressions, using instead holding period returns adjusted for commissions and taxes, give almost identical results: eleven of the sixteen coefficients on β^2 were negative. As a result, while expected long-run rates of return increase with beta, they do not increase as fast as theory would suggest if short-run expected rates of return are linearly related to risk as measured by beta.

1.3.3 Quality Rating vs. Beta

Quality rating, at least as given by Fitch Rating Services, seems to be a better measure of risk than beta estimated from historical data for portfolios with equal weights, while the reverse seems true but to a lesser extent for portfolios with proportional weights.[16] The criterion used in measuring "better" was the relative abilities of the risk measures to discriminate among securities according to subsequent returns. To apply this criterion, stocks having both measures of risk were classified into six groups with the same number of stocks in each for each five-year period using first, Fitch ratings, and second, beta coefficients. For equally weighted buy-and-hold portfolios over the 1928-1968 period, the rank order correlation between risk and average unadjusted five-year rates of return was 0.43 using beta as the measure of risk and 0.83 using Fitch ratings. For proportionally weighted buy-and-hold portfolios, the rank order correlation was 0.94 using beta and 0.77 using Fitch. Thus, Fitch ratings work better than betas for stocks of smaller market values and less well for stocks of larger market values. The same conclusion follows from other measures of discriminatory power.[17]

1.3.4. Rebalancing vs. Buy-and-Hold Strategies

Of the two equally weighted investment strategies, the five-year returns from rebalancing beat the returns from buy-and-hold on average over the 1926-1971 period (Table 1-1). This result obtains even after adjusting for transactions costs and taxes.

The reader should keep in mind two important qualifications in interpreting these numbers. First, the differences in performance between the equally weighted rebalanced and buy-and-hold portfolios are substantial only for portfolios with above-average risks. Second, and more important, of the three overlapping periods shown in Table 1-2, the superiority of rebalancing is most marked in the 1928-1948 period, is considerably smaller in 1938-58, and disappears in 1948-68. Indeed, in this last period the buy-and-hold policy may have been preferable after allowances for transactions costs and taxes. A breakdown of these periods into smaller time intervals indicates that the largest gap in returns between the rebalanced and buy-and-hold portfolios occurred in the 1928-1933 period and the second largest in the 1938-1943 period. The advantage of rebalancing over buy-and-hold vanished after World War II. The 1948-1958 and 1958-1968 periods saw a slight advantage for the buy-and-hold policy.[18]

There are at least three possible ways of explaining the superior performance of rebalancing to buy-and-hold in the first two decades of the 1928-1968 period and the disappearance of this phenomenon in the last two decades. One explanation would be an increase in market efficiency from the first to the second halves of this period, perhaps because of securities legislation (resulting in increased disclosure and curbs on manipulation) or because of other changes in the institutional environment. A second explanation might lie in the unique character of the stock market decline starting in 1929 and, to a lesser extent, in 1937. A third explanation might attribute the impressive differences between the returns from rebalancing and buy-and-hold strategies to chance, reflecting the very large dispersion of the underlying distribution of investment returns. The tests reported in note 18 are consistent with this last interpretation.

1.3.5. Return and Size of Issue

An earlier analysis[19] found that for the 1964-1968 period, portfolios of New York Stock Exchange stock with equal amounts invested in each issue performed much better than portfolios with amounts invested proportional to the market value of the shares. The implication is that in this period at least, the smaller issues far out-performed the larger issues. However, the differences were not as pronounced for the much longer period covered in this chapter.

Over the entire 1928-1968 period equally weighted portfolios outperformed the proportionally weighted ones, as measured by the average five-year returns, at least for investors with a buy-and-hold strategy (Table 1-1). However, a breakdown of the 1928-1968 period into three overlapping twenty-year intervals showed no systematic difference in performance between the equally and proportionally weighted portfolios (Table 1-2). In the first twenty years, equally weighted portfolios consistently and by large amounts outperformed proportionally weighted portfolios. In the other two intervals, there was no consistent tendency. The gap in performance between the equally and the proportionally weighted portfolios is more pronounced over shorter periods of time. Thus in each of the two decades 1938-1948 and 1958-1968, the equally weighted portfolios in every beta class substantially outperformed proportionally weighted portfolios (Table 1-3). The reverse situation characterized the years 1948-58.[20] The differences in performance associated with the two different weighting schemes are even more pronounced if the ten-year periods are further broken down into five-year intervals. The magnitude of these differences in returns for a particular risk, even if they do not prove statistically significant, should give pause to an investor in interpreting current measures of investment performance which are typically based on a single arbitrary weighting scheme.

These substantial period-dependent differences in performance between equally weighted and proportionally weighted portfolios, or equivalently between large and small stock issues, may indicate that there is another (or more than one) important factor affecting returns which is not allowed for in current return generating functions. In other words, a return generating function which assumes the existence of only one common factor may be inadequate to explain the differences between actual and expected returns. The gap in performance between equally weighted and proportionally weighted portfolios appears too great to be explained by the greater liquidity risks attached to equal weighting but of the wrong sign (in two out of three instances) if greater unique risks are attached to proportional weighting. Additional testing will be required to confirm whether a size-related factor is necessary in explaining the returns of individual securities.

1.4 CONCLUDING REMARKS

Lest the reader conclude that an investor with a long-term horizon, such as some eleemosynary institutions, would be well advised to assume the greater risks associated with larger expected returns, this last section will serve to dispel such a conclusion. It is true that if expected five-year returns are positively related to risk, if there are no transaction costs and if five-year returns are stochastically independent,[21] expected returns for horizons greater than five years would be positively related to risk.

Nonetheless, the investment results for any particular long period of time represent only a single drawing from a probability distribution and there is no guarantee that this drawing would be anywhere near the expected result. This is true even if investors have correctly assessed the distribution generating future returns. Indeed, aggregate returns which were realized by all investors over the 1928 to 1968 period illustrate that there is no necessary reward for bearing additional risk over any particular long period of time. As pointed out earlier, the returns from a value-weighted buy-and-hold strategy do correspond to what all investors would realize from their investments in all stocks covered by the strategy. It is impossible for all investors to realize the returns which would result from equally-weighted strategies.

For value-weighted buy-and-hold strategies, the returns realized over the forty-year period from July 1928 through June 1968 were, if anything, negatively related to risk. For example, one dollar invested in stocks of the lowest risk would have increased to $32.74 before adjustment for commissions or taxes, (Table 1-4), while the same dollar in stocks of the highest risk would have increased to only

Table 1-4. The Value of One Dollar in 40 Years Under a Value-Weighted Buy-and-Hold Strategy (July, 1928-June,1968)

Risk Class		Dollar Value	
	Unadjusted	Adjusted for Commissions	Adjusted for Commissions and Taxes
low	$32.74	$31.07	$4.84
2	27.24	25.19	3.67
3	51.66	46.89	8.61
4	55.88	51.40	9.69
5	43.74	39.66	7.09
6	43.76	38.86	7.49
7	42.63	37.53	7.38
8	46.50	41.17	7.72
9	42.27	36.83	5.53
high	26.65	22.68	3.43

$26.65. More generally, the unadjusted increases in value for all risk classes are not positively correlated with risk. The rank order correlation is in fact negative (−.14), though not significant. The same conclusions follow after adjusting for commissions or both commissions and all taxes.[22] This does not mean that in some other forty-year period it would not have been preferable in retrospect to be in high-risk securities.

These increases in value were calculated in a similar way as the returns for the five-year periods except for two major differences: First, both old and new stocks were reassigned every five years to portfolios according to the latest available assessments of beta. The returns, where indicated, were properly adjusted for the commissions and taxes which would have been incurred in such restructuring.[23] Second, each of the portfolios was converted to cash at the end of the forty-year period, which of course would have incurred commissions and possibly some taxes. The increases in value adjusted for commissions would therefore represent the cash-to-cash forty-year experience of any organization not paying taxes. Since the tax adjustment was based upon the maximum personal tax liability, an individual not subject to the maximum would have experienced a return between the two adjusted figures.

According to the New York Times,[24] a recent report to the Ford Foundation[25] was widely interpreted as a criticism of universities for not concentrating on "maximum long-term return." Such returns, as that report recognizes, are often associated with higher short-run volatility, i.e., higher betas. It might be argued that a forty-year horizon examined here is too short for a university but this argument is irrelevant. For any long horizon the realized change in wealth will be one drawing from a probability distribution with an extremely large dispersion. There is thus no guarantee that a high-risk investment strategy will produce greater wealth in any fixed period of time than a low-risk strategy—even if expected long-run returns are positively related to risk.

The forty-year results in Table 1-4 indicate that higher risk strategies do not dominate lower risk strategies for investors in aggregate. Except for the most bizarre dependencies among forty-year returns, one would not expect to find such dominance for longer horizons. The results in this chapter, utilizing the longest period of time for which data are available, thus give no clear guideline about the appropriate level of risk to be assumed by eleemosynary institutions or any other investors in managing their funds.

NOTES TO SECTION ONE

1. Three such studies include: Black, Jensen and Scholes (1972); Blume and Friend (1973) and Fama and MacBeth (1973).

2. Blume and Friend (1973).

3. Black, Jensen and Scholes (1972), and Blume and Friend (1973).

4. Fama and MacBeth (1973) have found some statistically significant but unpredictable nonlinearities in the cross-sectional relationship of one-month returns to beta. Since the nonlinearities are unpredictable from month to month, their finding is not inconsistent with a linear relationship between average monthly returns and beta.

5. The short-run finding mathematically takes the form $P[E(R) = a + b\beta] > 0.95$, where $\beta > 0$. Raising each side of the equality to the nth power yields $P\left\{[E(R)]^n = [a + b\beta]^n\right\} > 0.95$. Upon taking the derivative twice, the probability inequality becomes $P\left\{d^2 E(R)^n/d\beta^2 = n(n-1)\ [E(R)]^{n-2} b^2\right\} > 0.95$. Since $E(R)$ is greater than zero, the second derivative is nonnegative for n greater than 1.0, which establishes the proposition in the text.

6. A typical study would be Fama and Blume (1966).

7. For each of the eight nonoverlapping five-year periods from July 1928 through June 1968, the serial correlation of successive monthly returns was calculated for each common stock listed during an entire five-year period. The averages of these correlations were furthest from zero in the 1928-1933 and 1933-1938 periods, amounting to 0.137 and −.128, respectively. The averages were negative in each of the remaining five-year periods. All of these average correlations were statistically significant. Two tests of significance were carried out and gave similar results. One converted the serial correlation coefficients (ρ) into $Z = 1/2 \ln (1 + \rho/1 - \rho)$ statistics for each of the stocks included in a five-year period (ranging from 496 issues in 1928-1933 to 944 issues in 1963-1968) and then obtained t-values to measure the significance of the deviation of the average Z from zero. The t-statistics in absolute value ranged from a high of 25.4 in 1933-1938 to a low of 4.6 in 1958-1963. This test is discussed in Hoel (1958). A second test found that the number of positive or negative serial correlations in each of the periods differed significantly at the five percent level under the null hypothesis that a positive or negative number was equally likely. All significance tests reported in this chapter are at the five percent level.

8. In connection with these first two reasons why it is dangerous to infer long-run relationships between risk and return from observed short-run relationships, it might be noted that Cheng and Deets (1971) found that for the period December 31, 1937-February 2, 1969, a rebalancing strategy applied to the Dow Jones Industrials yielded very much higher rates of return prior to adjustment for commission and tax costs than a buy-and-hold strategy. Risk was not held constant in their analysis—unlike the procedures to be followed in this paper— but it is difficult to see how this could account for their result.

9. Blume (1974).

10. The Fitch ratings are a subjective measure of risk derived in the words of

the service as follows: "While the earnings and dividend record dominate in the primary stages of stock ratings, all factors bearing on immediate and more distant prospects must be considered. The financial position of the company is examined, and account is taken of the nature of the industry, and of the position of the enterprise in the industry. The competitive position of the company is analyzed, and due attention is given to the combined caution and progressiveness of its "policies." For an extensive analysis of the relationship of these subjective measures to past and future estimated betas and to accounting measures of risk, the reader is referred to Ofer (1973).

11. The beta coefficients for any month were calculated by regressing the immediately prior returns upon the Fisher Combination link relative index. These calculations typically used sixty prior months, but if the data did not permit this, the calculations were still performed using the maximum available data providing there were at least twenty-nine prior monthly returns. The Fitch ratings were collected for 1926, 1928, and every fifth year thereafter through 1958. By 1963, Fitch had stopped rating common stocks.

12. At the beginning of each five-year period, it was assumed that the investor purchased the portfolio with cash; but at the end, the portfolio was not liquidated.

13. Capital gain taxes were calculated on the assumption that the most recent purchase in the lowest tax category was sold first. Thus, long-term gains or losses were realized before shorter-term gains or losses. Under the particular rebalancing policy in this chapter, this rule for selling securities would tend to minimize taxes if the market were steady or rising. As with the portfolios adjusted only for commissions, the portfolios were assumed not to have been liquidated at the end of five years, so that unrealized gains or losses were untaxed.

14. For the Fitch ratings, the portfolios formed in the sixties were based upon 1958 ratings. Except for this big gap, the Fitch ratings were never dated more than three years before the formation of the portfolios. The β coefficients were always updated to the month at which the portfolios were formed.

15. The beta coefficients used in these regressions were not derived from the beta coefficients used in forming the portfolios but were estimated anew from the subsequent sixty monthly returns realized under the portfolio strategy. This technique will minimize order biases as discussed in Blume and Friend (1973). It makes the assumption that beta coefficients and more generally probability distributions of returns for well diversified portfolios can be assumed stationary over short periods of time. This is not an unreasonable assumption as shown by Blume (1970).

16. Ofer (1973) suggests that another subjective measure, Standard and Poor's ratings, are poorer measures of risk than the Fitch stock ratings over the postwar period for which they were both available.

17. For the unweighted portfolios, using Fitch ratings over the 1928-1968 period, the difference between the average five-year rates of return from the highest risk portfolio to the lowest risk portfolio was 0.26 compared to the 0.02 for the beta unweighted portfolios. The standard deviation of the six five-year average returns was 0.16 for Fitch and 0.11 for beta. For the weighted portfolios, the difference between high and low risk portfolios was 0.15 for

Fitch and 0.30 for beta, and the standard deviations were 0.106 and 0.114, respectively.

18. That rebalancing beats buy-and-hold strategies in the pre-World War II period might suggest that, contrary to the usual assumption of independence of rates of returns from one time interval to another, returns over this period were characterized by substantial negative serial dependence. As reported in Section 1.2, the average serial correlation between successive monthly rates of return for individual stocks over each of the five-year periods from 1928 to 1968 was generally negative and statistically significant. Yet, there was no apparent relationship between the sign and magnitude of the correlation and the relative performance of rebalancing and buy-and-hold strategies in the different periods. Indeed, in the 1928-1933 period when rebalancing outperformed buy-and-hold by a substantial margin, the average 60-month serial correlation coefficient for individual stocks was positive and highly significant.

When, instead of the customary time-series serial correlations for individual stocks, cross-sectional correlations were computed for each successive pair of months, the average serial correlation for each month is negative not only for every five-year period, including 1928-1933, but also for every beta class within each period. These average cross-sectional correlations, which are significant in each period, bear a somewhat closer relationship to the relative performance of rebalancing and buy-and-hold strategies than do time-series correlations, but the relationship is still not perfect.

A more satisfactory explanation of the difference in results between rebalancing and buy-and-hold strategies follows from recognizing that mathematically buy-and-hold would be expected to outperform rebalancing if on the average the returns on stocks in month t (R_{ti} where i represents any stock) are positively correlated with cumulative returns on the same stocks ($\prod_{\tau=1}^{t-1} R_{\tau i}$) from the beginning to the month immediately preceding t. The sign of such cross-sectional correlations, which were computed for each month in the periods 1928-1933 and 1933-1938 for each of ten stock portfolios classified by beta, explains the observed difference in performance between buy-and-hold and rebalancing strategies over these five-year periods quite well. However, while the observed differences in average returns for given beta between buy-and-hold and rebalancing strategies are extremely large for 1928-1933, the averages of the 59 monthly correlations between R_{ti} and $\prod_{\tau=1}^{t-1} R_{\tau i}$ are not significantly different from zero either for 1928-1933 or 1933-1938 for any of the ten beta stock portfolios using either a t-test or a binomial test of signs.

19. Friend, Blume, and Crockett (1970).

20. It should be noted that though only arithmetic averages of nonoverlapping 60-month period returns are presented for these shorter periods, the monthly arithmetic averages raised to the 60th power provided similar results.

21. This assumption seems more plausible for five-year returns than for daily, weekly, or monthly returns since a primary reason for short-run dependencies is transaction costs which make it unprofitable for investors to profit from short-run disequilibria of small magnitude. In the long run, such transaction costs are probably less critical.

22. A similar result for buy-and-hold strategies was obtained in Friend and Taubman (1966).
23. In calculating realized gains or losses, it was assumed that each share of a security held over five years had as its cost basis the average cost of all shares of that security currently in the portfolio and purchased more than five years before.
24. *The New York Times* (September 24, 1973).
25. *Managing Educational Endowments* (1972).

REFERENCES

Black, F., M.C. Jensen, and M. Scholes, "The Capital Asset Pricing Model: Some Empirical Tests," in Michael C. Jensen (ed.), *Studies in the Theory of Capital Markets* (New York: Praeger, 1972).

Blume, M., and I. Friend, "A New Look at the Capital Asset Pricing Model," *The Journal of Finance* (Mar. 1973).

_____, "Unbiased Estimators of Long-Run Expected Rates of Return," *Journal of the American Statistical Association* (Sept. 1974).

_____, "Portfolio Theory: A Step Towards Its Application," *Journal of Business* (Apr. 1970).

Cheng, P.L., and M.K. Deets, "Portfolio Returns and the Random Walk Theory," *The Journal of Finance* (Mar. 1971).

Fama, E., and M. Blume, "Filter Rules and Stock Market Trading," *The Journal of Business* (Supplement) (Jan. 1966).

_____, and J.D. MacBeth, "Risk, Return and Equilibrium: Empirical Tests," *Journal of Political Economy* (May 1973).

Friend, I., M. Blume, and J. Crockett, *Mutual Funds and Other Institutional Investors: A New Perspective* (New York: McGraw-Hill, 1970).

_____, and P.J. Taubman, "Risk and the Rate of Return on Common Stock," *Proceedings of the Seminar on the Analysis of Security Prices* (University of Chicago, Nov. 1966).

Hoel, P.G., *Introduction to Mathematical Statistics* (New York: John Wiley and Sons, Inc., 1958).

Ofer, A.R., *Return, Risk, and Growth Expectations: An Empirical Assessment of the Economic Performance of the Stock Market* (Ph.D. dissertation, University of Pennsylvania, 1973).

Managing Educational Endowments (Report to the Ford Foundation, July 1972).

The New York Times (Sept. 24, 1973) Business and Finance, p. 1.

✳ *Section Two*

Betas and Their Regression Tendencies

Marshall E. Blume*

2.1 INTRODUCTION

A previous study [3] showed that estimated beta coefficients, at least in the context of a portfolio of a large
number of securities, were relatively stationary over time.
Nonetheless, there was a consistent tendency for a portfolio with
either an extremely low or high estimated beta in one period to have
a less extreme beta as estimated in the next period. In other words,
estimated betas exhibited in that article a tendency to regress
towards the grand mean of all betas, namely one. This chapter will
examine in further detail this regression tendency.[1]
Section 2.2 presents evidence showing the existence of this
regression tendency and reviews the conventional reasons given in
explanation [1], [4], [5]. Section 2.3 develops a formal model of
this regression tendency and finds that the conventional analysis of
this tendency is, if not incorrect, certainly misleading. Accompany-
ing this theoretical analysis are some new empirical results which
show that a major reason for the observed regression is real
nonstationarities in the underlying values of beta and that the
so-called "order bias" is not of dominant importance.

2.2. THE CONVENTIONAL WISDOM

If an investor were to use estimated betas to group securities into

*The author wishes to thank Professors John Bildersee and Harry Markowitz
for their helpful comments and the Rodney L. White Center for financial
support.

portfolios spanning a wide range of risk, he would more than likely find that the betas estimated for the very same portfolios in a subsequent period would be less extreme or closer to the market beta of one than his prior estimates. To illustrate, assume that the investor on July 1, 1933, had at his disposal an estimate of beta for each common stock which had been listed on the NYSE (New York Stock Exchange) for the prior seven years, July 1926-June 1933. Assume further that each estimate was derived by regressing the eighty-four monthly relatives covering this seven-year period upon the corresponding values for the market portfolio.[2]

If this investor desired equally weighted portfolios of 100 securities, he might group those 100 securities with the smallest estimates of beta together to form a portfolio. Such a portfolio would of all equally weighted portfolios have the smallest possible estimated portfolio beta since an estimate of such a portfolio beta can be shown to be an average of the estimates for the individual securities [2, p. 169]. To cover a wide range of portfolio betas, this investor might then form a second portfolio consisting of the 100 securities with the next smallest estimates of beta, and so on.

Using the securities available as of June 1933, this investor could thus obtain four portfolios of 100 securities apiece with no security in common. Estimated over the same seven-year period, July 1926-June 1933, the betas for these portfolios[3] would have ranged from 0.50 to 1.53. Similar portfolios can be constructed for each of the next seven-year periods through 1954 and their portfolio betas calculated. Table 2-1 contains these estimates under the heading "Grouping Period."

The betas for these same portfolios, but reestimated using the monthly portfolio relatives adjusted for delistings from the seven years following the grouping period, illustrate the magnitude of the regression tendency.[4] Whereas the portfolio betas as estimated, for instance, in the grouping period 1926-33 ranged from 0.50 to 1.53, the betas as estimated for these same portfolios in the subsequent seven-year period 1933-40 ranged only from 0.61 to 1.42. The results for the other periods display a similar regression tendency.

An obvious explanation of this regression tendency is that for some unstated economic or behavioral reasons, the underlying betas do tend to regress towards the mean over time.[5] Yet, even if the true betas were constant over time, it has been argued that the portfolio betas as estimated in the grouping period would statistically be more extreme than those estimated in a subsequent period. This bias has sometimes been termed an order or selection bias.

Table 2-1. Beta Coefficients for Portfolios of 100 Securities

Portfolio	Grouping Period	First Subsequent Period
	7/26-6/33	7/33-6/40
1	0.50	0.61
2	0.85	0.96
3	1.15	1.24
4	1.53	1.42
	7/33-6/40	7/40-6/47
1	0.38	0.56
2	0.69	0.77
3	0.90	0.91
4	1.13	1.12
5	1.35	1.31
6	1.68	1.69
	7/40-6/47	7/47-6/54
1	0.43	0.60
2	0.61	0.76
3	0.73	0.88
4	0.86	0.99
5	1.00	1.10
6	1.21	1.21
7	1.61	1.36
	7/47-6/54	7/54-6/61
1	0.36	0.57
2	0.61	0.71
3	0.78	0.88
4	0.91	0.96
5	1.01	1.03
6	1.13	1.13
7	1.26	1.24
8	1.47	1.32
	7/54-6/61	7/61-6/68
1	0.37	0.62
2	0.56	0.68
3	0.72	0.85
4	0.86	0.85
5	0.99	0.95
6	1.11	0.98
7	1.23	1.07
8	1.43	1.25

The frequently given intuitive explanation of this order bias [1], [4], [5], parallels the following: Consider the portfolio formed of the 100 securities with the lowest estimates of beta. The estimated portfolio beta might be expected to understate the true beta or equivalently be expected to be measured with negative error. The reason the measurement error might be expected to be negative may best be explored by analyzing how a security might happen to have one of the 100 lowest estimates of beta. First, if the true beta were in the lowest hundred, the estimated beta would fall in the lowest 100 estimates only if the error in measuring the beta were not too large which roughly translates into more negative than positive errors. Second, if the true beta were not in the lowest 100, the estimated beta might still be in the lowest 100 estimates if it were measured with a sufficiently large negative error.[6]

Thus, the negative errors in the 100 smallest estimates of beta might be expected to outweigh the positive errors. The same argument except in reverse would apply to the 100 largest estimates. Indeed, it would seem that any portfolio of securities stratified by estimates of beta for which the average of these estimates is not the grand mean of all betas, namely 1.0, would be subject to some order bias. It would also seem that the absolute magnitude of this order bias should be greater, the further the average estimate is from the grand mean. The next section formalizes this intuitive argument and suggests that, if it is not incorrect, it is certainly misleading as to the source of the bias.

2.3 A FORMAL MODEL

The intuitive explanation of the order bias just given suggests that the way in which the portfolios are formed caused the bias. This section will argue that the bias is present in the estimated betas for the individual securities and is not induced by the way in which the portfolios are selected. Following this argument will be an analysis of the extent to which this order bias accounts for the observed regression tendency in portfolio betas over time.

A numerical example will serve to illustrate the logic of the subsequent argument and to introduce some required notation.[7] Assume for the moment that the possible values of beta for an individual security i in period t, β_{it}, are 0.8, 1.0 and 1.2 and that each of these values is equally likely. Assume further that in estimating a beta for an individual security, there is a 0.6 probability that the estimate $\hat{\beta}_{it}$ contains no measurement error, a 0.2 probability that it understates the true β_{it} by 0.2, and a 0.2 probability that it overstates the true value by 0.2. Now in a sample of ten securities whose true betas were all say 0.8, one would expect two estimates of beta to be 0.6, six to be 0.8, and two to be 1.0. These numbers have been transcribed to the first row of Table 2-2. The second and third rows are similarly constructed by first assuming that the ten securities all had a true value of 1.0 and then of 1.2.

The rows of Table 2-2 thus correspond to the distribution of the estimated beta, $\hat{\beta}_{it}$, conditional on the true value, β_{it}. It might be noted that the expectation of $\hat{\beta}_{it}$ conditional on β_{it}, $E(\hat{\beta}_{it} \mid \beta_{it})$, is β_{it}. However, in a sampling situation, an investigator would be faced with an estimate of beta and would want to assess the distribution of the true β_{it} conditional on the estimated $\hat{\beta}_{it}$. Such conditional distributions correspond to the columns of Table 2-2. It is easily verified that the expectation of β_{it} conditional on $\hat{\beta}_{it}$, $E(\beta_{it} \mid \hat{\beta}_{it})$, is generally not β_{it}. For example, if $\hat{\beta}_{it}$ were 0.8, $E(\beta_{it} \mid \hat{\beta}_{it} = 0.8)$ would be 0.85 since with this estimate the true beta would be 0.8 with probability 0.75 or 1.0 with probability 0.25.[8]

The estimate $\hat{\beta}_{it}$, therefore, would typically be biased, and it is biased whether or not portfolios are formed. The effect of forming large portfolios is to reduce the random component in the estimate, so that the difference between the estimated portfolio beta and the true portfolio beta can be ascribed almost completely to the magnitude of the bias.

In the spirit of this example, we will now develop explicit formulae for the order bias and real nonstationarities over time. Let it be assumed that the betas for individual securities in period t, β_{it}, can be thought of as drawings from a normal distribution with a mean of 1.0 and variance $\sigma^2(\beta_{it})$. The corresponding assumption for the numerical example just discussed would be a trinomial distribution with equal probabilities for each possible value of β_{it}.

Let it additionally be assumed that the estimate, $\hat{\beta}_{it}$, measures β_{it} with error η_{it}, a mean-zero independent normal variate, so that $\hat{\beta}_{it}$ is given by the sum of β_{it} and η_{it}. It immediately follows that β_{it} and

Table 2-2. Number of Securities Cross Classified by β_{it} and $\hat{\beta}_{it}$

		$\hat{\beta}_{it}$				
		.6	.8	1.0	1.2	1.4
	.8	2	6	2		
β_{it}	1.0		2	6	2	
	1.2			2	6	2

$\hat{\beta}_{it}$ are distributed by a bivariate normal distribution. It might be noted that, as formulated, $\sigma^2(\eta_{it})$ need not equal $\sigma^2(\eta_{jt})$, $i \neq j$. Since the empirical work will assume equality, the subsequent theoretical work will also make this assumption even though for the most part it is not necessary. The final assumption is that β_{it} and β_{it+1} are distributed as bivariate normal variates. Because η_{it} is independently distributed, $\hat{\beta}_{it}$ and β_{it+1} will be distributed by a bivariate normal distribution.

That $\hat{\beta}_{it}$ and β_{it+1} are bivariate normal random variables, each with a mean of 1.0, implies the following regression

$$E(\beta_{it+1} \mid \hat{\beta}_{it}) - 1 = \frac{\text{cov}(\beta_{it+1}, \hat{\beta}_{it})}{\sigma^2(\hat{\beta}_{it})} (\hat{\beta}_{it} - 1). \qquad (2.1)$$

This regression is similar to the procedure proposed in Blume [3] to adjust the estimated betas for the regression tendency. That procedure was to regress estimates of beta for individual securities from a later period on estimates from an earlier period and to use the coefficients from this regression to adjust future estimates.[9] The empirical evidence presented there indicated that this procedure did improve the accuracy of estimates of future betas, though no claim was made that there might not be better ways to adjust for the regression tendency.

The coefficient of $(\hat{\beta}_{it} - 1)$ in (2.1) can be broken down into two components: one of which would correspond to the so-called order bias and the other to a true regression tendency. To achieve this result, note that the covariance of β_{it+1} and $\hat{\beta}_{it}$ is given by $\text{cov}(\beta_{it+1}, \beta_{it} + \eta_{it})$, which because of the assumed independence of the errors, reduces to the covariance of β_{it+1} and β_{it}. Making this substitution and replacing $\text{cov}(\beta_{it+1}, \beta_{it})$ by $\rho(\beta_{it+1}, \beta_{it})\sigma(\beta_{it+1})$ $\sigma(\beta_{it})$, (2.1) becomes

$$E(\beta_{it+1} \mid \hat{\beta}_{it}) - 1 = \frac{\rho(\beta_{it+1}, \beta_{it})\sigma(\beta_{it+1})\sigma(\beta_{it})}{\sigma^2(\hat{\beta}_{it})} (\hat{\beta}_{it} - 1). \quad (2.2)$$

The ratio of $\sigma(\beta_{it})\sigma(\beta_{it+1})$ to $\sigma^2(\hat{\beta}_{it})$ might be identified with the order bias and the correlation of β_{it} and β_{it+1} with a true regression.

If the underlying values of beta are stationary over time, the correlation of successive values will be 1.0 and the standard deviations of β_{it} and β_{it+1} will be the same. Assuming such stationarity and noting then that β_{it+1} equals β_{it}, Equation (2.2) can be rewritten as[10]

$$E(\beta_{it+1} \mid \hat{\beta}_{it}) - 1 = E(\beta_{it} \mid \hat{\beta}_{it}) - 1$$

$$= \frac{\sigma^2(\beta_{it})}{\sigma^2(\hat{\beta}_{it})} \, (\hat{\beta}_{it} - 1). \qquad (2.3)$$

Since $\sigma^2(\beta_{it})$ would be less than $\sigma^2(\hat{\beta}_{it})$ if beta is measured with any error, the coefficient of $(\hat{\beta}_{it} - 1)$ would be less than 1.0. This means that the true beta for a security would be expected to be closer to one than the estimated value. In other words, an estimate of beta for an individual security except for an estimate of 1.0 is biased.[11]

In light of this discussion, the chapter now reexamines the empirical results of the previous section. The initial task will be to adjust the portfolio betas in the grouping periods for the order bias. After making this adjustment, it will be apparent that much of the regression tendency observed in Table 2-1 remains. Thus, if (2.2) is valid, the value of the correlation coefficient is probably not 1.0. The statistical properties of estimates of the portfolio betas in both the grouping and subsequent periods will be examined. The section ends with an additional test that gives further confirmation that much of the regression tendency stems from true nonstationarities in the underlying betas.

To adjust the estimates of beta in the grouping periods for the order bias using (2.3) would require estimates of the ratio of $\sigma^2(\beta_{it})$ to $\sigma^2(\hat{\beta}_{it})$. The sample variance calculated from the estimated betas for all securities in a particular cross-section provides an estimate of $\sigma^2(\hat{\beta}_{it})$. An estimate of $\sigma^2(\beta_{it})$ can be derived as the difference between estimates of $\sigma^2(\hat{\beta}_{it})$ and $\sigma^2(\eta_{it})$. If the variance of the error in measuring an individual beta is the same for every security, $\sigma^2(\eta_{it})$ can be estimated as the average over all securities of the squares of the standard error associated with each estimated beta.

In conformity with these procedures, estimates of the ratio of $\sigma^2(\beta_{it})$ to $\sigma^2(\hat{\beta}_{it})$ for the five seven-year periods from 1926 through 1961 were respectively 0.92, 0.92, 0.89, 0.82, and 0.75. In other words, an unbiased estimate of the underlying beta for an individual security should be eight to twenty-five percent closer to 1.0 than the original estimate. For instance, if $\sigma^2(\beta_{it})/\sigma^2(\hat{\beta}_{it})$ were 0.9 and if $\hat{\beta}_{it}$ were 1.3, an unbiased estimate would be 1.27.

To determine whether the order bias accounted for all of the regression, the estimated betas for the individual securities were adjusted for the order bias using (2.3) and the appropriate value of the ratio. For the same portfolios of 100 securities examined in the previous section, portfolio betas for the grouping period were recalculated as the average of these adjusted betas. These adjusted portfolio betas could alternatively be obtained by adjusting the unadjusted portfolio betas directly. These adjusted portfolio betas are given in Table 2-3. For the reader's convenience, the unadjusted portfolio betas and those estimated in the subsequent seven years are reproduced from Table 2-1.

Before comparing these estimates, let us for the moment consider the statistical properties of the portfolio betas, first in the grouping period and then in the subsequent period. Though unadjusted estimates of the portfolio betas in the grouping period may be biased, they would be expected to be highly "reliable" as that term is used in psychometrics. Thus, regardless of what these estimates measure, they measure it accurately or more precisely their values approximate those which would be expected conditional on the underlying population and how they are calculated. For equally-weighted portfolios, the larger the number of securities, the more reliable would be the estimate.

Specifically, for an equally-weighted portfolio of 100 securities, the standard deviation of the error in the portfolio beta would be one-tenth the standard error of the estimated betas for individual securities providing the errors in measuring these individual betas were independent of each other. During the 1926-33 period, the average standard error of betas for individual securities was 0.12 so that the standard error of the portfolio beta would be roughly 0.012. The average standard error for individual securities increased gradually to 0.20 in the period July 1954-June 1961. For the next seven-year period ending June 1968, the average declined to 0.17.

As pointed out, standard errors for portfolio betas calculated from those for individual securities assume independence of the errors in estimates. The standard error for a portfolio beta can however be calculated directly without making this assumption of independence by regressing the portfolio returns on the market index. The standard error for the portfolio of the 100 securities with the lowest estimates of beta in the July 1926-June 1933 period was, for instance, 0.018, which compares to 0.012 calculated assuming independence. The average standard error of the estimated betas for the four portfolios in this period was also 0.018. The average standard errors of the betas for the portfolios of 100 securities in the four subsequent seven-year periods ending June 1961 were respectively 0.025, 0.027, 0.024, and 0.027. Although these standard errors, not assuming independence, are about 50 percent larger than before, they are still extremely small compared to the range of possible values for portfolio betas.

Table 2-3. Beta Coefficients for Portfolios of 100 Securities

Portfolio	Grouping Period		First Subsequent Period	Second Subsequent Period
	Unadjusted for Order Bias	Adjusted for Order Bias		
	7/26-6/33		7/33-6/40	7/40-6/47
1	0.50	.54	0.61	0.73
2	0.85	.86	0.96	0.92
3	1.15	1.14	1.24	1.21
4	1.53	1.49	1.42	1.47
	7/33-6/40		7/40-6/47	7/47-6/54
1	0.38	.43	0.56	0.53
2	0.69	.72	0.77	0.86
3	0.90	.91	0.91	0.96
4	1.13	1.12	1.12	1.11
5	1.35	1.32	1.31	1.29
6	1.68	1.63	1.69	1.40
	7/40-6/47		7/47-6/54	7/54-6/61
1	0.43	.50	0.60	0.73
2	0.61	.65	0.76	0.88
3	0.73	.76	0.88	0.93
4	0.86	.88	0.99	1.04
5	1.00	1.00	1.10	1.12
6	1.21	1.19	1.21	1.14
7	1.61	1.54	1.36	1.20
	7/47-6/54		7/54-6/61	7/61-6/68
1	0.36	.48	0.57	0.72
2	0.61	.68	0.71	0.79
3	0.78	.82	0.88	0.88
4	0.91	.93	0.96	0.92
5	1.01	1.01	1.03	1.04
6	1.13	1.10	1.13	1.02
7	1.26	1.21	1.24	1.08
8	1.47	1.39	1.32	1.15
	7/54-6/61		7/61-6/68	
1	0.37	.42	0.62	
2	0.56	.67	0.68	
3	0.72	.79	0.85	
4	0.86	.89	0.85	
5	0.99	.99	0.95	
6	1.11	1.08	0.98	
7	1.23	1.17	1.07	
8	1.43	1.32	1.25	

For the moment, let us therefore assume that the portfolio betas as estimated in the grouping period before adjustment for order bias are extremely reliable numbers in that whatever they measure, they measure it accurately. In this case, adjusting these portfolio betas for the order bias will give extremely reliable and unbiased estimates of the underlying portfolio beta and therefore these adjusted betas can be taken as very good approximations to the underlying, but unknown, values. The greater the number of securities in the portfolio, the better the approximation will be.

The numerical example in Table 2-2 shows intuitively what is happening. Consider a portfolio of a large number of securities whose estimated betas were all 0.8 in a particular sample. It will be recalled that such an estimate requires that the true beta be either 0.8 or 1.0. As the number of securities with estimates of 0.8 increases, one can be more and more confident that 75 percent of the securities have true betas of 0.8 and 25 percent have true betas of 1.0 or equivalently that an equally-weighted portfolio of these securities has a beta of 0.85.

The heuristic argument in the prior section might lead some to believe that, contrary to the estimates in the grouping period, there are no order biases associated with the portfolio betas estimated in the subsequent seven years. This belief, however, is not correct. Formally, the portfolios formed in the grouping period are being treated as if they were securities in the subsequent period. To estimate these portfolio betas, portfolio returns were calculated and regressed upon some measure of the market. In this chapter, these portfolio returns were calculated under an equally-weighted monthly revision strategy in which delisted securities were sold at the last available price and the proceeds reinvested equally in the remaining. Other strategies are, of course, possible.

Since these portfolios are being treated as securities, formula (2.3) applies, so that there is still some "order bias" present. However, in determining the rate of regression, the appropriate measure of the variance of the errors in the estimates is the variance for the portfolio betas and not for the betas of individual stocks. This fact has the important effect of making the ratio of $\sigma^2(\beta_{it})$ to $\sigma^2(\hat{\beta}_{it})$ much closer to one than for individual securities. Estimating $\sigma^2(\hat{\beta}_{it})$ and $\sigma^2(\eta_{it})$ for the portfolios formed on the immediately prior period, the value of this ratio for each of the four seven-year periods from 1933 to 1961 was in excess of 0.99 and for the last seven-year period in excess of 0.98. Thus, for most purposes, little error is introduced by assuming that these estimated portfolio betas contain no "order bias" or equivalently that these estimates measure accurately the true portfolio beta.

A comparison of the portfolio betas in the grouping period, even after adjusting for the order bias, to the corresponding betas in the immediately subsequent period discloses a definite regression tendency. This regression tendency is statistically significant at the five percent level for each of the last three grouping periods, 1940-47, 1947-54, 1954-61.[12] Thus, this evidence strongly suggests that there is a substantial tendency for the underlying values of beta to regress towards the mean over time. Yet, it could be argued that this test is suspect because the formula used in adjusting for the order bias was developed under the assumption that the distributions of beta were normal. This assumption is certainly not strictly correct and it is not clear how sensitive the adjustment is to violations of this assumption.

A more robust way to demonstrate the existence of a true regression tendency is based upon the observation that the portfolio betas estimated in the period immediately subsequent to the grouping period are measured with negligible error and bias. These estimated portfolio betas can be compared to betas for the same portfolios estimated in the second seven years subsequent to the grouping period. These betas, which have been estimated in the second subsequent period and are given in Table 2-3, disclose again an obvious regression tendency. This tendency is significant at the five percent level for the last three of the four possible comparisons.[13]

2.4. SUMMARY

Beginning with a review of the conventional wisdom, the chapter showed that estimated beta coefficients tend to regress towards the grand mean of all betas over time. We presented two kinds of empirical analyses which showed that part of this observed regression tendency represented real nonstationarities in the betas of individual securities and that the so-called order bias was not of overwhelming importance.

In other words, companies of extreme risk—either high or low— tend to have less extreme risk characteristics over time. There are two logical explanations. First, the risk of existing projects may tend to become less extreme over time. This explanation may be plausible for high risk firms, but it would not seem applicable to low risk firms. Second, new projects taken on by firms may tend to have less extreme risk characteristics than existing projects. If this second explanation is correct, it is interesting to speculate on the reasons. For instance, is it a management decision or do limitations on the availability of profitable projects of extreme risk tend to cause the riskiness of firms to regress towards the grand mean over time?

Though one could continue to speculate on the forces underlying this tendency of risk—as measured by beta coefficients—to regress towards the grand mean over time, it remains for future research to determine the explicit reasons.

NOTES TO SECTION TWO

1. Quite apart from this regression tendency, it is reasonable to suppose that betas do change over time in systematic ways in response to certain changes in the structure of companies.

2. Such regressions were calculated only for securities with complete data. The relative for the market portfolio was measured by Fisher's Combination Link Relative [6].

3. These portfolio betas were derived by averaging the 100 estimates for the individual securities. Alternatively, as [2] shows, the same number would be obtained by regressing the monthly portfolio relatives upon the market index where the portfolio relatives are calculated assuming an equal amount invested in each security at the beginning of each month.

4. These portfolio betas were calculated by regressing portfolio relatives upon the market relatives. The portfolio relatives were taken to be the average of the monthly relatives of the individual securities for which relatives were available. These relatives represent those which would have been realized from an equally-weighted, monthly rebalancing strategy in which a delisted security is sold at the least available price and the proceeds reinvested equally in the remaining securities. This rather complicated procedure takes into account delisted securities and therefore avoids any survivorship bias. In [3], the securities analyzed were required to be listed on the NYSE throughout both the grouping period and the subsequent period, so that there was a potential survivorship bias. Nonetheless, the results reported there are in substantive agreement with the results in Table 2-1.

5. If the betas are continually changing over time, an estimate of beta as provided by a simple regression must be interpreted with considerable caution. For example, if the true beta followed a linear time trend, it is easily shown that the estimated beta can be interpreted as an unbiased estimate of the beta in the middle of the sample period. A similar interpretation would not in general hold if, for instance, the true beta followed a quadratic time trend.

6. It is theoretically possible that the estimated beta for a security whose true beta does not fall into the lowest 100 to be in the lowest 100 estimates with a positive measurement error if the betas for some of the improperly classified securities are measured with sufficiently large positive errors.

7. The author is indebted to Harry Markowitz for suggesting this numerical example as a way of clarifying the subsequent formal development.

8. For further and more detailed discussion of the distinction between $E(\beta_{it} \mid \hat{\beta}_{it})$ and $E(\hat{\beta}_{it} \mid \beta_{it})$, the reader is referred to Vasicek [7].

9. That the regression of estimated betas from a later period on estimates from an earlier period is similar to (2.1) follows from noting that $E(\hat{\beta}_{it+1} \mid \hat{\beta}_{it})$ equals $E(\beta_{it+1} \mid \hat{\beta}_{it})$ and that $\text{cov}(\hat{\beta}_{it+1}, \hat{\beta}_{it})$ equals $\text{cov}(\beta_{it+1}, \hat{\beta}_{it})$. In [3], the

grand mean of all betas was estimated in each period and was not assumed equal to 1.0.

10. Equation (2.3) can be derived alternatively from the assumption that β_{it} and $\hat{\beta}_{it}$ are bivariate normal variables and under the assumption of stationarity β_{it} will equal β_{it+1}. Vasicek [7] has developed using Bayes' Theorem, an expression for $E(\beta_{it} \mid \hat{\beta}_{it})$ which can be shown to be mathematically identical to the right hand side of (2.3). He observed that the procedure used by Merrill Lynch, Pierce, Fenner and Smith, Inc., in their Security Risk Evaluation Service is similar to his expression if $\sigma^2(\eta_{it})$ is assumed to be the same for all securities. Merrill Lynch's procedure, as he presented it, is to use the coefficient of the cross-sectional regression of $(\hat{\beta}_{it+1} - 1)$ on $(\hat{\beta}_{it} - 1)$ to adjust future estimates. This adjustment mechanism is in fact the same as (2.1) or (2.2) which shows that such a cross sectional regression takes into account real changes in the underlying betas. Only if betas were stationary over time would his formula be similar to Merrill Lynch's.

11. The formula for order bias given by (2.3) is similar to that which measures the bias in the estimated slope coefficient in a regression on one independent variable measured with error. Explicitly, consider the regression, $y = bx + \epsilon$, where ϵ is an independent mean-zero normal disturbance and both y and x are measured in deviate form. Now if x is measured with independent mean-zero error η and y is regressed on $x + \eta$, it is well known that the estimated coefficient, $\hat{b}$, will be biased toward zero and the probability limit of $\hat{b}$ is $\dfrac{b}{1 + \dfrac{\sigma^2(\eta)}{\sigma^2(x)}}$. This expression can be rewritten as $\dfrac{\sigma^2(x)}{\sigma^2(x + \eta)} b$. Interpreting x as the true beta less 1.0, the correspondence to (2.3) is obvious. In this type of regression, one could either adjust the independent variables themselves for bias and thus obtain an unbiased estimate of the regression coefficient or run the regression on the unadjusted variables and then adjust the regression coefficient. The final coefficient will be the same in either case.

12. This test of significance was based upon the regression $(\hat{\beta}_{it+1} - 1) = b(\hat{\beta}_{it} - 1) + \epsilon_{it}$ where $\hat{\beta}_{it}$ has been adjusted for order bias. The estimated coefficients with the t-value measured from 1.0 in parentheses were for the five seven-years chronologically 0.86 (−1.14), 0.94 (−0.88), 0.71 (−3.84), 0.86 (−3.23), and 0.81 (−2.57). Note that even if β_{it} were measured with substantial independent error contrary to fact, the estimated b would not be biased towards zero because, as note 10 shows, the adjustment for the order bias has already corrected for this bias.

13. Using the same regression as in the previous note, the estimated coefficient b with the t-value measured from 1.0 in parentheses were for the four possible comparisons in chronological order 0.92 (−0.69), 0.74 (−2.67), 0.62 (−6.86), and 0.58 (−5.51).

REFERENCES

1. Fischer Black, Michael C. Jensen and Myron Scholes. "The Capital Asset Pricing Model: Some Empirical Tests," in Michael C. Jensen, ed., *Studies in the Theory of Capital Markets*. New York: Praeger Publishing, 1972.

2. Marshall Blume, "Portfolio Theory: A Step Towards Its Practical Application," *Journal of Business* (April 1970).

3. _____ . "On the Assessment of Risk," *Journal of Finance* (March 1971).

4. _____ and Irwin Friend. "A New Look at the Capital Asset Pricing Model," *Journal of Finance* (March 1973).

5. Eugene F. Fama and James D. MacBeth, "Risk, Return and Equilibrium: Empirical Tests," *Journal of Political Economy* (May 1973).

6. Lawrence Fisher. "Some New Stock-Market Indexes," *Journal of Business* (January 1966), supplement.

7. Oldrich A. Vasicek. "A Note on Using Cross-Sectional Information in Bayesian Estimation of Security Betas," *Journal of Finance* (December 1973).

Section Three

Ex Ante and Ex Post
Measures of Return

Marshall E. Blume

This chapter presents some preliminary thoughts and empirical evidence on forecasting the future course of the stock market. Following a discussion of what in an efficient market may be possible to forecast and what may be impossible to forecast, the chapter goes on to propose a model to explain expected returns based upon the usual discounted cash flow model. The study then uses the capital asset pricing model to develop an alternative model to explain expected returns. Along with these models are some empirical tests which are not only interesting in their own right, but also illustrate how misleading some types of tests can be.

3.1 WHAT MAY BE POSSIBLE TO FORECAST

Unlike many macroeconomic variables, a correct forecast of the future level of the stock market can be used directly to make handsome profits. Over the forty-five year period from the beginning of 1927 to the end of 1972, a simple investment strategy which only assumes knowledge of whether the dividend-adjusted level of the market a month hence would be higher or lower than the current level would have produced after commissions an annual compounded rate of return of 51.4 percent—considerably higher than those reported by Fisher and Lorie.[1] This strategy involves the purchase or short sale of the market portfolio at the beginning of each month according to whether the market at the end of that month will be higher or lower than at the beginning.

In view of these potentially large returns from only limited knowledge of the future level of the market, many practitioners have attempted to forecast the market. The *New York Times*, as well as other publications, periodically report forecasts made by different members of the financial community. If it were easy and cheap to obtain accurate forecasts of the future level of the stock market, one would expect that all investors would be using such forecasts in managing their investments.

If investors could obtain accurate forecasts cheaply and if, for instance, all investors believed that the market would be lower at the end of a month or a year by a sufficient amount to cover transaction costs, each individual investor would try to sell his portfolio of stocks or even sell them short. The end result would be that no stocks would be held long. This situation is clearly inconsistent with market inventory constraints unless the prices of all securities go to zero.[2] That this has not happened empirically suggests that never have all investors believed with sufficient conviction that the stock market would be lower at some future point in time to liquidate their holdings of common stock.

More generally, if investors make intelligent choices, using all available information, it is most unlikely that a forecast of the market based upon any relatively simple econometric model would be of sufficient accuracy to produce superior investment performance consistently. Some might however take the position that econometric models require such a level of sophistication that only a few investors could use them. This position however receives no support from the empirical evidence. Certainly institutional investors have the resources to utilize econometric models in devising their strategies, but no comprehensive study has ever found that such institutional investors on average outperform individual investors.[3] For the more studied mutual funds, there is no reason to believe that the performance of any fund which historically has consistently outreturned other funds at the same level of risk could not be attributed solely to chance.

Despite these arguments, it is apparent that some academicians do believe that the signals from econometric models may potentially be accurate enough to justify an investment decision to sell the market short or at the minimum switch from equity holdings to risk free assets. For example, Homa and Jaffee[4] simulate an investment strategy using an econometric model based upon the money supply to signal shifts between the stock market and government bills. They conclude that their simulated results are "sufficiently encouraging to indicate the value of further research in this area." In interpreting their results, one might note two items: first, although the coefficients in their model are based upon prior data, the structure of the model appears to have been determined at least in part by the same data which were subsequently used in the simulation.[5] Second, the root-mean-squared error of using Standard & Poor's Composite Index to forecast the next quarter's value of that index was 4.86 over the sixties—the same period as their forecasts. The root-squared-errors of the forecasts using their monetary model were between 4.54 and 5.39.[6] The exact value hinges upon the way in which the money supply is predicted.

Accepting the extreme difficulty in an efficient market of forecasting the market with sufficient accuracy to generate larger than normal trading profits, an economist may nonetheless find econometric models useful in answering questions such as: How do investors form their assessments of future expected returns for the market? What do investors expect from the stock market in the future? Have the returns investors expected from the market, though probably not realized, changed over time? When bond yields are up, are investors' expectations for the stock market also up? The answers to several of these questions have, for instance, immediate implications for measuring a firm's cost of capital.

In summary, if the stock market is efficient, the application of econometric techniques to this market seems governed by the following principle: Any mechanical forecasting device will probably not succeed for long if the forecasts are of sufficient accuracy to obtain superior investment results.

3.2 THE DISCOUNTED CASH FLOW MODEL

This section explores the usefulness of the standard discounted cash flow model in explaining the expected returns on the market. In part for reasons discussed above, it does not attempt to design a model which might be capable of producing superior investment returns.

The presentation of the standard cash flow model requires the following definitions:

M_t the value of a share of the market portfolio at time t.

X_t the earnings per share of the market portfolio reported at time t (after allowance for depreciation).

m_t the price-earnings ratio at time t.

D_t the dividends per share paid at time t.

k_t . the retention rate defined as $\dfrac{X_t - D_t}{X_t}$

g_t the growth rate of earnings, defined as $(X_t/X_{t-1} - 1)$

ρ_t the risk adjusted discount rate applicable to period t.

It is assumed that ρ_t is known at time $t-1$. Uncertainty is introduced into the model through m_t and X_t, which are not assumed known until time t. Since it will ultimately be assumed in testing the final model that the retention rate is known and constant over time, the theoretical development to follow will also make this assumption. The subscript on k_t will therefore be dropped.

For an investor with an one-period horizon, the value of a share in the market portfolio at time $t-1$ according to the discounted cash flow model will be given by

$$M_{t-1} = \frac{E(D_t + M_t)}{1 + \rho_t} \qquad (3.1)$$

where the expectation operator is taken as of time $t-1$. Assuming a retention rate of $k,^7$ one obtains after multiplying by $1 + \rho_t$ and dividing by M_{t-1}:

$$1 + \rho_t = \frac{E(D_t)}{M_{t-1}} + \frac{E(M_t)}{M_{t-1}} \qquad (3.2)$$

The substitution of $m_t\, X_{t-1}(1 + g_t)$ for M_t in (3.2) yields

$$1 + \rho_t = E\left(\frac{D_t}{M_{t-1}}\right) + \frac{E[(m_t)(1+g_t)]}{m_{t-1}} \qquad (3.3)$$

since X_{t-1} is nonrandom and m_{t-1} equals M_{t-1}/X_{t-1}.

The first term after the equality represents the expected dividend yield. The second term may be rewritten as

$$E\left[\frac{m_t}{m_{t-1}}\right]\left[1 + E(g_t)\right],$$

if the assumption is made that m_t and g_t are distributed independently. This assumption may seem implausible at first glance. It is easy to conceive of a situation in which past growth rates might convey information about future growth rates and therefore about the value of m_t. It is even possible that past growth rates may convey information about changes in future risk. Nonetheless, previous growth rates for individual companies appear to have little value in forecasting future growth rates.[8] To the extent such a conclusion generalizes to the market as a whole, this assumption of independence has some empirical support.

Making this assumption of independence, (3.3) can be rewritten as

$$\rho_t = E\left(\frac{D_t}{M_{t-1}}\right) + E\left(\frac{m_t}{m_{t-1}}\right)E(g_t) + [E\left(\frac{m_t}{m_{t-1}}\right) - 1]. \qquad (3.4)$$

If it is assumed that the realized return on the market, $[(M_t - M_{t-1}) + D_t]/M_{t-1}$ can be expressed as ρ_t plus a mean-zero independent stationary normal disturbance term ϵ_t, (3.4) can be reexpressed in a model which will be tested below as

$$\frac{M_t - M_{t-1} + D_t}{M_{t-1}} = E\left(\frac{D_t}{M_{t-1}}\right) + E\left(\frac{m_t}{m_{t-1}}\right)E(g_t)$$

$$+ [E\left(\frac{m_t}{m_{t-1}}\right) - 1] + \epsilon_t \qquad (3.5)$$

The empirical adequacy of (3.5) to explain the expected returns—not realized returns—for a share of the market portfolio was examined with monthly data from March 1947 through January 1971. The market return was measured by the return on the Standard & Poor's Composite Index adjusted for dividends.[9]

In measuring the independent variables, it was assumed that the expected multiple next month would be unchanged from that of the current month.[10] This assumption, which amounts to setting $E(m_t/m_{t-1})$ to 1.0, has the pragmatic advantage of vastly simplifying (3.5), leaving only two variables to be measured. The assumption also has some empirical support. From January 1954 through December 1971, the correlation of successive changes in the monthly price earnings ratio of the Standard & Poor's Composite Index was 0.047, which is insignificantly different from zero. Thus, the past sequence of price-earnings ratios may be of little value in forecasting future changes. Although it may be possible to forecast such changes with data other than past price-earnings ratios, it is not implausible to assume that $E(m_t/m_{t-1})$ equals 1.0 as a first approximation.[11]

The dividend yield was measured by the dividend index for the Standard & Poor's Composite Index expressed on a monthly basis and divided by the previous month-end value of that index. Since the first order serial correlation of these yields was 0.991, the immediately previous value was assumed to be a good approximation of the expected value for the following month. Estimates of the expected growth rates were determined as averages of past growth rates in dividends defined as $(D_t/D_{t-1} - 1)$. Such averages were calculated over twelve months, twenty-four months, and so on up to 144 months. In addition, just the previous monthly value was used. This single observation would be appropriate if the growth rates followed a random walk over time.

Regressions of the monthly market return adjusted for dividends upon past dividend yields and growth rates of dividends conform in many respects to the implications of the theoretical model. Table 3-1 presents these results. The dependent variable is designated for brevity as $RM + RD$. Again for brevity, the lagged value of the dividend yield and the average growth rate obtained from immediately prior data are designated respectively RD_{t-1} and $\overline{G}$. The number of monthly growth rates used in calculating $\overline{G}$ is given in the left-hand column.

The constant term according to (3.5) should be zero. Regardless of how $\overline{G}$ is measured, the estimated constant terms are insignificantly different from zero. The coefficients on RD_{t-1} and $\overline{G}$ should both be positive. The estimated coefficients of RD_{t-1} are generally significant and always positive. The estimated coefficients of $\overline{G}$, though generally insignificant, are of the wrong sign when $\overline{G}$ is calculated with 72 or less observations.

If $\overline{G}$ were correctly measured, the coefficients on both RD_{t-1} and $\overline{G}$ should not only be positive but close to 1.0 according to (3.5). The values of the coefficients on RD_{t-1} are considerably larger than 1.0, while those on $\overline{G}$ are considerably less than 1.0. Further examination discloses a very high inverse relationship between the coefficients on RD_{t-1} and $\overline{G}$. What this suggests is that $\overline{G}$ and RD_{t-1} are interrelated in some way. Indeed, the correlation between RD_{t-1} and $\overline{G}$ range as high as 0.78 for the 48 month average. This interrelationship would suggest that the use of RD_{t-1} alone as an explanatory variable might possibly explain as much of the variation as the two variables combined after adjustment for degrees of freedom.

To examine this possibility, the following two regressions were calculated:

Table 3-1. Regressions for the Discounted Cash Flow Model

Number of Terms in G	Dependent Variable	Constant		RD_{t-1}		$\bar{G}$		$\bar{R}^2$	Autocorrelation of Residuals
		Estimate	t-value	Estimate	t-value	Estimate	t-value		
1	$RM + RD$	−0.0055	−0.80	4.94	2.61	−0.291	−2.26	0.028	0.014
12	$RM + RD$	−0.0050	−0.69	4.55	2.13	−0.119	−0.29	0.011	0.017
24	$RM + RD$	−0.0061	−0.83	5.43	2.36	−0.488	−0.88	0.013	0.004
48	$RM + RD$	−0.0099	−1.32	8.77	2.95	−1.979	−1.95	0.024	−0.007
72	$RM + RD$	−0.0046	−0.64	4.32	1.59	−0.037	−0.03	0.011	0.007
108	$RM + RD$	−0.0059	−0.77	3.81	1.80	0.564	0.46	0.011	0.006
144	$RM + RD$	−0.0069	−0.93	4.35	2.31	0.478	1.05	0.015	0.004
1	RM	−0.0055	−0.78	3.95	2.08	−0.290	−2.26	0.021	0.018
12	RM	−0.0050	−0.69	3.56	1.67	−0.122	−0.29	0.004	0.011
24	RM	−0.0061	−0.84	4.44	1.93	−0.491	−0.89	0.006	0.007
48	RM	−0.0100	−1.32	7.79	2.62	−1.935	−1.96	0.017	−0.003
72	RM	−0.0046	−0.65	3.32	1.22	−0.031	−0.28	0.003	0.010
108	RM	−0.0059	−0.78	2.81	1.32	0.576	0.47	0.004	0.010
144	RM	−0.0070	−0.94	3.36	1.78	0.483	1.06	0.007	0.007

$$RM_t + RD_t = -0.0046 + 4.25RD_{t-1} + \epsilon_t \quad \overline{R}^2 = 0.014 \quad (3.6)$$
$$ (-.65) \quad (2.26)$$

and

$$RM_t + RD_t = 3.10\,RD_{t-1} + \epsilon_t \qquad \overline{R}^2 = 0.016 \; (3.7)$$
$$ (5.38)$$

The second regression incorporates the a priori assumption that the constant term is zero. The coefficients of determination adjusted for degrees of freedom are of the same magnitude as those for the regressions using both RD_{t-1} and $\overline{G}$ as explanatory variables (Table 3-1).

The coefficients for this discounted cash flow appear remarkably stationary over the sample period. For example, the regression of the dividend adjusted market return on the prior month's dividend yield with the constant suppressed resulted in a coefficient of 3.164 for the first half of the sample and 2.907 for the last half.

In comparison to other studies, the coefficients of determination or "R-squareds" reported in this chapter appear quite low. The reason is that the model in this study used as the dependent variable changes in the level of the market, while those earlier studies which obtained high R-squareds used as the dependent variable the levels of the market, not the changes in those levels. A model similar to (3.5) but expressed in levels does produce a large R-squared when fitted to the same data. Thus was obtained the regression

$$M_t = 18.09 + 21.47D_{t-1} - 562.41\,\overline{G} \qquad \overline{R}^2 = 0.99 \; (3.8)$$
$$ (2.15) \quad (6.71) \quad\quad (-2.44)$$

The variable $\overline{G}$ was measured as the average growth rate over the prior 144 months and also has the wrong sign. In calculating these estimates, the Cochrane-Orcutt procedure was used to adjust for first-order serial correlation of the residuals which before adjustment was 0.95. After adjustment, the first order serial correlation dropped to 0.13. The $\overline{R}^2$ before adjustment was 0.92.

The coefficient of determination for this regression measures the capability of the independent variables to explain the level of M_t. If the level of an independent and a dependent variable possess similar time trends, the variables may be strongly correlated even though there is no causal effect between the two. The difficulty in interpreting regressions using levels is that it is difficult to assess how much correlation is due solely to common time trends. Since there appears to be no strong time trend in the rate of change of the market—at least in comparison to the time trend in levels, the rate of change regressions are more easily interpreted than the level regressions. The serial correlation coefficient is 0.997 for the levels of the market adjusted for dividends, while the correlation is 0.025 for the changes in these levels.

The independent variables in the rate of change regressions based upon (3.5) explain only the expected return, ρ_t, and not the deviations from this return which are measured by ϵ_t. The maximum variance which could be explained by regressions based upon (3.5) is therefore roughly $\sigma^2(\rho_t)$. The total variance in the dependent variable $\sigma^2(R_{Mt})$ is the sum of that due to ρ_t and ϵ_t. Thus, the value of the coefficient of determination, if the variables were properly measured, would be the ratio of $\sigma^2(\rho_t)$ to $\sigma^2(R_{Mt})$. The empirical evidence suggests that this ratio is somewhat greater than 0.01, or equivalently that the ratio of $\sigma(\rho_t)$ to $\sigma(R_{Mt})$ is somewhat greater than 0.1. Since $\sigma(R_{Mt})$ over the sample period is 0.037, the value of $\sigma(\rho_t)$ would be on the order of 0.0037 or .37 percent per month.

This measure of the standard deviation of the expected rate of return of .37 percent per month should be interpreted with extreme caution. First, it is based upon the assumption of normality which can be viewed as only a rough approximation to the underlying distribution of stock market returns. Second, it is difficult to restate this number on a quarterly or annual basis particularly if there is any time dependence in expected returns. The average monthly return over the sample period was 1.06 percent per month. Thus, if normality were assumed, the monthly expected rate of returns would be less than 0.32 percent or more than 1.80 percent five percent of the time. This magnitude of variability seems quite large. Much additional work will be required to determine whether such a large range stems purely from violations of statistical assumptions and if not, whether it is consistent with an efficient market.

That the coefficients of determination reported above are small is probably not unique to tests of the discounted cash flow model. Such low R squareds might be expected for tests of any model which attempts to explain the returns on the stock market expected, but not necessarily realized, by investors.

Consider any model developed to explain ρ_t. Let such a model be designated by $f(X)$ where X is a vector of variables whose values are available at time $t - 1$. Now if the realized return on the market can be expressed, as above, as ρ_t plus a mean-zero independent stationary normal disturbance term ϵ_t, we have by substitution in $\rho_t = f(X)$ the following:

$$\frac{M_t + M_{t-1} + D_t}{M_{t-1}} = f(X) + \epsilon_t. \qquad (3.9)$$

As with the discounted cash flow model, $\bar{R}$ will approximate the ratio of $\sigma(\rho_t)$ to $\sigma(R_{Mt})$. In the post-World War II period, it will be recalled that $\sigma(R_{Mt})$ is 0.037. During this same period, roughly two thirds of the average monthly total returns were due to capital gains. If the standard deviation of the total expected return were three times that of the dividend yield, the value of $\sigma(\rho_t)$ for this period would be roughly .003, which would imply an $\bar{R}^2$ of around .01. Even if the standard deviation of total return were ten times as large as that of the dividend yield, the value of $\bar{R}^2$ would only be as high as 0.1. Thus, this author at least would be surprised to see a large coefficient of determination in a test of a model designed to explain expected returns on the stock market using prior data.

3.3 THE CAPITAL ASSET PRICING MODEL

The capital asset pricing model provides at least theoretically an alternative method of explaining the variability in the expected rates of return on the stock market. Under assumptions which have been discussed extensively elsewhere,[1][2] this model shows that the expected risk premium on asset or portfolio i is given by

$$E(R_{it}) - R_{Ft} = \beta_i [E(R_{gt}) - R_{Ft}] \qquad (3.10)$$

The variable R_{gt} is the return on the entire market portfolio which we shall assume consists of equities and bonds. The variable β_i is defined as the $\mathrm{cov}(R_i, R_g)/\mathrm{var}(R_g)$. Several studies[1][3] have pointed out significant empirical deficiencies of the capital asset pricing model. The relationship of the analysis to be carried out in this section and these earlier studies will be discussed below. For the moment, we shall assume the validity of the model.

The interpretation of R_{it} first as the return from a portfolio of stocks and second as the return from a portfolio of bonds leads to the two equations

$$E\left(\frac{M_t - M_{t-1} + D_t}{M_{t-1}}\right) - R_{Ft} = \beta_M [E(R_{gt}) - R_{Ft}] \qquad (3.11)$$

and

$$E\left(\frac{B_t - B_{t-1} + C_t}{B_{t-1}}\right) - R_{Ft} = \beta_B [E(R_{gt}) - R_{Ft}] \qquad (3.12)$$

where B_t is the market price of a bond in the bond portfolio and C_t is the coupon paid per bond during period t. Eliminating $E(R_{gt}) - R_{Ft}$ from (3.11) and 3.12) gives

$$E\left(\frac{M_t - M_{t-1} + D_t}{M_{t-1}}\right) - R_{Ft} = \frac{\beta_M}{\beta_B}\left[E\left(\frac{B_t - B_{t-1} + C_t}{B_{t-1}}\right) - R_{Ft}\right]$$

(3.13)

It would be anticipated that the ratio of β_M to β_B would be positive and greater than 1.0.

As before, the assumption that the observed return on the market portfolio of common stocks is $\rho_t + \epsilon_t$ gives the testable model

$$RM_t + RD_t - R_{Ft} = \frac{\beta_M}{\beta_B}\left[E(RB_t + RC_t) - R_{Ft}\right] + \epsilon_t \quad (3.14)$$

where RB_t is the yield on bonds due to changes in the price of a bond and RC_t is the yield due to coupon payments.

If the capital market line were expected to remain unchanged for every period into the future and if the expected holding period return on a multiperiod instrument were the product of the future expected one-period returns,[14] the coupon yield on a default-free consol will measure its expected return over the next period. If, however, the capital market line were expected to change in the future, the coupon yield would reflect the anticipated capital gain or loss. For example, assume that for the risk of a particular consol paying one dollar, the expected return next period were 10 percent and thereafter only 5 percent. It can be shown the present price of this consol would be $5.45 for a stated yield of 18 percent. The expected return however would be only 10 percent as investors would anticipate a capital loss of 45 cents or 8 percent.

Thus, in order to use the stated yield as the one-period expected return, it will be assumed that the capital market line is expected to remain unchanged in the future. During periods when the term structure of interest is declining, this assumption may be totally inappropriate. Such would be the case, for instance, in the twenties. In the post-World War II period, this assumption is more plausible.

The yield on a consol was approximated by the yield on a long term bond index, namely the Standard & Poor's Composite Bond Index. The riskfree yield was measured by the monthly series for government bills developed by Bildersee.[15] The return on the stock market was measured as before. The sample period was also the same as before—March 1947 through January 1971. The value of the bond yield and riskfree rate would have been available prior to the period over which the return on the stock market was measured.

The regression of the market return less the riskfree rate on the expected risk premium for the bond market conformed to the theoretical model as given by (3.13) in two respects. The constant term was insignificantly different from zero and the coefficient on the risk premium for bonds was greater than 1.0. The regression itself was

$$RM_t + RD_t - R_{Ft} = -0.009 + 14.13\,(RB_{t-1} - R_{Ft}) \qquad \overline{R}^2 = 0.033$$
$$(-1.58) \quad (3.27)$$

$$(3.15)$$

The value of $\overline{R}^2$ relative to the sum of squares of the market return was 0.020 and the first order serial correlation of the residuals was 0.007. If one places the a priori restriction that the constant is zero to obtain a more efficient estimate, the regression becomes

$$RM_t + RD_t - R_{Ft} = 7.89\,(RB_{t-1} - R_{Ft}) \qquad \overline{R}^2 = 0.028 \qquad (3.16)$$
$$(4.85)$$

Thus, a 0.1 percent monthly risk premium on bonds is associated with a .78 percent risk premium on stocks. Equivalently, the beta on the average stock is 7.89 times as large as the beta for the average bond.

The coefficients of this model are less stationary than those of the discounted cash flow model. Suppressing the constant, the coefficient of the expected bond premium is 10.36 in the first half of the period, March 1947 through January 1959, and 4.87 in the second half ending January 1971. Both coefficients are significant. The value of the coefficient in the second half, if taken at face value, would indicate a narrowing of the gap between the beta on the average stock and that on the average bond.

The remainder of this section will comment on the relationship of these empirical results to previous tests of the capital asset pricing model. These previous tests have generally shown that the risk-return tradeoff which is implied by common stocks listed on the New York Stock Exchange predicts returns for riskfree assets which often differ by significant amounts from actual riskfree rates. These tests leave unanswered the question of what the relationship is, if any, between the bond and the stock markets. Equation (3.16) suggests that the expected risk premiums on common stocks vary directly with expected risk premiums on long-term bonds as indicated by the significant *t*-values. This is, of course, a much stronger statement than the statement that the expected risk premium on the portfolio of common stocks exceeds that expected on the portfolio of long term bonds. Whether the expected returns on long term bonds lie on, above, or below the risk-return tradeoff as determined by common stocks awaits further study.

3.4 CONCLUSION

Recognizing that in an efficient market it would be very difficult to use econometric models to devise investment strategies promising above average returns, the chapter explored the empirical properties of two models in explaining future expected returns on the stock market. The first was a traditional discounted cash flow model; the second was derived from the capital asset pricing model. Both of these models produced low coefficients of determination. The study pointed out that one should not expect large values for such coefficients in tests of models like these two. The preliminary results are sufficiently encouraging and interesting to justify further analyses of these models.

NOTES TO SECTION THREE

1. Fisher and Lorie (1970).
2. This argument makes the assumption that the risk free rate is positive and that investors are risk averse.
3. Cf. Friend, Blume, and Crockett (1970) for a bibliography.
4. Homa and Jaffee (1971).
5. For example, it is hard to visualize any a priori argument for including in an equation to forecast the growth of the money supply the square of the lagged value of unemployment but not the lagged value itself.
6. The root-mean-square errors reported by Homa and Jaffe (1971) were up to five percent larger than those reported in the text. These differences could be due to rounding errors or possibly to typographical errors in their Table 2.
7. Robichek and Bogue (1971) show that the price-earning ratio or multiple is a function of the retention rate. Likewise, the growth rate of X_t is a function of the retention rate. In a more general model which does not assume a fixed k, m_t and g_t would be explicit functions of k.
8. Cragg and Malkiel (1968).
9. The dividend adjustment was to add to $(M_t - M_{t-1})/M_{t-1}$ the ratio of one twelfth of the Composite dividend index at time t, D_t, to M_{t-1}.
10. This assumption is, of course, more plausible for the market as a whole than for segments of the markets such as stocks with high or low multiples.

11. It is planned in future work to relax this assumption. For example, the expected ratio of the multiples might be measured by the ratio of the current yield on high grade bonds to the yield which would be expected at the end of the month.

12. Blume and Friend (1973).

13. Friend and Blume (1970), Black, Jensen and Scholes (1972), Blume and Friend (1973), and Fama and MacBeth (1973).

14. The risk of a multiperiod instrument might be expected to change over time. Such changes, if stochastic, would invalidate except in special cases the traditional capital asset pricing model and limit the theoretical generality of the text.

15. Bildersee (1973).

REFERENCES

Bildersee, John S., "The Association Between a Market Determined Measure of Risk and Alternative Measures of Risk," Working Paper #8-73, Rodney L. White Center for Financial Research, (August 1973).

Black, Fischer, Michael C. Jensen, and Myron Scholes. "The Capital Asset Pricing Model: Some Empirical Tests," in Michael C. Jensen, ed. *Studies in the Theory of Capital Markets.* (New York: Praeger Publishing, 1972).

Blume, Marshall, "Portfolio Theory: A Step Towards Its Practical Application," *Journal of Business* (April 1970).

_____, "On the Assessment of Risk," *Journal of Finance*, (March 1971).

_____, and Irwin Friend, "A New Look at the Capital Asset Pricing Model," *Journal of Finance*, (March 1973).

_____, and Frank Husic, "Price, Beta and Exchange Listing," *Journal of Finance*, (May 1973).

Cragg, John G., and Burton G. Malkiel, "The Consensus and Accuracy of Some Predictions of the Growth of Corporate Earnings," *Journal of Finance*, (March 1968).

Cunningham, Stephen, "Improved Estimates and Forecasts of Beta Coefficients," Mimeograph, (1973).

Fama, Eugene, and James D. MacBeth, "Risk, Return and Equilibrium: Empirical Tests," *Journal of Political Economy*, (May 1973).

Fisher, Lawrence, and James H. Lorie, "Some Studies of Variability of Returns on Investments in Common Stocks," *Journal of Business*, (April 1970).

Friend, Irwin, Marshall E. Blume, and Jean Crockett, *Mutual Funds and Other Institutional Investors: A New Perspective*, (New York: McGraw Hill, 1970).

_____, and Marshall E. Blume, "Measurement of Portfolio Performance Under Uncertainty," *American Economic Review*, (September 1970).

Homa, Kenneth E., and Dwight M. Jaffee, "The Supply of Money and Common Stock Prices," *Journal of Finance*, (December 1971).

Malinvaud, E., *Statistical Methods of Econometrics:* second revised ed., (New York: American Elsevier, 1970).

Robichek, Alexander, A., and Marcus C. Bogue, "A Note on the Behavior of Expected Price/Earnings Ratios Over Time," *Journal of Finance*, (June 1971).

✳︎ *Section Four*

The Relation Between Real and Financial Measures of Risk and Return

Stewart C. Myers*

This chapter is concerned with the real determinants of the risk of common stocks, most specifically with the real determinants of "beta" (β), the key variable of the Capital Asset Pricing Model developed by Sharpe, Lintner and Mossin.[1] It is worth devoting a few introductory paragraphs to explaining why this is an important issue.

Modern portfolio theory, and particularly the capital asset pricing model (CAPM), have profoundly influenced economists' understanding of how capital markets work. They have also had a limited, but significant effect on the way portfolio managers and investment analysts do their jobs. Their effect on theory and practice in the real sector has been insignificant, however. It is true that one can use the CAPM to prove general theorems about corporate financing policy, but the model has yielded no new theorems, and more general proofs of the old ones are available.[2] The CAPM is potentially an operational framework for corporate capital budgeting decisions under uncertainty,[3] but its practical use has been limited to tentative studies using firms' betas to help estimate their costs of capital. It is also potentially useful in the area of public utility regulation, but again, there is only a handful of actual applications.[4]

One principal difficulty is directly evident from the most commonly used expression of the CAPM.

*The chapter was completed while I was Visiting Professor at the London Graduate School of Business, which I would like to thank for research support. I also thank Mr. Sudipto Bhattacharya and Dr. Stewart Turnbull for their perceptive comments.

$$E(\tilde{R}_j) - R_F = \beta_j [E(\tilde{R}_m) - R_F], \qquad (4.1)$$

where:

$E(\tilde{R}_j)$ = the expected one-period rate of return offered by asset j,

$E(\tilde{R}_m)$ = the expected one-period return on the market portfolio,

R_F = the one-period risk-free rate of interest, and

$$\beta_j = \text{cov}(\tilde{R}_j, \tilde{R}_m)/\text{var}(\tilde{R}_m), \text{ asset } j\text{'s "beta".}$$

This formula is expressed entirely in terms of market rates of return; for example, R_{jt} is defined as

$$\tilde{R}_{jt} = \frac{\tilde{D}_{jt} + \tilde{P}_{jt} - P_{j,t-1}}{P_{j,t-1}}.$$

Suppose a firm wanted to use this theory to assess the value of a potential capital investment requiring an outlay I at $t = 0$. The investment should be taken if the project's contribution to stock value exceeds I—that is, $\Delta P_0 > I$—but of course, ΔP_0 is observable only if the investment is financed as a separate enterprise, and only *after* that enterprise's stock has been sold. Thus in practice the firm must estimate ΔP_0. If it somehow knows the asset's beta, then the appropriate market capitalization rate, $E(R)$, can be calculated from (4.1), and ΔP_0 estimated by

$$\Delta P_o = \frac{E(\Delta D_1 + \Delta P_1)}{1 + E(R)}.$$

But this is not much help for an asset surviving for more than one period. Today's price cannot be obtained without an estimate of tomorrow's. Moreover, it is difficult to see how the firm could know the asset's beta, since in a multiperiod world the CAPM defines beta only in terms of the covariance of security prices over time, and offers no clues as to the determinants of the asset's price level or stochastic behavior.

To summarize, the capital asset pricing model is expressed primarily in terms of the prices of *financial* assets. It states a necessary equilibrium relationship between these prices, given their stochastic behavior over a period of time. But it says very little about how these prices are determined by real variables that the firm can estimate directly.

Developing a fully rigorous and operational theory of the real determinants of asset values is a task far too difficult to attempt here. This study is instead devoted to summing up progress to date and to identifying the likely next steps. It is divided into two parts dealing with the following issues:

1. What is the state of empirical knowledge about the real determinants of beta?
2. To what extent is this knowledge consistent with theory? Where do we go from here?

As I will show, there have been extensive investigations of the real or book characteristics of high risk firms. The results are mostly consistent with intuition, in that (various proxies for) earnings variability, growth, cyclicality and financial leverage are significantly correlated with beta. However, there is not much theory having more than intuitive content. The missing link is a dynamic model of a firm's earnings behavior, growth and market valuation. In Part II of this paper, I present a model which partly fills this gap.

4.1 EMPIRICAL WORK ON THE REAL DETERMINANTS OF BETA

In finance the normal methodology is model-building first and testing afterwards. In this case the order is reversed, as it is in this chapter. This part reviews and summarizes all the empirical work known to me relating to the real determinants of stocks' systematic risk. However, it is impossible to provide a full description of each study's experimental design. The following discussion is limited to the main ideas and results.

4.1.1 Beaver, Kettler, and Scholes

Beaver, Kettler, and Scholes (BKS, [2]) were the empirical pioneers, although Ball and Brown's work [1] preceded theirs. However, the Ball and Brown study is mostly devoted to other, broader issues, and the part investigating the real determinants of systematic risk is much less informative than the BKS study. In any event, Ball and Brown's results were confirmed by BKS.

BKS used seven accounting variables that intuition or tradition suggest are associated with high-risk firms.

1. *Dividend payout*, defined as total dividends per share paid by the firm over a nine-year period, divided by total earnings per share over the same period. Two arguments can be made for including payout as an independent variable. First, most firms attempt to achieve stable (or stable growth in) dividends, and in normal times regard them almost as a fixed liability. Nevertheless, earnings have to cover dividends, at least in the long run. The higher the variance of earnings, the lower must the normal dividend be set in order to keep the probability of "trouble" (earnings less than the normal dividend) acceptably low. Thus dividend payout should be a proxy for managements' uncertainty about future earnings. Second, firms which grow rapidly usually retain a greater proportion of earnings. Since there is a long tradition in the literature associating high growth with high risk, low dividend payout should be a proxy for high risk.[5]

2. *Growth*, measured by the log of the five-year change in net book assets. Again, the rationale is the traditional association between rapid growth and high business risk.

3. *Financial leverage*, measured by the ratio of book debt to net book assets. Given business risk, the CAPM predicts a positive linear relationship between beta and the ratio of the *market* value of debt to the total market value of the firm (debt plus equity).[6] However, this relationship will be difficult to observe if firms with low business risk find they can issue more debt.[7] In the limiting case where firms keep the *sum* of business and financial risk constant, there will be no evident relationship between the debt ratio and beta (until other variables successfully account for differences in business risk).

4. *Liquidity*, measured by ratio of current assets to current liabilities. This is widely used as measure of solvency by creditors.

5. *Size*, measured by the log of net book assets. Casual observation suggests a relationship between size and safety, and to the extent that size reflects diversification of activity, theory predicts that large firms will have lower *total* risk. There is no rigorous theory predicting that large firms have lower systematic risk, however.

6. *Earnings variability*, measured by the standard deviation of earnings per share over nine years, where each year's net earnings available to common is normalized by dividing by the value of the firm's stock at the end of the preceding year. It makes sense to predict that firms with highly volatile earnings will have highly volatile stock prices. This means high *total* risk, however, not necessarily high systematic risk. There is an empirical correlation between total and systematic risk, but this is to be expected, simply because the former includes the latter. It is not true that increased

total risk necessarily means increased systematic risk. Also, note that this variable is partly dependent on variable 3, financial leverage: the more debt the firm uses, the greater the variance of earnings available to common stockholders.

7. *The "Earnings Beta"*, which is the slope coefficient of the regression of the firm's net earnings (again normalized by the preceding period's stock value) on the average normalized earnings for the entire sample of firms. Thus it is a measure of *cyclicality*, that is, the extent to which fluctuations in the firm's earnings are correlated with fluctuations in earnings of firms generally. Since stock prices clearly respond to earnings, both individually and generally, the earnings beta and the stock beta ought to be strongly related.

I suspect that most readers will find this list of variables intuitively reasonable. The intuitive concept of risk, however, includes many things that are *not* necessarily related to risk as defined by the CAPM. A rigorous a priori hypothesis can be made with respect to only one of the seven variables, namely financial leverage. A less rigorous but very plausible case can be made for variable 7, the "Accounting Beta." As for the other five variables, there is no theory.

BKS tested the relationships between these variables and beta by cross-sectional tests on a sample of 307 firms for which complete accounting and stock price data were available for the period 1947-65. Actually, four separate tests were run. First, the data were split into two subperiods, 1947-56 and 1957-65. Within each period, tests were performed both on individual securities and on five-security portfolios. The portfolios were formed by ranking the stocks on basis of the relevant *accounting* variable, and then assigning firms ranked 1-5 to portfolio 1, those ranked 6-10 to portfolio 2, etc. Tests were then performed on portfolio averages of the accounting variables and betas.[8]

For each of the four cases, pairwise rank correlations were calculated between each of the seven variables and contemporaneous firm or portfolio betas. The results are shown in Table 4-1. It is gratifying that leverage and the accounting beta show the strong positive correlations expected on theoretical grounds. (In this case a rank correlation of ±.14 is significant at approximately the one percent confidence level.) Earnings variability and payout also have significant correlations in the expected direction. Size has a somewhat weaker correlation. Finally, growth and liquidity, although they were significantly correlated with beta in the first subperiod, are totally unrelated in the second. In view of this, it is hard to put much faith in these two variables.

Table 4-1. **Contemporaneous Association Between Market Determined Measure of Risk and Seven Accounting Risk Measures[a]**

| | Period One (1947-56) | | Period Two (1957-65) | |
	Individual Level	Portfolio[b] Level	Individual Level	Portfolio[b] Level
Variable				
Payout	−.49 (−.50)	−.79 (−.77)	−.29 (−.24)	−.50 (−.45)
Growth	.27 (.23)	.56 (.51)	.01 (.03)	.02 (.07)
Leverage	.23 (.23)	.41 (.45)	.22 (.25)	.48 (.56)
Liquidity	−.13 (−.13)	−.35 (−.44)	.05 (−.01)	.04 (−.01)
Size	−.06 (−.07)	−.09 (−.13)	−.16 (−.16)	−.30 (−.30)
Earnings Variability	.66 (.58)	.90 (.77)	.45 (.36)	.82 (.62)
Accounting Beta	.44 (.39)	.68 (.67)	.23 (.23)	.46 (.46)

[a]Rank correlation coefficients appear in top row, and product-moment correlations appear in parentheses in bottom row.

[b]The portfolio correlations are based upon 61 portfolios of 5 securities each.

Source: Beaver, Kettler, and Scholes [2], p. 669.

Viewed as a whole, the results are encouraging. Theory, what there is of it, is supported, and intuition is confirmed. However, one can obtain significant associations between variables without actually explaining very much, and to some extent that is the case here. BKS ran a second test in which they attempted to *predict* the 1957-65 betas by using the accounting variables from the earlier 1947-56 period. The best explanator of the 1947-56 betas, as determined by regression analysis, is a linear combination of dividend payout, asset growth and earnings variability. This procedure explains 44.7 percent of the variance in the first period's betas.[9] However, when this equation is used to predict the 1957-65 betas, using accounting variables from the first period, only 24 percent of the variance is explained. This is not too impressive, considering that 21 percent is explained by the "naive" prediction that the 1957-65 beta would be equal to the 1947-56 beta. Nevertheless, it is some improvement. Moreover, it must be remembered that 100 percent prediction accuracy is impossible. Even if we knew the exact, true betas of all firms for the second period, we could not predict the *measured* betas, for that would require an exact a priori prediction of the sampling errors encountered in estimation.

4.1.2 White

White [27] followed broadly the same methodology as BKS, but with important differences in variable definition and in the way the tests were carried out. He hypothesized three main factors characteristic of high-beta firms:

1. *High debt ratio.* This variable's effect on beta is predicted by theory and supported by the BKS results. However, White defined the debt ratio in terms of *market* values,[10] which is the specification called for by theory. BKS considered only variables that could be derived from accounting data, and so restricted their tests to the book debt ratio.

2. *Rapid growth* in sales or operating earnings, measured by the log of the relative change of the variable over the period examined. BKS examined growth in book assets but obtained mixed results.

3. *High asset beta*, defined as the slope coefficient of a regression of each firm's percentage change in sales on the contemporaneous percentage change in gross national product. This is analogous to BKS's "accounting beta" in that each measures firms' cyclicality. However, there are two important differences. First, the index used is a national one, not simply an average taken over the firms in the sample under consideration. Since the investor is concerned with the covariance of each stock's return with the rate of return on the entire market (and in principle with its covariance with changes in aggregate national wealth), he should likewise be concerned with the covariance of each firm's income with *national* income. It is true that the average earnings of any reasonably large sample of firms will be highly correlated with national income, but errors will necessarily enter if the sample average is used.

The second difference between White and BKS's definition of cyclicality is that White used sales rather than earnings. It is true that investors are more concerned with earnings than sales per se. But it is *expected* earnings which determine stock prices, and changes in sales may be a better proxy for changes in expected earnings than is the one-period change in accounting earnings. Accounting procedures induce various lags and biases in reported income, for example.

Aside from differences in variable definition, White's study differs from BKS's in the use of relatively large portfolios of securities as the basis for his cross-sectional tests. This has become standard operating procedure in tests of the CAPM, since it vastly reduces errors in measurements of individual firms' betas; these errors otherwise attenuate the observed relationship between firms' betas and their average returns. The aim in the present context is to reduce errors both in measuring beta and in measuring the three hypothesized determinants of beta.

The regressions summarized in Table 4-2 are typical of White's results. In these tests the 210 securities in White's sample were grouped into 10 portfolios of 31 securities each. (The 31 stocks with the highest betas were put in portfolio 1, the 31 with the next highest betas in portfolio 2, etc.) Then four cross-sectional regressions were run, using as independent variables various combinations of the portfolio's asset betas, debt ratios, and rates of sales or earnings growth. As is obvious from the table, White found significant relationships, in the expected direction, for all variables. He also explained a much higher proportion of the variance in the betas, although it must be remembered that in this test there are only 10 portfolio betas to be explained.

These tests were successfully repeated for various subperiods within the 1951-68 period,[11] but I will not attempt to present all the results here. It should be noted, however, that the coefficients of the growth variables dropped to insignificant levels when White repeated his tests for the 1961-1968 subperiod. This matches BKS's findings. However, since the asset beta—the "cyclicality" variable—and the debt ratio both have a strong positive relationship with beta, it is fair to say that White's results support the conclusions of the BKS study, and of course vice versa.

Table 4-2. White's Regression Results for 10 Portfolios of 31 Securities Each, 1951-68

		Variable			
Regression	Constant	Asset Beta	Market Debt Ratio	Sales Growth	Earnings Growth
1	0.505	0.325			
$(R^2 = .71)$	$(4.54)^a$	(4.38)			
2	0.153	0.247	2.45		
$(R^2 = .85)$	(0.969)	(3.88)	(2.62)		
3	−0.347	0.274	2.35	7.16	
$(R^2 = .96)$	(−2.31)	(7.65)	(4.56)	(4.10)	
4	−0.294	0.220	1.69		7.68
$(R^2 = .97)$	(−2.53)	(7.22)	(3.62)		(5.03)

[a]T-statistics in parenthesis below coefficients
Source: White [27], Table 4.6.

4.1.3 Gonedes

Gonedes's work [9] provides additional, and somewhat discouraging, evidence on the importance of BKS's accounting beta as a determinant of firms' stock betas. He dealt with a random sample of 99 firms for the period 1946-67, and three seven-year subperiods, 1946-52, 1953-59, and 1961-67. (The data for 1960 were reserved for various statistical tests which will not be reviewed here.) The accounting betas were measured by regressions of the form

$$\tilde{X}_j = a + b_j \tilde{X}_m + C_j \tilde{X}_I + \tilde{e}_j, \qquad (4.2)$$

where:

$\tilde{X}_j$ = firm j's earnings,

$\tilde{X}_M$ = aggregate earnings of all firms for which complete data were available over the 1946-68 period,

$\tilde{X}_I$ = that part of the aggregate earnings of all other firms in j's industry which could not be explained by X_M, and

$\tilde{e}_j$ = an error term reflecting unsystematic risk.

The 99 firms in the sample were randomly selected from industries for which adequate indexes could be constructed.

Regressions were run using net income (after interest and taxes), net income normalized by net book assets, and first differences of these two variables. As it turned out only the first differences gave significant results.

Gonedes tested for correlation between stock betas and accounting betas measured in terms of scaled net income and found no significant relationship for any subperiods. This is exactly counter to the BKS results. However, some positive relationship was found for accounting betas derived from first differences in scaled income. This is again counter to BKS, who found that this procedure gave poorer results for their sample.[12]

Table 4-3 shows the correlations obtained using accounting betas derived from first differences of scaled net income. Significant relationships are found for the 1946-52 and 1953-59 subperiods when accounting betas are derived from the full 21 years of data, but the relationship disappears in the 1960s. There is no relationship at all when the accounting betas are measured from seven year's data, but this probably indicates only that accounting betas are hard to measure with a handful of observations.

Gonedes also tested for correlation between the coefficients of determination (R^2's) of the equations used to estimate the account-

Table 4-3. Correlation Between Accounting and Stock Betas—Gonedes's Results (Accounting betas derived from first differences in net income scaled by net book assets)

Accounting Beta Measured Over:	Stock Beta Measured Over:		
	1946-52	1953-59	1961-68
1946-68 (Excluding 1960)	.32[b] (.22)[a]	.41[b] (.34)[b]	.08 (.0)
1946-52	.29[b] (.05)		
1953-59		.0 (.04)	
1961-68			.07 (.0)

[a]Significant at 5 percent confidence level.
[b]Significant at 1 percent confidence level.
Source: Gonedes [9], Table 5, pp. 434-35.

ing and stock betas. The proposition is that if the earnings index explains a large proportion of the variance of a firm's earnings, then the stock market index ought to explain a large proportion of the variance in returns on the firm's stock. Gonedes found this to be true, so long as accounting betas were derived from first differences in accounting income. This is certainly evidence of an association between the cyclicality of a firm's earnings and its stock's market prices. However, correlating R^2's and correlating betas are not the same thing, since a firm can have a low R^2 and high beta, or conversely. Thus it is no paradox to find significant correlation of R^2's but insignificant correlation of accounting and stock betas.

There is no obvious reason for the differences between BKS and Gonedes.[13] Particularly in view of White's results, it seems fair to claim that cyclicality, somehow measured, is a determinant of beta. But the measurement of cyclicality and the exact specification of its relationship to beta still pose difficult problems.

4.1.4 Rosenberg and McKibben
One interesting aspect of the tests described so far is that they have uniformly assumed (1) substantial cross-sectional variance of betas and the real determinants of beta, but (2) stability of these variables across time for each firm. Assumption (2) is implicit in the way the betas and the independent variables are measured. However, it is obviously questionable. There is no reason to expect the

determinants of beta to be strictly constant across time, and if the determinants change, beta ought to change too.

Rosenberg and McKibben [26] use an interesting test which explicitly assumes that beta shifts over time. Space is insufficient for a full presentation, but the idea is this. Suppose beta at time t is linearly related to certain real determinants W_{nt}. For firm j,

$$\beta_{jt} = \sum_{n=1}^{N} W_{jnt} b_j. \qquad (4.3)$$

This relationship is assumed to apply to all firms and to be constant over time. However the real determinants vary across firms and time, and thus will beta.

Substituting Equation (4.3) in Equation (4.1) we have:

$$E(\tilde{R}_{jt}) - R_{Ft} = \sum_{n=1}^{N} W_{jnt} b_j \left(E(\tilde{R}_{mt}) - R_{Ft} \right) \qquad (4.4)$$

Normally beta is estimated by fitting the regression equation

$$\hat{r}_{jt} = \hat{\alpha}_j + \hat{\beta}_j \tilde{r}_{mt} + \tilde{e}_{jt}, \qquad (4.5)$$

where the $\tilde{r}_t$'s are returns in excess of the risk free rate. But if Equation (4.4) is correct, (4.5) is incorrect, since it assumes the true value of beta is constant. Instead we should run the regression

$$r_{jt} = \alpha_j + \sum_{n=1}^{N} b_j (\tilde{W}_{jnt} \tilde{r}_{mt}) + e_{jt}, \qquad (4.6)$$

where the independent variables are $(\tilde{W}_{jnt} \tilde{r}_{mt})$, the *products* of the market excess returns and the hypothesized determinants of beta. This procedure allows a direct measurement of the b_j's in Equation (4.3). This one-step procedure is in contrast to the three studies cited above, in which a two-step test was required—one step to estimate the betas and their hypothesized determinants, and another to see whether the hypothesized variables explain the cross-sectional differences in firms' betas.

The results of most interest here were obtained by pooling time series data (yearly observations) and cross-sectional data for 558 firms over the 1954-66 period. (The data have to be pooled because the b_j's in Equations (4.3) and (4.6) are assumed to be the same for all firms.) Unfortunately, the results are hard to compare with those of BKS, White or Gonedes, since Rosenberg and McKibben tried *thirty-one* independent variables, of which eleven are based on stock market data. Thus if we find that a variable which we expect to work does not, this may simply be due to its collinearity with one or more of the other 30 variables. There are four direct measures of firm growth, for example, and at least three other variables which might reasonably be expected to proxy for growth. What is one to conclude from the failure or success of any one of these variables?

Moreover, the inclusion of variables derived from stock market data hampers our quest for the real determinants of beta, since the market behavior of the firm's stock responds to the real variables and to some extent proxies for them. In any case, these financial variables are not usually available for specific real assets. (They are for firms, which are collections of assets, but in many instances are of no help.)

However, Rosenberg and McKibben do confirm the results of BKS, White, and Gonedes in several respects. First, financial leverage is again found to have a significant positive relationship with beta. Second, a positive and highly significant relationship is found for volatility in earnings, measured by the standard deviation of changes in earnings per share over time. Third, strong positive relationships are found for *growth* in sales and earnings (confirming White and BKS).

On the other hand, no significant relationship is found for either the accounting beta or the dividend payout ratio, which is generally contrary to the other authors I have cited. Whether this is an actual failure of these variables given the Rosenberg-McKibben sample and methodology, or whether it is simply a matter of multicollinearity, is hard to say.

There are several other variables tested. Most were insignificant and some of those that were significant had unexpected signs. Rosenberg and McKibben note that the pattern of signs does not correspond to their a priori expectations.[14]

4.1.5 A Tentative Summary

There are several other studies which clarify the real determinants of beta, but it seems inefficient to show the results of each. Instead I will propose a tentative summary at this point, and then note whether the other studies support or weaken this view. It seems safe to identify four factors which contribute to high stock betas.

1. *Cyclicality*. This broad term is meant to include BKS's "accounting beta" and the corresponding risk measures used in the other

studies discussed above. Specific definitions vary, but each study started from the same hypothesis, namely that beta depends on the covariance between swings in the firm's earnings and swings in earnings in the economy generally. This hypothesis is not based on a fully rigorous model, but it is so much in the spirit of the CAPM that it is hard not to hold it a priori. The empirical results of BKS and White strongly support the idea and Gonedes's work partly supports it. Rosenberg and McKibben do not find the accounting beta to be significantly related to the stock beta, but I am inclined to think that the effect was stolen by one of their 30 other independent variables.

2. *Earnings Variability.* Both BKS and Rosenberg-McKibben find earnings volatility to be strongly related to beta. This is mildly disturbing from a theoretical point of view, since earnings volatility represents the total, not the systematic risk of earnings; we would expect it to be less important than the "accounting beta" or some other measure of cyclicality. Nevertheless, earnings variability corresponds closely to the popular, intuitive idea of firm risk, and it is a sensible proxy for cyclicality. Thus it certainly belongs on any tentative list of real factors associated with beta.

However, it is unfortunate that no studies have separated the variance of firms' earnings into systematic and unsystematic components, and tested which component is more strongly related to beta. If the CAPM is right, the systematic component ought to be more important.

3. *Financial Leverage.* Theory specifies a relationship between the market debt ratios and beta, but the effect comes through strongly even when the book debt ratio is used.

4. *Growth*, which can be measured in a variety of ways. BKS, White and Rosenberg-McKibben all found growth to be important, although the effect seems less strong in the 1960s than earlier. BKS also found dividend payout to be important, which is consistent, since rapid growth normally is associated with low payout, and there is no reason for dividend policy per se to affect risk.[15]

It is not at all clear how best to *measure* growth. Moreover, the studies cited have not drawn a clear distinction between growth as expansion and growth defined as the opportunity to invest in projects offering expected rates of return exceeding the cost of capital.

Several other comments should be made before turning to other studies. First, none of the four investigations described above has a complete theoretical base. The authors would of course agree, and note their willingness to use one as soon as it is discovered. But we must bear in mind that the puzzles they encountered may be due to use of the wrong functional specification. Rosenberg and McKibben do at least assume a specific, plausible specification and develop consistent tests, but they would agree that their choice of independent variables is not based on any clear theory.

In the absence of theory there are many intuitively appealing variables and several plausible ways to measure each of them. This naturally makes it difficult to compare the studies cited, except by thinking in terms of general factors like "growth" or "cyclicality."

4.1.6 Other Studies

Several other empirical studies investigate the real determinants of beta. I will briefly describe whether they support or weaken the case for the four general determinants of beta suggested above.

Cyclicality. The work of Pettit and Westerfeld [24] and Gordon and Halpern [11] deals primarily with cyclicality as a possible determinant of beta. The former derived an "earnings beta" by first fitting a trend line to firms' earnings per share, scaled by average earnings per share over the period investigated, and also to the scaled earnings of the Standard and Poor's 500 Stock Index. Then the earnings beta was defined as the covariance of the residuals from these trend lines. A highly significant pairwise correlation was found between this statistic and the firms' stock betas. The relationship persisted when the earnings beta was combined with several other independent variables in a multiple regression. Finally, these tests were successfully repeated with a different earnings beta based on operating income.

Gordon and Halpern provide additional evidence as a byproduct of their application of the CAPM to the problem of estimating the cost of capital for a division of a firm. Their earnings beta was based on the covariance between the rates of growth of firms' earnings per share and growth rates for economy-wide corporate profits. Again, a strong positive correlation between earnings betas and stock betas was found.

Earnings variability. Lev and Kunitsky [16] find that stock betas are significantly related to the degree of "smoothness" of various operating and financial series, principally earnings, dividends, sales, and capital expenditure. Smoothness is measured as the mean absolute deviation of the actual values of the variable from its trend. (If smoothness is S, then a perfectly smooth series will have $S = 0$.) Clearly this is another way of defining volatility; thus the discovery of a significant positive relationship between S and the stock beta confirms the results reported earlier in this chapter.

On the other hand, it is not obvious why the smoothness of

dividends, sales and capital expenditures should matter at all once earnings volatility is accounted for. There are two possible lines of response. The first, and simplest, is to say that any simple measure of earnings volatility is an imperfect representation of investors' actual uncertainty about the firm's future earnings. In this case we can regard the other smoothness measures as useful additional proxies. Lev and Kunitsky see something deeper, however. They argue that firms' managers are engaged in a continual battle to control the environment, and that the greater their success, the lower their firms' stocks' beta. Control of environment is effected by reducing the variance of each of the firm's major activities, not just the variance of the end result, earnings. Thus, smoothness of sales would have a place even if there were no problems in measuring earnings volatility directly. Unfortunately, these explanations are not mutually exclusive, and there is no way to distinguish between them from the results at hand.

The role of earnings volatility is also supported by Lev [12] who shows that firms with high operating leverage (that is, high ratios of fixed to total costs) tend to have high betas. This is sensible since high operating leverage is by definition associated with high earnings volatility and high earnings betas.

Both Pettit and Westerfeld [24] and Melicher [18] confirm that firms with low dividend payout ratios tend to have high betas. This too supports the case of earnings volatility, since low dividend payout is a natural response of a management that is uncertain about future earnings.

The only authors who do not find a reliable positive association between earnings volatility and beta are Breen and Lerner [5]. However, their results can be attributed to an inappropriate measure of volatility and to their attempt to measure volatility from severely limited time series data.[16]

Financial leverage. The debt ratio performs somewhat erratically in the studies of Pettit-Westerfeld, Breen and Lerner, and Melicher. In the first case the book debt ratio is not significant in a multiple regression with several other independent variables. In Breen and Lerner, the debt ratio is significant, but inexplicably of the wrong sign in two out of twelve subsamples. Melicher found it significant only when the square of the debt ratio was also introduced.

These results are not fatal to the theoretical prediction of a positive relationship between the debt ratio and stock beta, other things being equal. One can argue that other things are not equal, so that other variables may be obscuring or proxying for the hypothesized effect. Nevertheless these results introduce the seed of doubt.

Fortunately for theory, Hamada [14] devised an indirect test which isolates the effect of financial leverage on beta. There is, of course, substantial variance in the cross-sectional distribution of stocks' betas, even for firms in the same industry. Since debt ratios also vary, theory would predict that part of the dispersion is due to different debt policies. Therefore Hamada grouped a sample of firms into nine reasonably homogenous industries and computed "unlevered betas" for each firm. The unlevered betas were estimates, based on theory, the stock beta and the observed debt ratio, of the beta the firms would have had if their debt ratios were zero. Hamada's prediction was that the dispersion of the firms' betas would be reduced by this unlevering process. (If the stock beta were unrelated to leverage, then the dispersion would be unaffected by unlevering. Since each industry group was chosen to hold other determinants of beta roughly constant, the unlevered beta estimates should cluster more closely around some true, "industry beta.") Hamada's prediction is confirmed by his results, which justify substantial confidence in the link between financial leverage and the stock beta.

Growth. Growth is the weakest of the four candidates which I tentatively proposed as real determinants of beta. Its weaknesses show up again in Pettit and Westerfeld's study. Although they find a significant pairwise correlation between the growth rate of earnings per share and the stock beta, the variable is insignificant in multiple regressions. Breen and Lerner find a generally significant relationship but again it has the wrong sign (negative) in two of the twelve subsamples examined.

On the other hand, the dividend payout ratio is negative and significant in these two studies, as well as in Melicher's. Perhaps this ratio is simply a better proxy for the firm's growth prospects. Unfortunately, none of the studies cited in this chapter have attempted to determine what the dividend payout ratio is really proxying for, or whether it has an independent effect on beta.

4.1.7 Summary

The empirical evidence on the real determinants of beta can be summed up in two sentences. At least three real factors can be identified with relative confidence, namely financial leverage, cyclicality, and volatility of operating earnings (although the third may be proxying for the second). Growth is a possible fourth variable, but its performance in the empirical work cited has been erratic.

The summary *has* to be brief, because there is very little to say once the four factors are noted. Despite the substantial number of studies cited, there is scant agreement on how the factors are to be measured and the exact specification of their effects on beta. Theory gives no guidance (except in the case of financial leverage), so there is little to say beyond the generalities in the paragraph above. Further progress in understanding the real determinants of beta depends on the development of a theory which specifies the relevant variables and how they should in principle be measured. A modest beginning is made in Section 4.2.

4.2 A PARTIAL THEORY

The existing tests of the relationship between book and market risk measures are attempts to find simple short cuts through a complicated causal sequence. The task of theory is to trace out that sequence more carefully. A convenient place to start is at the qualitative, abstract description of the process, given in Figure 4-1. At the top of the figure is the firm, which acquires labor, capital goods, raw materials, and other resources in factor markets, transforms these resources into a product, and sells the product. The result is a real return, composed of the immediate cash flow, less economic depreciation, plus any change in the present value of future investment opportunities.

All this occurs in the real sector of the economy. Crossing the dotted line into the financial sector, we find the return transformed into a financial return (dividends plus capital gains or losses) received by the firm's shareholders. Finally, we can observe the time series of stock returns and calculate summary risk measures like beta.

The problem is that the real return on an asset is never observed directly unless shares in it are traded in a rational and efficient financial market. Even in that case, the capital asset pricing model gives only limited insight into the *components* of the total return (cash flow, economic depreciation, and the change in the value of future investment), or in the determinants of these variables. The empirical studies summarized in Section 4.1 have helped to remedy this problem. However, since they attempt to shortcut the causal sequences described in Figure 4-1, the potential gain in knowledge from further, purely empirical tests seems limited.

The partial theory presented in this section consists of an explicit valuation formula for a long-lived asset in terms of investors' expectations about the asset's future cash flows. The real determinants of the asset's risk are evident from the formula.

The model is a development of the work of Merton [19], and is in many respects similar to a model developed by Bogue and Roll [4]. There is another promising line of theory, developed by Black [3],

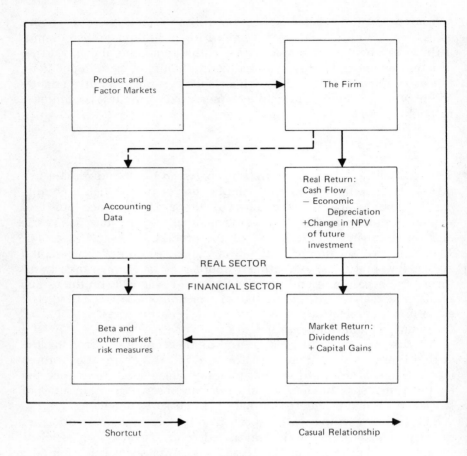

Figure 4-1.   Determinants of Market Risk Measures

Brennan [6], and Turnbull [29], which I have not attempted to review here.

4.2.1 Assumptions and Notation

Let us suppose that the capital asset pricing model is true now and will be in every relevant future period. Consider a real asset which generates an uncertain stream of cash flows, $\tilde{X}_1, \tilde{X}_2, \ldots, \tilde{X}_t$, out to some terminal period $t = T$. The problem is to determine the current equilibrium value of this asset, P_0.

Since the CAPM holds, we know that P_t will be given by:

$$P_t = \frac{(\overline{X}^t_{t+1} + \overline{P}^t_{t+1})(1 - \lambda \rho \, \sigma_{t+1})}{1 + r} \tag{4.7}$$

where:

$\overline{X}^t_{t+1}$ = investors' expectation of $\tilde{X}_{t+1}$ based on information available at t;

$\overline{P}^t_{t+1}$ = investors' expectation of $\tilde{P}_{t+1}$ based on information available at t;

λ = the market price of risk, assumed constant over time;

r = the one-period risk-free rate of interest, likewise assumed constant over time;

ρ = the correlation of the asset's rate of return with the market return, assumed constant, and

σ_{t+1} = the standard deviation of $(\tilde{X}_{t+1} + \tilde{P}_{t+1})/(\overline{X}^t_{t+1} + \overline{P}^t_{t+1})$.

Equation (4.7) illustrates the usual problem with the CAPM: today's price cannot be calculated without knowing the probability distribution of tomorrow's price. The key to solving this problem is a specification of how investors' expectations are formed. To simplify, first assume that, at any point in time, the project offers a level stream of expected cash flows, i.e., $\overline{X}^t_{t+1} = \overline{X}^t_{t+2} = \ldots = \overline{X}^t_T = X^t$. However, investors revise their expectation of the mean income $\overline{X}$ as time progresses and they observe the asset's actual performance. Specifically, suppose that a simple adaptive-expectations model is appropriate for the asset. Let $\overset{\sim}{\delta}_t \overline{X}^{t-1}$ represent the deviation of the actual cash flow in t from the cash flow that was expected one period previously:

$$\tilde{X}_t = \overline{X}^{t-1}(1 + \overset{\sim}{\delta}_t). \tag{4.8}$$

$\overset{\sim}{\delta}_t$ has a zero mean, constant standard deviation σ_δ, and $\mathrm{cov}(\overset{\sim}{\delta}_t, \overset{\sim}{\delta}_{t+1}) = 0$.

Given the actual cash flow $\tilde{X}_t$, investors revise their expectation about $\overline{X}$ by

$$\overline{X}_t = \overline{X}^{t-1}(1 + \eta \delta_t). \tag{4.9}$$

That is, the deviation of $\tilde{X}_t$ from the expectatio ^{t-1} is assumed to be partly "noise" and partly a signal of a ifting mean. The elasticity of expectations, η, is the ratio of signal to the sum of noise and signal. For convenience of the algebra to follow, also define $\overset{\sim}{\epsilon}_t = \eta\overset{\sim}{\delta}_t$ and $1 + \gamma = 1/\eta$, so that $\overset{\sim}{\delta}_t = \overset{\sim}{\epsilon}_t(1 + \gamma)$ and $\sigma_\delta = \sigma_\epsilon(1 + \gamma)$.

By specifying a process by which expectations are updated in reponse to information, we have also specified how uncertainty is resolved over time. If we ask investors for their estimate of $\tilde{X}_{10}$ as of $t = 0$, they will say that $\overline{X}^0_{10} = \overline{X}^0$, the current expectation of every period's cash flow. The variance of $\tilde{X}_{10}$, given information available at $t = 0$, will of course be much greater than that of $\tilde{X}_1$. However, as $\tilde{X}_1$, $\tilde{X}_2$ ... are actually observed, the perceived variance of $\tilde{X}_{10}$ becomes progressively smaller.

4.2.2 Derivation of the Valuation Formula

Now the price of the asset at any time t, given expected income at that time, can be obtained by dynamic programming—i.e., by solving Equation (4.7) "backwards." Recall that the cash flow stream stops at time T. Thus $P_T = 0$. Therefore, P_{T-1} can be determined from Equation (4.7) given $\overline{X}^{T-1}$:

$$P_{T-1} = \frac{\overline{X}^{T-1}(1 - \lambda\rho\sigma_\delta)}{1 + r}. \tag{4.10}$$

Now consider P_{T-2}, given $\overline{X}^{T-2}$. Let $\tilde{V}_{T-1} = \tilde{X}_{T-1} + \tilde{P}_{T-1}$. From Equation (4.10) and the specification of the way investor' expectations are formed,

$$\tilde{V}_{T-1} = \overline{X}^{T-2}(1 + \overset{\sim}{\epsilon}_{T-1} + \gamma\overset{\sim}{\epsilon}_{T-1}) + \overline{X}^{T-2}(1 + \overset{\sim}{\epsilon}_{T-1})\left(\frac{1 - \lambda\rho\sigma_\delta}{1+r}\right). \tag{4.11}$$

The expected value and standard deviation of $\tilde{V}_{T-1}$ are derived as follows. Since $E(\overset{\sim}{\epsilon}_t) = 0$ and $\sigma_\epsilon + \gamma\sigma_\epsilon = \sigma_\delta$,

$$\overline{V}^{T-2}_{T-1} = \overline{X}^{T-2}\left(1 + \frac{1 - \lambda\rho\sigma_\epsilon}{1+r} - \frac{\lambda\rho\gamma\sigma_\epsilon}{1+r}\right).$$

We define the last two terms in brackets as q and z respectively, so that

$$\overline{V}_{T-1}^{T-2} = \overline{X}^{T-2}(1 + q - z).$$ (4.12)

From Equations (4.10) and 4.11), we find

$$\sigma(\tilde{V}_{T-1}) = \overline{X}^{T-2}\sigma_\epsilon(1 + \gamma + q - z).$$ (4.13)

Now we can solve for P_{T-2} given $\overline{X}^{T-2}$. Substituting in Equation (4.7),[17]

$$
\begin{aligned}
P_{T-2} &= \frac{\overline{V}^{T-2} - \lambda\rho\sigma_\epsilon(\tilde{V}_{T-1})}{1 + r} \\
&= \frac{\overline{X}^{T-2}}{1 + r}[(1 + q - z) - \lambda\rho\sigma_\epsilon(1 + \gamma + q - z)] \\
&= \overline{X}^{T-2}\left[(1 + q - z)\left(\frac{1 - \lambda\rho\sigma_\epsilon}{1 + r}\right) - \frac{\lambda\rho\gamma\sigma_\epsilon}{1 + r}\right] \\
&= \overline{X}^{T-2}[(q - z)(1 + q)].
\end{aligned}
$$ (4.14)

Here we are assuming that λ, ρ and r are constant over time.

Exactly the same logic can be applied to find P_{T-3} given $\overline{X}^{T-3}$. We find:

$$P_{T-3} = \overline{X}^{T-3}[(q - z)(1 + q + q^2)].$$

One can find P_{T-4}, P_{T-5}, etc. by similar logic. In the end we reach $P_{T-T} = P_0$, the current equilibrium value of the asset, which is:

$$P_0 = \overline{X}^0\left[(q - z)\sum_{t=0}^{T-1}q^t\right].$$ (4.15)

For a very long lived asset, $T \to \infty$, and since q is less than 1, Equation (4.15) approaches the value

$$
\begin{aligned}
P_0 &= \overline{X}^0\left(\frac{q - z}{1 - q}\right). \\
&= \overline{X}^0\left(\frac{1 - \lambda\rho\sigma_\delta}{r + \lambda\rho\eta\sigma_\delta}\right).
\end{aligned}
$$ (4.16)

4.2.3 Discussion

Equations (4.15) and (4.16) are the most basic part of the theory presented in this chapter. They are two valuation formulas for single assets (or for firms that can be regarded as single assets), given investors' current expectation of the normal cash flow, $\overline{X}_0$. As we will now see, these two equations provide useful insights into the real determinants of risk and behavior of asset prices over time.

The formulas in effect discount the expected future cash flows $\overline{X}_t^0$ for two separate sources of risk: first, for the risk associated with next period's actual cash flow, and, second, for the risk associated with revision of expectations about the normal cash flow $\overline{X}$. Suppose that $\eta = 0$, so that the second source of risk disappears. In this case, normal earnings never change, so there are no capital gains or losses. (Note we have assumed λ, ρ, r and σ_δ to be constant over time.) In this case Equation (4.15) reduces to:

$$P_0 = \frac{\overline{X}^0 \, (1 - \lambda \rho \sigma_\delta)}{1 + r} \sum_{t=0}^{T-1} \frac{1}{(1 + r)^t}$$

If we define $CEQ(\tilde{X})$ as $\overline{X}^0 \, (1 - \lambda \rho \sigma_\delta)$, and rearrange, this becomes the well-known "certainty equivalent approach" to valuation.[18]

$$P_0 = \sum_{t=1}^{T} \frac{CEQ(\tilde{X})}{(1+r)^t} \tag{4.17}$$

But under the more reasonable assumption of $\eta > 0$, there is a two-stage discounting process.

$$P_0 = \frac{CEQ(\tilde{X})}{1 + r} \sum_{t=0}^{T-1} \left(\frac{1 - \lambda \rho \eta \sigma_\delta}{1 + r} \right)^t \tag{4.18}$$

This can of course be written in the usual certainty-equivalent format,

$$P_0 = \sum_{t=1}^{T} \frac{\alpha_t \, \overline{X}^0}{(1+r)^t} \, ,$$

where $\alpha_t = (1 - \lambda \rho \sigma_\delta) \, (1 - \lambda \rho \eta \sigma_\delta)^{t-1}$. However, the discounted cash flow formula, using a single risk-adjusted discount rate, will *not* generally be appropriate.[19]

The next step is to consider the one-period rate of return earned by an asset's owners. Let Q_t be its "cash flow multiplier," defined as $P_t/\overline{X}^t$. By definition, the actual rate of return earned from $t = 0$ to $t = 1$ is

$$1 + \tilde{R}_1 = \tilde{V}_1/P_0 = (\tilde{X}_1 + \tilde{P}_1)/P_0.$$

We can express $\tilde{X}_1$ and $\tilde{P}_1$ in terms of $\overset{\sim}{\delta}$ and solve for $\tilde{R}_1$.

$$1 + \tilde{R}_1 = \frac{\tilde{X}_0 (1 + \overset{\sim}{\delta}) + \overline{X}^0 (1 + \eta\overset{\sim}{\delta})Q_1}{\overline{X}^0 Q_0} \tag{4.19}$$

$$= (1 + \overset{\sim}{\delta})/Q_0 + (1 + \eta\overset{\sim}{\delta})/Q_1/Q_0. \tag{4.20}$$

For an asset of indefinite life ($T = \infty$), $Q_1 = Q_0$ and

$$\tilde{R}_1 = (1 + \overset{\sim}{\delta})/Q_0 + \eta\delta. \tag{4.20a}$$

The expected rate of return is in general

$$E(\tilde{R}_1) = 1/Q_0 + (Q_1/Q_0 - 1), \tag{4.21}$$

where $(Q_1/Q_0 - 1)$ can be interpreted as the expected rate of economic depreciation. For an asset of indefinite life, expected economic depreciation is zero, and

$$E(\tilde{R}_1) = 1/Q_0. \tag{4.21a}$$

Equations (4.20) through (4.21a) reveal an important potential advantage of this theory: it should provide a means to eliminate some of the difficulties encountered by the empirical tests reviewed in Section 4.1 of this chapter. Those tests attempted to relate estimated betas to estimates of (investors' expectations about) diverse real or accounting variables. Equations (4.20) through (4.21a) in principle allow a more direct test. If they are correct it should be possible to explain stock rates of return directly in terms of η and $\overset{\sim}{\delta}$.

Of course η and $\overset{\sim}{\delta}$ will likewise be estimates, obtained by fitting a forecasting model to the firm's prior earnings history. Consequently errors in observation of the independent variables are not eliminated. Another difficulty is that the model as developed here leaves out several obvious sources of variability and covariability in stock returns, namely changes in the capitalized value of future growth, in financial leverage, in r, the risk-free interest rate, and in λ, the market price of risk. Although a more complete model seems feasible, that will have to wait for another study.

4.2.4 Determinants of Beta

The valuation formulas developed in this chapter also imply a theory of the determinants of beta. It is clear from the model's assumptions that asset betas should be related to cyclicality and (given the correlation coefficient ρ) to earnings volatility. But there are several other variables affecting beta which have not been correctly identified in the empirical studies.

The ith firm's beta is defined as:

$$\beta_i = \frac{\text{cov}(\tilde{R}_i, \tilde{R}_M)}{\sigma_M^2} = \frac{\rho\, \sigma_M\, \sigma(\tilde{R}_i)}{\sigma_M^2},$$

where $\tilde{R}_M$ is the rate of return on the market portfolio (in principle, on national wealth) and σ_M is the standard deviation of $\tilde{R}_M$. Since σ_M is common to all securities and ρ is exogenous to the model, beta essentially depends on $\sigma(\tilde{R}_i)$.

From Equation (4.20) we see that $\sigma(\tilde{R})$ is related to σ_δ:[20]

$$\sigma(R) = \sigma_\delta (1/Q_0 + \eta Q_1/Q_0) \tag{4.22}$$

As might be expected, $\sigma(R)$ is positively related to σ_δ. This is immediately obvious when Equation (4.22) is written out for a project of indefinite life ($T = \infty$): Since $Q_1/Q_0 = 1$ in this case.

$$\sigma(\tilde{R}) = \sigma_\delta (1/Q_0 + \eta)$$

$$= \sigma_\eta \left(\frac{r + \eta}{1 - \lambda\rho\sigma_\delta}\right) \tag{4.22a}$$

clearly $\delta\sigma(\tilde{R})/\delta\sigma_\delta > 0$. Also, $\delta\sigma(R)/\delta\eta > 0$, although this result holds in general only for $T > 1$. Finally it can be shown that $\delta\sigma(\tilde{R})/\delta T < 0$ for $0 < \eta < 1$; this occurs essentially because an increase in asset life increases the cash flow multiplier Q_0.

The relationship of beta to T and η is illustrated by the numerical results in the top panel of Table 4-4. These were calculated from Equation (4.22), the definition of beta, given a risk-free interest rate of $r = .05$, a correlation coefficient of $\rho = .10$, a market price of risk of $\lambda = 5/3$, and a standard deviation for the market return of

σ_M = .042. The impact of asset life on beta is very dramatic for low values of η. However, for assets of moderately long life (say, $T > 10$), beta is approximately proportional to η.

4.2.5 Growth

As pointed out in Section 4.1, there are two distinct financial usages of the word "growth." In one, growth is simply the rate of expansion of the firm's assets, sales, or earnings. In the other, growth is the opportunity to make future investments with positive net present values. Empirical studies do not distinguish these two meanings carefully, but their measurements of growth suggest mainly the first interpretation.

Growth as extra-profitable future investment is extremely difficult to bring into the model presented here, since including it would require explicit consideration of how the firm's investment policy responds to random shifts in the firm's investment opportunity set. But it is relatively simple to include an exogenous *trend* in the cash flow $\hat{X}_t$.

Suppose there is an exogenous growth rate g. This might be due to inflation or other factors. Specify X_t as

Table 4-4. Determinants of Beta—Example

A. Beta as a function of asset life (T) and elasticity of expectations (η).

	$T = 1$	2	5	10	20	40	∞
$\eta = 0$	1.36	.70	.300	.168	.104	.076	.065
$\eta = .5$	1.36	1.02	.821	.756	.726	.716	.714
$\eta = 1.0$	1.36	1.36	1.36	1.36	1.36	1.36	1.36

B. Beta as a function of growth rate (g) and elasticity of expectations (η), for infinite lived project ($T = \infty$).

	$g = 0$	.02	.05	.08	.12
$\eta = 0$	.065	.039	a	a	a
$\eta = .5$	.714	.701	.682	.662	a
$\eta = 1.0$	1.36	1.36	1.36	1.36	1.36

[a]Asset value not defined.

Assumptions

$\rho = .5$ $\lambda = 5/3$
$\sigma_\delta = .1$ $\sigma_M = .042$

$$\tilde{X}_t = \overline{X}_{t-1} (1 + g) (1 + \tilde{\delta}),$$

where $\tilde{\delta}$ has the same properties as before, and $\overline{X}^{t-1}$ is now interpreted as "normal" cash flow for $t - 1$. Investors' expectations of the normal cash flow are updated by

$$\overline{X}^t = \overline{X}^{t-1} (1 + g) (1 + \eta\tilde{\delta}).$$

Now P_0 can be obtained, as before, by solving for P_{T-1} given $\overline{X}^{T-1}$, P_{T-2} given $\overline{X}^{T-2}$, etc. However, it is necessary to define the discounting factors q and z a little differently, i.e. as:

$$q = \frac{1 + g}{1 + r} (1 - \lambda\rho\sigma_\epsilon),$$

$$z = \frac{1 + g}{1 + r} (\lambda\rho\gamma\sigma_\epsilon).$$

Having done this, we obtain a valuation equation identical in form to Equation (4.14). Substituting the new definitions of q and z in Equation (4.14) we obtain

$$P_0 = \overline{X}^0 \left(\frac{q - z}{1 - q} \right) = \left(\frac{(\frac{1 + g}{1 + r}) (1 - \lambda\rho\sigma_\delta)}{1 - (\frac{1 + g}{1 + r}) (1 - \lambda\rho\eta\sigma_\delta)} \right)$$

$$= \overline{X}^0 (1 + g) \left(\frac{1 - \lambda\rho\sigma_\delta}{r - g + \lambda\rho\eta (1 + g)\sigma_\delta} \right). \tag{4.23}$$

In the certainty case ($\sigma_\delta = 0$) this reduces to the well known constant growth model of Gordon and Shapiro [12] and Williams [28].

The equations for $\tilde{R}$ and $\sigma(\tilde{R})$ are the same as for the no-growth case, providing that Q_t is redefined as $P_t / \overline{X}_t (1 + g)$. Thus for an infinite-lived asset

$$\tilde{R} = (1 + \tilde{\delta})/Q_0 + \eta$$

$$\sigma(\tilde{R}) = \sigma_\delta (1/Q_0 + \eta)$$

$$\beta = \frac{\rho \sigma_\delta}{\sigma_M} (1/Q_0 + \eta) \qquad (4.24)$$

In this case $(T = \infty)$ the effects of growth on beta are easily calculated. Substituting for Q_0 and differentiating,

$$\delta\beta/\delta g = -\frac{\rho \sigma_\delta}{\sigma_M} (\frac{1 - \eta}{1 - \lambda\rho\sigma_\delta}),$$

which is always negative. That is, beta decreases as the rate of growth increases; the rate of decrease is a positive linear function of ρ, η and σ_δ.

This is a particularly interesting result because it goes exactly contrary to the usual view. All of the empirical studies cited in Section 4.1 hypothesized that rapidly growing firms have *high* betas. Moreover, some of the studies' results seem actually to support this idea, although the growth variable performed erratically, and was the weakest of the four factors tentatively identified as real determinants of beta.

Equations (4.23) and (4.24) provide a plausible explanation of these empirical results. First, note from the bottom panel of Table 4-4 that the absolute effect of g on beta is relatively small for reasonable values of the growth rate and other parameters. It is doubtful that this effect could have been picked up by the empirical tests, given their vague specifications and the inevitable errors in measuring investors' expectations about g. It seems much more likely that g is a relatively unreliable proxy for something else. What that something else may be is not clear. Perhaps it is earnings volatility, but perhaps g is proxying for "growth" in the second financial sense of the term. That is, rapidly expanding firms may also tend to have greater opportunities for extra-profitable future investment, and it *may* turn out that firms enjoying high growth, in this second sense of the term, also have high betas. Pending careful investigation of these possibilities, the only prudent course is to strike growth from the tentative list of the real determinants of beta.

4.2.6 Conclusions

That cuts the tentative list to three, namely cyclicality, earnings volatility, and financial leverage. The last two do not require any significant further discussion. Leverage was not included in my valuation model because this variable already has rigorous theoretical justification. As to earnings volatility, it does not appear important per se, but only as a proxy for cyclicality. In fact, it should be totally irrelevant if the earnings stream is uncorrelated with the return on the market portfolio ($\rho = 0$). However, earnings volatility is likely to be an excellent proxy for cyclicality, and it may be directly important in a way not captured by the model presented here.

The model's assumptions guarantee cyclicality a major role in determining beta. Difficulties arise, however, when we attempt to *measure* cyclicality and to specify its relationship to beta in a simple, testable form. Consider again the formula for beta for a no-growth ($g = 0$), infinite lived ($T = \infty$) asset.

$$\beta = \frac{\rho\sigma_\delta}{\sigma_M} (1/Q_0 + \eta)$$

Substituting for Q_0 and simplifying, we obtain

$$\beta = \frac{\rho\sigma_\delta}{\sigma_M} \left(\frac{r+\eta}{1-\lambda\rho\sigma_\delta} \right). \tag{4.25}$$

Now, the closest analogue to the "accounting beta" used in the empirical tests is $\text{cov}(\hat{R}_M, \hat{\delta})/\sigma_M^2 = \rho\sigma_\delta/\sigma_M$.[21] Call this B. Then Equation (4.25) becomes

$$\beta = B\left(\frac{r+\eta}{1-\lambda\rho\sigma_\delta} \right). \tag{4.25a}$$

Unfortunately this is not a simple linear function, and thus it is not easy to test directly. More important, Equation (4.25a) could not be fitted cross-sectionally, since there is no reason to expect η, the elasticity of earnings expectations, to be the same for all firms at any point in time.

In a way it makes more sense to define cyclicality as ηB, the covariance of shifts in investors' earnings *expectations* with the market return $\hat{R}_M$. Surely it is not the variance of next year's earnings, but the variance of investors' forecasts of "normal" earnings, which accounts for the bulk of the variance in stock returns. But although ηB would no doubt perform better than B, problems in cross-sectional tests are by no means eliminated.

In summary, the model confirms cyclicality as a determinant of beta, but unfortunately it also raises the issue of whether cyclicality can be adequately measured by any single statistic. In this and other respects, the valuation model makes clear the difficulties in simple regressions or correlations of observed betas with various real variables. There is not only the problem of measuring cyclicality, but also its rather complicated relationship with beta, and finally the simultaneous effects on beta of asset life and the rate of growth of "normal" cash flows or earnings. It seems fair to suggest that this type of "short-cut" test is premature. More progress may be made by taking the longer road, that is by attempting to explain the time series of stock rates of return in terms of the errors experienced in forecasting firms' earnings, and in terms of forecast revisions over time.

NOTES TO SECTION FOUR

1. See [27], [17] and [22] respectively.

2. For example, Hamada [13] has proved Modigliani and Millers' [21] well-known Proposition I in the context of the CAPM, but much more general proofs are available, for example Stiglitz [28].

3. See Hamada [13].

4. For an example, see Myers and Pogue [23].

5. The best-known proponent of this view is Gordon [10].

6. Hamada [14].

7. Dyer [7] has found evidence of this effect.

8. Errors in observing true values of beta and the accounting variables ought to be reduced by forming portfolios.

9. The explanatory power was only slightly less when the accounting beta was substituted for earnings volatility.

10. Actually, White used the ratio of the book value of debt to the market value of equity. It is the divergence between book and market values of equity which causes most of the error in the book debt ratio.

11. And also for various portfolio sizes, variable definitions, etc.

12. Beaver, Kettler and Scholes [2], p. 667.

13. It might be noted that Gonedes's sample was smaller than that of BKS or White, and moreover that his sample was concentrated in a few specific industries. Gonedes properly criticizes BKS for normalizing the earnings of firms in their sample by past market values of equity. Firms with high betas will tend to have more volatile equity values, and under BKS's procedure, will automatically tend to have more volatile earnings and higher accounting betas. Thus BKS

are not correlating beta solely with accounting variables, but also with stock price volatility.

14. Rosenberg and McKibbin, p. 327.

15. This follows from Miller and Modigliani's well-known proof of the irrelevance of dividend policy [20].

16. They first fitted a trend line to five years' earnings per share data, and then measured volatility as the proportion of the variance explained by the trend. This is a poor procedure, not only because of the small number of earnings observations, but because there is no necessary relationship between R^2 and the standard deviation of the series. A firm's earnings could have a low standard deviation but no trend and an R^2 of essentially zero. Breen and Lerner would take the low R^2 as evidence of high volatility in earnings.

17. There are two reasons for keeping λ and r constant. The first is a desire for simplicity. The second is the fact that the CAPM is not generally correct in a many-period world unless investors' opportunity set is stable over time. See Fama[8].

As to ρ, the basic assumption is that the correlation of $\tilde{\delta}$ and $\tilde{R}_M$ is constant across time. Now if there is another variable y which is a linear function of $\tilde{\delta}$ (i.e. $y = a + b\,\tilde{\delta}$) the correlation coefficient of y with $\tilde{R}_M$ will also be ρ. Since V_t is always a linear function of $\tilde{\delta}$, it is appropriate to take ρ as a constant, exogenous parameter.

18. See Robicheck and Myers [25].

19. The only case in which it would be appropriate occurs when $\eta = 1$. In this case Equation (4.19) satisfies Robichek and Myers's conditions for discounting at a single risk-adjusted rate. See [22].

20. The subscript i is eliminated whenever no confusion will follow.

21. Strictly speaking, the covariance should be measured between $\tilde{\delta}$ and forecast errors on national income, rather than between $\tilde{\delta}$ and $\tilde{R}_M$. However, if all stocks are priced according to Equations (4.15) or (4.16), $\tilde{R}_M$ will be perfectly correlated with forecast errors in national income.

REFERENCES

1. R. Ball and P. Brown, "Portfolio Theory and Accounting." *Journal of Accounting Research*, 7 (Autumn 1969), 300-323.

2. W.H. Beaver, P. Kettler and M. Scholes, "The Association Between Market Determined and Accounting Determined Risk Measures." *Accounting Review*, XLV (October 1970), 654-82.

3. F. Black, "Corporate Investment Decisions." Associates in Finance, Note 2B (unpublished), 1969.

4. M. Bogue and R. Roll, "Capital Budgeting of Risky Projects with 'Imperfect' Markets for Physical Capital." *Journal of Finance*, XXIX (May 1974), 601-13; also reprinted in Vol. II of *Risk and Return in Finance*.

5. W.J. Breen and E.M. Lerner, "Corporate Financial Strategies and Market Measures of Risk and Return." *Journal of Finance*, XXVIII (May 1974), 339-52.

6. M.J. Brennan, "An Approach to the Valuation of Uncertain Income Streams." *Journal of Finance*, XXVIII (June 1973), 661-74.

7. J. Dyer, "Financial Leverage, Business Risk and the Tax Subsidy to Debt: An Empirical Study." Unpublished M.Sc. Thesis, M.I.T., 1974.

8. E. Fama, "Multiperiod Consumption-Investment Decisions." *American Economic Review*, 60 (March 1970), 163-74.

9. N.J. Gonedes, "Evidence on the Information Content of Accounting Numbers: Accounting-Based and Market-Based Estimates of Systematic Risk." *Journal of Financial and Quantitative Analysis*, VIII (June 1973), 407-44.

10. M.J. Gordon, *The Investment, Financing and Valuation of the Corporation.* (Homewood, Ill.: Richard D. Irwin, 1962).

11. _____ and P. Halpern, "Cost of Capital for a Division of a Firm." *Journal of Finance*, XXIX (September 1974), 1153-64.

12. _____ and E. Shapiro, "Capital Equipment Analysis: The Required Rate of Profit." *Management Science*, 3 (October 1956), 102-10.

13. R. Hamada, "Portfolio Analysis, Market Equilibrium and Corporate Finance." *Journal of Finance*, XXIV (March 1969), 13-31.

14. _____, "The Effect of the Firm's Capital Structure on the Systematic Risk of Common Stocks." *Journal of Finance*, XXVII (May 1972), 435-52.

15. B. Lev, "On the Association Between Operating Leverage and Risk." *Journal of Financial and Quantitative Analysis*, IX (September 1974), 627-42.

16. _____ and S. Kunitzky, "On the Association Between Smoothing Measures and the Risk of Common Stocks." *Accounting Review*, XLIX (April 1974), 259-70.

17. J. Lintner, "The Valuation of Risk Assets and the Selection of Risky Investment in Stock Portfolios and Capital Budgets." *Review of Economics and Statistics*, 47 (February 1965), 10-31.

18. R.W. Melicher, "Financial Factors which Influence Beta Variations within a Homogeneous Industry Environment." *Journal of Financial and Quantitative Analysis*, IX (March 1974), 231-43.

19. R.C. Merton, "Capital Budgeting in the Capital Asset Pricing Model." Unpublished note, 1973.

20. M.H. Miller and F. Modigliani, "Dividend Policy, Growth and the Valuation of Shares." *Journal of Business*, 34 (October 1961), 411-53.

21. F. Modigliani and M.H. Miller, "The Cost of Capital, Corporation Finance and the Theory of Investment." *American Economic Review*, 48 (June 1958), 261-97.

22. J. Mossin, "Equilibrium in a Capital Asset Market." *Econometrica*, 34 (October 1966), 768-83.

23. S.C. Myers and G.A. Pogue, "An Evaluation of the Risk of Comsat Common Stock."

24. R. Pettit and R. Westerfeld, "A Model of Capital Asset Risk." *Journal of Financial and Quantitative Analysis*, 7 (March 1972), 1649-68.

25. A.A. Robichek and S.C. Myers, "Conceptual Problems in the Use of Risk-Adjusted Discount Rates." *Journal of Finance*, XXI (December 1966), 727-30.

26. B. Rosenberg and W. McKibbin, "The Prediction of Systematic and Specific Risk in Common Stocks." *Journal of Business and Quantitative Analysis*, VIII (March 1973), 317-34.

27. W.F. Sharpe, "Capital Asset Prices: A Theory of Market Equilibrium Under Conditions of Risk." *Journal of Finance*, XIX (September 1964), 425-42.

28. J. Stiglitz, "A Re-Examination of the Modigliani-Miller Theorem." *American Economic Review*, 59 (December 1969), 784-93.

29. S.M. Turnbull, "An Approach to the Determinants of Systematic Risk." Working Paper, London Graduate School of Business Studies, 1975.

30. R. White, "On the Measurement of Systematic Risk." Unpublished Ph.D. Dissertation, M.I.T., 1972.

31. J.B. Williams, *The Theory of Investment Value.* (Cambridge, Massachusetts: Harvard University Press, 1938).

Section Five

The Usefulness of Beta Risk for Estimating the Cost of Capital

James L. Bicksler*

5.1 BETA RISK IN A MEAN-VARIANCE EQUILIBRIUM WORLD

The mean-variance general equilibrium framework of asset prices under uncertainty has important implications for corporate investment decision making, ex ante portfolio selection, ex post portfolio performance evaluation, governmental capital budgeting, and rate of return regulation.

The basic assumptions underlying the market equilibrium relationship of security prices in a mean-variance world are:

1. All investors are risk averse and choose portfolios in a manner consistent with maximizing expected utility of single-period terminal wealth.
2. Portfolio investment opportunities can be described solely in terms of means and variances (or standard deviations) of the ex ante distribution of one-period portfolio returns.
3. Investors have homogenous expectations regarding means, variances, and covariances of returns for all securities in the investment opportunity set and, in addition, all investors have identical investment opportunity sets.
4. Capital markets are efficient in the sense that borrowing and lending rates are equal. There are no restrictions to short sales, no taxes, no transactions costs, and capital assets are perfectly divisible, et cetera.

*The author wishes to thank Irwin Friend, Amir Barnea, and Richard Roll for helpful comments on an earlier draft of this chapter.

5. The supply of all capital assets is given.

Under these, and other less restrictive conditions, equilibrium relationships for risky capital assets have been derived. The fundamental result of risk, return, and market equilibrium at the level of the individual asset or security is:

$$E(\tilde{R}_i) = R_f + B_i\,[E(\tilde{R}_m) - R_f] \tag{5.1}$$

where $E(\tilde{R}_i)$ is the expected return on the individual security for the single period being considered, $E(\tilde{R}_m)$ is the expected return on the market portfolio, R_f is the riskless rate of return, and B_i is the systematic risk of the ith security. Equation (5.1) says that the equilibrium expected return on an asset equals the riskless rate of return (the rate of time preference) plus a risk premium.

The beta of a security or capital asset measures the marginal contribution of that individual risky asset to the dispersion or variance of the *ex ante* return distribution of the market portfolio, R_m. Formally, beta or the marginal risk of an asset is:

$$B_i = \text{cov}(\tilde{R}_i, \tilde{R}_m)/\sigma^2(\tilde{R}_m). \tag{5.2}$$

From (5.1) and (5.2), we see that:

$$E(\tilde{R}_i) = R_f + \frac{[E(\tilde{R}_m) - R_f]}{\sigma^2(\tilde{R}_m)}\,(\text{cov}\,\tilde{R}_i, \tilde{R}_m). \tag{5.3}$$

This is the equivalent to saying that the equilibrium expected return for a risky asset is equal to a riskless rate of interest plus a linear risk premium equal to the product of the risk premium per unit of risk, commonly called the proportionality factor or $[E(R_m) - R_f]/\sigma^2(R_m)$, and the asset's covariance with the market portfolio, or $\text{cov}(\tilde{R}_i, \tilde{R}_m)$.

This linear expected risk-return relationship for securities was derived from a market scenario where investors choose only mean-variance efficient portfolios and market conditions imply a set of clearing prices for all assets in the investment opportunity set. Under these conditions, the expected risk-return market equilibrium relationship for such portfolios can be described by the capital market line:

$$E(\tilde{R}_p) = R_f + \lambda(\sigma[\tilde{R}_p]) \tag{5.4}$$

where $(\sigma \tilde{R}_p)$ is the standard deviation of the expected return distribution for efficient portfolios and λ is the price of risk reduction and is equal to:

$$(E(\tilde{R}_p) - R_f)/\sigma(\tilde{R}_m).$$

It is clear that under conditions of mean-variance market equilibrium and given a world of positive but not perfectly correlated securities' returns, an individual security's contribution to the risk of an efficient portfolio is not the asset's variance of return. Instead, the asset's variance of return can be dichotomized into two components which are (1) systematic risk or the asset's covariation with the return on the market portfolio and (2) the unsystematic risk or the asset's variation due to residual elements. This relationship can be expressed as:

$$\sigma^2(\tilde{R}_i) = B_i^2 \sigma^2(\tilde{R}_m) + \sigma^2(\tilde{e}_i) \tag{5.5}$$

where $\sigma^2(\tilde{e}_i)$ is that portion of $\sigma^2(\tilde{R}_i)$ which is uncorrelated with the market portfolio. This is the diversifiable or unsystematic risk. The unsystematic risk component of the variance of returns of a security is eliminated in the formation of efficient portfolios.[2] Hence, the total risk of an efficient portfolio is equal to the portfolio's systematic risk. Alternatively stated, any portfolio having unsystematic or residual risk is nonefficient inasmuch as there is always an alternative portfolio having equivalent expected return and less risk.[3]

The above briefly indicates that the risk of an asset must be measured from a portfolio viewpoint and that the mean-variance equilibrium model of market prices implies that beta is the appropriate measure of a risky asset's volatility or sensitivity.

5.2 EXTENSIONS OF THE SIMPLE FORM OF THE CAPITAL ASSET PRICING MODEL

For a variety of theoretical and empirical reasons, there have been proposed recently some exciting extensions such as the two-factor model of both Black and Ross and a model by Merton which indicates that the simple form of the CAPM model is tractable and offers avenues of investigation that are of interest to the profession.[4]

The two-factor model proposed independently by Black and Ross and empirically tested by Black-Jensen-Scholes (hereafter B-J-S) may be expressed as:[5]

$$E(\tilde{R}_i) = E(\tilde{R}_z)(1 - B_i) + E(\tilde{R}_m)B_i. \qquad (5.6)$$

It postulates that in a world in which there is no borrowing or lending of the riskless asset as well as no restrictions on short selling, capital market equilibrium relationships can be described via investors holding a linear combination of two funds or portfolios.[6],[7] These two funds are the market portfolio, m, and the minimum-variance zero-beta portfolio, z. The products $E(\tilde{R}_m)\beta_i$ and $E(\tilde{R}_z)$ $(1 - \beta_i)$ represent, respectively, the contributions to expected return on a risky asset of both the market portfolio and the riskless asset, which in this context is the zero-beta minimum variance portfolio. The expected equilibrium return on a risky asset is thus the returns on the two portfolios weighted by beta and its complement.

A potentially interesting extension of the basic Sharpe-Lintner model is the model of Merton. The model postulates that investors' portfolios are linear combinations of three portfolios, the market portfolio, the riskless portfolio, and a portfolio which is perfectly negatively correlated with the riskless asset. Merton argues that this model can conceptually explain the Friend-Blume and Black-Jensen-Scholes phenomenon of low (high) beta portfolios earning more (less) than predicted by the traditional capital market line. Further, this analysis has the appealing properties of being intertemporal in nature and allowing for changes in the investment opportunity set. That is, Merton sets forth an equilibrium scenario under conditions where a single-period model does not hold. Until empirical tests are made of this version of the capital asset pricing model, conjectures about its empirical robustness must remain unsubstantiated.[8]

5.3. THE BETA FRAMEWORK OF THE COST OF CAPITAL

The normative capital budgeting decision of the firm may be viewed as the determination of whether the acceptance of new physical investment projects improves the ex ante optimal risky portfolios. That is, the investment decision of the firm is a determination of whether the new project should represent a portion of the market value of all capital assets (e.g., the market portfolio). In this sense, corporate investment choices are decisions as to whether new securities should be issued where these securities are viewed as claims to possible returns-covariances from the projects being considered.

One common formulation of the firm's investment decision is that projects are acceptable if, and only if, their expected marginal rate of return exceeds the cost of capital or the cutoff rate. In this context, the cost of capital is viewed as the minimum yield necessary for the price of the stock to increase. The correct specification of this rate must be based on market equilibrium relationships that emerge out of the portfolio balancing decisions of investors.[9] In addition to the previously enumerated four assumptions underlying the two-parameter capital asset pricing model, the following assumptions will be made.[10]

1. The one-period horizon of the project proposals of the firm is identical to the one-period portfolio horizon of investors.[11]
2. Investment projects are technologically independent in the sense that their return-covariance characteristics are invariant to the firm screening the proposal.

The individual investor's budget equation is:

$$W_i = M_i + \sum_j Z_{ij} P_j \qquad (5.7)$$

where W is the wealth of the investor at the start of the period, M is the investor's net riskless lending, Z is the fraction owned of the equity of a firm, P is the market value of the total equity of a firm, and the subscripts i and j represent respectively the individual and the firm. The investor's single period terminal wealth is

$$Y_i = rM_i + \sum_j Zij (X_j - rd_j) \qquad (5.8)$$

where Y is the investor's terminal wealth, r is the pure rate of interest, X is the firm's total gross returns, and d is the market value of debt. Via the assumptions of efficient markets, homogenous expectations, and investors choosing mean-variance efficient portfolios, the optimal portfolio for the individual is derived by solving a system of n linear equations in n variables Z_{ij}. The solution to these equations:

$$\sum_k Z_{ik} \sigma_{jk} = B_i(u_j - rv_j) \ (j = 1, \ldots, n) \qquad (5.9)$$

where u is the expected gross returns, $E(\hat{X})$, to the firm is:

$$Z_j^* B_i = Z_{ij} \qquad (j = 1, \ldots, n). \qquad (5.10)$$

Equation (5.10) says that the separation theorem holds for the individual and that the optimal portfolio decision is comprised of choosing (1) the optimal risky portfolio and (2) the appropriate amount of borrowing (levering) or lending (unlevering). Thus, the risky holdings of investors differ not in composition but only by a scale factor.

It follows from our assumption of efficient markets that the demand for securities by investors is such that (1) all market assets are purchased (Equation (5.11)) and (2) net borrowing equals net lending (Equation 5.12)).

$$\sum_i Z_{ij} = 1 \qquad\qquad (j = 1, \ldots, n) \qquad\qquad (5.11)$$

$$\sum_i M_i = \sum d_j \qquad\qquad (5.12)$$

A general equilibrium solution to Equations (5.8), (5.11), and (5.12) combined with our prior assumptions gives

$$Z_{i1} = Z_{i2} = \ldots Z_{in}. \qquad\qquad (5.13)$$

This says that a given investor holds a constant proportion of every risky stock.[12,13]

If $R = 1/\sum B_i$, then substituting into (5.10) and (5.9), rearranging and solving for v_j we have:

$$v_j = \frac{1}{r}(u_j - Rb_j) \qquad\qquad (5.14)$$

where v is the market value of the firm and R can be interpreted as the price of risk reduction.[14,15]

Equation (5.14) says that the market value of the firm equals its gross return minus a correction for risk with this quantity then being discounted at the pure rate of interest. The correction for risk is equal to the product of R and b_j. The certainty equivalent of the firm's gross cash flows equals the firm's expected gross returns minus a risk discount. The risk discount is the market price per unit of risk, R, times the risk output of the firm, b. Thus, gross returns are decomposed into corporate market value by discounting for (1) uncertainty and (2) futurity.[16]

The condition for an investment to increase the price of equity shares, given that financial policy does not matter, is

$$dV_j - I \geqslant 0 \qquad\qquad (5.15)$$

or

$$\frac{1}{r}(u - Rb) \geqslant I \qquad (5.16)$$

If the market risk aversion factor, R, equals

$$R = \frac{u_j - rv_j}{b_j} \qquad (5.17)$$

and if the investment is debt financed, then the project is acceptable if

$$\frac{u_z - rI}{b_j} > \frac{u_j - rv_j}{b_j} \qquad (5.18)$$

The decision rule implied by Equation (5.18) is that if the ratio of expected returns net of interest cost to systematic risk is larger for the project than for the aggregate firm then the acceptance of the project will increase the price of equity shares. This investment rule is independent of the form of project financing.

More generally, for investment projects having arbitrary return patterns, the cost of capital is

$$r + \frac{Rb_z}{I} \qquad (5.19)$$

This follows directly from Equation (5.16) and states that the appropriate cost of capital equals the risk free rate of return plus a risk premium equal to the product of R and b_z divided by I.[17] That is, the cost of capital depends upon the market price of risk, (R), the covariance relationship of the project's stochastic returns with the market's returns, (b), and the pure rate of interest, (r).[18] The cost of capital therefore increases (decreases), ceteris paribus, with increases (decreases) in the beta of the project. This increase (decrease) in the cost of a capital results from an increase (decrease) in the risk premium component of the hurdle rate.

It should be noted that the appropriate cost of capital of a "diversifying" project is a marginal rate inasmuch as the beta of the project will differ from the beta of the firm.[19] Thus, the average cost of capital for the firm is only a relevant concept for corporate investment decisions under conditions where the risk characteristics of the projects are identical to the risk properties of the firm (e.g., for the case of a nondiversifying project).

An exception to this generalization is the determination of the fair rate of return for public utility regulation. In this regulation scenario, the average cost of capital, rather than the marginal cost of capital, has far more economic relevance inasmuch as the determined rate is applicable to the entire rate base.[20,21,22]

To summarize, the present state of market equilibrium theory of capital asset prices suggests that beta is a highly useful concept for analyzing the cost of capital. Specifically, the conceptual usefulness of beta is that it is a necessary variable in specifying the magnitude of the risk premium.

5.4 SOME PREVIOUS EMPIRICAL EVIDENCE OF RISK-RETURN

The possible usefulness of beta in decision making cannot be evaluated in the abstract, but depends upon the empirical validity of the two-parameter capital asset pricing model as a description of the stochastic process generating security returns. An all-too-brief summary of the simple version of the Sharpe-Lintner model might be that the empirical evidence indicates that it is not a "complete" explanation of the structure of yields and risk of capital market instruments. Specifically, the studies of Douglas, Lintner, Miller-Scholes, Friend-Blume and Black-Jensen-Scholes indicate, if properly interpreted, that the intercepts are positive (negative) for low (high) risk assets.[23]

However, the evidence of virtually all of the recent studies is strongly suggestive of a linear relationship between a common stock's expected return and its beta risk.[24] It follows that (1) the risk premia for NYSE stocks within a given period varies systematically in proportion to the security's nondiversifiable covariance risk, and (2) that beta is an appropriate measure of a common stock's risk even if the simple form of the CAPM is not a complete description of the structure of security returns. In other words, given the linear relationship between beta and expected return, the model is capable of determining ratios between risk premia on different common stocks, but not their absolute expected yields. Further, there is no conclusive evidence that measures of risk other than beta systematically affect equity returns.

For example, tests by Fama-MacBeth of their four-factor model converted to a portfolio basis yields inferences regarding, among other things, (1) whether there are any systematic nonlinearities in risk-return relationships, and (2) the importance of nonbeta risk in the structure of yields. Specifically, Fama-MacBeth set forth a capital market valuation equation that tests hypotheses embedded in the two-factor model of Black and Ross.[25] The expected return on a security via the four-factor model is:

$$E(\tilde{R}_{it}) = \tilde{Y}_{0t} + \tilde{Y}_{1t}B_i + \tilde{Y}_{2t}B_i^2 + \tilde{Y}_{3t}s_i + \tilde{e}_{it}. \tag{5.20}$$

$\tilde{R}_{it}$ is the one-period return on company i in the period from $t-1$ to t. Y_0 is the equivalent of the return on the riskless asset. B_i represents security i's beta. S_i is the standard deviation of the residuals of security i. The random disturbance term $(\hat{e})$ has a mean value of zero and it is independent of the other variables. $\tilde{Y}_0$, $\hat{Y}_1$, $\hat{Y}_2$, and $\hat{Y}_3$ are stochastic regression coefficients.

The model states that the expected return on an asset is the sum of the expected return on a zero-beta security, the risk premia of linear and quadratic beta risk, the risk premium of nonbeta risk and a residual component.

Their empirical results indicated that on the average $\tilde{Y}_{2t} = 0$ and $\tilde{Y}_{3t} = 0$. This evidence is consistent with the hypotheses that there are no systematic nonlinearities in the risk-return trade off and that there are no systematic effects of nonbeta risk on the risk-return relationships of securities.

5.5 EMPIRICAL TESTS AND RESULTS

Some surrogate evidence derived from the following test is also consistent with the results implied by market-line theory. The research design employed was:

1. Using five years (60 months) of monthly returns, the beta of each stock was estimated by regressing returns on the Fisher Combination Link Relative Index.[26]
2. Securities were ranked from high to low according to the magnitude of their beta.
3. Ten equal size and contiguous portfolios were formed with the highest ten percent beta securities forming portfolio 1, the next highest ten percent beta securities forming portfolio 2, etc.[27]
4. Using data from the next five years, the betas, the standard error of the residual term of the market model, and variance of the return distribution for individual securities were estimated.[28]

5. The estimates of the beta, standard error of the residual term, and the variance of the return distribution were calculated for each of the ten portfolios. These calculations were averages derived from the betas, standard errors of the residual term and the variances of the return distribution for the individual securities within each of the ten portfolios.
6. The coefficient of determination between mean return and each of (1) beta, (2) standard error of the residual term, and (3) variance of the return distribution were calculated using the ten portfolio observations. These R^2's are presented in Table 5-1.

The data seems to indicate that the relationship between returns and risk is more systematic if beta represents the measure of risk employed. Likewise, the risk-return relationship is least systematic when the measure of risk utilized is the standard deviation of the portfolio residuals. Both of these results are consistent with market-line theory.

In his review article, Jensen concludes that "the recent evidence presented by Black, Jensen, and Scholes and Fama and MacBeth seems to indicate that the two-factor equation for equilibrium expected returns involving the market factor and the beta factor suggested by B-J-S and later derived theoretically by Black, Vasicek, and Brennan may be an adequate representation of the unconditional

Table 5-1.   Coefficients of Determination for Selected Estimation Periods

Time Interval	Mean Returns Beta	Mean Returns se (e)	Mean Returns Std. Dev.
January, 1931, to December, 1967	.993	.314	.992
January, 1931, to December, 1935	.964	.456	.962
January, 1936, to December, 1940	.710	.698	.831
January, 1941, to December, 1945	.980	.541	.979
January, 1946, to December, 1950	.000	.103	.102
January, 1951, to December, 1955	.616	.024	.165
January, 1956, to December, 1960	.696	.010	.474
January, 1961, to December, 1967	.834	.023	.776

expected returns on assets, even though it is far from a complete specification of the stochastic structure of asset returns."[29,30]

In short, our empirical knowledge of capital market phenomena for common stocks is consistent with a number of important properties of the extended two-parameter model and this framework has comparative advantages from a positive standpoint over alternative capital market equilibrium models.[31,32]

Indeed, Fama states that "the important basis for the conclusion that the two-parameter model is useful is that it does well, relative to any other capital market model of which I am aware, in describing actual return data. Although there is some disagreement on matters of detail, the implications of the model for the measurement of risk and the relationship between risk and average return seem to stand up well in the empirical tests of Friend and Blume, and Black, Jensen, and Scholes, and in the test of Fama and MacBeth. . . ."[33]

5.6 REMARKS CONCERNING APPLICABILITY OF BETA TO CORPORATE DECISION MAKING

Despite the considerable empirical appeal of the two-parameter, one should not infer that the straightforward application of beta analysis to estimating the cost of capital is without problems. First, the nonstationarity of beta from period to period for individual securities is well documented.[34] Second, the slope of the security market line may and often does shift over time. Third, a forecast of expected market returns is not endogenously given in capital market-line theory. Thus, for unique capital budgeting projects an efficient unbiased assessment of the expected equilibrium risk-adjusted yield appears to be a nonsimple and nonmechanical task.[35]

One viewpoint is, given that the betas of individual projects are nonstationary, widespread operational usefulness of systematic risk would require a dynamic theory to account for changes in beta. However, since our understanding of the determinants of beta risk and changes therein is still in its infancy, this point of view concludes that the use of a nonstationary variable (e.g., the beta time series of the firm) is not appropriate for decision making purposes. The additional requirement that the assessed beta is for the project and not for the firm further complicates matters.

An alternative viewpoint and approach is that of Bayesianism.[36] It argues that inductive reasoning and behavior are similar activities and are identical to coherent and admissible decision making.[37] The Bayesian approach is a learning model of great value in accomplishing one of the major objectives of science, namely learning from experience. Also, it has the appealing property of being consistent with Jeffrey's rules for a theory of inductive inference.[38] Hence, in a fundamental sense, the Bayesian approach presents a unified and operational approach to the problem of inference in general and to estimating the beta and subsequently the equilibrium rate of return (e.g., the cost of capital or cutoff rate) for the project in particular. Bayes' theorem sets forth a specific manner in which a decision maker's prior knowledge is revised with the arrival of new sample information to obtain one's posterior probability.[39] The assessment of the prior beta can reflect the particular set of knowledge about the determinants of relative market risk that the decision maker possesses.[40]

Unfortunately, while there have been a number of studies investigating the determinants of beta risk, equation specification is still somewhat of an *ad hoc* task.[41] Myers suggests that "the missing link seems to be a dynamic model of a firm's earnings behavior, growth, and market valuation."[42] In any case, we have just a preliminary idea of the stochastic process generating beta.

The point here is to suggest that as our empirical understanding of the determinants of beta increases then we may want to incorporate our assessments of the probability distributions of these underlying and causal factors into our Bayesian forecast of the B for the project.[43]

5.7 CONCLUSION

To conclude, beta is an elegant and highly appealing way to formulate the concept of the cost of capital within a market equilibrium scenario. The empirical robustness of several important properties of the two-parameter model adds to its appropriateness. However, the use of "mechanical" procedures in deriving the cost of capital is likely to lead to biased, inconsistent, and highly inefficient estimates. It would appear, however, that the Bayesian approach to the inferential or decision problem of assessing the beta of individual projects has much to commend it. A more complete specification awaits a better understanding of the determinants of beta.[44]

NOTES TO SECTION FIVE

1. In the abstract, the magnitude of a security's beta could range from plus infinity to negative infinity. In reality, there are few securities that have negative betas.

2. The Evans-Archer investigation concluded "that there was little economic justification of increasing portfolio sizes beyond 10 or so securities." Their

investigation was based on both t and F tests computed on sample standard deviations of the log of the wealth relatives for portfolios containing different numbers of securities. See Evans, J.L., and Archer, S.J., "Diversification and the Reduction of Dispersion: An Empirical Analysis," *Journal of Finance*, 1968, pp. 761-767.

3. There is some ad hoc evidence consistent with the view that investors hold portfolios fairly close to the efficiency locus. The argument is: First, Friend shows via data of both the New York Stock Exchange Public Transaction Study and the Crockett-Friend Study "that institutions and individuals with reasonably well-diversified portfolios own well over 63 percent of NYSE stock." Second, the Evans-Archer study indicates that most of the gains of diversification can be achieved by a portfolio comprised of 10 randomly chosen stocks." Since, by definition, portfolios having no unsystematic risk are efficient and since the Friend concept of well-diversified portfolios (a portfolio having 10 or more different dividend payment stocks) can be viewed as consistent with the Evans-Archer empirical finding, it appears that investor portfolios are approximately mean-variance efficient. See Friend, I., Prepared Testimony, New York Telephone Company, June, 1973, pp. 9-13, and Evans-Archer, *op. cit.*

4. Black, F., "Capital Market Equilibrium with Restricted Borrowing," *Journal of Business*, July, 1972; Ross, S.A., "Portfolio and Capital Market Theory with Arbitrary Preferences and Distributions—The General Validity of the Mean-Variance Approach in Large Markets," Rodney L. White Center for Financial Research, Working Paper 6-71, University of Pennsylvania; and Merton, R.C., "An Intertemporal Capital Asset Pricing Model," in this volume.

5. Black, F., Jensen, M.C., and Scholes, M., "The Capital Asset Pricing Model: Some Empirical Tests," in M.C. Jensen, ed., *Studies in the Theory of Capital Markets*, Praeger Publishers, New York, 1972.

6. Black's assumptions are identical to those enumerated previously except that there is no riskless asset and hence no riskless borrowing or lending. See Black, *op. cit.*, p. 446.

7. Intuitively, a zero-beta portfolio is a portfolio whose returns are uncorrelated with the returns of the market portfolio.

8. For a further explanation of the intricacies of his framework, see Merton, *op. cit.*

9. Many of the ideas in this section are based on Mossin's and Hamada's treatments of the cost of capital. See Mossin, J., *Theory of Financial Markets*, Prentice-Hall, Englewood Cliffs, N.J., 1973; Mossin, J., *Security Pricing Theory and Its Implications for Corporate Investment Decisions*, General Learning Press, Morristown, N.J., 1972; and Hamada, R.S., "Portfolio Analysis, Market Equilibrium, and Corporation Finance," *Journal of Finance*, March, 1969, pp. 13-31.

10. Some slight amplifications of these four assumptions are made. First, it is postulated that all investors have the same horizons and make portfolio choices at the same time. Second, there is an absence of risk of ruin or bankruptcy at the level of the firm and the investor.

11. Some preliminary beginnings towards a multiperiod theory of capital budgeting under uncertainty are contained in Brennan, M.J., "An Approach to the Valuation of Uncertain Income Streams," *Journal of Finance*, June, pp.

661-674; and Bogue, M., and Roll, R., "Capital Budgeting of Risky Projects with 'Imperfect' Markets for Physical Capital," in this volume.

12. The intuitive rationale for the same percentage, likely varying from investor to investor, of each stock in the portfolio of a given individual is that if all securities are fairly priced, and if there are homogenous expectations, then all investors hold a constant percentage of the most inclusive portfolio (e.g., the market portfolio).

13. The constant proportion property of investor behavior is much stronger than the separation theorem of Tobin inasmuch as the former is derived from general equilibrium conditions of the capital market while the latter emerges out of the procedure of deriving the optimal portfolio for a single investor. For an exposition of the conditions under which this property holds, see Hakansson, N., "Risk Disposition and the Separation Property in Portfolio Selection," *Journal of Financial and Quantitative Analysis*, December, 1969, pp. 401-416.

14. More formally, R is the harmonic mean of the tradeoff between expected risk and expected return divided by the number of investors.

15. For a discussion of the price of risk and the size of the market, see Lintner, J., "The Market Price of Risk, Size of Market and Investors' Risk Aversion," *Review of Economics and Statistics*, February, 1970, pp. 87-99; Budd, A.P., and Litzenberger, R.H., "The Market Price of Risk, Size of Market and Investors' Risk Aversion: A Comment," *Review of Economics and Statistics*, February, 1972, pp. 204-206; and Lintner, J., "The Market Price of Risk, Size of Market and Investors' Risk Aversion: A Reply," *Review of Economics and Statistics*, February, 1972, pp. 206-208.

16. While there is a certain superficial similarity between this valuation model and those of traditional finance, the discount rates for this framework are derived from a market equilibrium scenario and are not simply *ad hoc* definitions without any meaningful positive implications.

17. As an example, the appropriate cost of capital for a riskless asset is the pure rate of interest. That is, when b_z is zero, the cutoff rate is r.

18. The hurdle rate has two components. They are a risk adjustment factor and a time discount rate. These components can be utilized, in conjunction with a firm's net cash flow, to calculate the net present value of a project proposal.

19. For recent finance literature espousing essentially the same point of view, see Rubenstein, M.E., "A Synthesis of Corporate Financial Theory," *Journal of Finance*, March, 1973, pp. 167-181; Weston, J.F., "Investment Decisions Using the Capital Asset Pricing Model," *Financial Management*, Spring, 1973, pp. 25-33; and, Black, F., "Corporate Investment Decisions," Financial Note No. 2B, May 29, 1969.

20. From this, it follows that it is more compatible with the Supreme Court's decision in the *Federal Power Commission* v. *Hope Natural Gas*.

21. Of course, in setting rates for public utility regulation, the fair rate of return should be higher than the cost of capital in order to be consistent with normative micro capital budgeting.

22. For public utility rate case testimony utilizing beta along with views concerning the relevance of beta for such decision, see

Friend, I., Prepared Testimony, New York Telephone Company, June, 1973; Hess, P., "A Proposed Aid in Determination of a Firm's Cost of Equity," Iowa Commerce Commission, August 9, 1973; Morrison, G.R., New York State Public Service Commission Case No. 26370, 1973, pp. 11-14; Myers, S.C., "The Application of Finance Theory to Public Utility Rate Cases," *Bell Journal of Economics and Management Science*, Spring, 1972, pp. 58-97; Myers, S.C., "What Was A.T.&T's Cost of Capital in 1971?", undated; and Woods, D.L., "Beta Risk Measures for Mountain Bell," American Telephone and Telegraph Company, Corporate Planning Organization, August, 1973;

Breen, W.J., and Lerner, E.M., "On the Use of B in Regulatory Proceedings," *Bell Journal of Economics and Management Science*, Autumn, 1972, pp. 612-621; and Myers, S.C., "On the Use of B in Regulatory Proceedings: A Comment," *Bell Journal of Economics and Management Science*, Autumn, 1972, pp. 622-627.

23. See Douglas, G.W., "Risk in the Equity Markets: An Empirical Appraisal of Market Efficiency," *Yale Economic Essays:* Spring, 1969, 3-45; Lintner, J., "Security Prices and Risk: The Theory and a Comparative Analysis of A.T.&T. and Leading Industrials," a paper presented at the conference on the Economics of Regulated Public Utilities, June 24, 1965, Chicago, as cited by Douglas, G.W.; Miller, M.H. and Scholes, M., "Rates of Return in Relation to Risk: A Reexamination of Some Recent Findings," M.C. Jensen, ed., *Studies in the Theory of Capital Markets*, N.Y., Praeger Publishing Company, 1972; and Friend, I., and Blume, M., "Measurement of Portfolio Performance Under Uncertainty," *The American Economic Review*, September, 1970, 561-575.

24. However, the Blume-Friend study suggests that if the opportunity set is expanded to include 20-year AA corporate bonds that the relationship between return and nondiversifiable risk is nonlinear. See Blume, M.E., and Friend, I., "A New Look at the Asset Pricing Model," *Journal of Finance*, March, 1973, F.N. 24, p. 31.

25. Fama, E.F., and MacBeth, J., "Risk, Return, and Equilibrium: Empirical Tests," *Journal of Political Economy*, May-June, 1973, pp. 607-636.

26. The stocks utilized were those listed on the New York Stock Exchange for the relevant period. The price relatives for delisted stocks included the closing price of the stock on the month preceding the delisting.

27. Portfolios were equal weighted rather than value weighted.

28. With the passage of time, the composition of the portfolios changes as beta is recalculated annually and reranked on a different data base.

29. Jensen, M.C., "Capital Markets: Theory and Evidence," *Bell Journal of Economics and Management Science*, Autumn, 1972, p. 391.

30. Note also Black-Jensen-Scholes comment that "the empirical results suggest that the returns of different securities can be written as a linear function of two factors" and that "it seems to us that we have established the presence and significance of the beta factor in explaining security returns." See Black-Jensen-Scholes, *op. cit.* pp. 100 and 115.

31. The CAPM's comparative advantages can be illustrated by (1) noting that

the time-state preference theory is essentially nonoperational with regard to testing capital market equilibrium phenomena, (2) noting that the empirical investigations of the capital growth model are just beginning, (3) noting that traditional models of valuation, such as the Gordon dividend model, are based on ad hoc assumptions about the discounting process inasmuch as they are not derived from a capital market equilibrium scenario, and (4) recalling the two-factor model's robustness for explaining the unconditional returns on assets.

32. Consistent with this stance is the comment of Haley-Schall regarding the usefulness of the risk-adjusted discount model. "For theoretical purposes the model is much less appealing because there is no direct means of determining r_y. It must be considered a derived quantity resulting from some unspecified process. . . . The theoretical issue is how equilibrium prices (or rates of return) are determined." See Charles W. Haley and Lawrence D. Schall, *The Theory of Financial Decisions*, McGraw-Hill Book Company, New York, N.Y., p. 187.

33. See Fama, E.F., "Risk, Return, and Portfolio Analysis: Reply," *Journal of Political Economy*, May-June, 1973, p. 754.

34. See, for example, Blume, M.E. "On the Assessment of Risk," *Journal of Finance*, March, 1971, pp. 1-10; Campanella, F., *The Measurement of Portfolio Risk Exposure*, Lexington Books, Lexington, Mass., 1972, pp. 26-28; Jacob, N., "The Measurement of Systematic Risk for Securities and Portfolios: Some Empirical Results," *Journal of Financial and Quantitative Analysis*, March, 1971, pp. 815-834, and Sharpe, W.F. and Cooper, G.M., "Risk-Return Classes of New York Stock Exchange Common Stocks, 1931-1967," *Financial Analysts Journal*, March-April, 1972. Evidence on the nonstationarity thesis using time series date and the two-factor model is documented in Black, Jensen, and Scholes, *op. cit.*, pp. 99-121.

35. For capital budgeting projects of the acquisition of the firm genre, then an additional complication is that the variance of the estimated beta of the project (e.g., acquired firm) is likely to be high.

36. The Bayesian approach for the assessment of capital budgeting parameter has also been prescribed by Bogue and Roll, *op. cit.*, p. 3. Papers that integrate the Bayesian approach into investment portfolio decision making are Kalymon, B.A., "Estimation Risk in the Portfolio Selection Model," *Journal of Financial and Quantitative Analysis*, 1971, pp. 559-582; Mao, J.C.T. and Sarndal, C.E., "A Decision Theory Approach to Portfolio Selection," *Management Science B*, 1966, pp. 323-333; and Winkler, R.L., "Bayesian Models for Forecasting Security Prices," *Journal of Financial and Quantitative Analysis*, June, 1973, pp. 387-405. The only paper utilizing a Bayesian framework of estimating beta is Vasicek, O.A., "Using Cross-Sectional Information in Bayesian Estimation of Security Betas," *Journal of Finance*, December, 1973.

37. An exposition of the foundations of utility and subjective probability are contained in de Finetti, B., "La Prevision: Ses Lois Logiques, Ses Sources Subjectives," *Annales de l'Institut Henri Poincare 7*, pp. 1-68. English translation in Kyburg, H.E., and Smokler, H.E., eds., *Studies in Subjective Probability*, Wiley, New York, 1964, pp. 93-158, and Savage, L.J., *The Foundation of Statistics*, Wiley, New York, 1954.

38. For an exposition of this, see Zellner, A., *An Introduction to Bayesian Influence in Economics*, John Wiley and Sons, New York, 1971, Chapter 1, and Zellner, A., "The Bayesian Approach and Alternatives in Econometrics," in M.D.

Intriligator (ed.), *Frontiers of Quantitative Economics*, North-Holland, 1971, 178-193.

39. Bayes' theorem, commonly referred to as the principle of inverse probability, utilizes information from sample data and combines it with prior information to make inferences about the parameters of a stochastic process. Thus, the posterior distribution makes inferences about parameters based on both the likelihood function and the prior probability density function.

40. From a normative standpoint these assessments should be compatible with (1) knowledge of capital market risk relationships and (2) the laws of probability. See Tversky, A., and Kaheman, D., "Judgment under Uncertainty: Heuristics and Biases," paper presented to the Fourth Conference on Subjective Probability, Utility, and Decision Making," Rome, Italy, September, 1973, pp. 1-6.

41. For insights into the present state of empirical knowledge about beta, see the studies by Beaver-Kettler-Scholes, Breen-Lerner, Hamada, Petit-Westerfield, Rosenberg-McKibben, and White. Beaver, W., Kettler, P., and Scholes, "Association Between Market Determined Risk Measures," *The Accounting Review*, October, 1970, pp. 654-681; Breen, W.J., and Lerner, E.M., "Corporation Financial Strategies and Market Measures of Risk and Return," *Journal of Finance*, May, 1973; Hamada, R., "The Effect of the Firm's Capital Structure on the Systematic Risk of Common Stocks," *Journal of Finance*, May, 1972, pp. 435-452; Petit, R.R. and Westerfield, R., "A Model of Capital Market Risk," *Journal of Financial and Quantitative Analysis*, March, 1972, pp. 1649-1668; Rosenberg, B., and McKibben, W., "The Prediction of Systematic and Specific Risk in Common Stocks," *Journal of Financial and Quantitative Analysis*, March, 1973, pp. 317-334; and White, R.W., "On the Measurement of Systematic Risk," Ph.D. dissertation M.I.T. 1972.

42. See Myers, S.C., "The Relation Between Real and Financial Measures of Risk and Return," in this volume.

43. There may also be other desirable adjustments such as the regression toward the mean beta phenomena. See, for example, the discussion in Blume, M.E., "Betas and Their Regression Tendencies," in this volume.

44. For insights into the methods and techniques for deriving subjective probability distributions see Winkler, R.L., "The Assessment of Prior Distributions in Bayesian Analysis," *Journal of the American Statistical Association*, 1967, pp. 776-800 and Savage, L.J., "The Elicitation of Personal Probabilities and Expectations," *Journal of the American Statistical Association*, March, 1971, pp. 783-801.

REFERENCES

1. Beaver, W., Kettler, P. and Scholes, M., "The Association Between Market Determined and Accouting Determined Risk Measures," *The Accounting Review*, October, 1970.

2. Black, F., "Capital Market Equilibrium with Restricted Borrowing," *Journal of Business*, July, 1972.

3. Black, F., Jensen, M.C., and Scholes, M., "The Capital Asset Pricing

Model: Some Empirical Tests," in M.C. Jensen, ed., *Studies in the Theory of Capital Markets*, Praeger Publishers, New York, 1972.

4. Black, F., "Corporate Investment Decisions," Financial Note No. 2B, May 29, 1969.

5. Blume, M.E., "On the Assessment of Risk," *Journal of Finance*, March, 1971.

6. Blume, M.E., "Betas and Their Regression Tendencies," in this volume.

7. Blume, M.E., and Friend, I., "A New Look at the Capital Asset Pricing Model," *Journal of Finance*, March, 1973.

8. Bogue, M., and Roll, R., "Capital Budgeting of Risky Projects with 'Imperfect' Markets for Physical Capital," in this volume.

9. Breen, W.J., and Lerner, E.M., "On the Use of B in Regulatory Proceedings," *Bell Journal of Economics and Management Science*, Autumn, 1972.

10. Breen, W.J., and Lerner, E.M., "Corporate Financial Strategies and Market Measures of Risk and Return," *Journal of Finance*, May, 1973.

11. Brennan, M.J., "An Approach to the Valuation of Uncertain Income Streams," *Journal of Finance*, June, 1973.

12. Budd, A.P., and Litzenberger, R.H., "The Market Price of Risk, Size of Market and Investors' Risk Aversion: A Reply," *Review of Economics and Statistics*, February, 1972.

13. Campanella, F., *The Measurement of Portfolio Risk Exposure*, Lexington Books, Lexington, Mass., 1972.

14. de Finetti, B., "La Prevision: Ses Lois Logiques, Ses Sources Subjectives," *Annales de l'Institut Henri Poincare 7*. English translation in Kyberg, H.E., and Smokler, H.E., eds., *Studies in Subjective Probability*, Wiley, New York, 1964.

15. Douglas, G.W., "Risk in the Equity Markets: An Empirical Appraisal of Market Efficiency," *Yale Economic Essays*, Spring, 1969.

16. Evans, J.L., and Archer, S.J., "Diversification and the Reduction of Dispersion: An Empirical Analysis," *Journal of Finance*, 1968.

17. Fama, E.F., "Risk, Return, and Portfolio Analysis: Reply," *Journal of Political Economy*, May-June, 1973.

18. Fama, E.F., and MacBeth, J., "Risk, Return and Equilibrium: Empirical Tests," *Journal of Political Economy*, May-June, 1973.

19. Friend, I., Prepared Testimony, New York Telephone Company, June, 1973.

20. Friend, I., and Blume, M., "Measurement of Portfolio Performance Under Uncertainty," *The American Economic Review*, September, 1970.

21. Hakansson, N., "Risk Disposition and the Separation Property in Portfolio Selection," *Journal of Financial and Quantitative Analysis*, December, 1969.

22. Haley, C.W., and Schall, D., *The Theory of Financial Decisions*, McGraw-Hill Book Company, New York, N.Y., 1973.

23. Hamada, R.S., "Portfolio Analysis, Market Equilibrium, and Corporation Finance," *Journal of Finance*, March, 1969.

24. Hamada, R., "The Effect of the Firm's Capital Structure on the Systematic Risk of Common Stocks," *Journal of Finance*, May, 1972.

25. Hess, P., "A Proposed Aid in Determination of Firm's Cost of Equity," Iowa Commerce Commission, August 9, 1973.

26. Jacob, N., "The Measurement of Systematic Risk for Securities and Portfolio: Some Empirical Results," *Journal of Financial and Quantitative Analysis*, March, 1971.

27. Jensen, M.C., "Capital Markets: Theory and Evidence," *Bell Journal of Economics and Management Science*, Autumn, 1972.

28. Kalymon, B.A., "Estimation Risk in the Portfolio Selection Model," *Journal of Financial and Quantitative Analysis*, 1971.

29. Lintner, J., "The Market Price of Risk, Size of Market and Investors' Risk Aversion," *Review of Economics and Statistics*, February, 1970.

30. Lintner, J., "The Market Price of Risk, Size of Market and Investors' Risk Aversion: A Reply," *Review of Economics and Statistics*, February, 1972.

31. Mao, J.C.T., and Sarndal, C.E., "A Decision Theory Approach to Portfolio Selection," *Management Science B*, 1966.

32. Merton, R.C., "An Intertemporal Capital Asset Pricing Model," *Econometrica*, September, 1973; also reprinted in this volume.

33. Miller, M.H., and Scholes, M., "Rates of Return in Relation to Risk," in M.C. Jensen, ed., *Studies in the Theory of Capital Markets* New York, 1972, Praeger Publishing Company, 1972.

34. Morrison, G.R., New York State Public Service Commission, Case No. 26370, 1973.

35. Mossin, J., *Security Pricing Theory and Its Implications for Corporate Investment Decisions*, General Learning Press, Morristown, N.J., 1972.

36. Myers, S.C., "What was A.T.&T's Cost of Capital in Early 1971," Undated.

37. Myers, S.C., "The Application of Finance Theory to Public Utility Rate Cases," *Bell Journal of Economics and Management Science*, Spring, 1972.

38. Myers, S.C., "On the Use of B in Regulatory Proceedings: A Comment," *Bell Journal of Economics and Management Science*, Autumn, 1972.

39. Pettit, R., and Westerfield, R., "A Model of Capital Market Risk," *Journal of Financial and Quantitative Analysis*, March, 1972.

40. Rosenberg, B., and McKibben, W., "The Prediction of Systematic and Specific Risk in Common Stocks," *Journal of Financial and Quantitative Analysis*, March, 1973.

41. Ross, S.A., "Portfolio and Capital Market Theory with Arbitrary Preferences and Distributions—The General Validity of the Mean-Variance Approach in Large Markets," Rodney L. White Center for Financial Research, Working Paper, University of Pennsylvania.

42. Rubenstein, M.E., "A Synthesis of Corporate Financial Theory," *Journal of Finance*, March, 1973.

43. Savage, L.J., *The Foundations of Statistics*, Wiley, New York, 1954.

44. Savage, L.J., "The Elicitation of Personal Probabilities and Expectations," *Journal of the American Statistical Association*, March, 1971.

45. Scholes, M., "Resolved: Beta is a Useful Tool in Managing Money," *Proceeding of the Seminar on the Analyses of Security Prices*, University of Chicago, 1973.

46. Sharpe, W.F., and Cooper, G.M., "Risk-Return Classes of New York Stock Exchange Common Stocks, 1931-1967," *Financial Analysts Journal*, March-April, 1972.

47. Tversky, A., and Kaheman, D., "Judgment Under Uncertainty: Heuristics and Biases," paper presented to the Fourth Conference on Subjective Probability, Utility, and Decision Making, Rome, Italy, September, 1973.

48. Vasicek, O.A., "A Note on Using Cross-Sectional Information in Bayesian Estimation of Security Betas," *Journal of Finance*, December, 1973.

49. Weston, J.F., "Investment Decision Using the Capital Asset Pricing Model," *Financial Management*, Spring, 1973.

50. White, R.W., "On the Measurement of Systematic Risk," Ph.D. dissertation, M.I.T., 1972.

51. Winkler, R.L., "The Assessment of Prior Distributions in Bayesian Analysis," *Journal of the American Statistical Association*, 1967.

52. Winkler, R.L., "Bayesian Models for Forecasting Security Prices," *Journal of Financial and Quantitative Analysis*, June, 1973.

53. Woods, D.L., "Beta Risk Measures for Mountain Bell," American Telephone and Telegraph Company, Corporate Planning Organization, August, 1973.

54. Zellner, A., *An Introduction to Bayesian Inference in Econometrics*, John Wiley and Sons, New York, 1969.

55. Zellner, A., "The Bayesian Approach and Alternatives in Econometrics," in M.D. Intriligator (ed.), *Frontiers of Quantitative Economics*, North-Holland, 1971.

The Demand for Risky Assets

Irwin Friend and Marshall E. Blume*

A striking characteristic of recent research on capital asset pricing is the paucity of empirical work on the determinants of the market price of risk[1] in contrast to the abundance of work on the interrelationships of the risk premiums among different risky assets. The market price of risk will in part depend on the utility functions of individual investors and, except for a special class of functions, on the distribution of wealth among investors.

The relationship between utility functions and wealth of all investors is obviously basic to constructing an aggregate demand function for risky assets. However, there are a multiplicity of other important potential uses, including the derivation of the form of household consumption or saving functions, measurement of the impact of different government, fiscal, or insurance measures on economic welfare, and assessment of the problems in extending single period financial and economic investment decisions to a multiperiod world.

Until recently, most interested economists believed that utility functions of individuals were characterized either by constant or decreasing absolute risk aversion and by increasing proportional risk aversion (Section 6.1). The measure of proportional risk aversion used in this chapter is the same as the elasticity of the marginal utility of wealth. In recent years, this traditional view of increasing proportional risk aversion has been vigorously questioned by advo-

*We wish to thank the National Science Foundation and the Rodney L. White Center for Financial Research for financial support.

cates of the *log* utility function which, while still maintaining decreasing absolute risk aversion, implies that proportional risk aversion is constant rather than increasing.

This study will, for the first time, systematically exploit cross-sectional data on household asset holdings to assess the nature of households' utility functions. The data used are detailed information on assets, income, and other socioeconomic-demographic characteristics for a large sample of households.

Prior to analyzing the survey data, the study will adapt and extend existing theory to obtain the relationships between the composition of household wealth (both human and nonhuman) and their utility functions. These relationships are suitable for statistical analyses at both the micro and macro levels (Section 6.2). Part of the empirical work is based upon these survey data (Section 6.3). Other work analyzes *ex post* and *ex ante* market returns since the latter part of the nineteenth century to estimate the market price of risk (Section 6.4). The last part of the chapter synthesizes the analyses of the household and market data (Section 6.5).

Our main conclusions are: First, regardless of their wealth level, the coefficients of proportional risk aversion for households are on average well in excess of one and probably in excess of two. Thus, investors require a substantially larger premium to hold equities or other risky assets than they would if their attitudes toward risk were described by logarithmic utility functions.

Second, the study concludes that the assumption of constant proportional risk aversion for households is as a first approximation a fairly accurate description of the market place. These first two findings imply that the utility function of a representative investor is quite different from those which have often been assumed in the literature. However, it should be pointed out that our conclusion of constant proportional risk aversion follows from our treatment of investment in housing. Other plausible treatments would imply either moderately increasing or moderately decreasing proportional risk aversion.

Third, under tenable assumptions, including that of constant proportional risk aversion, we develop a simple form of the aggregate equilibrium relationship between the relative demand for risky assets and the market price of risk. To determine the actual values of the required rate of return on risky assets, the market price of risk, and the relative value of risky assets would of course entail the specification of supply conditions. For a constant physical supply of both risky and nonrisky assets, the relationship developed in this chapter indicates how the required rate of return on risky assets as a whole is determined.

6.1 EARLIER STUDIES

Economists have generally been convinced that the market utility function has risk-aversion properties somewhere between a negative exponential utility function with constant absolute risk aversion and increasing relative risk aversion, and a constant elasticity utility function with decreasing absolute risk aversion, but with constant proportional risk aversion. The authority generally cited for asserting these bounds for the utility function is Kenneth Arrow (for example, see S.C. Tsiang).

While no one is likely to argue with the plausibility of decreasing absolute risk aversion, the widely held assumption of increasing (or at most constant) relative risk aversion is open to question. At the theoretical level, the denial of the tenability of decreasing relative risk aversion is based on the assumed implausibility of a utility function which is unbounded either from above or from below (see Arrow). However, arguments based upon such bounding conditions may be economically empty. The ultimate justification for such an assumption must rest on the empirical data. The only direct evidence we know of that has been cited to support the assumption of increasing or constant relative risk aversion are the studies which conclude that either the income elasticity or the wealth elasticity of demand for cash balances (usually money narrowly or broadly defined) is at least one (see Arrow). Of this evidence, only the wealth elasticity is at all relevant. Moreover, in view of the existence of liabilities or negative assets in investors' balance sheets, it is more appropriate to relate the total of risky assets, rather than the customary cash balances, to net worth, but this has not been done in the relevant literature.

The available cross-section studies based on household surveys of assets and liabilities point to a wealth elasticity of liquid assets of well below or close to one if all tangible assets including consumer durables are included in wealth, and lower figures if tangible assets are excluded (for example, see Jean Crockett and Friend, pp. 37 and 55-57). The aggregate time-series data reflecting changes in supply and demand conditions, including those arising from changes in wealth distribution, among different groups in the population, appear to be much less pertinent than the cross-section information.[2]

In recent years, the major challenge to the widely held assumption of a market utility function characterized by increasing relative risk aversion has been posed by proponents of the *log* utility function which implies constant relative risk aversion (again associated with decreasing absolute risk aversion). The *log* utility function has been justified in this literature mainly on grounds of the reasonableness of the implicit growth maximization criterion as contrasted with the alleged unreasonableness of mean-variance efficient portfolios.[3]

More recently, in Richard Roll's study a new set of empirical tests of the implications of the growth-optimum and mean-variance models found that the former performs well in comparison with the latter "but the test results are clouded by the close operational similarity of the two models" (p. 552). Still another set of empirical tests obtained from experimental games suggested that a *log* utility function might characterize individuals with wealth in excess of $200,000, but below that level increasing relative (and decreasing absolute) risk aversion was exhibited. (See M.J. Gordon, G.E. Paradis, and C.H. Rorke.)

6.2 THEORETICAL BACKGROUND FOR THE EMPIRICAL ANALYSIS

The literature has shown under various conditions that in equilibrium the market price of risk—the ratio of the expected risk premium on risky assets to the variance of return on those assets—equals the market value of all risky assets times a function of each individual's measure of absolute risk aversion. More precisely, this relationship can be developed for discrete planning periods by assuming either that investors' utility functions are quadratic or that their utility functions are exponential or logarithmic and end-of-period wealth is normally distributed.[4] This relationship takes the form

$$\frac{E(r_m - r_f)}{\sigma^2(r_m)} = V_{mo} \left[\sum_k E\left(\frac{1}{R_k}\right) \right]^{-1} \qquad (6.1)$$

where r_m is the return on the market portfolio of all risky assets, r_f is the return on the risk-free asset, R_k is Pratt's measure of absolute risk aversion for the kth investor, and V_{mo} is the market value of all risky assets at the beginning of the planning period. Stephen Ross has obtained a similar expression by assuming an infinitesimal planning horizon and no finite changes in value of any asset in an infinitesimal period.[5]

Although the various developments of (6.1) assumed that the net supply of the risk-free asset was zero, they can easily be generalized to the situation in which this asset has a positive net supply. For mathematical convenience, this generalization will be based upon an infinitesimal horizon model and will make the same assumptions as those made by Ross. Besides the assumption about the distribution of returns mentioned above, perhaps the most critical assumptions include homogeneity of expectations and a frictionless capital market. In a frictionless capital market, all financial assets—both risk-free and risky—are infinitely divisible, can be traded with no transaction costs, and can be sold short with the proceeds available to purchase another asset.

In parallel with Ross's development, the wealth conservation equation for the kth investor, assuming no taxes, would be[6]

$$W_{k,t+dt} = W_{kt} \left\{ 1 + [r_f + \alpha_k E(r_m - r_f)] dt + \alpha_k \sigma_m y(t) \sqrt{dt} \right\} \quad (6.2)$$

where α_k is the proportion of the net worth of investor k placed in the portfolio of risky assets, σ_m is the standard deviation of the returns on the portfolio of risky assets, and $y(t)$ is a standardized normal random variate.[7] By expanding $U(W_{k,t+dt})$ about W_{kt}, taking expected values and dropping terms involving dt to the power of 2 or more, one obtains

$$E[U(W_{k,t+dt})] = U(W_{kt}) + U'(W_{kt})W_{kt} [r_f + \alpha_k E(r_m - r_f)] dt$$

$$+ \tfrac{1}{2} U''(W_{kt})W_{kt}^2 \alpha_k^2 \sigma_m^2 dt \quad (6.3)$$

To determine the optimal value of α_k, the derivative of $E[U]$ is set to zero:

$$U'(W_{kt})E(r_m - r_f) + U''(W_{kt})W_{kt}\alpha_k \sigma_m^2 = 0 \quad (6.4)$$

Recalling that Pratt's measure of relative risk aversion C_k is defined as $W_{kt}[-U''(W_{kt})/U'(W_{kt})]$,[8] (6.4) can be rewritten as[9]

$$\alpha_k = \frac{E(r_m - r_f)}{\sigma_m^2} \cdot \frac{1}{C_k} \quad (6.5)$$

In the absence of taxes, (6.5) could be used to estimate the coefficient of relative risk aversion for investor k given estimates of a_k and the market price of risk. However, if returns from both risky and risk-free assets are taxed at the same rates in any tax bracket[10] and if t_k is the average rate of tax for investor k, Equation (6.2) could be modified to incorporate the tax effect. Repeating the logic underlying (6.2) through (6.5) would yield the tax adjusted relationship:

$$\alpha_k = \frac{E(r_m - r_f)}{\sigma_m^2} \cdot \frac{1}{(1 - t_k)C_k} \tag{6.6}$$

Since r_m and r_f are measured before personal taxes, the assumption of homogeneous expectations assures that if $(1 - t_k)\alpha_k$ is constant over all investors, C_k will also be constant. This observation will be used in the next section in conjunction with cross-sectional survey data to assess how C_k varies with net worth.

So far, it has been explicitly assumed that all assets are liquid in that they can be purchased or sold at no cost in any quantity. This assumption is clearly unrealistic for human wealth. David Mayers has shown in a mean-variance world of finite horizons how this assumption can be relaxed to allow for the nonmarketability of human wealth. His insight can be readily applied to the continuous case. To do this, redefine r_m as the return on the portfolio of liquid risky assets and α_k as the proportion of investor k's liquid net worth (total net worth less human wealth) placed in the portfolio of liquid risky assets. Further, define the new terms: h_k as the ratio of the value of the human wealth of the kth investor to his net worth and r_{hk} as the rate of return on the kth investor's human wealth.

Under these definitions, the wealth conservation equation adjusted for taxes t_k, again assumed the same for all types of income, would be

$$
\begin{aligned}
W_{k,t+dt} = W_{kt} &\left\{ 1 + (1 - t_k) \cdot \left\{ (1 - h_k)[r_f + \alpha_k E(r_m - r_f)] \right. \right. \\
&\left. + h_k E(r_{hk}) \right\} dt + (1 - t_k) \cdot [(1 - h_k)^2 \alpha_k^2 \sigma_m^2 \\
&+ h_k^2 \sigma_{hk}^2 + 2\alpha_k h_k (1 - h_k) \\
&\left. \cdot \operatorname{cov}(r_m, r_{hk})]^{1/2} y(t) \sqrt{dt} \right\}
\end{aligned}
\tag{6.7}
$$

The covariance term allows for the presence of dependencies between the returns on liquid and human wealth. That both the variance of human wealth and the covariances are subscripted by k means that these statistics can vary from one individual to another. Repeating the logic underlying (6.2) through (6.5) would yield

$$\alpha_k = \frac{E(r_m - r_f)}{\sigma_m^2} \cdot \frac{1}{(1 - t_k)(1 - h_k)C_k} - \frac{h_k}{1 - h_k} \beta_{hk,m} \quad (6.8)$$

where $\beta_{hk,m}$ is the ratio of $\text{cov}(r_m, r_{hk})$ to σ_m^2. Thus, $\beta_{hk,m}$ can be interpreted as the slope coefficient of the regression of r_{hk} on r_m. It is interesting to note that the ratio α_k does not depend upon $E(r_{hk})$ but only upon the dependence between r_m and r_{hk}.[11]

Equations (6.6) and (6.8) are micro functions for the individual investor and are not the same kinds of relationships as (6.1), which is an equilibrium condition for the market as a whole—a macro-economic concept. Such macro relationships can be developed from these micro functions by forming a weighted average of α_k over all investors, the weights defined as the ratio of the investor's liquid wealth to the total liquid wealth in the market. If γ_k equals this proportion, if a is defined as the ratio of liquid risky assets to all liquid assets, and if all assets are liquid, the micro relationship would imply

$$\Sigma \gamma_k \alpha_k = \alpha = \frac{E(r_m - r_f)}{\sigma_m^2} \Sigma \frac{\gamma_k}{(1 - t_k)C_k} \quad (6.9)$$

Relation (6.9), which is easily solved for the market price of risk, differs from (6.1) mainly in that it takes into account taxes, allows the net supply of the risk-free asset to be positive, and is expressed in terms of relative rather than absolute risk aversion.

If one includes human wealth and further assumes that this wealth is illiquid, a similar macro relationship to (6.9) can be derived by averaging α_k given by (6.8). The resulting average is

$$\Sigma \gamma_k \alpha_k = \alpha = \frac{E(r_m - r_f)}{\sigma_m^2} \left[\Sigma \frac{\gamma_b}{(1 - t_k)(1 - h_k)C_k} \right] \quad (6.10)$$

$$- \Sigma \gamma_k \frac{h_k}{1 - h_k} \beta_{hk,m}$$

The macro relationship (6.10), again easily solved for the market price of risk, is quite different from (6.1) and (6.9) in that it takes explicit account of the nonmarketability of human wealth.

It should be noted that Equations (6.9) and (6.10), and the simplifications of these equations presented subsequently, represent aggregate equilibrium relationships between the relative demand for risky assets and the market price of risk. The market price of risk at the macro level is not given, as it may be at the micro level, but is determined jointly with the aggregate ratio α of liquid risky assets to all liquid assets. For example, assuming a constant physical supply of both risky and nonrisky assets, α is determined by $E(r_m)$ and r_f. Equations (6.9) and (6.10) indicate how $E(r_m)$ and α are related to C_k, the distribution of wealth γ_k, tax rates t_k, σ_m^2, and r_f. [1] [2]

If an investor's coefficient of relative risk aversion is assumed independent of γ_k and this coefficient is also independent of his average tax rate, (6.9) can be vastly simplified. This assumption of constant proportional risk aversion on the average is considerably more general than the assumption that all investors have the same value for C_k in that C_k can be a function of characteristics of investors which are independent of γ_k and t_k.

Specifically, let it be assumed that C_k is given by

$$\frac{1}{C_k} = \frac{1}{C} + \epsilon_{ck} \tag{6.11}$$

where ϵ_{ck} is a mean-zero disturbance independent of γ_k and t_k. The symbol C defined by (6.11) can be interpreted as the harmonic mean of C_k. Let us first simplify (6.9) by substituting (6.11) into it to obtain

$$\alpha = \frac{E(r_m - r_f)}{\sigma_m^2} \cdot \left[\frac{1}{C} \Sigma \frac{\gamma_k}{1 - t_k} + \Sigma \frac{\gamma_k \epsilon_{ck}}{1 - t_k} \right] \tag{6.12}$$

The application of expected value operators to (6.12) causes the second summation in the brackets to go to zero. Since the sum of the γ_ks is one, the reciprocal of the first summation might be termed the weighted harmonic mean of $(1 - t_k)$. Designating this mean as $1 - t$ and solving for the market price of risk, (6.12) takes the simplified form

$$\frac{E(r_m - r_f)}{\sigma_m^2} = \alpha C(1 - t) \tag{6.13}$$

If in addition to the assumption of constant proportional risk aversion (on the average) it can further be assumed that $\beta_{hk,m}$ and ϵ_{ck} are independent of the level of human wealth of the kth individual, (6.10) can likewise be vastly simplified. To do this, note first that the terms α $(\gamma_k h_k)/(1 - h_k)$, and $\gamma_k/(1 - h_k)$ can be written as R/L, H_k/L and W_k/L, respectively, where H_k is the value of the kth investor's human wealth, W_k his net worth, R the total value of all risky liquid assets, and L the total value of all liquid assets. With these identities, the simplification of (6.10) proceeds by substituting (6.11) into (6.10), taking expected values, substituting these identities, and solving for the market price of risk. The resulting expression is

$$\frac{E(r_m - r_f)}{\sigma_m^2} = \left[\frac{R}{W^*} + \beta_{hm} \frac{H}{W^*} \right] C \tag{6.14}$$

where W^* is $\Sigma W_k/(1 - t_k)$ or a tax adjusted sum of all wealth and β_{hm} is defined as $E(\beta_{hk,m} \mid H_k)$, assumed the same for all investors.[13]

These simple equilibrium expressions are valid if investors' utility functions are characterized by constant proportional risk aversion on the average as specified in (6.11). If valid, (6.13) and (6.14) would seem to offer tractable ways to estimate C from time-series data.[14] They also provide extremely simple forms of the aggregate equilibrium relationship between the relative demand for risky assets and the market price of risk.

6.3 THE ANALYSIS OF THE SURVEY DATA

The micro relationships just developed lend themselves to the use of cross-sectional data in ascertaining whether or not C_k, the coefficient of proportional risk aversion, is invariant on the average to investors' net worth. After describing the cross-sectional data, we will first examine the behavior of C_k employing (6.6) which implicitly assumes that all wealth is liquid and then will assess it employing

(6.8) which explicitly accounts for the nonmarketability of human capital.

The cross-sectional data to be analyzed come from the 1962 and 1963 Federal Reserve Board (FRB) Surveys of the Financial Characteristics of Consumers and Changes in Family Finances. These surveys, which oversampled the upper income groups, collected for more than 2,100 households detailed information on the value of their assets and liabilities at the end of both 1962 and 1963 and on the sources and amounts of income in both of these years.

From these data, the study constructed three different types of balance sheets at the end of 1962. The first type included all assets and associated liabilities with the exception of human wealth and homes.[15] The second excluded only human wealth. The third included not only homes, but also an estimate of human wealth. These balance sheets, expressed as ratios to the corresponding measures of net worth, are summarized in Tables 6-1 through 6-3 by net worth categories. Changes in the definition of wealth will, of course, move households from one wealth class to another.

In checking the validity and reasonableness of the data, it was observed that a few households received substantial salaries from closely held businesses in which they had active interests. Since some part of these salaries might more properly be classified as dividends or return on capital, any salaries from such closely held businesses in excess of $25,000 were valued as perpetuities at 10 percent and added to equity. To determine how sensitive the results are to this adjustment, the subsequent analyses were replicated on a subsample which excludes any households which own such businesses. The conclusions were virtually unchanged.[16]

Only households with a net worth in excess of $1,000 were included. Since such households have a predominant impact upon the market for assets, this restriction would have little effect upon the value of the variables in the macro relationships (6.13) or (6.14). Yet, it appears to improve the quality of the survey data by eliminating those households who may have underreported their assets or whose assets were temporarily lower than normal.

A crude estimate of human wealth was given by the discounted value of the average labor income in 1962 and 1963 which was then assumed to grow at 4 percent per year. The discount rate was taken to be 10 percent. If a person was less than 65, he was assumed to retire at 65. If he was working and over 65, he was assumed to continue to work for four years; if over 69, three years, if over 74, two years; and if over 79, one year. The sensitivity of the subsequent results to this arbitrary method of calculating human wealth will be examined, and it will turn out that within broad ranges of discount rates and growth rates the results are substantially unaffected.

If the micro relationship (6.6) were to hold, an estimate of the market price of risk times the reciprocal of the coefficient of relative risk aversion $[E(r_m - r_f)/\sigma_m^2] C_p^{-1}$ is given by $\alpha_k(1 - t_k)$. The assumption made in the last section that all investors agree on the value of the market price of risk means that $\alpha_k(1 - t_k)$ provides an estimate of C_k^{-1} up to a multiplicative positive constant, so that $\alpha_k(1 - t_k)$ can be used to assess how C_k^{-1} and, thereby, how C_k varies with net worth.[17] Using either of the first two balance sheets, which do not include human capital, the cross-sectional data provide estimates of $\alpha_k(1 - t_k)$. Since (6.6) does not take account of the nonmarketability of human wealth, the analysis based upon (6.6) will not include this kind of wealth. It might be mentioned that virtually all empirical applications of portfolio theory have ignored human wealth in spite of its obvious importance to the demand for risky assets.

In interpreting the meaning of these numbers, it should be noted that the derivation of (6.6) assumed that all assets are acquired for investment purposes, can be unambiguously dichotomized as risky or risk-free, are subject to the same schedule of income taxes, and are infinitely divisible. For analyses of the composition of wealth inclusive of homes, these assumptions may be so unrealistic as to place serious restrictions on the validity of (6.6).

Contrary to the implicit treatment of assets in our model and in capital asset pricing theory generally, homes are typically acquired by households for consumption as well as investment purposes. Moreover, the lack of tax on the imputed income from owning a home as well as other subsidies make the tax rate assumption highly questionable. Furthermore, a house involves a substantial investment and for a person with limited liquid assets, the incurrence of more debt than he might normally want to have. In the absence of an adequate rental market, the purchase of a home may be the only way of obtaining the desired type of housing. Holding utility functions constant, these factors would tend to increase the values of α_k for the lower wealth groups relative to those for the upper wealth groups if the investment in a home is assumed to be risky.[18]

Since investments in homes are not strictly compatible with the assumptions underlying (6.6), homes have been treated in three different ways in the empirical work: not as an investment asset; as a risky asset where the relevant investment is measured by the household's equity in the home; and as a risky asset where the investment is measured by the gross market value of the home.

Table 6-1. Average Ratios of Assets and Selected Items to Household Net Worth Exclusive of Homes (and Associated Mortgages) for Households Classified by Net Worth[a]

December 31, 1962

Type of Item	Net Worth (Thousands of Dollars)					
	1-10	10-100	100-200	200-500	500-1,000	Over 1,000
Risk-Free Assets to Net Worth						
Checking Accounts	0.079	0.026	0.020	0.014	0.018	0.009
Other Cash Balances[b]	0.301	0.192	0.062	0.029	0.027	0.021
Savings Bonds	0.069	0.040	0.034	0.012	0.012	0.003
Life Insurance (Cash Value)	0.238	0.071	0.042	0.025	0.031	0.013
Other Risk-Free Assets[c]	0.127	0.053	0.004	0.010	0.017	0.012
	0.814	0.382	0.163	0.089	0.103	0.057
Mixed-Risk Assets to Net Worth						
State and Local Bonds	0.0	0.001	0.001	0.013	0.014	0.032
Other Mixed-Risk Assets[d]	0.042	0.077	0.131	0.084	0.064	0.099
	0.042	0.078	0.132	0.098	0.078	0.131
Risky Assets to Net Worth						
Common and Preferred Stock	0.050	0.111	0.272	0.363	0.283	0.316
Equity in Uninc. Business	0.081	0.308	0.286	0.370	0.315	0.328
Other Risky Assets[e]	0.140	0.167	0.186	0.104	0.265	0.225
	0.271	0.586	0.743	0.838	0.863	0.869
Total Assets to Net Worth	1.128	1.046	1.039	1.025	1.004	1.057
Liabilities to Net Worth	0.128	0.046	0.039	0.025	0.044	0.057
Ancillary Statistics						
$(1 - t_k)\alpha_k^f$	0.285	0.601	0.749	0.763	0.677	0.650
Number of Households	523.	477.	68.	100.	69.	103.

aThese averages are weighted by the inverse of the sampling probability for each household. These sampling probabilities have been adjusted for bIncludes checking and other commercial bank accounts, savings and loan savings accounts, credit union savings accounts, and mutual savings accounts.

cIncludes U.S. Treasury Bills, notes and certificates, the withdrawal value of profit sharing and retirement plans, credit balances in brokerage accounts, and risk-free assets held in trust accounts. Risky assets held in trust accounts are included in the appropriate category of direct holdings, except that when they could not be classified in this manner, they were included in miscellaneous risky assets.

dIncludes long-term corporate, state and local and U.S. government bonds (other than savings bonds).

eIncludes investment real estate assets and miscellaneous assets, such as patents, etc.

fThe symbol α_k is defined as the ratio of the sum of the mixed-risk and risky assets to net worth for investor k. The symbol t_k is the average federal tax rate for investor k as estimated by the procedure devised by the Survey of Financial Characteristics of Consumers. The only difference was that realized capital gain income or losses were included in adjusted gross income in this paper unlike the original procedure. The original survey ignored this type of income in calculating the tax rate.

Table 6-2.   Average Ratios of Assets and Selected Items to Household Net Worth Inclusive of Homes for Households Classified by Net Worth[a]

December 31, 1962

Type of Item	Net Worth (Thousands of Dollars)					
	1-10	10-100	100-200	200-500	500-1,000	Over 1,000
Risk-Free Assets to Net Worth						
Checking Accounts	0.040	0.019	0.017	0.012	0.023	0.009
Other Cash Balances	0.138	0.109	0.084	0.032	0.023	0.019
Savings Bonds	0.029	0.025	0.020	0.020	0.009	0.003
Life Insurance (Cash Value)	0.097	0.056	0.033	0.025	0.033	0.013
Other Risk-Free Assets	0.055	0.033	0.013	0.008	0.010	0.012
	0.359	0.243	0.167	0.096	0.097	0.056
Mixed-Risk Assets to Net Worth						
State and Local Bonds	0.0	0.000	0.001	0.005	0.037	0.029
Other Mixed-Risk Assets	0.016	0.038	0.084	0.077	0.043	0.090
	0.016	0.039	0.085	0.082	0.081	0.119
Risky Assets to Net Worth						
Market Value of Homes	1.539	0.657	0.216	0.098	0.112	0.046
Common and Preferred Stock	0.012	0.052	0.208	0.289	0.306	0.292
Equity in Uninc. Business	0.045	0.147	0.271	0.395	0.235	0.339
Other Risky Assets	0.035	0.101	0.108	0.084	0.213	0.216
	1.631	0.957	0.803	0.866	0.866	0.892
Total Assets To Net Worth	2.006	1.238	1.055	1.044	1.043	1.067
Liabilities to Net Worth						
Mortgage Liabilities	0.924	0.204	0.041	0.016	0.008	0.003
Other Liabilities	0.083	0.034	0.014	0.028	0.035	0.064
	1.006	0.238	0.055	0.044	0.043	0.067

Ancillary Statistics

$(1 - t_k)\alpha_k$ (Equity in Homes)[b]	0.669	0.718	0.724	0.780	0.642	0.665
$(1 - t_k)\alpha_k$ (Investment in Homes)[b]	1.495	0.897	0.758	0.793	0.648	0.667
Number of Households	459.	731.	94.	103.	76.	108.

[a]See fn. for Table 6-1.
[b]Includes automobiles.

Table 6-3. Average Ratios of Assets and Selected Items to Household Net Worth Inclusive of Human Wealth and Homes Classified by Net Worth[a]

December 31, 1962

Type of Item	Net Worth (Thousands of Dollars)					
	1-10	10-100	100-200	200-500	500-1,000	Over 1,000
Risk-Free Assets to Net Worth	0.181	0.077	0.036	0.061	0.068	0.052
Checking-Accounts	0.027	0.007	0.003	0.005	0.014	0.008
Other Cash Balances	0.116	0.042	0.014	0.021	0.019	0.016
Savings Bonds	0.011	0.011	0.003	0.008	0.005	0.003
Life Insurance (Cash Value)	0.027	0.013	0.010	0.014	0.021	0.013
Other Risk-Free Assets	0.000	0.004	0.006	0.013	0.009	0.012
Mixed-Risk Assets to Net Worth	0.013	0.014	0.008	0.003	0.041	0.093
State and Local Bonds	0.0	0.000	0.000	0.001	0.019	0.023
Other Mixed-Risk Assets	0.013	0.014	0.008	0.032	0.023	0.070
Risky Assets to Net Worth	0.878	0.964	1.006	0.958	0.926	0.910
Market Value of Homes	0.470	0.183	0.101	0.104	0.086	0.043
Common and Preferred Stock	0.002	0.017	0.018	0.085	0.171	0.253
Equity in Uninc. Business	0.055	0.070	0.022	0.085	0.220	0.277
Human Capital	0.334	0.656	0.850	0.649	0.349	0.148
Other Risky Assets	0.018	0.038	0.014	0.035	0.100	0.189
Total Assets to Net Worth	1.072	1.056	1.049	1.052	1.035	1.055
Liabilities to Net Worth						
Mortgage Liabilities	0.052	0.044	0.043	0.039	0.013	0.004

Other Liabilities	0.021	0.012	0.006	0.013	0.022	0.051
	0.072	0.056	0.049	0.052	0.035	0.055
Ancillary Statistics						
Number of Households	114.	819.	485.	200.	90.	135.

aSee fn. for Table 6-2.

Another possibility would be to assume that households consider homes to be riskless assets, but this seems a less tenable assumption than the ones we have utilized.

Within the context of the model embodied in (6.6), perhaps the most appropriate measure of a household's investment in housing is its equity value. First, if an investor views a mortgage and a house as a package, it may well be that he regards only his equity at risk. Second, the use of equity is more in the spirit of infinitely divisible assets than the use of total assets. Nonetheless, the results of alternative assumptions are presented.

Tables 6-1 and 6-2 present averages of the estimated tax adjusted ratio $(1 - t_k)\alpha_k$ by net worth classes for varying treatments of housing. Human wealth is not included. In addition, Table 6-4 presents the slope coefficients of the regressions of $(1 - t_k)\alpha_k$ on the logarithm of net worth.[19] The α_k in these tables are ratios of risky and mixed-risk assets to net worth. Both simple regressions and regressions which control with dummy variables for the possible interaction between net worth and three socioeconomic factors (age, education, and occupation) are presented. Whether or not these dummy variables are included, the slope coefficients on the logarithm of net worth are not much different.[20]

Table 6-4.   Regressions of $(1 - t_k)\alpha_k$ on the Logarithm of Net Worth with and Without Holding Constant Age, Education, and Occupation

December 31, 1962

tc128,c132,c21,c130,, Net Worth Including Homes	Housing[a] Measured by	Simple Regression Coefficient on ln(NW)			Regression with Dummy Variables for Age, Education, and Occupation[b] Coefficient on ln (NW)		
		estimate	t-value	$\bar{R}^2$	estimate	t-value	$\bar{R}^2$
No		0.063	11.27	0.09	0.055	7.76	0.15
Yes	Equity	−0.006	−1.52	0.00	−0.001	−0.23	0.05
Yes	Full Value	−0.185	−15.30	0.13	−0.155	−9.77	0.18

[a]Includes automobiles.

[b]The dummy variables, assuming the value of 1.0 if the characteristic is applicable to the head of the household and 0.0 otherwise, are for age (less than or equal to 25 and 5-year intervals from 25 to 65), for education (grade school or less, some high school, high school graduate, some college, or college graduate), and for occupation (self-employed, employed by others, retired, farm operator, not gainfully employed, and employer unknown).

The relationship of $(1 - t_k)\alpha_k$ to net worth varies according to whether housing is included, and if included, how measured. For the narrowest definition of wealth exclusive of human wealth and homes, there is overall a significant positive relationship to net worth (see Table 6-4). A closer analysis, however, indicates that most of this positive relationship stems from households with net worth of less than $500,000 and that for households of greater means, the ratio shows a slight tendency to decrease (see Table 6-1). This behavior would be consistent with decreasing proportional risk aversion at least through net worth classes up to $500,000. This result is not affected appreciably if mixed assets were combined with risk-free rather than with risky assets. For the broader definition of wealth including housing as a risky asset but excluding human wealth, the ratio of $(1 - t_k)\alpha_k$ is practically invariant to net worth if housing is measured by its equity value, and negatively related to net worth if housing is measured by its full value (see Table 6-4). These findings are consistent with constant proportional and increasing proportional risk aversion, respectively.[2][1] If housing is included as a risk-free asset, the tendency toward decreasing proportional risk aversion would be even greater than indicated by Table 6-1.

There are several potentially important biases in these findings. First, contrary to the assumptions of the model, individuals do not all hold the same portfolio of risky assets. Consider an individual whose portfolio of risky assets is perfectly correlated with the market portfolio of risky assets but is less volatile—that is, has a portfolio *beta* coefficient of less than 1.0. Since the risky portfolio of reference is the market portfolio, the calculated value of α_k would overstate the relative degree of risk in his portfolio. Likewise, if he were to hold a portfolio of risky assets with a *beta* greater than one, the calculated value of α_k would understate the degree of risk. The evidence in our 1975 study indicates that households with lower incomes and presumably less wealth tend to hold portfolios of stocks with smaller portfolio *betas* than their richer counterparts although their portfolios are less well diversified.

Second, life insurance is not handled satisfactorily in this analysis since only the immediately realizable portion is treated as a risk-free asset. Life insurance does not conveniently fit into the dichotomy of risk-free and risky assets, and some other mode of analysis is required to handle this type of asset. However, the net surrender value of life insurance probably represents a significant understatement of the value of insurance as a device for reducing risk. Since life insurance is relatively much more important in the lower than in the upper net worth classes, correction for this deficiency of the model would again tend to change the results in the direction of decreasing proportional risk aversion.

Third, the calculated α_k might differ from its permanent value because of transitory elements. If a transitory reduction in net worth left unchanged the value of risky assets, the calculated α_k would be biased upwards. This situation might apply to an individual who was faced with a temporary reduction in net worth and because of transaction costs chose to reduce his risk-free assets. However, if he reduced only risky assets, the calculated α_k would be biased downwards. Since the former case is probably more prevalent for families of lower net worth and this type of transitory phenomenon is more likely to apply to these households, correcting for this possible bias would be expected to change the results in the same way as the previous bias.

Fourth, the model made the assumption that the tax rate on risky assets was the same as that on risk-free assets. In fact, the tax rate on risky assets tends to be less than that on risk-free assets. While the magnitude of this bias seems to be small, it results in an understatement of C_k.[22] However, it is not clear how this understatement varies with net worth.

To this point, the empirical analyses have ignored human wealth. The micro relationship (6.8) incorporates such wealth and can be used to examine the behavior C_k. Rearranging (6.8) yields

$$\frac{E(r_m - r_f)}{\sigma_m^2} \frac{1}{C_k} = (1 - h_k)(1 - t_k)\alpha_k + h_k(1 - t_k)\beta_{hk,m} \quad (6.15)$$

If $\beta_{hk,m}$ were known, the right-hand side of (6.15) could be used to analyze the relationship of C_k^{-1} to net worth. The variable $\beta_{hk,m}$, however, is not known, so that some other tack must be taken.

This other tack will be to assume the validity of two stochastic relationships and use these in conjunction with (6.15) to derive an empirically estimable regression. For the net worth class i, the first relationship takes the form

$$(C_k)^{-1} = (C^i)^{-1} + \eta_{ck} \quad (6.16)$$

where η_{ck} is a mean-zero disturbance independent of h_k and t_k, and C_i is the harmonic mean of C_k in the ith net worth class. This assumption is like the assumption of constant proportional risk aversion on the average, as embodied in (6.11), except that it only pertains to a single net worth class. Again for net worth class i, the second relationship takes the form

$$\beta_{hk,m} = \beta^i_{hm} + \eta_{hk} \tag{6.17}$$

where η_{hk} is a mean-zero disturbance independent of h_k and t_k, and β^i_{hm} is the mean of $\beta_{hk,m}$ in the ith net worth class.

The substitution of (6.16) and (6.17) into (6.15) with some simplification yields the regression

$$(1 - h_k)(1 - t_k)\alpha_k = \frac{E(r_m - r_f)}{\sigma^2_m}\frac{1}{C^i} - \beta^i_{hm} h_k (1 - t_k) + \mu_k \tag{6.18}$$

where μ_k is defined to be $[E(r_m - r_f)/\sigma^2_m]\eta_{ck} + h_k(1 - t_k)\eta_{hk}$. The independent variable, $h_k(1 - t_k)$, and the dependent variable, $(1 - h_k)(1 - t_k)\alpha_k$, can be estimated from the cross-sectional data. The constant term allows an analysis of the relationship of the coefficient of proportional risk aversion to net worth class, and the slope coefficient gives an estimate of β_{hm}. It is easily verified that under the assumed stochastic processes, μ_k has an expected value of zero and is uncorrelated with the independent variable, so that the estimated coefficients will be unbiased.[2][3]

Using the total sample of households, regression (6.18) was first estimated for each of the six net worth classes inclusive of human wealth and with homes measured by their equity value (see Table 6-5).[24] If unbiased, the constant terms indicate that the coefficient of proportional risk aversion on the average increases with net worth. The magnitude of the increase is not large. The estimate of $(C^i)^{-1}$ for those households with net worth in excess of $1 million is 33 percent less than the estimate for those households with net worth between $1 and $10 thousand. The estimates of β^i_{hm} tend to decrease as net worth increases starting at 0.775 for the lowest net worth class and ending at 0.603 for the highest net worth class.

There are several potentially important biases in these results. The first type pertain to violations of the assumptions used in developing (6.18). The second type pertain to limitations of the survey data. Turning to the first type, the assumptions implied that μ_k, which is a weighted sum of the deviations of $(C_k)^{-1}$ and $\beta_{hk,m}$ from their group means, is independent of $h_k(1 - t_k)$ within a net worth class. This implication probably is not strictly true. For instance, households in the same net worth class with a lower proportion of their wealth in human capital might be expected to have lower tax rates which would tend to induce a correlation between η_k and $h_k(1 - t_k)$. The possibility that the coefficient of proportional risk aversion might vary with socioeconomic factors would only cause a misspecification of (6.19) if these factors were correlated to h_k and

Table 6-5. Estimated Coefficients and Other Statistics for Regressions of the Form[a]

$$(1 - h_k)(1 - t_k)\alpha_k = \frac{E(r_m - r_f)}{\sigma_m^2}\frac{1}{C^i} - \beta_{hm}h_k(1 - t_k) + \eta_k$$

Net Worth Class[b]	Estimate of $\dfrac{E(r_m-r_f)}{\sigma_m^2}\dfrac{1}{C^i}$	Estimate of β_{hm}^i	$\bar{R}^2$	Unweighted Means $(1-t_k)\alpha_k$	$(1-h_k)\cdot(1-t_k)\alpha_k$	$h_k(1-t_k)$	$(1-t_k)$	Number of Households
A. Total-Sample[c]								
1-10	0.742 (0.035)	0.775 (0.069)	0.52	0.582	0.496	0.319	0.982	114
10-100	0.707 (0.009)	0.775 (0.014)	0.80	0.595	0.255	0.583	0.912	819
100-200	0.611 (0.010)	0.697 (0.013)	0.85	0.675	0.145	0.668	0.867	485
200-500	0.612 (0.016)	0.743 (0.029)	0.76	0.602	0.292	0.431	0.814	200
500-1000	0.529 (0.020)	0.613 (0.072)	0.44	0.584	0.412	0.192	0.705	90
over 1000	0.499 (0.021)	0.603 (0.146)	0.11	0.525	0.440	0.097	0.616	135
B. Households with Income from Salaries or Wages								
1-10	0.759 (0.048)	0.796 (0.071)	0.66	0.466	0.314	0.559	0.976	65
10-100	0.650 (0.012)	0.704 (0.015)	0.76	0.564	0.153	0.706	0.908	676

100-200	0.595 (0.010)	0.676 (0.014)	0.83	0.678	0.113	0.712	0.869	455
200-500	0.565 (0.018)	0.671 (0.031)	0.73	0.590	0.227	0.504	0.615	171
500-1000	0.567 (0.022)	0.712 (0.070)	0.60	0.615	0.387	0.254	0.714	68
over 1000	0.515 (0.024)	0.676 (0.154)	0.13	0.536	0.441	0.110	0.522	119

aSee fn. for Table 6-1.

bShown in thousands of dollars.

cNumbers in parentheses are standard errors.

t_k within a net worth class. Perhaps the most obvious socioeconomic factor which might be correlated with h_k and probably t_k within a class is the employment status of the members of the household. To determine the importance of this obvious misspecification, regression (6.18) was rerun on the sample of households reporting some income from salaries or wages. The results are not much different from the regressions for the total sample (see Table 6-5). For three out of six classes, the constant term was larger than before, while for the other three it was less, and the changes are not systematically related to net worth.

Let us now turn to the second type of biases which stem from limitations of the sample data. There are at least five principal problems. First, the balance sheets collected to not contain any estimate of the value of social security or pension fund benefits. Second, the value of relief payments is omitted. The importance of this omission is likely to be significant only in the lowest net worth class. Third, the value of human wealth may be misstated due to incorrectly assumed discount rates and growth rates.[25] Fourth, there may be transitory elements in the value of human capital. Fifth, the data do not allow an unambiguous determination of the return from closely held businesses attributable to wages. Taking the last problem first, (6.18) was reestimated for households with no closely held businesses. The results were unchanged.[26]

The first four problems all reduce logically to misstatements of the values of h_k and $\beta_{hk,m}$. In the model, social security and pension funds are assets over which a household has no control, so that formally these assets should enter into a more broadly construed h_k and would increase the value of this term. If it is assumed that the return on social security is uncorrelated with the return on the market portfolio of liquid risky assets, the inclusion of social security would reduce the value of a more broadly defined $\beta_{hk,m}$. Since pension funds are generally tied more directly to wage income, as a first approximation it is probably not too far from the mark to assume that their inclusion would not change $\beta_{hk,m}$ by much. The use of an incorrect discount rate or the inclusion of transitory elements would probably cause a misstatement in h_k but not necessarily in $\beta_{hk,m}$.

The total differential of (6.15) provides a way to measure the impact of these potential problems. Assuming dt_k and $d\alpha_k$ are zero in that t_k and α_k, derived from the household data, are known, the total differential takes the form

$$d \frac{E(r_m - r_f)}{\sigma_m^2} \frac{1}{C_k} = [(1 - t_k)\beta_{hk,m} - (1 - t_k)\alpha_k] \, dh_k$$

$$(6.19)$$

$$+ h_k(1 - t_k)d\beta_{hk,m}$$

The coefficients on $d\beta_{hk,m}$ can be estimated by net worth class as the means of $h_k(-t_k)$ given in Table 6-5. Likewise from Table 6-5, the coefficients on dh_k by net worth class starting with the lowest can be estimated as: 0.179, 0.112, —0.071, 0.003, —0.152, and —0.154.

Replacing the total differentials in (6.19) by finite differences and recalling that h_k is measured as a proportion, it is seen that $|\Delta h_k|$ would have to be extremely large to have much effect upon the relationship of the market price of risk times $(C^i)^{-1}$ to net worth. Thus, the conclusions would appear robust to large errors in the assumed discount and growth rates.

Correcting for the omission of social security benefits may have an important impact and together with the biases previously discussed might easily change the conclusion to one of constant proportional risk aversion on the average. To determine the magnitude of such a correction, let us assume that the average value of social security benefits within a net worth class in 1962 was $15,000.[27] Also assume that the value of social security does not change in any predictable way with changes in the value of the market portfolio, and that the net worth of the typical household in a net worth class is the midpoint except for $2 million for the class with the largest net worth. On the basis of these assumptions, the estimates of $[E(r_m - r_f)/\sigma_m^2](C^i)^{-1}$ would change to 0.609 for the 1-10 thousand dollar class,[28] 0.583 for the 10-100 class, 0.561 for the 100-200 class, 0.592 for the 200-500 class, 0.521 for the 500-1,000 class, and 0.495 for the class of greatest wealth. These adjusted figures show considerably less evidence of increasing proportional risk aversion on the average. Assigning a larger value to social security benefits and adjusting for the other biases discussed above might even change the conclusion to decreasing proportional risk aversion.

To summarize, for what we regard as the most appropriate treatment of investment in homes and human wealth within the context of our model, the unadjusted results give some evidence of increasing proportional risk aversion on the average. Yet, the magnitude of this increase is not great. Corrections for the various deficiencies of the theoretical model, the econometric analyses, and the sample data would on balance tend to make the results closer to constant proportional risk aversion and might even produce evidence of moderately decreasing proportional risk aversion. Perhaps the most accurate single statement is: if there is any tendency for increasing or decreasing proportional risk aversion, the tendency is so slight that for many purposes the assumption of constant proportional risk aversion is not a bad first approximation.

6.4 THE MARKET PRICE OF RISK

To assess numerical values for the coefficients of proportional risk aversion, the results in the previous section must be augmented with an assessment of the market price of risk, namely $E(r_m - r_f)/\sigma^2(r_m)$. This section will employ two different techniques to formulate such an assessment. The first will utilize realized rates of return on stocks and fixed interest obligations, while the second will attempt to develop direct *ex ante* measures. Common stocks on the New York Stock Exchange (NYSE) will be used as the principal proxy for the market portfolio of risky assets partially because of the importance of these stocks in the actual market portfolio, but more pragmatically because of the lack of data on returns for most other risky assets. Nonetheless, the market price of risk will also be estimated using similar techniques with data from the bond market to confirm the estimates from the NYSE data.

For both industrial and all or composite NYSE common stocks, Table 6-6 shows for the past 100 years, 1872-1971, and selected subperiods, arithmetic averages of annual realized rates of return[29] as well as the standard deviations of these rates. The annual returns, which assume the quarterly reinvestment of dividends, are estimated from the work of the Cowles Commission prior to 1926 and, thereafter, from Standard and Poor's sources. The returns prior to 1926 may be less accurate. Over the past hundred years, the average annual return for the composite stocks was 9.7 percent and for the industrial stocks, 11.3 percent. The standard deviations of these annual returns were 0.19 and 0.22, respectively.

Also included in Table 6-6 are corresponding mean annual returns and standard deviations for high grade corporate bonds. The only differences are that coupons are reinvested seminannually rather than quarterly and only the last 70 years are covered. The mean annual return on these bonds over the years 1902-71 was 4.0 percent which compares to a range of 10.7 to 12.8 percent for common stocks over the same period. In fact, in every one of the seven decades covered, stocks beat bonds and sometimes by substantial margins. However, the standard deviations of annual returns on bonds were always less than on stocks.

As a further check on the relationship of the bond and the stock markets, the semiannual returns for the bonds were regressed upon the corresponding returns for the NYSE composite stocks.[30] The slope coefficients or *beta* coefficients are displayed in Table 6-6 and indicate that the returns on bonds usually tend to fluctuate with those on stocks except in the 1952-61 decade when the coefficient is negative. Over the entire 70-year period, the *beta* coefficient is 0.078 which would imply, if the capital asset pricing model held, that the expected risk premium on bonds is 7.8 percent of that on stocks.[31]

Using the mean annual returns and the standard deviations calculated in the corresponding period, estimates of the market price of risk were derived. These estimates—as well as the risk-free rates—are contained in Table 6-6. The availability of a reliable series for the risk-free rate confined these estimates to the period after 1902. The estimates of the market price of risk over the longest period 1902 to 1971 were 1.7 for the composite stocks and 1.5 for the industrials, with not much different values for the 1902-61 period immediately preceding the date of the FRB survey. The estimate for the bond market was 2.3. It might be argued that these estimates are biased downwards because the variance of returns is estimated from a segment of the market of risky assets which would not reflect the full benefits from diversification. Additionally, assets which are both more and less risky than NYSE common stocks have been excluded in deriving the average risk premiums. It is difficult to assess the bias associated with these exclusions.[32]

The sampling errors in these estimates are undoubtedly large. To obtain some idea of the magnitude, the estimates of the market price of risk might be conceived of as drawings from some underlying probability distribution. Using this approach, the average of the seven decade estimates for the composite stocks is 2.4 which is somewhat larger than the estimate derived from the total period reflecting the large sampling error and possibly some nonstationarities in the distribution over time. The standard deviation of this average is 1.2. If the market price of risk were normally distributed, this would mean that there is an 0.88 probability that the true value of this parameter is greater than 1.0. The corresponding average and standard deviation for the industrials are 3.2 and 1.9, respectively.

An alternative way to assess the market price of risk is to develop *ex ante* measures of the expected returns on risky assets and the

Table 6-6.   Average Annual Arithmetic Rates of Return and Standard Deviations of Annual Returns 1872-1971

| | New York Stock Exchange Stocks[a] | | | | High Grade Corporate Bonds[b] | | | Risk-free[d] Rate | Calculated Market Price of Risk | | |
| | Composite | | Industrial | | | | | | Stocks | | Bonds |
Period	Mean Annual Return	Standard Deviation	Mean Annual Return	Standard Deviation	Mean Annual Return	Standard Deviation	Bond[c] Beta		Composite	Industrial	
1872-1881	0.0953	0.177	0.0820	0.129							
1882-1891	0.0429	0.130	0.0720	0.117							
1892-1901	0.0879	0.118	0.0773	0.163							
1902-1911	0.0794	0.218	0.1111	0.318	0.0436	0.0391	0.136	0.0409	0.808	0.692	1.712
1912-1921	0.0532	0.195	0.1128	0.296	0.0415	0.0545	0.179	0.0495	0.097	0.721	−2.718
1922-1931	0.1020	0.268	0.1108	0.289	0.0572	0.0369	0.061	0.0447	0.798	0.789	9.226
1932-1941	0.0866	0.282	0.1255	0.348	0.0672	0.0376	0.081	0.0138	0.925	0.915	37.782
1942-1951	0.1725	0.136	0.1697	0.105	0.0244	0.0289	0.044	0.0127	8.673	14.136	14.084
1952-1961	0.1804	0.189	0.1859	0.203	0.0177	0.0456	−0.055	0.0315	14.165	3.740	−6.623
1962-1971	0.0742	0.130	0.0779	0.136	0.0259	0.0596	0.131	0.0512	1.372	1.447	−7.125
1902-1961	0.1124	0.216	0.1360	0.263	0.0419	0.0431	0.072	0.0322	1.716	1.504	5.249
1902-1971	0.1069	0.206	0.1277	0.249	0.0396	0.0457	0.078	0.0349	1.702	1.501	2.276
1926-1971	0.1155	0.212	0.1256	0.234	0.0381	0.0420		0.0232	1.963	1.788	8.487
1872-1971	0.0974	0.188	0.1125	0.221							

[a]From 1926, the fitures are estimated from the Standard & Poor's Stock Indexes. For earlier years, the data are from Common-Stock Indexes. The Cowles Index was converted to the Standard & Poor's base by adjusting overlapping figures. The relative for the first quarter of the t-th year was taken to be $i_1 = [P_1 + \frac{1}{4}(D_1/P_1)P_1]/P_0$ where P_1 and D_1/P_1 are stock price and annualized dividend yield at end of quarter and the return for the year derived from the product of the four quarterly returns.

[b]Semiannual relatives were estimated as $(P + \frac{1}{2}C)/100$, where C is the coupon rate on a new 20-year bond sold at par and P is the price at the end of the 6 months. The coupon rate C was estimated as the yield to maturity given by Standard & Poor's for High Grade Corporate Bonds. The price

P was calculated using the coupon rate C and the yield to maturity given by the Standard & Poor's at the end of the 6 months on the assumption that such a yield would be appropriate for a bond with 19 years and 6 months to maturity. Multiplying successive pairs of these relatives yields estimates of the annual returns.

cThe βs are derived from semiannual regressions of the form $r_b = \alpha + \beta r_m$ where r_b and r_m are annual rates of return on corporate high grade bonds and composite stocks, respectively.

dPrime Corporate Bonds 1-Year Maturity February Average from Sidney Homer, pp. 366-67, updated by Salomon Brothers.

variance of those returns. To this end, *ex ante* measures of expected return were developed by adding the current yield to an estimate of the future growth rate of earnings per share.[33] The future growth rate was estimated by the arithmetic and by the geometric mean of the annual growth rates over the prior 10 years.[34] For the 70 years ending in 1971, the mean estimate of the expected annual return for the composite stocks ranged from 13.0 to 9.0 percent, depending upon the way in which the future growth rate of earnings was estimated.[35] It might be recalled that the corresponding mean of annual realized returns was 10.7 percent. For comparison, the yield to maturity on high grade corporate bonds is also given in Table 6-7.

These estimates of expected rates of return for composite stocks were used to derive an estimate of the market price of risk for each of the 70 years from 1902 through 1971. Subtracting the risk-free

Table 6-7. "Expected" Annual Rates of Return for Common Stocks and Bonds 1902-71

Period	High Grade Corporate Bonds Yields to Maturity	New York Stock Exchange Composite Stocks		Calculated Market Price of Risk for Stocks Using	
		Arithmetic Estimate[a]	Geometric Estimate[b]	Arithmetic Estimate	Geometric Estimate
1902-1911	0.0452	0.157	0.132	6.090	4.674
1912-1921	0.0519	0.132	0.097	1.989	1.120
1922-1931	0.0486	0.177	0.059	3.639	0.319
1932-1941	0.0363	0.064	0.011	0.518	−0.042
1942-1951	0.0270	0.160	0.126	3.829	3.075
1952-1961	0.0362	0.137	0.122	4.472	3.843
1962-1971	0.0562	0.086	0.080	1.228	1.047
1902-1961		0.138	0.091	4.423	2.165
1902-1971	0.0431	0.130	0.090	3.109	2.005

[a]The Arithmetic Estimate is the arithmetic mean of annual expected returns where the expected return for the t-th year is taken to be $i_t = D_t/P_t + GE_t$, where GE_t = arithmetic mean of previous 10 years of earnings growth. Dividends yields were obtained and earnings growth rates calculated from Standard and Poor's Quarterly "Earnings, Dividends and Price Earnings Ratios."

[b]The Geometric Estimate is the same except that GE_t is the geometric mean of the previous 10 years of earnings growth.

rate appropriate to the year from these expected returns yielded 70 risk premiums, which were then divided by estimates of the variance of the return for these stocks. These variances were estimated from the 10 realized annual returns immediately preceding the year for which the expected return was assessed. Table 6-7 presents the average of these 70 estimates of the market price of risk as well as averages for selected subperiods. The average covering the 70 years ending in 1971 was 3.1 using the arithmetic estimate of *ex ante* expected return and 2.0 using the geometric, which are again greater than 1.0 though somewhat higher than the figures derived from realized returns.

To obtain some feeling for the magnitude of the sampling errors associated with these averages for the overall period, the standard deviation of the mean was calculated using every tenth estimate of the market price of risk from 1901 through 1971. Using every estimate instead of every tenth would have resulted in a downward biased estimate of the standard deviation unless explicit account was taken of the fact that successive estimates are based in part upon the same data. The standard deviation of the mean was 0.99 for the market price of risk based upon the arithmetic rate of growth in earnings and 0.87 for the geometric rate of growth. Assuming these standard deviations of the mean can be applied to the means of the 70 annual estimates (though there is reason to believe the true standard deviations would be less), the probability that the market price of risk using arithmetic rates of growth is greater than 1.0 would be 98 percent. The corresponding probability for the market price of risk based upon geometric rates of growth would be 87 percent.

This section has used several different approaches to estimating the market price of risk. All of these methods indicate that the market price of risk is greater than 1.0. The probabilities attached to this conclusion were assessed and, while not always at the frequently cited 5 percent level of significance, were consistent with a high level of significance. To the extent that there is some independence among the various estimates, the probability that the market price of risk is greater than 1.0 would be considerably larger than those reported for each of the individual estimates.

6.5 THE SYNTHESIS

The empirical results in Section 6.3 indicate that the assumption of constant proportional risk aversion for households is a fairly accurate description of the market place. More specifically, the study found that with a plausible treatment of investment in homes the net worth of a household had little value in explaining the level of its coefficient of relative risk aversion. Before taking account of potential biases, there was a slight tendency of this coefficient to increase with net worth. After adjusting for the biases, little such tendency remained.[36]

The main exception to this finding of constant proportional risk aversion occurred in the analysis based upon an extremely narrow definition of wealth which excluded homes, the associated mortgages, and human wealth. In this case, there was evidence of decreasing proportional risk aversion. This tendency would be more pronounced if homes were considered a risk-free asset. Since an investor probably considers the value of his home and at least to some extent his human wealth in formulating his investment decisions, the analyses based upon broader definitions of wealth are more pertinent in assessing how the coefficient of proportional risk aversion varies with net worth.

In addition, Section 6.3 derived various estimates of the product of the market price of risk and the reciprocal of the coefficient of proportional risk aversion. Regardless of how broadly wealth was defined, the estimate of this product was, with one unimportant exception, always less than 1.0. Though the value obtained depends on the definition of wealth, the product of the market price of risk times the reciprocal of the coefficient of proportional risk aversion appears to be between 0.5 and 0.8.

Coupling this conclusion with an estimate of the market price of risk allows an assessment of the coefficient of relative risk aversion. The evidence in Section 6.4 showed with a high level of significance that the market price of risk is in excess of 1.0. The implication is that the coefficient of relative risk aversion for the typical household is in excess of 1.0—contrary to the properties of the *log* utility function. Since the market price of risk is probably around 2.0 or more, the coefficient of proportional risk aversion is more likely to be in excess of two.[37]

Households, of course, only represent part of the demand for risky marketable assets. The aggregate demand function would have to take into account the impact of other investors such as eleemosynary institutions and financial intermediaries. Regardless of how their utility or, more accurately, decision functions are derived, the fact that the ratios of risky assets to net worth for these institutions are usually less than 1.0 and not uncommonly considerably less than 1.0 would seem to imply that their coefficients of relative risk aversion would tend to be at least 2.0. If, as is probably correct, the riskiness of institutional portfolios as a whole has remained less than that of households, their coefficients of relative risk aversion would tend to be greater than those of households.

In concluding, it is worthwhile to review some of the more important limitations of the models under which the empirical data were interpreted. Such limitations point the way to further work. First, the model made no adjustment for inflation. The presence of unanticipated inflation would mean that no asset denominated in nominal dollars could be considered risk free. Second, the model, in assuming that the changes in the value of an asset were continuous, could not properly incorporate insurance. Third, the model did not incorporate adequately the unique characteristics of housing. Fourth, the model assumed that an investor made his portfolio choice in a one-period context. Thus, the model, in contrast to a multiperiod model, is not rich enough to capture the possibilities of hedging against future changes in the investment opportunity set.[38] For households, perhaps the most widely available hedges are homes which protect against future changes in the cost of housing.

NOTES TO SECTION SIX

1. The market price of risk is the difference between the expected rates of return on the market portfolio of risky assets as a whole and on a risk-free asset per unit of risk of the market portfolio. For purposes of this study, it turns out that the relevant measure of risk is the variance of returns.

2. Even the time-series analyses are not consistent in indicating a wealth elasticity of cash balances, broadly defined, equal to or greater than one in the period following World War II. See Allan Meltzer, p. 236.

3. See Henry A. Latané; Nils Hakansson; and Harry Markowitz. For a different theoretical position, see Paul Samuelson and Robert Merton.

4. See Jan Mossin; John Lintner; and A.P. Budd and R.H. Litzenberger.

5. This assumption is nontrivial and would exclude such distributions of returns of individual assets as nonnormal stable.

6. An intuitive explanation for the appearance of the standard deviation with $\sqrt{dt}$ rather than with dt is that if a time period is subdivided into n subperiods each of duration $\tau = 1/n$, and if the returns over each of these subperiods are independently distributed, then the variance of returns over τ, σ_τ^2 is equal to $1/n$ times the variance of returns σ^2 over the initial period. As n approaches ∞, $1/n$ approaches dt, so that σ_τ approaches $\sigma_t \sqrt{dt}$.

7. Equation (6.2) implies that the kth individual invests α_k of his assets in risky assets and $1 - \alpha_k$ in the risk-free asset. In the type of continuous time model used in this study, the separation theorem holds.

8. This measure of relative risk aversion can also be interpreted as the wealth elasticity of the marginal utility of wealth as indicated in the introduction.

9. Samuelson has obtained a similar expression for the individual investor.

10. This assumption is tantamount to assuming that capital gains and ordinary income are taxed identically and abstracts from the special tax treatment of homes and tax-exempt securities. However, see fn. 37.

11. Since the dependence between r_m and r_{hk} is a factor in determining the optimum ratio of risky liquid assets to all liquid assets, it would be anticipated that an investor might be able to improve his expected utility by altering the proportions of the risky liquid assets he holds from those implicit in the market portfolio to take into account differences in the values of the covariances of human wealth and individual liquid assets in the market portfolio. The work of Y. Landskroner indeed shows this to be the case. Whether (6.8) results in an expected utility close to the optimum depends upon the correlation of the optimal portfolio of risky liquid assets and the market portfolio. If this correlation were very close to 1.0, for instance, it would be possible to construct a portfolio of the market and the risk-free asset which would have a probability distribution very similar to the optimal portfolio of liquid assets. Numerous empirical studies have demonstrated that the returns on portfolios of a large number of securities are highly correlated with the market portfolio.

12. This can easily be seen by writing in a one-period model

$$\alpha = \frac{E(R_m)}{1 + E(r_m)} \div \left[\frac{E(R_m)}{1 + E(r_m)} + \frac{F}{1 + r_f} \right]$$

where $E(R_m)$ represents the expected dollar return over the period on the available supply of liquid risky assets at the beginning of the period, and F represents the corresponding known dollar return on riskless assets. The constant physical supply of liquid risky assets and risk-free assets are measured by $E(R_m)$ and F, respectively.

13. Though (6.14) was developed under the restrictive assumptions that the sole decision of the individual was how much of his liquid assets to place in the market portfolio of liquid risky assets, Landskroner has shown that if r_0, the return on an asset uncorrelated with the return on the market portfolio of risky assets, is substituted for r_f and is also uncorrelated with the return on human capital, (6.14) holds in the more general case where an investor's decision variables include not only how much to put into risky liquid assets, but also how much to place into each risky liquid asset.

14. To utilize (6.13) in a time-series, the weighted harmonic mean of $(1 - t_k)$ might be approximated by the ratio of total disposable income to total adjusted gross income. For the survey of households to be examined in the next section, the weighted harmonic mean would be 0.787 while the ratio of total disposable income to total adjusted gross income would be 0.859 which is close to the 0.871 implied by the *Statistics of Income*. Thus, if this harmonic mean is representative of the population, the ratio of total disposable income to total adjusted gross income would be about 10 percent greater than the harmonic mean. This figure of 10 percent might be useful in adjusting the time-series available from the *Statistics of Income* to that required by (6.13).

15. With homes are included automobiles which represent only a minor proportion of assets except possibly for the lowest wealth groups.

16. See fn. 21.

17. If $E[C_k^{-1}]$ were to decrease with increases in net worth W_k, it is not necessary that $E(C_k)$ would increase. Yet, if the distributions of C_k given $W_k, P(C_k|W_k)$, remain unchanged as W_k increases except for location, it can be shown that $E(C_k)$ would increase with increases in W_k. This proposition follows from noting that if for fixed ϵ_k, $[E(C_k) + \epsilon_k]^{-1} > [E(C_k)' + \epsilon_k]^{-1} > 0$, $E(C_k) + \epsilon_k < E(C_k)' + \epsilon_k$. Since $P(C_k|W_k)$ is unchanged except for location, the distributions of ϵ_k will be the same at each level of W_k. Taking the definite integral of these two inequalities with respect to the distribution of ϵ_k yields the desired result.

18. Housing presents other difficulties in applying the micro relationships developed in the last section. First, since an investor values a house not only for its monetary rewards but also for its consumption value, it may be difficult to aggregate returns from housing with those from other assets. Second, the purchase of a home with a large mortgage permits an investor to hedge against changes in housing costs and in the costs of borrowing funds.

19. In the first attempt at running these regressions, the sampling probability associated with each household was used to adjust for heteroscedasticity on the assumption that the reciprocal of the sampling probabilities in each stratum was picked to be negatively related to the variation within the stratum. The correlations of the absolute value of the residuals with these reciprocals revealed that there was substantial heteroscedasticity present in the regressions. All regressions reported in the study are unweighted and exhibited little evidence of heteroscedasticity.

20. Though these comparative results indicate that the socioeconomic factors are roughly orthogonal to the logarithm of net worth, this does not mean that C_k^{-1} could not vary with these factors.

21. The qualitative results are unchanged if households with closely held businesses are excluded. For instance, following the same order as in Table 6-4, the estimated coefficients on the logarithm of net worth would be: 0.076, −0.004, and −.250 with respective t-values of 8.4, −.61, and −11.48. These coefficients are roughly the same as those reported for the full sample. The regressions were also rerun with dummy variables included for age, education, and occupation. There is little change in the estimated coefficients on the logarithm of net worth.

22. See fn. 37.

23. The formula for μ_k would on the surface suggest that (6.19) suffers from some form of heteroscedasticity. Though this is true because of the way in which (6.17) and (6.18) were defined, it would be easy to redefine the variance of η_{hk} as a function of $h_k(1-t_k)$ so as to make (6.19) homoscedastic. Thus, the apparent heteroscedasticity of (6.19) is artificial. Further, the discussion of (6.19) at this point abstracts from measurement error in h_k.

24. If housing is measured instead by market value, the results are not much different. From lowest to highest net worth class, the constant terms would have been 0.810, 0.793, 0.634, 0.623, 0.530, and 0.500.

25. The calculation of the value of human wealth made no adjustment for the probability of death before normal retirement. Formally, this is equivalent to assuming an incorrect discount rate and will be subsumed under this problem.

26. From lowest to highest net worth class, the constant terms were estimated respectively as 0.711, 0.635, 0.541, 0.580, 0.522, and 0.449.

27. This estimate of value is based upon the following assumptions: The average household is headed by a person 45 years old and consists of a spouse and two children with average age of 10 years. Using the 1941 CSO table as in *CRC Standard Mathematical Tables* with a 2.5 percent interest rate and assuming maximum benefits with no increases in the future, the retirement portion was estimated roughly to be $13,000 which represents an overstatement in view of the assumption of maximum benefits. The ancillary survivorship and disability benefits are more difficult to estimate but seem well under the 50 percent of retirement benefits as shown in government compilations. As a result, we have used an overall, probably somewhat conservative estimate of $15,000 for the combined value of retirement and ancillary benefits. The use of 2.5 percent interest rate is consistent with the maintenance of the real value of the benefits over time.

28. This number was calculated by noting that the inclusion of social security benefits would cause an increase of 0.487 in the value of h_k and a decrease of 0.690 in the value of β_{hm}. Applying these changes to (6.19) results in a decrease of 0.133, which when subtracted from 0.742 gives the adjusted estimate in the text.

29. These average rates of return would represent unbiased estimates of one-period holding returns if stationarity is assumed. To assess the sensitivity of these numbers to different horizons and since the arithmetic mean raised to the appropriate n^{th} power to obtain an n-year return can yield a seriously upward biased estimate of expected return over an n-year period (see Blume, 1974), an average of five-year returns over the 1872-1971 period (yielding a return relative of 1.587 for the composite index) was compared with the fifth power of the average annual returns (1.592), with little difference in results.

30. For a discussion of the specification of this type of regression, the reader is referred to Blume (1970).

31. Over the 1902-71 period, the average annual risk premium on NYSE composite stocks was 0.0720. Multiplying this figure by 0.078 would yield an expected risk premium for bonds of 0.0056, which compares to the actual average annual risk premium on bonds of 0.0047.

32. The market price of risk was also estimated using, instead of variance of returns, the variance of the difference of the annual return and the risk-free rate. If the risk-free rate were constant over time, the two variances would, of course, be the same. These alternative estimates were marginally lower. For the period 1902-71, this alternative estimate was, for instance, 0.04 smaller for the composite stocks than that presented in Table 6-6.

33. Implicit in this formulation are the assumptions: 1) Earnings grow at a constant rate in perpetuity. 2) The payout ratio and discount rates are constant.

34. Estimates using only 5 prior years of data gave unreasonably low rates of return in the early 1920s and middle 1930s which with the appropriate dividend

yield would have implied expected returns as low as -22 percent. As long as cash is available, no investor if he really held this belief would hold stock. Using 10 years of prior data yielded negative estimates of the expected market return in only a few cases and then only with the geometric.

35. This range is consistent with that found in a survey of stockholders by W.G. Lewellen, R.C. Lease, and G.C. Schlarbaum.

36. These conclusions do not preclude the possibility that the coefficient of proportional risk aversion varies with socioeconomic factors which are uncorrelated with net worth.

37. This conclusion is based upon the assumption that the tax rates on all sources of income are the same when in fact tax rates differ. The effect is that the estimates of the coefficients of proportional risk aversion reported in the text are downward biased, although the bias is not large and does not vary much among net worth classes. With differential taxes and not including human wealth, an estimate of $\alpha_k C_k$ would be

$$\frac{(1 - t_m)E(r_m) - (1 - t_f)r_f}{(1 - t_m)^2 \sigma_m^2}$$

where t_m is the tax rate on risky liquid assets and t_f the tax rate on risk-free assets. Assuming the same tax rate on both kinds of assets, the estimate of $\alpha_k C_k$ would be given by

$$\frac{E(r_m) - r_f}{(1 - t_c) \sigma_m^2}$$

where t_c is a weighted average of t_f and t_m. Noting that $(1 - t_m) > (1 - t_f)$ and $E(r_m) > r_f$, the following inequality holds

$$\frac{(1 - t_c)(1 - t_m)}{(1 - t_m)^2} E(r_m) - \frac{(1 - t_c)(1 - t_f)}{(1 - t_m)^2} r_f > E(r_m) - r_f$$

Upon dividing by $(1 - t_c)\sigma_m^2$, the inequality shows that the estimate of $\alpha_k C_k$ derived under the assumption of the same tax for both kinds of assets is biased downwards.

If human wealth is included and assumed taxed at the same rate t_{hw} as risk-free assets, $\alpha_k C_k$ would be given by the same formula as the first one in the footnote times the quantity

$$\left[(1 - h_k) + \frac{h_k}{\alpha_k} \cdot \frac{1 - t_f}{1 - t_m} \cdot \beta_{hk,m} \right]^{-1}$$

If the same rate is applied to all assets, $\alpha_k C_k$ is given by the second formula times the quantity

$$\left[(1 - h_k) + \frac{h_k}{\alpha_k} \cdot \beta_{hk,m} \right]^{-1}$$

Since $(1 - t_f) < (1 - t_m)$, not taking account of differential taxes will result in a downward biased estimate of the second term in the product. Since the first term is subject to the same biases as before, the net effect will be that estimates of C_k which do not adjust for the differential taxes associated with human and risk-free wealth will be downward biased.

Under reasonable estimates of the relevant variables, it can be shown that the assumption that tax rates on all sources of income are the same biases downward the coefficient of proportional risk aversion for the broadest definition by wealth by about 8 percent for the $10,000-$100,000 net worth class and by 9 percent for the $500,000-$1,000,000 class. These results assume: $E(r_m) = 0.10$, $r_f = .05$, and $\sigma_m^2 = .025$ for all households; for the low net worth households, $t_f = t_{hw} = .10$, $t_m = .02$ in view of the heavy weight of housing in the marketable risky assets of this group, and $t_c = .08$; and for the high net worth households, $t_f = t_{hw} = .35$, $t_m = .25$ in view of the heavy weight of unincorporated business and the small weight of housing and tax-exempts.

38. Merton has developed a theoretical multiperiod model which does incorporate continuous changes in the investment opportunity set. E.F. Fama and J.D. MacBeth have developed some preliminary tests of the economic content of Merton's model. It might be noted that a utility function characterized by constant proportional risk aversion is consistent with myopic behavior so long as investment yields in different periods are serially independent.

REFERENCES

K.J. Arrow, *Essays in the Theory of Risk-Bearing*, Chicago 1971.

M.E. Blume, "Portfolio Theory: A Step Towards Its Practical Application," *J. Bus., Univ. Chicago*, Apr. 1970, *43*, 152-73.

————, "Unbiased Estimators of Long-Run Expected Rates of Return," *J. Amer. Statist. Assn.*, Sept. 1974, *69*, 634-38.

———— and I. Friend, "The Asset Structure of Individual Portfolios and Some Implications for Utility Functions," *J. Finance*, May 1975, *30*, 585-603.

A.P. Budd and R.H. Litzenberger, "The Market Price of Risk, Size of Market and Investor's Risk Aversion: A Comment," *Rev. Econ. Statist.*, May 1972, *54*, 204-06.

J. Crockett and I. Friend, "Consumer Investment Behavior," in R. Ferber, ed., *Determinants of Investment Behavior*, Nat. Bur. Econ. Res. Conference Report, New York 1967, 15-127.

E.F. Fama and J.D. MacBeth, "Tests of the Multiperiod Two-Parameter Model," *J. Finance Econ.*, May 1974, *1*, 43-66.

I. Friend, "Rates of Return on Bonds and Stocks, the Market Price of Risk and the Cost of Capital," Rodney L. White Center for Financial Research Working Paper No. 23-73 (University of Pennsylvania, Philadelphia, Pa.).

M.J. Gordon, G.E. Paradis, and C.H. Rorke, "Experimental Evidence on Alternative Portfolio Decision Rules," *Amer. Econ. Rev.*, Mar. 1972, *62*, 107-18.

N.H. Hakansson, "Capital Growth and the Mean-Variance Approach to Portfolio Selection," *J. Finance. Quant. Anal.*, Jan. 1971, *6*, 517-57.

S. Homer, *The History of Interest Rates*, New Brunswick 1963.

Y. Landskroner, "The Determinants of the Market Price of Risk," unpublished doctoral dissertation, Univ. Pennsylvania 1975.

H.A. Latané, "Criteria for Choice Among Risky Ventures," *J. Polit. Econ.*, Apr. 1959, *67*, 144-55.

W.G. Lewellen, R.C. Lease, and G.C. Schlarbaum, "Patterns of Investment Strategy and Behavior Among Individual Investors," mimeo., Purdue Univ. 1974.

J. Lintner, "The Market Price of Risk, Size of Market and Investor's Risk Aversion," *Rev. Econ. Statist.*, Feb. 1970, *52*, 96-99.

H. Markowitz, "Investment for the Long Run," in I. Friend and J. Bicksler, eds., *Risk and Return in Finance*, Cambridge 1976.

D. Mayers, "Non-marketable Assets and Capital Market Equilibrium Under Uncertainty," in M.C. Jensen, ed., *Studies in the Theory of Capital Markets*, New York 1972.

A.H. Meltzer, "The Demand for Money: The Evidence from the Time-Series," *J. Polit. Econ.*, June 1963, *71*, 219-46.

R. Merton, "An Intertemporal Capital Asset Pricing Model," *Econometrica*, Sept. 1973, *41*, 867-87.

J. Mossin, "Security Pricing and Investment Criteria in Competitive Markets," *Amer. Econ. Rev.*, Dec. 1969, *59*, 749-57.

R. Roll, "Evidence on the Growth-Optimum Model," *J. Finance*, June 1973, *28*, 551-66.

S.A. Ross, "Uncertainty and the Heterogeneous Capital Goods Model," *Rev. Econ. Stud.*, Jan. 1975, *42*, 133-146.

P.A. Samuelson, "The Fundamental Approximation Theorem of Portfolio Analysis in Terms of Means, Variances, and Higher Moments," *Rev. Econ. Stud.*, Oct. 1970, *37*, 537-43.

_____ and R. Merton, "Fallacy of the Log-Normal Approximation to Optimal Portfolio Decision-Making Over Many Periods," in I. Friend and J. Bicksler, eds., *Risk and Return in Finance*, Cambridge 1976.

S.C. Tsiang, "The Rationale of the Mean-Standard Deviation Analysis, Skewness Preference, and the Demand for Money," *Amer. Econ. Rev.*, June 1972, *62*, 354-71.

Cowles Commission for Research in Economics, *Common-Stock Indexes*, 2d ed., Bloomington 1939.

CRC Standard Mathematical Tables, 11th ed., Cleveland 1957.

Internal Revenue Service, *Statistics of Income*, Washington 1962.

✳ *Section Seven*

A Reexamination of the Capital Asset Pricing Model

Robert C. Merton*

7.1 INTRODUCTION

Much of the theoretical and most of the empirical research in modern capital market theory has been based on the Sharpe-Lintner-Mossin mean-variance, equilibrium model of exchange commonly called the Capital Asset Pricing Model (CAPM). However, the model has recently come under criticism from many sides. In an excellent survey article, Jensen [9] outlines the many controversies (both theoretical and empirical) and discusses a number of proposed alternatives. Briefly, the principal theoretical criticisms of the model have centered on (1) the assumption that investors choose their portfolios according to the Markowitz mean-variance criterion; (2) the perfect market assumptions; (3) the static or single-period nature of the model. On the empirical side, the main result of the CAPM that has been tested is the Security Market Line which specifies a relationship between the equilibrium expected return on an individual security to the expected return on the market portfolio. This relationship can be written as

$$E(\tilde{R}_i) = r + \beta_i[E(\tilde{R}_M) - r] \tag{7.1}$$

where $\tilde{R}_i$ is the random variable return on the ith security; $\tilde{R}_M$ is the return on the market portfolio; r is the rate of interest; E is the expectation operator; $\beta_i \equiv \sigma_{iM} / \sigma_M^2$ with σ_{iM} equal to the covariance

*Presented in Vail, Colorado, August 1973. Aid from the National Science Foundation is gratefully acknowledged.

between $\hat{R}_i$ and $\hat{R}_M$ and σ_M^2 equal to the variance of $\hat{R}_M$. Extensive testing by Friend and Blume [7] and Black, Jensen, and Scholes [2] seem to reject the hypothesis that assets are priced so as to satisfy Equation (7.1). In particular, the empirical security market line is too "flat." I.e., "low beta" ($\beta_i < 1$) securities have a larger return on average and "high beta" ($\beta_i > 1$) securities have a smaller return on average than is forecast by (7.1).

The approaches to the resolution of this controversy can be roughly classified into four groups: (1) those who believe that the CAPM is basically correct (or at least, that the security market line specification (7.1) does describe the relationship among expected returns) on a period-by-period basis and that the empirical discrepancies are caused by using the wrong index, missing assets, or by not taking into account that the (time-series for the) coefficients fluctuate in a stochastic manner (cf. Fama and MacBeth [6]); (2) those who believe that the CAPM is basically correct but that the perfect market assumptions are not. Hence, the model must be modified to allow for differentials between borrowing and lending rates, no short-sales, taxes, or the possibility of no riskless asset (cf. Black [1], Brennan [3]); (3) those who believe that due to intertemporal effects not considered in the one-year period CAPM, other sources of uncertainty besides market risk are significant in portfolio choice and hence the expected return on an asset will depend on more than its covariance with the market (cf. Merton [12]); (4) those who believe that the returns on assets are generated by a weighted linear combination of "common" or "systematic" factors plus an uncorrelated random term and that by "arbitrage" the expected return on an asset can be written in a general form similar to the Security Market Line specification, but that the CAPM itself has no relevance (cf. Ross [16].

In Section 7.2 of this chapter an expositional discussion of the results in Merton [12] are presented and suggestions are made as to what other sources of uncertainty are likely to affect equilibrium expected returns on assets. In Section 7.3, a simple model is presented to provide an analytical framework for the discussion in Section 7.2.

Section 7-4 gives a brief discussion of why models of the type presented in Section 7-2 will, in general, give results different from the one-period, max-expected-utility-of-wealth models. It also explains the distinction between the "consumer services" model of Section 7-2 and the Ross [16] "Arbitrage-Factor" model.

7.2 A "CONSUMER SERVICES" MODEL OF ASSET PRICING

Most models of consumer choice postulate that each consumer acts so as to:

$$\text{Max}\, E \quad U[C_1, C_2, \ldots, C_T; W_T] \qquad (7.2)$$

where U is a well-behaved concave utility function; E is the expectation operator over the probability distributions of relevant random variables; $C_t = (C_{1t}, \ldots, C_{nt})$ is a vector bundle of consumption goods in period t of the consumer's life and end-of-life wealth; W_T, enters because of possible bequest motives. Since the cornerstone for much of economic theory is the assumption that all economic activities and institutions exist solely as the means to the ends of consumer satisfaction, a logical starting place for understanding why certain capital markets and financial securities exist is a study of the consumer-choice problem to determine the roles each of these markets or securities plays in helping consumers to maximize satisfaction. While this is certainly not a new idea, much of portfolio theory and capital market theory has been deduced based on the criterion of maximizing the expected utility of end-of-period wealth. While under certain conditions (cf. Fama [5]) (7.2) reduces to this type criterion, these condtions are rather specialized, and it will clarify much of the current controversy to return to the more basic criterion (7.2).

Even in the early work of Irving Fisher in a world of certainty and full information, it was recognized that the creation of financial securities and an exchange market for trading them would improve economic efficiency because endowments of individual economic units may not match optimal consumption plans in a temporal sense (i.e., financial securities make it possible to have savings by an individual economic unit not equal to investment). Moreover, the existence of such a market along with "bonds" for every maturity were sufficient for efficient intertemporal resource allocation as well as providing the appropriate "signals" for the efficient decentralization of the production and consumption decisions. Further, the return structure on all assets is completely determined by the prices of these bonds, and in particular, the one-period returns on all assets are equal to the one-period rate of interest.

When uncertainty is introduced, the problem became substantially more complicated. For the same efficiency to obtain, it is necessary to have securities and markets for every possible state of the world. While in such an Arrow-Debreu "complete markets" model the return structure on all assets is completely determined by the prices of these contingent claims, the model is so general that it is not empirically testable, and the enormous costs in running so many markets and processing the necessary information make its prescriptions economically infeasible. Because most of its theorems do not carry over for incomplete markets, care should be used in applying the model even as a "theoretical approximation." Nonetheless, in contrast to the CAPM which says that the consumer-investor requires only two financial securities (a one-period riskless bond and a mutual fund containing all assets in proportion to their value) for efficiency, the Arrow-Debreu model does demonstrate that financial securities may serve other roles for the consumer beyond that of providing an "efficient" risk-return tradeoff for end-of-period wealth.

Since the consumer does face relevant uncertainties in addition to the uncertainty of his end-of-period wealth, the natural inclination is to develop a model which explicitly takes into account the effects of these other uncertainties on asset pricing (as does the Arrow-Debreu model) while at the same time, introducing enough structure and restrictions to the model to give it the same analytical simplicity and empirical tractability as the CAPM. In [12], an equilibrium model of this type was developed based on intertemporal utility maximization in continuous-time where the uncertainties were described by diffusion-type stochastic processes. However, because of the rather specialized technical tools required for that analysis, an expositional development of the basic results of that model along with some extensions would seem appropriate.

We start with the Arrow-Debreu model with complete markets where there are more securities[1] (N) than states of nature (n). Cass and Stiglitz [4] have proved a "mutual fund" or "separation" theorem which states that there can be constructed n mutual funds or (composite) securities made up of linear combinations of the N securities such that (1) all consumer-investors would be indifferent between having available just these n mutual funds or all the N securities; (2) the construction of these composite securities requires no knowledge of consumer preferences, wealth allocations, or their subjective probabilities for each of the states of nature.

While the theorem states "indifference" when there are no transactions costs and information is freely available to everyone, it is reasonable to presume strict preference for the mutual funds if $N \gg n$. Economies of scale in transactions costs and information gathering and processing make it more sensible to have a centralized compilation of the distributions for each of the N securities rather than have each investor do it for himself. For the same reason, it would make sense to have each mutual fund have the property of paying a positive amount in one state of nature and zero otherwise (i.e., basic contingent claims) rather than some other more complicated combination which in theory would be equivalent.

Since the number of possible states of nature is very large, such a complete set of markets is economically unfeasible. There are three basic reasons: (1) the direct costs of operation of so many separate mutual funds; (2) despite the reduction from N to n, the large size of n would make the consumer's information processing costs very large; (3) the occurrence of certain states may be controllable by some consumers (i.e., the moral hazard problem). Hence, some "compromise" is obviously required. To do so, we retain the notion that the mutual fund approach is preferred when there are large numbers of securities and large numbers of relatively small economic units (e.g., consumers), but we restrict the number of funds. Consumers have access to limited amounts of information and have limited abilities to process the information that they have. Further, because of the costs of information gathering and processing, one would expect the consumer to center his attentions on the major sources of uncertainty which affect his consumption plan. Therefore, it is reasonable to assume that these sources of uncertainty can be represented by a finite and not very large number of state variables. One would expect the number and type of mutual funds[2] that would be created to correspond roughly to the number and type of major uncertainties which consumers face. The primary prerequisites for such a fund to be created are: (1) the source of uncertainty must be important to a sufficient number of consumers; (2) it must be possible to have a standardized contract with payoffs in contingencies which are easily recognizable; (3) the source of uncertainty must not be controllable by the consumer(s). Thus, for some of the major uncertainties, it is virtually impossible to construct a financial security which would allow the consumer to hedge against them. Broadly, we would expect to find two types of securities traded: (1) "natural" securities such as common stocks which are issued by firms to finance production of real output; and (2) financial securities or financial intermediaries created to serve the purposes of the "mutual funds" discussed above. These purposes are to aid the consumer in achieving a higher (expected) consumption level (through a return to capital), a better intertemporal allocation of resources (by not requiring that savings equals investment at each point in time), and a lower level of risk (by providing hedges against the major (common) sources of uncertainty faced by the consumer).

The individual consumer's demand for assets can be categorized as follows: for those important sources of uncertainty which he faces in common with other consumers, he will take positions in the mutual funds or financial securities created for that purpose. For those important sources of uncertainty for which no mutual fund exists (either because it is specialized to him or there is inherent moral hazard), he will take positions in those primary securities, if they exist, to hedge. For those sources of uncertainty for which no security is a hedge and for those sources which he neglects in his analysis, no security position can help so his (differential) demand for securities will be unaffected.

As an example, if the consumers are one-period maximizers of the utility of mean and variance of end-of-period wealth, then the well-known separation or two-fund theorem obtains. Namely, each investor will be indifferent between selecting a portfolio from all the primary securities and from two funds: (1) the market portfolio of risky assets and (2) a riskless asset. Presumably, such funds would be created since there is an obvious common demand. However, suppose one investor also has (uncertain) labor income which he cannot sell forward to eliminate its risk because of the moral hazard problem. Suppose further that it is a very highly-specialized form of labor which can only be used by one (or a small number of similar) company. Then, from risk-aversion, it would be natural to suppose that this investor would want to hold less of this company's stock than is represented in the market portfolio. Hence, in addition to the two mutual funds, he would want to short-sell some amount of this particular company's stock to hedge against unfavorable changes in his labor income. If on the other hand, there was no security whose outcome was correlated with this particular source of uncertainty, his optimal portfolio would be generated by the two mutual funds alone.

Thus, to a reasonable approximation, most of the aggregate demand for the individual primary securities can be viewed as coming in an "indirect way through the mutual funds." I.e., individual consumers for the most part only purchase a relatively small number of composite financial securities or mutual funds. Mutual fund managers purchase the primary securities to form the portfolios necessary to perform these services. Therefore, the aggregate demand for a primary security will depend on how its return contributes to the formation of these "service" portfolios.

Since the equilibrium expected return on an asset is "determined" by the aggregate demand for it, one would expect to find a correspondence between its expected return and the statistical dependence between the asset's return and the various major sources of uncertainty. All risk-averse consumers would prefer to have less uncertainty for the same expected consumption stream, and would "give up" some (expected) return on an asset in return for that asset.

providing a hedge against some of these uncertainties. Hence, to the extent that any asset's return contributes to (or aggravates) the consumers' attempts to hedge against these uncertainties, one would expect the equilibrium return on that asset to be affected. If, on average, a particular asset's return contributes to consumers' attempts to hedge against a common source of uncertainty, then one would expect that the equilibrium expected return on that asset to be differentially lower than on a similar asset which does not provide that "service." This negative differential in expected return can be interpreted as the market "cost" to the consumer for the hedging service provided by this asset. If, on average, an asset's return would aggravate consumers' attempts to hedge, then the equilibrium expected return would be differentially higher, and this positive differential in expected return can be interpreted as the market "premium" to the consumer in return for bearing the extra risk caused by holding this asset. A simple illustration of this principle can be found in the CAPM. Since the only source of uncertainty is end-of-period wealth and all investors are assumed to be risk-averse, a given investor would view an asset as providing a ("diversification") service if it lowers the variance of his end-of-period wealth and, hence, would accept a lower expected return on this asset than on one which did not provide this service. However, since all investors' optimal portfolios are perfectly-correlated, an asset which aids diversification for one investor does so for all investors, and therefore, all investors would accept a lower expected return on this asset. Inspection of the security market line, (7.1), shows this is the case.

However, with respect to most sources of uncertainty, such unanimity among investors' views of whether an asset contributes to risk or not will be the exception. Thus, one group of consumers may consider a *long* position in an asset as contributing to a reduction of the risks it perceives while another group may view a *short* position as contributing to a reduction in its risks. Thus, whether the market expected return on the asset represents a differential cost or premium will depend on the aggregation of investor's demands, and unless there is a systematic "weak side" to the market, the sign of the differential may fluctuate through time. One example of this type is the Modigliani-Sutch [13] Habitat theory of bond pricing. If a consumer has preferences which induce risk-aversion with respect to wealth, then he will view long-term bonds as risky and would require a market premium over short-term bonds to hold them. If a consumer has preferences which induce risk-aversion with respect to income, then short-term bonds are risky to him, and he would require a market premium over long-term bonds to hold them. Thus, with respect to the uncertainty about future interest rates, the differential expected return between long- and short-term bonds could be of either sign.

To determine the types of securities one would expect to find and the sources of differentials in expected returns, it is necessary to establish what the important uncertainties are facing a typical consumer making a plan according to the criterion in (7.2). Although not a complete listing, the following seven items would seem to cover most of the important common sources of uncertainty for consumers:

(S.1) uncertainty about his own future tastes;
(S.2) uncertainty about the menu of possible consumption goods that will be available in the future;
(S.3) uncertainty about relative prices of consumption goods;
(S.4) uncertainty about his labor income;
(S.5) uncertainty about future values of nonhuman assets;
(S.6) uncertainty about the future investment opportunity set, i.e., the future rates of return which can be earned on capital;
(S.7) uncertainty about the age of death.

While all of these have probably been considered in one model or another, it is important to note that all models which use the criterion of maximizing the expected utility of end-of-period wealth explicitly take into account only the uncertainty in (S.5). Included in this class of models is the CAPM.

Even though all these uncertainties are important to the consumer, not all will differentially affect security prices or returns. It is difficult to image a financial security which could reduce the uncertainties associated with (S.1) or (S.2). While (S.7) is an important problem for all consumers and life insurance was created in response to this demand, the event of death is probably reasonably statistically independent among people, and it is unlikely that the returns on securities (other than life insurance policies) would be statistically dependent on the event of an individual's death. Hence, one would not expect (S.7) to cause differential effects on security prices. The risks associated with (S.4) could be completely eliminated if the consumer could sell forward his wage income in the same way shares are issued on nonhuman capital. Because of the moral hazard problem, it is difficult for the consumer to sell forward his wage income. While some of the individual risk can be eliminated by disability and life insurance and by "investing" in education to make his labor more substitutable across firms, there still will be systematic risk due to (unanticipated) shifts in capital and labor's relative shares (i.e., the wage-rental ratio). This could produce a differential demand for shares in labor-intensive versus capital-intensive industries. Inflation risk (S.3) may cause differentials in demand between different maturity "money" securities. Although information costs and the uncertainties (S.1) and (S.2) prohibit complete future markets for consumption goods, it is reasonable to expect consumers to differentiate broad classes of consumption (e.g., housing, food, transportation, clothing, and recreation) and hence, differentials in demand for shares in different industries could occur as the result of (S.3). (S.5) is the standard end-of-period wealth uncertainty and hence, differential demands will occur for securities which aid diversification. Finally, as is discussed in [12], if there is uncertainty about the rates of return which will be available in the future, differential demands may occur between long and short-term bonds and between shares of firms whose returns are sensitive to shifts in capitalization rates versus ones that are not.

If these are the sources of uncertainty common to most investors, then we can identify a set of mutual funds which would be (approximately) sufficient to span the space of consumers' optimal portfolios. Specifically, we might identify these funds to be: (1) the "market" portfolio; (2) a (short-term) riskless asset; (3) hedging portfolios for *unanticipated* shifts in rates of return; (4) shifts in the wage/rental ratio; and (5) changes in prices for basic groups of consumption goods. Further, consumer demand for individual securities can be written as if they came indirectly through the demands for these mutual funds. Hence, the equilibrium expected return on a security will be a function of the expected return on each of these funds and the statistical dependence between the security's return and the return on each of these funds.

In the special case of continuous-trading examined in Merton [12], the equilibrium expected return on the kth security satisfies

$$E(\tilde{R}_k) - r = \sum_{i=1}^{m} \beta_{ik}[E(\tilde{R}_{im}) - r] \tag{7.3}$$

where $\tilde{R}_{im}$ is the return on the ith mutual fund and β_{ik} is the instantaneous multiple regression coefficient between the return on the kth security and the return on the ith mutual fund, and m is the number of mutual funds necessary to span the space of optimal portfolios.

To empirically test the model, it may be necessary to construct portfolios (in a fashion similar to the Black, Jensen, and Scholes [2] method for the "zero-beta" portfolio) which have the properties of the hypothesized mutual funds when no such portfolio already exists. Further, the specification (7.3) does not rule out changes over time in the $\{\beta_{ik}\}$ or the $E(\hat{R}_{im})$. Hence, care must be taken in choosing sufficiently small observation intervals to avoid (or at least limit) the nonstationarity problem.

7.3 A SIMPLE EXAMPLE

Consider a consumer-investor who lives for two periods and consumes only at the end of the second period. At the beginning of period one (time zero), he receives a wage income of $y(0)$. This and his initial wealth, $W(0)$, are then allocated in a portfolio among four assets: shares in two firms, a two-period discount bond, which pays $1 at the end of period two with certainty, and a riskless one-period bond. At the beginning of period two (time one), he receives a wage income of $y(1)$. This and his wealth at that time, $W(1)$, are then allocated in a portfolio among three assets: the shares in the two firms and a riskless one-period bond. At the end of period two (time two), he allocates his wealth among two consumption goods so as to maximize a strictly concave utility function of consumption.

The uncertainties that he faces as of time zero are in addition to uncertainty of returns on the risky assets, uncertainty about next period's wage income, next period's rate of interest, and the end-of-period price of consumption good number two. Consumption good number one is numeraire, and hence, by definition, its price is always one.

We postulate a very simple set of stochastic processes for the change in wage income, consumption prices, and interest rates. Namely,

$$\tilde{P}(t+1) - P(t) = v_2 \tilde{Z}_2(t) \qquad (7.4a)$$

$$\tilde{y}(t+1) - y(t) = v_1 \tilde{Z}_1(t) \qquad (7.4b)$$

$$\tilde{r}(t+1) - r(t) = -v_3 \tilde{Z}_3(t) \qquad (7.4c)$$

where $P(t)$ is the price of good two at time t; $y(t)$ is the wage income at time t; $r(t)$ is the interest rate at time t. Further, it is assumed that the v_i are constants and

$$E\left\{\tilde{Z}_i(t)\right\} = 0 \quad \text{for all } i \text{ and } t, \tag{7.5a}$$

$$E\left\{\tilde{Z}_i^2(t)\right\} = 1 \quad \text{for all } i \text{ and } t, \tag{7.5b}$$

$$E\left\{\tilde{Z}_i(t)\tilde{Z}_j(t)\right\} = 0 \quad \text{for } i \neq j \text{ and all } t, \tag{7.5c}$$

$$E\left\{\tilde{Z}_i(t)\tilde{Z}_j(t+\tau)\right\} = 0 \quad \text{for all } i, j \text{ and } \tau \neq 0 \tag{7.5d}$$

Thus, the expected change in these variables is zero and the changes have zero serial and cross-sectional correlations.

The return structure on the assets can be written as

$$\tilde{R}_1(t) = r(t) + \alpha_1 + a_1\tilde{Z}_1(t) + \tilde{\epsilon}_1(t) \tag{7.6a}$$
$$\text{(firm \#1)}$$

$$\tilde{R}_2(t) = r(t) + \alpha_2 + a_2\tilde{Z}_2(t) + \tilde{\epsilon}_2(t) \tag{7.6b}$$
$$\text{(firm \#2)}$$

$$\tilde{R}_3(t) = r(t) + \alpha_3 + a_3\tilde{Z}_3(t) \tag{7.6c}$$
$$\text{(two-period bond)}$$

where α_i and a_i are constants with $a_i > 0$
and

$E\left\{\tilde{\epsilon}_i(t)\right\} = 0; E\left\{\tilde{\epsilon}_i(t)\tilde{\epsilon}_j(t)\right\} = 0$ for $i \neq j$;

$E\left\{\tilde{\epsilon}_i(t)\tilde{Z}_j(t)\right\} = 0$ for all i, j;

$E\left\{\tilde{\epsilon}_i(t)\tilde{\epsilon}_j(t + \tau)\right\} = E\left\{\tilde{\epsilon}_i(t)\tilde{Z}_j(t + \tau)\right\} = 0$ for all i, j and $\tau \neq 0$;

Variance $(\tilde{R}_i(t)) \equiv \sigma_i^2$.

Thus, the return on firm #1 is positively correlated with changes in wage income; the return on firm #2 is positively correlated with changes in the price of consumption good two; the return on the two-period bond is (perfectly) negatively correlated with changes in the interest rate.

To solve the consumption-investment problem, we use the standard method of stochastic dynamic programming (cf. Hakansson [8] or Samuelson [14]) which requires us to start at the end of the program and work backwards.

At time two, the investor will know his wealth, $W(2)$, and the price of consumption good two, $P(2)$, and will act so as to

$$\underset{\{C_1, C_2\}}{\text{Max}} \quad U[C_1, C_2] \tag{7.7}$$

subject to the budget constraint: $W(2) = C_1 + P(2)C_2$, where $U[C_1, C_2]$ is a strictly concave utility function. The first-order condition to be satisfied by the optimal choice, $\{C_i^*\}$, is

$$\frac{\partial U}{\partial C_1} \Big/ \frac{\partial U}{\partial C_2} = 1/P(2) \tag{7.8}$$

From (7.8), we can solve for $C_i^* = C_i^*[W(2), P(2)]$. Define the indirect utility function, ϕ, to be

$$\phi[W(2), P(2)] \equiv U[C_1^*, C_2^*] \tag{7.9}$$

As time one, the investor will know his wealth (which includes his period-one wage income, $y(1)$), $W(1)$, the price of consumption good two, $P(1)$, and the interest rate, $r(1)$. Since he does no consuming at that time, his only decision is to choose a portfolio allocation $\{w_1(1), w_2(1), w_3(1)\}$ so as to

$$\text{Max } E_1 \left\{ \phi[\tilde{W}(2), \tilde{P}(2)] \right\} \tag{7.10}$$

Subject to the constraint $\Sigma_1^3 w_i(1) = 1$ where $w_i(1)$ is the fraction of his wealth invested in the ith asset and "E_1" is the conditional expectation operator, conditional on knowing all (relevant) events as of time one. We can write end-of-period wealth, $W(2)$, in terms of the decision variables as

$$\tilde{W}(2) = W(1) + W(1)[\Sigma_1^2 w_i(1)[\tilde{R}_i(1) - r(1)] + r(2)]$$

$$= W(1) + W(1)[\Sigma_1^2 w_i(1)\alpha_i + r(1)] \tag{7.11}$$

$$+ W(1) \left\{ \Sigma_1^2 w_i(1)a_i\tilde{Z}_i(1) + \Sigma_1^2 w_i(1)\tilde{\epsilon}_i(1) \right\}$$

where the constraint has been substituted out (i.e., $w_3(1) = 1 - \Sigma_1^2 w_i(1)$) and $\tilde{R}_i(1)$ has been substituted for from (7.6).

To provide explicit solutions and to relate them to the standard mean-variance analysis, we make a quadratic approximation of the type described in Samuelson [15] and justified for "short-time intervals" in Merton [10,11,12]. Namely,

$$E_1\left\{\phi[\tilde{W}(2),\tilde{P}(2)]\right\} \doteq E_1\left\{\phi[W(1),P(1)] + \phi_1[W(1),P(1)]\,\Delta\tilde{W}\right.$$

$$+ \phi_2[W(1),P(1)]\,\Delta\tilde{P} + 1/2[\phi_{11}(\Delta\tilde{W})^2$$

$$\left. + 2\phi_{12}(\Delta\tilde{W}\Delta P)\phi_{22}(\Delta\tilde{P})^2]\right\} \qquad (7.12)$$

where subscripts denote partial derivatives and "Δ" denotes change over the period. From (7.4), (7.5), (7.6), and (7.11), we have that

$$E_1[\Delta\tilde{W}] = W(1)[\Sigma_1^2 w_i(1)\alpha_i + r(1)], \qquad (7.13)$$

$$E_1[\Delta\tilde{P}] = 0,$$

and

$$E_1\left\{(\Delta\tilde{W})^2\right\} = W^2(1)\left\{(\Sigma_1^2 w_i(1)\alpha_i + r(1))^2 + \Sigma_1^2 w_i^2(1)\sigma_i^2\right\} \quad (7.14a)$$

$$\doteq W^2(1)\Sigma_1^2 w_i^2(1)\sigma_i^2,$$

$$E_1\left\{(\Delta\tilde{P})^2\right\} = v_2^2, \qquad (7.14b)$$

$$E_1\left\{\Delta\tilde{W}\Delta\tilde{P}\right\} = W(1)w_2(1)a_2 v_2 \qquad (7.14c)$$

where the approximation in (7.14a) is valid for short-time intervals since asymptotically, $(\Sigma^2 w_i(1)\alpha_i + r(1))^2 << \Sigma_1^2 w_i^2(1)\sigma_i^2$. Taking the expectation term-by-term in (7.12) (and noting that because $\phi[\hat{W},\hat{P}]$ and its derivatives are evaluated at the $[W(1),P(1)]$, they are nonstochastic) and substituting from (7.13) and (7.14), we can rewrite (7.12) as

$$E_1\left\{\phi[\widetilde{W}(2),\widetilde{P}(2)]\right\} \doteq [\phi + 1/2\phi_{22}v_2^2 + \phi_1 W(1)[\Sigma_1^2 w_i(1)\alpha_i + r(1)]$$

$$+ \ \phi_{12} W(1)w_2(1)a_2 v_2$$

$$+ \frac{W^2(1)}{2}\ \phi_{11}\Sigma_1^2 w_i^2(1)\sigma_i^2\,]. \tag{7.15}$$

The first-order conditions for an interior maximum in (7.15) are

$$0 = \phi_1 W(1)\alpha_1 + W^2(1)\phi_{11}w_1^*(1)\sigma_1^2 \tag{7.16a}$$

and

$$0 = \phi_1 W(1)\alpha_2 + \phi_{12} W(1)a_2 v_2 + W^2(1)\phi_{11}w_2^*(1)\sigma_2^2 \tag{7.16b}$$

Solving (7.16) for the optimal demands for risky assets, $d_i^*(\equiv w_i^*(1)W(1))$, we have that

$$d_1^*(1) \ = \ A\left(\frac{\alpha_1}{\sigma_1^2}\right) \tag{7.17a}$$

$$d_2^*(1) \ = \ A\left(\frac{\alpha_2}{\sigma_2^2}\right) \ + \ H\left(\frac{a_2 v_2}{\sigma_2^2}\right) \tag{7.17b}$$

where

$$A \equiv -\phi_1[W(1),P(1)]/\phi_{11}[W(1),P(1)] \tag{7.18a}$$

and

$$H \equiv -\phi_{12}[W(1),P(1)]/\phi_{11}[W(1),P(1)] \tag{7.18b}$$

Note that unlike in the standard mean-variance, the ratio of $d_1^*(1)/d_2^*(1)$ is not independent of preferences (unless $H \equiv 0$), and hence, the separation theorem does not obtain. Therefore, all investors will not hold the same (relative) proportions of risky assets. The reason for this is that due to the end-of-period price uncertainty between the consumption goods, the indirect utility function depends on other variables in addition to end-of-period wealth.

Substituting from (7.17) into (7.15), we can define a new "indirect" utility function

$$\psi[W(1),P(1),r(1)] \equiv \text{Max } E_1 \quad \phi[\tilde{W}(2),\tilde{P}(2)] \tag{7.19}$$

subject to the constraint $\Sigma_1^4 w_i(0) = 1$. End-of-period wealth can be written as

$$\tilde{W}(1) - W(0) = \tilde{y}(1) + W(0)[\Sigma_1^3 w_i(0)\alpha_i + r(0)]$$

$$+ W(0)\left\{\Sigma_1^3 w_i(0)a_i\tilde{Z}_i(0) + \Sigma_1^2 w_i(0)\tilde{\epsilon}_i(0)\right\} \tag{7.20}$$

As was done in (7.15), we can use a similar quadratic expansion for ψ by expanding around $[W(0) + y(0),P(0),r(0)]$. Namely,

$$E\left\{\psi[\tilde{W}(2), \tilde{P}(1), \tilde{r}(1)]\right\} \doteq E_0\left\{\psi + \psi_1\Delta\tilde{W} + \psi_2\Delta\tilde{P} + \psi_3\Delta\tilde{r}\right.$$

$$+ 1/2[\psi_{11}(\Delta\tilde{W})^2 + \psi_{22}(\Delta\tilde{P})^2$$

$$+ \psi_{33}(\Delta\tilde{r})^2 + 2(\psi_{12}(\Delta\tilde{W}\Delta\tilde{P})$$

$$+ \psi_{13}(\Delta\tilde{W}\Delta\tilde{r}) + \psi_{32}(\Delta\tilde{P}\Delta\tilde{r}))]\right\} \tag{7.21}$$

Taking expectations term-by-term, substituting from (7.4), (7.5), (7.6), and (7.20), and eliminating terms which do not involve the decision variables, we have that maximizing (7.21) is equivalent to

$$\underset{\{w_1,w_2,w_3\}}{\text{Max}} \left\{\psi_1 W(0)(\Sigma_1^3 w_i(0)\alpha_i + r(0))\right.$$

$$+ 1/2\psi_{11}[(\Sigma_1^3 w_i^2(0)\sigma_i^2)W^2(0) + 2v_1 a_1 w_1(0)W(0)]$$

$$+ \psi_{12}W(0)w_2(0)a_2 v_2 - \psi_{13}W(0)w_3(0)a_3 v_3\right\} \tag{7.22}$$

The first-order conditions for an interior maximum are

$$0 = \psi_1\alpha_1 + \psi_{11}[w_1^*(0)\sigma_1^2 W(0) + a_1 v_1] \tag{7.23a}$$

$$0 = \psi_1 \alpha_2 + \psi_{11}[w_2^*(0)\sigma_2^2 W(0)] + \psi_{12}a_2 v_2 \qquad (7.23b)$$

$$0 = \psi_1 \alpha_3 + \psi_{11}[w_3^*(0)\sigma_3^2 W(0)] - \psi_{13}a_3 v_3 \qquad (7.23c)$$

Solving (7.23) for the optimal demands for risky assets, $d^*(\equiv w_i^*(0)W(0))$, we have that

$$d_1^*(0) = A\left(\frac{\alpha_1}{\sigma_1^2}\right) - \frac{a_1 v_1}{\sigma_1^2} \qquad (7.24a)$$

$$d_2^*(0) = A\left(\frac{\alpha_2}{\sigma_2^2}\right) + H\left(\frac{a_2 v_2}{\sigma_2^2}\right) \qquad (7.24b)$$

$$d_3^*(0) = A\left(\frac{\alpha_3}{\sigma_3^2}\right) + K\left(\frac{a_3 v_3}{\sigma_3^2}\right) \qquad (7.24c)$$

where $A \equiv -\psi_1/\psi_{11}$, $H \equiv -\psi_{12}/\psi_{11}$, and $K \equiv +\psi_{13}/\psi_{11}$. Note that the portfolio demands for the "usual," one-period mean-variance maximizer would be $A\alpha_i/\sigma_i^2$. However, the multiperiod nature of the plan coupled with price, interest rate, and (future) wage income uncertainty results in differential demands and since $d_i^*(0)/d_j^*(0)$ are not independent of preferences, the separation theorem does not obtain. These differential demands can be interpreted as "hedging" demands induced by uncertainties about important variables other than terminal wealth. Note, for example, that because the return on security number one is positively correlated with future wage income, the investor holds less of this security than he would have if he had no wage income.

While a full discussion and derivation of the equilibrium relationship among expected returns in the presence of these additional uncertainties can be found in Merton [12], we can easily demonstrate the failure of the classical security market line (7.1) for the case leading to the demand functions in (7.24). Suppose that the aggregate supply of two-period bonds is zero (i.e., all such debt is "inside" debt). Then, in equilibrium, the aggregate demand for bonds must be zero. Since by construction, the returns on these bonds are uncorrelated with all other assets, these two conditions imply that these bonds will have a "zero beta" (zero covariance with the market). By the CAPM, the equilibrium expected return, $E(\tilde{R}_3)$, must equal the riskless rate, r, or in other words, $\alpha_3 = 0$. By summing

Equation (7.24c) over all investors with $\alpha_3 = 0$, we have that the aggregate demand for the bonds, D_3, will equal

$$D_3 \equiv \Sigma d_3^j (0) = \left(\frac{a_3 v_3}{\sigma_3^2}\right) \Sigma K^j \qquad (7.25)$$

where j denotes the jth investor. Unless $\Sigma K^j \equiv 0$, $D_3 \neq 0$, and hence $\alpha_3 = 0$ will not be the equilibrium expected excess return. Thus, one should not expect the security market line relationship to obtain except in very specialized cases. However, a generalized security market plane of the type specified in (7.3) might well provide an adequate description of equilibrium expected returns.

7.4 CONCLUSION

As illustrated in the example in the previous section, the consumer services model leads to demand functions and an equilibrium structure of returns for assets that are fundamentally different from those derived in models where investors maximize the expected utility of end-of-period wealth. While the stochastic dynamic programming technique produces a "derived" utility function of end-of-period wealth[3] whose expected value is maximized at each stage in the program, this "derived" utility function is not only a function of wealth but also of the other state variables of the problem (e.g., in the example of Section 7.3, these variables included relative consumption good prices and interest rates). Thus, the portfolio combination that maximizes the expected value of this utility function might be one that would never be chosen by a maximizer of expected utility of wealth. I.e., the optimal portfolio could be "inefficient" as measured by the usual methods of stochastic dominance. Moreover, these differences in the optimal portfolio holdings will appear unless the marginal utility with respect to wealth does not depend on the other state variables or unless the distribution of returns on assets is independent of the other state variables.

The specific linear structure of equilibrium expected returns described at the end of Section 7.2 depends on the validity of the local quadratic approximation of the derived utility function at each stage in the dynamic program. As mentioned in the example of Section 7.3, such an approximation is valid if the length of time between successive decisions is "small" and becomes more accurate as the asymptotic limit of continuous trading is approached. Moreover, I know of no other assumption justifying this approximation that is not severely at variance with economic facts (e.g., quadratic utility globally or gaussian-distributed returns). The Ross "Arbitrage Factor" model deduces a similar linear equilibrium structure of expected returns without the explicit assumption of the quadratic approximation. However, this model assumes that the stochastic returns on assets are generated in a linear fashion by one or more exogenous, stochastic factors. Careful analysis shows that such a' specification can only be a reasonable approximation to economic reality if the time interval between successive changes is small as well. Hence, as in the usual mean-variance model, this model requires the assumption of (approximate) continuous trading as a necessary condition for its economic validity.

NOTES TO SECTION SEVEN

1. It is assumed that there is at least one security with a positive payoff in at least one of each of the states of nature.
2. "Mutual fund" is used here in the broad sense including financial security or financial intermediary.
3. More generally, in the literature of optimal control, this function is called the Bellman function. The ϕ and ψ functions of the example in Section 7.3 are examples of this derived utility function.

REFERENCES

1. Black, F., "Capital Market Equilibrium with Restricted Borrowing," *Journal of Business*, 45 (1972), pp. 444-455.
2. _____, M.C. Jensen, and M. Scholes, "The Capital Asset Pricing Model: Some Empirical Tests," in *Studies in the Theory of Capital Markets*, M.C. Jensen, ed., New York: Praeger Publishers, 1972.
3. Brennan, M.J., "Capital Market Equilibrium with Divergent Borrowing and Lending Rates," *Journal of Financial and Quantitative Analysis*, 6 (1971), pp. 1197-1205.
4. Cass, D. and J.E. Stiglitz, "The Structure of Investor Preferences and Asset Returns, and Separability in Portfolio Allocation: A Contribution to the Pure Theory of Mutual Funds," *Journal of Economic Theory*, 2 (1970), pp. 122-160.
5. Fama, E.F., "Multiperiod Consumption-Investment Decisions," *American Review* 60 (1970), pp. 163-174.
6. _____ and J. MacBeth, "Risk, Return, and Equilibrium: Empirical Tests," *Journal of Political Economy*, 81,(1973), pp. 607-636.
7. Friend, I. and M. Blume, "Measurement of Portfolio Performance under Uncertainty," *American Economic Review*, 60 (1970), pp. 561-575.
8. Hakansson, N.H., "Optimal Investment and Consumption Strategies under Risk for a Class of Utility Functions," *Econometrica*, 38 (1970), pp. 587-607.

9. Jensen, M.C., "Capital Markets: Theory and Evidence," *Bell Journal of Economics and Management Science*, 2 (1972), pp. 357-398.

10. Merton, R.C., "Lifetime Portfolio Selection under Uncertainty: The Continuous-Time Case," *Review of Economics and Statistics*, 51 (1969), pp. 247-257.

11. _____, "Optimum Consumption and Portfolio Rules in a Continuous-Time Model," *Journal of Economic Theory*, 3 (1971), pp. 373-413.

12. _____, "An Intertemporal Capital Asset Pricing Model," *Econometrica*, 41 (1973), pp. 867-887; also reprinted in this volume.

13. Modigliani, F. and C.R. Sutch, "Innovations in Interest Rate Policy," *American Economic Review*, 56 (1966), pp. 178-197.

14. Samuelson, P.A., "Lifetime Portfolio Selection by Dynamic Stochastic Programming," *Review of Economics and Statistics*, 51 (1969), pp. 239-246.

15. _____, "The Fundamental Approximation Theorem of Portfolio Analysis in Terms of Means, Variances, and Higher Moments," *Review of Economic Studies*, 37 (1970), pp. 537-542.

16. Ross, S.A., "The Arbitrage Theory of Capital Asset Pricing," *Journal of Economic Theory* (forthcoming).

✳ *Section Eight*

An Intertemporal Capital Asset Pricing Model[1]

Robert C. Merton

8.1 INTRODUCTION

One of the more important developments in modern capital market theory is the Sharpe-Lintner-Mossin mean-variance equilibrium model of exchange, commonly called the capital asset pricing model.[2] Although the model has been the basis for more than one hundred academic papers and has had significant impact on the nonacademic financial community,[3] it is still subject to theoretical and empirical criticism. Because the model assumes that investors choose their portfolios according to the Markowitz [21] mean-variance criterion, it is subject to all the theoretical objections to this criterion, of which there are many.[4] It has also been criticized for the additional assumptions required,[5] especially homogeneous expectations and the single-period nature of the model. The proponents of the model who agree with the theoretical objections, but who argue that the capital market operates "as if" these assumptions were satisfied, are themselves not beyond criticism. While the model predicts that the expected excess return from holding an asset is proportional to the covariance of its return with the market portfolio (its "beta"), the careful empirical work of Black, Jensen, and Scholes [3] has demonstrated that this is not the case. In particular, they found that "low beta" assets earn a higher return on average and "high beta" assets earn a lower return on average than is forecast by the model.[6] Nonetheless, the model is still used because it is an equilibrium model which provides a strong specification of the relationship among asset yields that is easily interpreted, and the empirical evidence suggests that it does explain a significant fraction of the variation in asset returns.

This chapter develops an equilibrium model of the capital market which (i) has the simplicity and empirical tractability of the capital asset pricing model; (ii) is consistent with expected utility maximization and the limited liability of assets; and (iii) provides a specification of the relationship among yields that is more consistent with empirical evidence. Such a model cannot be constructed without costs. The assumptions, principally homogeneous expectations, which it holds in common with the classical model, make the new model subject to some of the same criticisms.

The capital asset pricing model is a static (single-period) model although it is generally treated as if it holds intertemporally. Fama [9] has provided some justification for this assumption by showing that, if preferences and future investment opportunity sets are not state-dependent, then intertemporal portfolio maximization can be treated as if the investor had a single-period utility function. However, these assumptions are rather restrictive as will be seen in later analysis.[7] Merton [25] has shown in a number of examples that portfolio behavior for an intertemporal maximizer will be significantly different when he faces a changing investment opportunity set instead of a constant one.

The model presented here is based on consumer-investor behavior as described in [25], and for the assumptions to be reasonable ones, it must be intertemporal. Far from a liability, the intertemporal nature of the model allows it to capture effects which would never appear in a static model, and it is precisely these effects which cause the significant differences in specification of the equilibrium relationship among asset yields that obtain in the new model and the classical model.

8.2 CAPITAL MARKET STRUCTURE

It is assumed that the capital market is structured as follows.

Assumption 1: All assets have limited liability.
Assumption 2: There are no transactions costs, taxes, or problems with indivisibilities of assets.
Assumption 3: There are a sufficient number of investors with comparable wealth levels so that each investor believes that he can buy and sell as much of an asset as he wants at the market price.
Assumption 4: The capital market is always in equilibrium (i.e., there is no trading at nonequilibrium prices).

Assumption 5: There exists an exchange market for borrowing and lending at the same rate of interest.

Assumption 6: Short-sales of all assets, with full use of the proceeds, is allowed.

Assumption 7: Trading in assets takes place continually in time.

Assumptions 1-6 are the standard assumptions of a perfect market, and their merits have been discussed extensively in the literature. Although Assumption 7 is not standard, it almost follows directly from Assumption 2. If there are no costs to transacting and assets can be exchanged on any scale, then investors would prefer to be able to revise their portfolios at any time (whether they actually do so or not). In reality, transactions costs and indivisibilities do exist, and one reason given for finite trading-interval (discrete-time) models is to give implicit, if not explicit, recognition to these costs. However, this method of avoiding the problem of transactions costs is not satisfactory since a proper solution would almost certainly show that the trading intervals are stochastic and of nonconstant length. Further, the portfolio demands and the resulting equilibrium relationships will be a function of the specific trading interval that is chosen.[8] An investor making a portfolio decision which is irrevocable ("frozen") for ten years will choose quite differently than the one who has the option (even at a cost) to revise his portfolio daily. The essential issue is the market structure and not investors' tastes, and for well-developed capital markets, the time interval between successive market openings is sufficiently small to make the continuous-time assumption a good approximation.[9]

8.3 ASSET VALUE AND RATE OF RETURN DYNAMICS

Having described the structure of the capital market, we now develop the dynamics of the returns on assets traded in the market. It is sufficient for his decision making that the consumer-investor know at each point in time: (i) the transition probabilities for returns on each asset over the next trading interval (the *investment opportunity set*); and (ii) the transition probabilities for returns on assets in future periods (i.e., knowledge of the stochastic processes of the changes in the investment opportunity set). Unlike a single-period maximizer who, by definition, does not consider events beyond the present period, the intertemporal maximizer in selecting his portfolio takes into account the relationship between current period returns and returns that will be available in the future. For example, suppose that the current return on a particular asset is negatively correlated with changes in yields ("capitalization" rates). Then, by holding this asset, the investor expects a higher return on the asset if, ex post, yield opportunities next period are lower than were expected.

A brief description of the supply side of the asset market will be helpful in understanding the relationship between current returns on assets and changes in the investment opportunity set.

An asset is defined as a production technology which is a probability distribution for cash flow (valued in consumption units) and physical depreciation, as a function of the amount of capital, $K(t)$ (measured in physical units, e.g., number of machines), employed at time t. The price per unit capital in terms of the consumption good is $P_k(t)$, and the value of an asset at time t, $V(t)$, equals $P_k(t)K(t)$. The return on the asset over a period of length h will be the cash flow, X, plus the value of undepreciated capital, $(1-\lambda)P_k(t+h)K(t)$ (where λ is the rate of physical depreciation of capital), minus the initial value of the asset, $V(t)$. The total change in the value of the asset outstanding, $V(t+h) - V(t)$, is equal to the sum of the return on the asset plus the value of gross new investment in excess of cash flow, $P_k(t+h)[K(t+h) - (1-\lambda)K(t)] - X$.

Each firm in the model is assumed to invest in a single asset and to issue one class of securities, called equity.[10] Hence, the terms "firm" and "asset" can be used interchangeably. Let $N(t)$ be the number of shares of the firm outstanding and let $P(t)$ be the price per share, where $N(t)$ and $P(t)$ are defined by the difference equations.

$$P(t+h) \equiv [X + (1-\lambda)P_k(t+h)K(t)]/N(t) \qquad (8.1)$$

and

$$N(t+h) \equiv N(t) + [P_k(t+h) - (1-\lambda)K(t)] - X]/P(t+h), \qquad (8.2)$$

subject to the initial conditions $P(0) = P$, $N(0) = N$, and $V(0) = N(0)P(0)$. If we assume that all dividend payments to shareholders are accomplished by share repurchase, then from (8.1) and (8.2), $[P(t+h) - P(t)]/P(t)$ is the rate of return on the asset over the period, in units of the consumption good.[11]

Since movements from equilibrium to equilibrium through time involve both price and quantity adjustment, a complete analysis would require a description of both the rate of return and change in asset value dynamics. To do so would require a specification of firm behavior in determining the supply of shares, which in turn would require knowledge of the real asset structure (i.e., technology; whether capital is "putty" or "clay"; etc.). In particular, the current returns on firms with large amounts (relative to current cash flow) of nonshiftable capital with low rates of depreciation will tend to be strongly affected by shifts in capitalization rates because, in the short run, most of the adjustment to the new equilibrium will be done by prices.

Since this study examines only investor behavior to derive the demands for assets and the relative yield requirements in equilibrium[12] only the rate of return dynamics will be examined explicitly. Hence, certain variables, taken as exogeneous in the model, would be endogeneous to a full-equilibrium system.

From the assumption of continuous trading (Assumption 7), it is assumed that the returns and the changes in the opportunity set can be described by continuous-time stochastic processes. However, it will clarify the analysis to describe the processes for discrete trading intervals of length, h, and then, to consider the limit as h tends to zero.

We assume the following:

Assumption 8: The vector set of stochastic processes describing the opportunity set and its changes, is a time-homogeneous[13] Markov process.

Assumption 9: Only local changes in the state variables of the process are allowed.

Assumption 10: For each asset in the opportunity set at each point in time t, the expected rate of return per unit time, defined by

$$\alpha \equiv E_t[P(t+h) - P(t)/P(t)/h,$$

and the variance of the return per unit time, defined by

$$\sigma^2 \equiv E_t[([P(t+h) - P(t)]/P(t - \alpha h)^2]/h,$$

exist, are finite with $\sigma^2 > 0$, and are (right) continuous functions of h, where "E_t" is the conditional expectation operator, conditional on the levels of the state variables at time t. In the limit as h tends to zero, α is called the instantaneous expected return and σ^2 the instantaneous variance of the return.

Assumption 8 is not very restrictive since it is not required that the stochastic processes describing returns be Markov by themselves, but only that by the "expansion of the state" (supplementary variables) technique [7, p. 262] to include (a finite number of) other variables describing the changes in the transition probabilities, the entire (expanded) set be Markov. This generalized use of the Markov assumption for the returns is important because one would expect that the required returns will depend on other variables besides the price per share (e.g., the relative supplies of assets).

Assumption 9 is the discrete-time analog to the continuous-time assumption of continuity in the state variables (i.e., if $X(t + h)$ is the random state variable, then, with probability one, $\lim_{h \to 0} [X(t + h) - X(t)] = 0$). In words, it says that over small time intervals, price changes (returns) and changes in the opportunity set are small. This restriction is nontrivial since the implied "smoothness" rules out Pareto-Levy or Poisson-type jump processes.[14]

Assumption 10 ensures that, for small time intervals, the uncertainty neither "washes out" (i.e., $\sigma^2 = 0$) nor dominates the analysis (i.e., $\sigma^2 = \infty$). Actually, Assumption 10 follows from Assumptions 8 and 9 (see [13, p. 321]).

If we let $\{X(t)\}$ stand for the vector stochastic process, then Assumptions 8-10 imply that, in the limit as h tends to zero, $X(t)$ is a diffusion process with continuous state-space changes and that the transition probabilities will satisfy a (multidimensional) Fokker-Planck or Kolmogorov partial differential equation.

Although these partial differential equations are sufficient for study of the transition probabilities, it is useful to write down the explicit return dynamics in stochastic difference equation form and then, by taking limits, in stochastic differential equation form. From the previous analysis, we can write the returns dynamics as

$$\frac{P(t + h) - P(t)}{P(t)} = \alpha h + \sigma y(t)\sqrt{h}, \tag{8.3}$$

where, by construction, $E_t(y) = 0$ and $E_t(y^2) = 1$, and $y(t)$ is a purely random process; that is, $y(t)$ and $y(t + s)$, for $s > 0$, are identically distributed and mutually independent.[15] If we define the stochastic process, $z(t)$, by

$$z(t + h) = z(t) + y(t)\sqrt{h}, \tag{8.4}$$

then $z(t)$ is a stochastic process with independent increments. If it is further assumed that $y(t)$ is Gaussian distributed,[16] then the limit as h tends to zero of $z(t + h) - z(t)$ describes a Wiener process or Brownian motion. In the formalism of stochastic differential equations,

$$dz \equiv y(t)\sqrt{dt}. \tag{8.5}$$

In a similar fashion, we can take the limit of (8.3) to derive the stochastic differential equation for the instantaneous return on the ith asset as

$$\frac{dP_i}{P_i} = \alpha_i \, dt + \sigma_i \, dz_i. \tag{8.6}$$

Processes such as (8.6) are called Itô processes and while they are continuous, they are not differentiable.[17]

From (8.6), a sufficient set of statistics for the opportunity set at a given point in time is $\{\alpha_i, \sigma_i, \rho_{ij}\}$ where ρ_{ij} is the instantaneous correlation coefficient between the Wiener processes dz_i and dz_j. The vector of return dynamics as described in (8.6) will be Markov only if α_i, σ_i, and ρ_{ij} were, at most, functions of the P's. In general, one would not expect this to be the case since, at each point in time, equilibrium clearing conditions will define a set of implicit functions between equilibrium market values, $V_i(t) = N_i(t)P_i(t)$, and the α_i, σ_i, and ρ_{ij}. Hence, one would expect the changes in required expected returns to be stochastically related to changes in market values, and dependence on P solely would obtain only if changes in N (changes in supplies) were nonstochastic. Therefore, to close the system, we append the dynamics for the changes in the opportunity set over time: namely,

$$d\alpha_i = a_i \, dt + b_i \, dq_i,$$

$$\tag{8.7}$$

$$d\sigma_i = f_i \, dt + g_i \, dx_i,$$

where we do assume that (8.6) and (8.7), together, form a Markov system,[18] with dq_i and dx_i standard Wiener processes.

Under the assumptions of continuous trading and the continuous Markov structure of the stochastic processes, it has been shown that the instantaneous, first two moments of the distributions are sufficient statistics.[19] Further, by the existence and boundedness of α and σ, P equal to zero is a natural absorbing barrier ensuring limited liability of all assets.

For the rest of the study, it is assumed that there are n distinct[20] risky assets and one "instantaneously risk-less" asset. "Instantaneously risk-less" means that, at each instant of time, each investor knows with certainty that he can earn rate of return $r(t)$ over the next instant by holding the asset (i.e., $\sigma_{n+1} = 0$ and $\alpha_{n+1} \equiv r(t)$). However, the future values of $r(t)$ are not known with certainty (i.e., $b_{n+1} \neq 0$ in (8.7). We interpret this asset as the exchange asset and $r(t)$ as the instantaneous private sector borrowing (and lending) rate. Alternatively, the asset could represent (very) short government bonds.

8.4 PREFERENCE STRUCTURE AND BUDGET EQUATION DYNAMICS

We assume that there are K consumer-investors with preference structures as described in [25]: namely, the kth consumer acts so as to

$$\max E_0 \left[\int_0^{T^k} U^k [c^k(s),s] ds + B^k [W^k(T^k), T^k] \right], \qquad (8.8)$$

where "E_0" is the conditional expectation operator, conditional on the current value of his wealth, $W^k(0) = W^k$ are the state variables of the investment opportunity set, and T^k is the distribution for his age of death (which is assumed to be independent of investment outcomes). His instantaneous consumption flow at age t is $c^k(t)$.[2 1] U^k is a strictly concave von Neumann-Morgenstern utility function for consumption and B^k is a strictly concave "bequest" or utility-of-terminal wealth function.

Dropping the superscripts (except where required for clarity), we can write the accumulation equation for the kth investor as[2 2]

$$dW = \sum_1^{n+1} w_i W \, dP_i/P_i + (y - c) \, dt, \qquad (8.9)$$

where $w_i \equiv N_i P_i/W$ is the fraction of his wealth invested in the ith asset, N_i is the number of shares of the ith asset he owns, and y is his wage income. Substituting for dP_i/P_i from (8.6), we can rewrite (8.9) as

$$dW = \left[\sum_1^n w_i(\alpha_i - r) + r \right] W \, dt + \sum_1^n w_i W \sigma_i dz_i + (y - c)dt, \qquad (8.10)$$

where his choice for $w_1, w_2 \ldots, w_n$ is unconstrained because w_{n+} can always be chosen to satisfy the budget constraint $\sum_1^{n+1} w_i = 1$.

From the budget constraint, $W = \Sigma^{n+1} N_i P_i$, and the accumulation equation (8.9), we have that

$$(y - c)dt = \sum_{1}^{n+1} dN_i(P_i + dP_i),\qquad(8.11)$$

i.e., the net value of new shares purchased must equal the value of savings from wage income.

8.5 THE EQUATIONS OF OPTIMALITY: THE DEMAND FUNCTIONS FOR ASSETS

For computational simplicity, we will assume that investors derive all their income from capital gains sources (i.e., $y \equiv 0$),[23] and for notational simplicity, we introduce the state-variable vector, X, whose m elements, x_i, denote the current levels of P, α, and σ. The dynamics for X are written as the vector Itô process,

$$dX = F(X)dt + G(X)dQ,\qquad(8.12)$$

where F is the vector $[f_1, f_2, \ldots, f_m]$, G is a diagonal matrix with diagonal elements $[g_1, g_2, \ldots, g_m]$, dQ is the vector Wiener process $[dq_1, dq_2, \ldots, dq_m]$, η_{ij} is the instantaneous correlation coefficient between dq_i and dz_j, and v_{ij} is the instantaneous correlation coefficient between dq_i and dq_j.

I have shown elsewhere[24] that the necessary optimality conditions for an investor who acts according to (8.8) in choosing his consumption-investment program are that, at each point in time,

$$0 = \max_{(c,w)} \left[U(c,t) + J_t + J_w \left[\left(\sum_{1}^{n} w_i(\alpha_i - r) + r \right) W - c \right] \right.$$

$$+ \sum_{1}^{m} J_i f_i + \tfrac{1}{2} J_{ww} \sum_{1}^{n}\sum_{1}^{n} w_i w_j \sigma_{ij} W^2$$

$$+ \sum_{1}^{m}\sum_{1}^{n} J_{iW} w_j W g_i \sigma_j \eta_{ij} + \frac{1}{2}\sum_{1}^{m}\sum_{1}^{m} J_{ij} g_i g_j v_{ij} \Bigg],\qquad(8.13)$$

subject to $J(W, T, X) = B(W, T)$, where subscripts on the "derived" utility of wealth function, J, denote partial derivatives. The σ_{ij} are the instantaneous covariances between the returns on the ith and j^{th} assets $(\equiv \sigma_i \sigma_j \rho_{ij})$.

The $n + 1$ first-order conditions derived from (8.13) are

$$0 = U_c(c,t) - J_W(W,t,X), \tag{8.14}$$

$$0 = J_w(\alpha_i - r) + J_{ww} \sum_1^n w_j W \sigma_{ij} + \sum_1^m J_{jw} g_j \sigma_i \eta_{ji} \quad (i = 1,2,\ldots,n), \tag{8.15}$$

where $c = c(W,t,X)$ and $w_i = w_i(W,t,X)$ are the optimum consumption and portfolio rules as functions of the state variables. Equation (8.14) is the usual intertemporal envelope condition to equate the marginal utility of current consumption to the marginal utility of wealth (future consumption). The manifest characteristic of (8.15) is its linearity in the portfolio demands; hence, we can solve explicitly for these functions by matrix inversion,

$$w_i W = A \sum_1^n v_{ij}(\alpha_j - r) + \sum_1^m \sum_1^n H_k \sigma_j g_k \eta_{jk} v_{ij} \quad (i = 1,2,\ldots,n), \tag{8.16}$$

where the v_{ij} are the elements of the inverse of the instantaneous variance-covariance matrix of returns, $\Omega = [\sigma_{ij}]$, $A \equiv -J_W/J_{WW}$, and $H_k \equiv -J_{kW}/J_{WW}$.

Some insight in interpreting (8.16) can be gained by expressing A and H_k in terms of the utility and consumption functions: namely, by the implicit function theorem applied to (8.14),

$$A = -U_c \left/ \left(U_{cc} \frac{\partial c}{\partial W} \right) \right. > 0, \tag{8.17}$$

and

$$H_k = -\frac{\partial c}{\partial x_k} \left/ \frac{\partial c}{\partial W} \right. \lessgtr 0. \tag{8.18}$$

From (8.17) and (8.18), we can interpret the demand function of (8.16) as having two components. The first term, $A\sum_1^n v_{ij}(\alpha_j - r)$, is the usual demand function for a risky asset by a single-period mean-variance maximizer, where A is proportional to the reciprocal of the investor's absolute risk aversion.[25] The second term $\sum_1^m \sum_1^n H_k \sigma_j g_k \eta_{jk} v_{ij}$, reflects his demand for the asset as a vehicle to hedge against "unfavorable" shifts in the investment opportunity set. An "unfavorable" shift in the opportunity set variable x_k is defined as a change in x_k such that (future) consumption will fall for a given level of (future) wealth. An example of an unfavorable shift would be if $\partial c/\partial x_k < 0$ and x_k increased.

It can be shown, by differentiating (8.16) with respect to η_{ij}, that all risk-averse utility maximizers will attempt to hedge against such shifts in the sense that if $\partial c/\partial x_k < (>)0$, then, ceteris paribus, they will demand more of the ith asset, the more positively (negatively) correlated its return is with changes in x_k. Thus, if the ex post opportunity set is less favorable than was anticipated, the investor will expect to be compensated by a higher level of wealth through the positive correlation of the returns. Similarly, if ex post returns are lower, he will expect a more favorable investment environment.

Although this behavior implies a type of intertemporal consumption "smoothing," it is not the traditional type of maintenance of a constant level of consumption, but rather it reflects an attempt to minimize the (unanticipated) variability in consumption over time. A simple example will illustrate the point. Assume a single risky asset, a riskless asset with return r, and X a scalar (e.g., $X = r$). Further, require that $\alpha = r$. Standard portfolio analysis would show that a risk-averse investor would invest all his wealth in the riskless asset (i.e., $w = 0$). Consider the (instantaneous) variance of his consumption which, by Itô's Lemma,[2 6] can be written as $[c_x^2 g^2 + c_W^2 w^2 W^2 \sigma^2 + 2 c_x c_W w W g \sigma \eta]$, where subscripts denote partial derivatives of the (optimal) consumption function. Simple differentiation will show that this variance is minimized at $wW = -c_x \eta g/\sigma c_W$, which is exactly the demand given by (8.16), and for $c_x < 0$ and $\eta > 0$, $w > 0$. Thus, an intertemporal investor who currently faces a five percent interest rate and a possible interest rate of either two or ten percent next period will have portfolio demands different from a single-period maximizer in the same environment or an intertemporal maximizer facing a constant interest rate of five percent over time.

While we have derived explicit expressions for the portfolio demands and given some interpretation of their meaning, further analysis at this level of generality is difficult. While some further results could be gained by restricting the class of utility functions (see Merton [25, p. 402]), a more fruitful approach is to add some additional (simplifying) assumptions to restrict the structure of the opportunity set.

8.6 CONSTANT INVESTMENT OPPORTUNITY SET

The simplest form of the model occurs when the investment opportunity set is constant through time (i.e., α, r, and Ω are constants), and from (8.6), the distributions for price per share will be log-normal for all assets. This form of the model is examined in detail in Merton [25, p. 384-88], and hence, the main results are presented without proof.

In this case, the demand for the ith asset by the kth investor, (8.16), reduces to

$$w_i^k W^k = A^k \sum_1^n v_{ij}(\alpha_j - r) \qquad (i = 1,2, \ldots, n), \quad (8.19)$$

which is the same demand that a one-period[2][7] risk-averse mean-variance investor would have. If all investors agree on the investment opportunity set (homogeneous expectations), then the ratio of the demands for risky assets will be independent of preferences, and the same for all investors. Further, we have the following theorem.

Theorem 1:[2][8] Given n risky assets whose returns are log-normally distributed and a riskless asset, then (i) there exists a unique pair of efficient portfolios ("mutual funds") one containing only the riskless asset and the other only risky assets, such that, independent of preferences, wealth distribution, or time horizon, all investors will be indifferent between choosing portfolios from among the original $n + 1$ assets or from these two funds; (ii) the distribution of the return on the risky fund is log-normal; (iii) the proportion of the risky fund's assets invested in the kth asset is

$$\left. \sum_1^n v_{kj}(\alpha_j - r) \middle/ \sum_1^n \sum_1^n v_{ij}(\alpha_i - r) \right. \qquad (k = 1,2, \ldots, n).$$

Theorem 1 is the continuous-time version of the Markowitz-Tobin separation theorem and the holdings of the risky fund correspond to the optimal combination of risky assets (see Sharpe [39, p. 69]).

Using the condition that the market portfolio is efficient in equilibrium, it can be shown (see Merton [26]) that, for this version of the model, the equilibrium returns will satisfy

$$\alpha_i - r = \beta_i(\alpha_M - r) \qquad (i = 1,2, \ldots, n), \quad (8.20)$$

where $\beta_i \equiv \sigma_{iM}/\sigma_M^2$, σ_{iM} is the covariance of the return on the ith asset with the return on the market portfolio, and α_M is the expected return on the market portfolio. Equation (8.20) is the continuous-time analog to the security market line of the classical capital asset pricing model.

Hence, the additional assumption of a constant investment opportunity set is a sufficient condition for investors to behave as if they were single-period maximizers and for the equilibrium return relationship specified by the capital asset pricing model to obtain. Except for some singular cases, this assumption is also necessary.

8.7 GENERALIZED SEPARATION: A THREE-FUND THEOREM

Unfortunately, the assumption of a constant investment opportunity set is not consistent with the facts, since there exists at least one element of the opportunity set which is directly observable: namely, the interest rate, and it is definitely changing stochastically over time. The simplest form of the model consistent with this observation occurs if it is assumed that a single state variable is sufficient to describe changes in the opportunity set. We further assume that this variable is the interest rate (i.e., $\alpha_i = \alpha_i(r)$ and $\sigma_i = \sigma_i(r)$).

The interest rate has always been an important variable in portfolio theory, general capital theory, and to practitioners. It is observable, satisfies the condition of being stochastic over time, and while it is surely not the sole determinant of yields on other assets,[29] it is an important factor. Hence, one should interpret the effects of a changing interest rate in the forthcoming analysis in the way economists have generally done in the past: namely, as a single (instrumental) variable representation of shifts in the investment opportunity set. For example, $\partial c/\partial r$ is the change in consumption due to a change in the opportunity set for a fixed level of wealth.

This assumed, we can write the kth investor's demand function for the ith asset, (8.16), as

$$d_i^k = A^k \sum_1^n v_{ij}(\alpha_j - r) + H^k \sum_1^n v_{ij}\sigma_{jr} \qquad (i = 1, 2, \ldots, n), \quad (8.21)$$

where $d^k \equiv w^k W^k$; $H^k \equiv -(\partial c^k/\partial r)/(\partial c^k/\partial W^k)$, and σ_{jr} is the (instantaneous) covariance between the return on the jth asset and changes in the interest rate ($\equiv \rho_{jr}\sigma_j g$). By inspection of (8.21), the ratio of the demands for risky assets is a function of preferences, and hence, the standard separation theorem does not obtain. However, generalized separation (see [5]) does obtain. In particular, it will be shown that all investors' optimal portfolios can be represented as a linear combination of three mutual funds (portfolios).

Although not necessary for the theorem, it will throw light on the analysis to assume there exists an asset (by convention, the nth one) whose return is perfectly negatively correlated with changes in r, i.e., $\rho_{nr} = -1$. One such asset might be riskless (in terms of default), long-term bonds.[30] In this case, we can rewrite the covariance term σ_{jr} as

$$\sigma_{jr} = \rho_{jr}\sigma_j g, \qquad (8.22)$$

$$= -g(\rho_{jn}\sigma_j\sigma_n)/\sigma_n, \text{ because } \rho_{jr} = -\rho_{jn},$$

$$= -g\sigma_{jn}/\sigma_n,$$

where g is the standard deviation of the change in r. From (8.22), we can write the second term in the demand function (8.21), $\Sigma_1^n v_{ij}\sigma_{jr}$, as $-g(\Sigma_1^n v_{ij}\sigma_{jn})/\sigma_n$ which equals zero for $i \neq n$ and equals $(-g/\sigma_n)$ for $i = n$, because the v_{ij} are the elements of the inverse of the variance-covariance matrix of returns.[31] Hence, we can rewrite (8.21) in the simplified form,

$$d_i^k = A^k \sum_1^n v_{ij}(\alpha_j - r) \qquad\qquad (i = 1,2,\ldots,n-1), \qquad (8.23)$$

$$d_n^k = A^k \sum_1^n v_{nj}(\alpha_j - r) - gH^k/\sigma_n.$$

Theorem 2 ("Three Fund" Theorem): Given n risky assets and a riskless asset satisfying the conditions of this section, then there exist three portfolios ("mutual funds") constructed from these assets, such that (i) all risk-averse investors, who behave according to (8.8), will be indifferent between choosing portfolios from among the original $n + 1$ assets or from these three funds; (ii) the proportions of each fund's portfolio invested in the individual assets are purely "technological" (i.e., depend only on the variables in the investment opportunity set for individual assets and not on investor preferences); and (iii) the investor's demands for the funds do not require knowledge of the investment opportunity set for the individual assets nor of the asset proportions held by the funds.

Proof: Let the first fund hold the same proportions as the risky fund in Theorem 1: namely, $\delta_k = \Sigma_1^n v_{kj}(\alpha_j - r)/\Sigma_1^n \Sigma_1^n v_{ij}(\alpha_j - r)$, for $k = 1,2,\ldots,n$. Let the second fund hold only the nth asset and the third fund only the riskless asset. Let λ^k be the fraction of the kth investor's wealth invested in the ith fund, $i = 1,2,3 (\Sigma_1^3 \lambda^k = 1)$. To prove (i), we must show that there exists an allocation $(\lambda_1^k, \lambda_2^k)$ which exactly replicates the demand functions, (8.23), i.e., that

$$\lambda_1^k \delta_i = (A^k/W^k)\sum_1^n v_{ij}(\alpha_j - r) \qquad\qquad (i = 1,2,\ldots,n-1), \qquad (8.24)$$

$$\lambda_1^k \delta_n + \lambda_2^k = (A^k/W^k)\sum_1^n v_{nj}(\alpha_j - r) - gH^k/\sigma_n W^k.$$

From the definition of δ_j, the allocation $\lambda^k = (A^k/W^k)$ $\Sigma_1^n \Sigma_1^n v_{ij}(\alpha_j - r)$ and $\lambda_2^k = -gH^k/\sigma_n W^\pi$ satisfied (8.24). Part (ii) follows from the choice for the three funds. To prove (iii), we must show that investors will select this allocation, given only the knowledge of the (aggregated) investment opportunity set, i.e., given $(\alpha, \alpha_n, r, \sigma, \sigma_n, \rho, g)$ where α and σ^2 are expected return and variance on the first fund's portfolio and ρ is its covariance with the return on the second fund. From the definition of δ_j, it is straightforward to show that

$$(\alpha - r)/\sigma^2 = \Sigma_1^n \Sigma_1^n v_{ij}(\alpha_i - r)$$

and

$$\rho = \sigma(\alpha_n - r)/\sigma_n(\alpha - r).$$

The demand functions for the funds will be of the same form as (8.23) with $n = 2$, and the proportions derived from these equations are λ_1^k and λ_2^k where λ_1^k can be rewritten as $A^k(\alpha - r)/\sigma^2 W^k$ Q.E.D.

Theorem 2 is a decentralization theorem which states that if investors believe that professional portfolio managers' estimates of the distribution of returns are at least as good as any the investor might form, then the investment decision can be separated into two parts by the establishment of three financial intermediaries (mutual funds) to hold all individual assets and to issue shares of their own for purchase by individual investors. Funds one and three provide the "service" to investors of an (instantaneously) efficient, risk-return frontier while fund two allows investors to hedge against unfavorable intertemporal shifts in the frontier. Note that the demand for the second fund by the kth investor, $\lambda_2^k W^k$, will be $\gtrless 0$, depending on whether $\partial c^k/\partial r$ is $\lessgtr 0$, which is consistent with the hedging behavior discussed in the general case of Section 8.5.

8.8 THE EQUILIBRIUM YIELD RELATIONSHIP AMONG ASSETS

Given the demand functions (8.23), we now derive the equilibrium market clearing conditions for the model of Section 8.7, and from these, derive the equilibrium relationship between the expected return on an individual asset and the expected return on the market.

From (8.23), the aggregate demand functions, $D_i = \Sigma_1^K d_i^k$, can be written as

$$D_i = A \sum_1^n v_{ij}(\alpha_j - r) \qquad\qquad (i = 1, 2, \ldots, n-1), \qquad (8.25)$$

$$D_n = A \sum_1^n v_{nj}(\alpha_j - r) - Hg/\sigma_n,$$

where $A \equiv \sum_1^K A^k$ and $H \equiv \sum_1^K H^k$. If N_i is the number of shares supplied by the ith firm and if it is assumed that the asset market is *always* in equilibrium, then

$$N_i = \sum_1^K N_i^k, \qquad\qquad (8.26)$$

$$dN_i = \sum_1^K dN_i^k \qquad\qquad (i = 1, 2, \ldots, n+1).$$

Furthermore, $\sum_1^{n+1} N_i P_i = \sum_1^{n+1} D_i \equiv M$, where M is the (equilibrium) value of all assets, the market.

The equilibrium dynamics for market value can be written as

$$dM = \sum_1^{n+1} N_i dP_i + \sum_1^{n+1} dN_i(P_i + dP_i) \qquad\qquad (8.27)$$

$$= \sum_1^K dW^k$$

$$= \sum_1^{n+1} D_i dP_i/P_i + \sum_1^K (y^i - c^i) dt.$$

Hence, changes in the value of the market come about by capital gains on current shares outstanding (the first term) and by expansion of the total number of shares outstanding (the second term). To separate the two effects, we use the same technique employed to solve this problem for the individual firm: namely, let P_M be the price per "share" of the market portfolio and let N be the number of shares where $N P_M \equiv M$. Then, $dM = N\, dP_M + dN(P_M + dP_M)$, and P_M and N are defined by the stochastic differential equations

$$N\, dP_M \equiv \sum_1^{n+1} N_i dP_i, \qquad\qquad (8.28)$$

$$dN(P_M + dP_M) \equiv \sum_1^{n+1} dN_i(P_i + dP_i),$$

where, by construction, dP_M/P_M is the rate of return on the market (portfolio).

Substituting from (8.27) into (8.28) and using (8.11), we have

$$dN(P_M + dP_M) = \sum_1^K (y^i - c^i)dt, \qquad (8.29)$$

$$N\, dP_M = \sum_1^{n+1} D_i dP_i/P_i.$$

If $w_i \equiv N_i P_i/M = D_i/M$, the percentage contribution of the ith firm to total market value, then, from (8.6) and (8.29), the rate of return on the market can be written as

$$\frac{dP_M}{P_M} = \left[\sum_1^n w_j(\alpha_j - r) + r\right]dt + \sum_1^n w_j \sigma_j dz_j. \qquad (8.30)$$

Substituting $w_i M$ for D_i in (8.25), we can solve for the equilibrium expected returns on the individual assets:

$$\alpha_i - r = (M/A)\sum_1^n w_j \sigma_{ij} + (Hg/A\sigma_n)\sigma_{in} \qquad (i = 1,2,\ldots,n). \qquad (8.31)$$

As with any asset, we can define $\alpha_M (\equiv \sum_1^n w_j(\alpha_j - r) + r)$, $\sigma_{iM}(\equiv \sum_1^n w_j \sigma_{ij})$, and $\sigma_M (\equiv \sum_1^n w_j \sigma_{jM})$ as the (instantaneous) expected return, covariance, and variance of the market portfolio. Then (8.31) can be rewritten as

$$\alpha_i - r = (M/A)\sigma_{iM} + (Hg/A\sigma_n)\sigma_{in} \qquad (i = 1,2,\ldots,n), \qquad (8.32)$$

and multiplying (8.32) by w_i and summing, we have

$$\alpha_M - r = (M/A)\sigma_M^2 + (Hg/A\sigma_n)\sigma_{Mn}. \qquad (8.33)$$

Noting that the nth asset satisfies (8.32), we can use it together with (8.33) to rewrite (8.32) as

$$\alpha_i - r = \frac{\sigma_i[\rho_{iM} - \rho_{in}\rho_{nM}]}{\sigma_M(1-\rho_{nM}^2)}(\alpha_M - r) + \frac{\sigma_i[\rho_{in} - \rho_{iM}\rho_{nM}]}{\sigma_n(1-\rho_{Mn}^2)}(\alpha_n - r)$$

$$(i = 1,2,\ldots,n-1). \qquad (8.34)$$

Equation (8.34) states that, in equilibrium, investors are compensated in terms of expected return, for bearing market (systematic) risk, and for bearing the risk of unfavorable (from the point of view of the aggregate) shifts in the investment opportunity set; and it is a natural generalization of the security market line of the classical capital asset pricing model. Note that if a security has no market risk (i.e., $\beta_i = 0 = \rho_{iM}$), its expected return will not be equal to the riskless rate as forecast by the usual model.

Under what conditions will the security market plane Equation (8.34) reduce to the (continuous-time) classical security market line, Equation (8.20)? From inspection of the demand Equations (8.21), appropriately aggregated, the conditions are

$$H = \sum_{1}^{K} - (\partial c^k/\partial r)/(\partial c^k/\partial W^k) \equiv 0 \qquad (8.35a)$$

or

$$\sigma_{ir} \equiv 0 \qquad\qquad (i = 1,2,\ldots,n). \qquad (8.35b)$$

There is no obvious reason to believe that (8.35a) should hold unless $\partial c_k/\partial r \equiv 0$ for each investor, and the only additive utility function for which this is so is the Bernoulli logarithmic one.[32] Condition (8.35b) could obtain in two ways: $g \equiv 0$, i.e., the interest rate is nonstochastic, which is not so; or $\rho_{ir} \equiv 0$, i.e., all assets' returns are uncorrelated with changes in the interest rate. While this condition is possible, it would not be a true equilibrium state.

Suppose that by a quirk of nature, $\rho_{ir} \equiv 0$ for all available real assets. Then, since the nth asset does not exist, (8.34) reduces to (8.20). Consider constructing a "man-made" security (e.g., a long-term bond) which is perfectly negatively correlated with changes in the interest rates, and hence, by assumption, not correlated with any other asset or the market (i.e., $\beta_n = 0$). Since $D_n = 0$, we have, from (8.25), that $(\alpha_n - r) = Hg\sigma_n \neq 0$, if $g \neq 0$ and $H \neq 0$. Thus, even though security n has a zero beta, investors will pay a premium (relative to the riskless rate) to other investors for creating this security.

An implication of this analysis for the theory of the term structure of interest rates, is that long-term, riskless bonds will not satisfy the expectations hypothesis ($\alpha_n = r$), even if they have no market risk. The premium charged is not a liquidity premium, and it will be either positive or negative depending on the sign of H. These results are consistent with the "habitat" theory (see [28]), if one interprets habitat as a stronger (or weaker) preference to hedge against changes in future investment opportunities.

8.9 EMPIRICAL EVIDENCE

Although the model has not been formally tested, we can do some preliminary analysis using the findings of Black, Jensen, and Scholes (BJS) [3] and some later, unpublished work of Scholes [37]. As mentioned earlier, they found that portfolios constructed to have zero covariance with the market (i.e., $\beta = 0$) had average returns that significantly exceeded the riskless rate which suggests that there is (at least) another factor besides the market that systematically affects the returns on securities. They call this second factor the "beta factor" because an individual security's covariance with it is a function of the security's beta. In particular, high-beta ($\beta > 1$) stocks had negative correlation and low-beta ($\beta < 1$) stocks had positive correlation. We can summarize the BJS specification and empirical findings as follows:

$$\alpha_i - r = \beta(\alpha_M - r) + \gamma_i(\alpha_0 - r), \qquad (8.36)$$

where α_0 is the expected return on the "zero-beta" portfolio, and

$$\alpha_0 > r; \qquad (8.37a)$$

$$\gamma_i = \gamma_i(\beta_i) \text{ with } \gamma_i(1) = 0, \text{ and } \partial\gamma_i/\partial\beta_i < 0. \qquad (8.37b)$$

While the finding of a second factor is consistent with the a priori specification of our model, it cannot be said that their specific findings are in agreement with the model without some further specification of the effect of a shift in r on the investment opportunity set. However, if a shift in r is an instrumental variable for a shift in capitalization rates generally, then an argument can be made that the two are in agreement.

The plan is to show that qualitative characteristics of the coefficient $(\rho_{in} - \rho_{iM}\rho_{nM})\sigma_i/\sigma_n(1 - \rho_{nM}^2)$ in (8.34) as a function of β_i would be the same as γ_i in (8.37b), and that the empirical characteristics of the zero-beta portfolio are similar to those of a portfolio of long term bonds.

If we take the classical security market line $\alpha_i = r + \beta_i\lambda$, where $\lambda \equiv (\alpha_M - r)$, as a reasonable approximation to the relationship among capitalization rates, α_i, then we can compute the logarithmic elasticity of α_i with respect to r as a function of β_i, to be

$$\psi(\beta_i) \equiv r(1 + \beta_i\lambda')/(r + \beta_i\lambda), \qquad (8.38)$$

where $\lambda' \equiv \partial\lambda/\partial r$, the change in the slope of the security market line with a change in r. From (8.27) we have that this elasticity is almost certainly a monotone decreasing function of β_i since $\psi'(\beta_i) \equiv \partial\psi/\partial\beta_i < 0$ if $\psi(1) < 1$.[33]

If we write the value of firm i as $V_i \equiv \overline{X}_i/\alpha_i$ where $\overline{X}_i$ is the "long-run" expected earnings and α_i, the rate at which they are capitalized, then the percentage change in firm value due to a change in r can be written as

$$\left(\frac{dV_i}{V_i}\right)_r \equiv \left[\frac{\partial\overline{X}_i}{\partial r}\bigg/\overline{X}_i - \frac{\partial\alpha_i}{\partial r}\bigg/\alpha_i\right] dr. \qquad (8.39)$$

If we neglect, as second-order, the effect of a shift in r on expected future earnings, then the residual effect on return due to a change in r, after taking out the common market factor, will be a systematic function of β_i:

$$d\epsilon(\beta_i) \equiv \left(\frac{dV_i}{V_i}\right)_r - \beta_i\left(\frac{dV_M}{V_M}\right)_r \qquad (8.40)$$

$$= -\psi(\beta_i)\frac{dr}{r} + \beta_i\psi(1)\frac{dr}{r}$$

$$= -\phi(\beta_i)\frac{dr}{r}$$

where $\phi(\beta_i) \equiv \psi(\beta_i) - \beta_i\psi(1)$ satisfies $\phi(1) = 0$ and $\phi'(\beta_i) < 0$. From (8.40), the correlation coefficient between $d\epsilon$ and dr, $\rho_{\epsilon r}$, will satisfy

$$\rho_{\epsilon r} \lessgtr 0 \text{ as } \beta_i \lessgtr 1. \qquad (8.41)$$

From the definition of $d\epsilon$ in (8.40), $\rho_{\epsilon r}$ is the partial correlation coefficient, $\rho_{ir} - \rho_{iM}\rho_{rM}$. By definition the nth asset in (8.34) is perfectly negatively correlated with changes in r. Hence (8.41) can be rewritten as

$$\rho_{in} - \rho_{iM}\rho_{nM} \lessgtr 0 \text{ as } \beta_i \lessgtr 1. \qquad (8.42)$$

Hence the coefficient of $(\alpha_n - r)$ in (8.34) could be expected to have the same properties as γ_i in (8.36) and (8.37b).

It still remains to be determined whether the zero-beta portfolio is a proxy for our long-term bond portfolio. Since there are no strong theroetical grounds for $(\alpha_n - r)$ to be positive[34] and since the zero-beta portfolio is an empirical construct, we resort to an indirect empirical argument based on the findings of BJS and Scholes.

Since Scholes found the correlation between the market portfolio and the bond portfolio, ρ_{Mn}, to be close to zero and the correlation between the zero-beta portfolio and the bond portfolio to be significantly positive, it then follows from (8.36) that one would expect to find $(\alpha_n - r)$ significantly positive.

While the analysis of this section can only be called preliminary, the model specification of Section 8.7 does seem to be more consistent with the data than the capital asset pricing model.[35]

8.10 CONCLUSION

An intertemporal model of the capital market has been developed which is consistent with both the expected utility maxim and the limited liability of assets. It was shown that the equilibrium relationships among expected returns specified by the classical capital asset pricing model will obtain only under very special additional assumptions. Whether the special form of the general model presented in Sections 8.7-8.9 will explain the empirical discrepancies found in the BJS study is an empirical question as yet unanswered. However, whether it does or not, the main purposes were to illustrate how testable specifications can be generated from the model and to induce those who do it best to pursue further empirical testing.

The model is robust in the sense that it can be extended in an obvious way to include effects other than shifts in the investment opportunity set. Two important factors not considered are wage income and many consumption goods whose relative prices are changing over time. In a more complete model the three-fund theorem of Section 8.7 will generalize to an m-fund theorem. Although there was no discussion of the supply side, given a micro theory of the firm, (8.1), (8.2), and (8.29) could be used to close the model.

NOTES TO SECTION EIGHT

1. This chapter is a substantial revision of parts of [24] presented in various forms at the NBER Conference on Decision Rules and Uncertainty, Massachu-

setts Institute of Technology, February, 1971, and at the Wells Fargo Conference on Capital Market Theory, San Francisco, July, 1971. I am grateful to the participants for helpful comments. I thank Myron Scholes and Fischer Black for many useful discussions, and Robert K. Merton for editorial assistance. Aid from the National Science Foundation is gratefully acknowledged.

2. See Sharpe [38 and 39], Lintner [19 and 20], and Mossin [29]. While more general and elegant than the capital asset pricing model in many ways, the general equilibrium model of Arrow [1] and Debreu [8, Ch.7] has not had the same impact, principally because of its empirical intractability and the rather restrictive assumption that there exist as many securities as states of nature (see Stiglitz [41]). The "growth optimum" model of Hakansson [15] can be formulated as an equilibrium model although it is consistent with expected utility maximization only if all investors have logarithmic utility functions (see Samuelson [36] and Merton and Samuelson [27]). However, Roll [32] has shown that the model fits the data about as well as the capital asset pricing model.

3. For academic references, see Sharpe [39] and Jensen [17] survey article. For a summary of the model's impact on the financial community, see [42].

4. See Borch [4], Feldstein [12], and Hakansson [15]. For a list of the conditions necessary for the validity of mean-variance, see Samuelson [34 and 35].

5. See Sharpe [39, pp. 77-78] for a list of the assumptions required.

6. Friend and Blume [14] also found that the empirical capital market line was "too flat." Their explanation was that the borrowing-lending assumption of the model is violated. Black [2] provides an alternative explanation based on the assumption of no riskless asset. Other less important, stylized facts in conflict with the model are that investors do not hold the same relative proportions of risky assets, and short sales occur in spite of unfavorable institutional requirements.

7. Fama recognizes the restrictive nature of the assumptions as evidenced by discussion in Fama and Miller [11].

8. A simple example of the expectations theory of the term structure will illustrate the point. It is well known (see, e.g., Stiglitz [40]) that bonds cannot be priced to equate expected returns over *all* holding periods. Hence, one must select a "fundamental" period (usually one "trading" period, our h) to equate expected returns. Clearly, the prices which satisfy this relationship will be a function of h. Similarly, the demand functions of investors will depend on h. We have chosen for our interval the smallest h possible. For processes which are well defined for every h, it can be shown that the limit of every discrete-time solution as h tends to zero, will be the continuous solutions derived here (see Samuelson [35]).

9. What is "small" depends on the particular process being modeled. For the orders of magnitude typically found for the moments (mean, variance, skewness, etc.) of annual returns on common stocks, daily intervals ($h = 1/270$) are small. The essential test is: for what h does the distribution of returns become sufficiently "compact" in the Samuelson [35] sense?

10. It is assumed that there are no economies or diseconomies to the

"packaging" of assets (i.e., no "synergism"). Hence, any "real" firm holding more than one type of asset will be priced as if it held a portfolio of the "firms" in the text. Similarly, it is assumed that all financial leveraging and other capital structure differences are carried out by investors (possibly through financial intermediaries).

11. In an intertemporal model, it is necessary to define two quantities, such as number of shares and price per share, to distinguish between the two ways in which a firm's value can change. The return part, (1), reflects new additions to wealth, while (2)reflects a reallocation of capital among alternative assets. The former is important to the investor in selecting his portfolio while the latter is important in (determining) maintaining equilibrium through time. The definition of price per share used here (except for cash dividends) corresponds to the way open-ended, mutual funds determine asset value per share, and seems to reflect accurately the way the term is normally used in a portfolio context.

12. While the analysis is not an equilibrium one in the strict sense because we do not develop the supply side, the derived model is as much an equilibrium model as the "exchange" model of Mossin [29]. Because his is a one-period model, he could take supplies as fixed.

13. While it is not necessary to assume that the processes are independent of calendar time, nothing of content is lost by it. However, when a state variable is declared as constant in the text, we really mean nonstochastic. Thus, the term "constant" is used to describe variables which are deterministic functions of time.

14. While a similar analysis can be performed for Poisson-type processes (see Kushner [18] and Merton [25]) and for the subordinated processes of Press [30] and Clark [6], most of the results derived under the continuity assumption will not obtain in these cases.

15. It is sufficient to assume that the $y(t)$ are uncorrelated and that the higher order moments are $0(1/\sqrt{h})$. This assumption is consistent with a weak form of the efficient markets hypothesis of Samuelson [33] and Fama [10]. See Merton and Samuelson [27] for further discussion.

16. While the Gaussian assumption is not necessary for the analysis, the generality gained by not making the assumption is more apparent than real, since it can be shown that all continuous diffusion processes can be described as functions of Brownian motion (see Feller [13, p. 326] and Itô and Mc-Kean [16]).

17. See Merton [25] for a discussion of Itô processes in a portfolio context. For a general discussion of stochastic differential equations of the Itô type, see Itô and McKean [16], McKean [22], and Kushner [18].

18. It is assumed that the dynamics of α and σ reflect the changes in the supply of shares as well as other factors such as new technical developments. The particular derivation of the dz_i in the text implies that the ρ_{ij} are constants. However, the analysis could be generalized by appending an additional set of dynamics to include changes in the ρ_{ij}.

19. Since these are sufficient statistics, if there are $n + 1$ assets and n is finite, then our assumption of a finite vector for X is satisfied.

20. "Distinct" means that none of the assets' returns can be written as an

(instantaneous) linear combination of the other assets' returns. Hence, the instantaneous variance-covariance matrix of returns, $\Omega = [\sigma_{ij}]$, is nonsingular.

21. Because the study is primarily interested in finding equilibrium conditions for the asset markets, the model assumes a single consumption good. The model could be generalized by making c^k a vector and introducing as state variables the relative prices. While the analysis would be similar to the one-good case, there would be systematic effects on the portfolio demands reflecting hedging behavior against unfavorable shifts in relative consumption goods prices (i.e., in the consumption opportunity set).

22. See Merton [25] for a derivation of (8.9).

23. The analysis would be the same with wage income, provided that investors can issue shares against future income, since we can always redefine wealth as including capitalized future wage income. However, since institutionally this cannot be done, the introduction of wage income will cause systematic effects on the portfolio and consumption decisions.

24. See Merton [23 and 25].

$$J(W,t,X) \equiv \max E_t \left\{ \int_t^T U(c,s)ds + B[W(T),T] \right\}$$

and is called the "derived" utility of wealth function. Substituting from (8.14) and (8.15) to eliminate w_i and c in (8.13) makes (8.13) a partial differential equation for J, subject to the boundary condition $J(W,T,X) = B(W,T)$. Having solved for J, we then substitute for J and its derivatives in (8.14) and (8.15) to find the optimal rules (w_i, c).

25. See Merton [26, Equation (36)].

26. Itô's Lemma is the analog to the Fundamental Theorem of the calculus for Itô processes. See Merton [25, p. 375] for a brief description and McKean [22, p. 32] for a formal proof.

27. Of course, since "one period" is an instant, a meaningful interpretation is that investors behave myopically.

28. Theorem 1 is stated and proved in a more general form, including the possibility of no riskless asset, in Merton [25, p. 384]. The uniqueness of the two funds is ensured by the requirement that one fund hold only the riskless asset and the other only risky assets, and that both funds be efficient. Otherwise, the funds are unique only up to a non-singular, linear transformation. A further requirement is that

$$r < \left. \sum_1^n \sum_1^n v_{ij}\alpha_j \middle/ \sum_1^n \sum_1^n v_{ij} \right.$$

However, since this is a necessary condition for equilibrium, it is assumed to be satisfied. See Merton [26] for a complete discussion of this point.

29. The reader should not interpret this statement as implying a causal relationship between interest rates and yields. All that is questioned is whether

there exists an implicit functional relationship between the interest rate and other yields.

30. We only interpret this asset as a long-term bond as a conceptual device. Although long-term bonds will be highly correlated with short rate changes, it is quite likely that they are not perfectly correlated.

31. I am indebted to Fischer Black for pointing out this simplification.

32. Hence (8.20) would be the correct specification for the equilibrium relationships among expected returns in the "growth optimum" model even when the investment opportunity set is not constant through time.

33. $\psi(1) \geq 1$ would imply that $\lambda'/\lambda \geq 1/r$ which, for typical values of r, would imply a very large, positive increase in the slope of the security market line. It is contended that such a shift would be highly unlikely.

34. One could argue that $\alpha_n > r$ on the grounds that current consumption is a normal good and, hence, $\partial c/\partial r < 0$ for most people. Also, the existence of wage income would tend to force $\alpha_n > r$. Finally, in a number of studies of the term structure, investigators have found positive premiums on long-term bonds, implying that $\alpha_n > r$.

35. M. Scholes is in the process of testing the model of Section 8.7. D. Rie [31] has also examined the effect of capitalization rate changes on the classical capital asset pricing model.

REFERENCES

1. Arrow, K.J.: "The Role of Securities in the Optimal Allocation of Risk Bearing," *Review of Economic Studies*, 31 (1964), 91-96.

2. Black, F.: "Capital Market Equilibrium with Restricted Borrowing," *Journal of Business*, 45 (1972), 444-455.

3. Black, F., M.C. Jensen, and M. Scholes: "The Capital Asset Pricing Model: Some Empirical Tests," in *Studies in the Theory of Capital Markets*, M.C. Jensen, ed. New York: Praeger Publishers, 1972.

4. Borch, K.: "A Note on Uncertainty and Indifference Curves," *Review of Economic Studies*, 36 (1969), 1-4.

5. Cass, D., and J.E. Stiglitz: "The Structure of Investor Preferences and Asset Returns, and Separability in Portfolio Allocation: A Contribution to the Pure Theory of Mutual Funds," *Journal of Economic Theory*, 2 (1970), 122-160.

6. Clark, P.K.: "A Subordinated Stochastic Process Model with Finite Variance for Speculative Prices," *Econometrica* 41 (1973), 135-155.

7. Cox, D.A., and H.D. Miller: *The Theory of Stochastic Processes*. New York: John Wiley, 1968.

8. Debreu, G.: *Theory of Value: An Axiomatic Analysis of Economic Equilibrium*. New York: John Wiley, 1959.

9. Fama, E.F.: "Multiperiod Consumption-Investment Decisions," *American Economic Review*, 60 (1970), 163-174.

10. _____ : "Efficient Capital Markets: A Review of Theory and Empirical Work," *Journal of Finance*, 25 (1970), 383-417.

11. Fama, E.F., and M.H. Miller: *The Theory of Finance*, New York: Holt, Rhinehart, Winston, 1972.

12. Feldstein, M.S.: "Mean-Variance Analysis in the Theory of Liquidity Preference and Portfolio Selection," *Review of Economic Studies*, 36 (1969), 5-12.

13. Feller, W.: *An Introduction to Probability Theory and Its Applications.* Volume 2. New York: John Wiley, 1966.

14. Friend, I., and M. Blume: "Measurement of Portfolio Performance under Uncertainty," *American Economic Review*, 60 (1970), 561-575.

15. Hakansson, N.H.: "Capital Growth and the Mean-Variance Approach to Portfolio Selection," *Journal of Financial and Quantitative Analysis*, 6 (1971), 517-557.

16. Itô, K., and H.P. McKean, Jr.: *Diffusion Processes and Their Sample Paths.* New York: Academic Press, 1964.

17. Jensen, M.C.: "Capital Markets: Theory and Evidence," *Bell Journal of Economics and Management Science*, 2 (1972), 357-398.

18. Kushner, H.J.: *Stochastic Stability and Control.* New York: Academic Press, 1967.

19. Lintner, J.: "The Valuation of Risk Assets and the Selection of Risky Investments in Stock Portfolios and Capital Budgets," *Review of Economics and Statistics*, 47 (1965), 13-37.

20. _____ : "Security Prices, Risk and Maximal Gains from Diversification," *Journal of Finance*, 20 (1965), 587-615.

21. Markowitz, H.: *Portfolio Selection: Efficient Diversification of Investment.* New York: John Wiley, 1959.

22. McKean, H.P., Jr.: *Stochastic Integrals.* New York: Academic Press, 1969.

23. Merton, R.C.: "Lifetime Portfolio Selection under Uncertainty: The Continuous-Time Case," *Review of Economics and Statistics*, 51 (1969), 247-257.

24. _____ : "A Dynamic General Equilibrium Model of the Asset Market and Its Application to the Pricing of the Capital Structure of the Firm," Working Paper 497-70, Sloan School of Management, Massachusetts Institute of Technology, December, 1970.

25. _____ : "Optimum Consumption and Portfolio Rules in a Continuous-time Model," *Journal of Economic Theory*, 3 (1971), 373-413.

26. _____ : "An Analytic Derivation of the Efficient Portfolio Frontier," *Journal of Financial and Quantitative Analysis*, 7 (1972), 1851-1872.

27. Merton, R.C., and P.A. Samuelson: "Fallacy of the Asymptotic Log-Normal Approximation in Portfolio Decision Making Over Many Periods," in *Risk and Return in Finance.* I. Friend and J. Bicksler, eds. Cambridge: Ballinger, 1976.

28. Modigliani, F., and C.R. Sutch: "Innovations in Interest Rate Policy," *American Economic Review*, 56 (1966), 178-197.

29. Mossin, J.: "Equilibrium in a Capital Asset Market," *Econometrica*, 34 (1966), 768-783.

30. Press, S.J.: "A Compound Events Model for Security Prices," *Journal of Business*, 40 (1967), 317-335.

31. Rie, D.: "Single Parameter Risk Measures and Multiple Sources of Risk: A Re-Examination of the Data Based on Changes in Determinants of Price Over

Time." Working Paper #14-72, Rodney L. White Center for Financial Research, Wharton School of Finance and Commerce, University of Pennsylvania.

32. Roll, R.: "Some Preliminary Evidence on the 'Growth Optimum' Model," Working Paper 3-71-2, Graduate School of Industrial Administration, Carnegie-Mellon University, July, 1971.

33. Samuelson, P.A.: "Proof that Properly Anticipated Prices Fluctuate Randomly," *Industrial Management Review*, 6 (1965), 41-49.

34. _____ : "General Proof that Diversification Pays," *Journal of Financial and Quantitative Analysis*, 2 (1967).

35. _____ : "The Fundamental Approximation Theorem of Portfolio Analysis in Terms of Means, Variances, and Higher Moments," *Review of Economic Studies*, 37 (1970), 537-542.

36. _____ : "The 'Fallacy' of Maximizing the Geometric Mean in Long Sequences of Investing or Gambling," *Proceedings of the National Academy of Sciences*, 68 (1971).

37. Scholes, M.: "The Relationship Between the Returns on Bonds and the Returns on Common Stocks," Mimeograph, Massachusetts Institute of Technology, November, 1971.

38. Sharpe, W.F.: "Capital Asset Prices: A Theory of Market Equilibrium under Conditions of Risk," *Journal of Finance*, 19 (1964), 425-442.

39. _____ : *Portfolio Theory and Capital Markets*. New York: McGraw-Hill, 1970.

40. Stiglitz, J.E.: "A Consumption-Oriented Theory of the Demand for Financial Assets and the Term-Structure of Interest Rates," *Review of Economic Studies*, 37 (1970), 321-351.

41. _____ : "Some Aspects of the Pure Theory of Corporate Finance, Bankruptcies, and Take-Overs," *Bell Journal of Economics and Management Science* 2 (1972), 458-482.

42. Welles, C.: "The Beta Revolution: Learning to Live with Risk," *Institutional Investor* (1971).

Return, Risk, and Arbitrage

Stephen A. Ross*

One of the strongest statements that can be made in positive economics is the assertion that if two riskless assets offer rates of return of ρ and ρ', then (in the absence of transactions costs):

$$\rho = \rho'. \tag{9.1}$$

As an arbitrage condition, this equality of rates of return may be expected to hold in all but the most profound disequilibrium. If economic agents can both borrow and lend at the rates ρ and ρ', then infinite profits are envisioned if rates diverge and (9.1) must obtain to prevent such arbitrage possibilities. Furthermore, even when the rates are both only lending rates, for example, if (9.1) did not hold then there would be no (gross) demand for the asset with the lower rate of return. The introduction of risk, however, alters these strong conclusions. Under neoclassical theory if an asset is risky its expected return will equal the riskless rate plus a premium to compensate the holder of the asset for bearing risk. The explanations that have been advanced in an effort to understand this premium have focused on somewhat special forms of equilibrium theories and have essentially abandoned the robust sort of argument that supports (9.1). The intent of this chapter is to develop an arbitrage theory for risky

*This work was supported by a grant from the Rodney L. White Center for Financial Research at the University of Pennsylvania and by National Science Foundation grant GS-35780. The author is grateful to Marshall Blume and Irwin Friend for helpful comments.

assets analogous to that for riskless assets, and, in so doing, to analyze the nature of risk premiums.

There are at present two major theoretical frameworks for the analysis of markets for risky assets; the state space preference approach and, the mean variance model and its variants. The arbitrage model which we will develop is a third approach to capital market theory, empirically distinguishable from the mean variance theory and more directly related to the state space approach. While formally all models may be viewed as special cases of the state space preference framework, it is in the restrictions imposed either on preferences or distributions that the empirical content of the various theories lie. The mean variance equilibrium model of Treynor, Sharpe and Lintner, for example, is derived by either assuming quadratic preferences or that assets are multivariate normally distributed. Neither of these assumptions, however, is particularly appealing on intuitive economic grounds; normality has only an inappropriate (and careless) application of the central limit theorem to recommend it and quadratic utility functions are implausible for any agents, let alone for all of them. We will examine the mean variance model and the assumptions of normality and quadratic preferences in detail in the sections below.

Much recent work has focused on the implications of alternative restrictions on the nature of investor preferences. Yet to obtain useful capital market results by restricting preferences requires severe assumptions on the homogeneity of investors' attitudes towards risk (as well as returns). A priori, it would seem more acceptable to place restrictions on probability structures rather than on preferences if only because there is a single ex post realization and a large body of commonly held information. It is the consequences of this approach that we will explore.[1]

In Section 9.1 a brief but unusual development of the mean variance capital market equilibrium model is given including the role of the zero-beta portfolio as a substitute for a riskless asset. It is to be emphasized that this model is a consequence of special restrictions on the state space preference framework. Section 9.2 introduces and develops the basic alternative model, the arbitrage model. Section 9.3 extends the general state space preference model developed by Arrow and Debreu and extended by Hirschleifer, Diamond, and others. With the aid of some familiar results from the theory of cones, we will examine the full implications of the assertion that a market for risky assets is in equilibrium in the absence of any of the usual constraints on preferences or distributions. In Section 9.4 the arbitrage model's relation to the mean variance model and the underlying state space framework is examined in detail. Section 9.4 also presents a somewhat novel derivation of the mean variance model by the use of the arbitrage theory. Section 9.5 summarizes and concludes the chapter.

SECTION 9.1

The mean variance model of capital market equilibrium represents a very strong restriction on the structure of asset returns across states. In particular, to develop the model we assume that all agents subjectively, and ex ante, view the n assets as being jointly normally distributed with a vector of means, E, and covariance matrix V.[2] It is well known (see, e.g., Sharpe [1970]) and easy to show that the feasible set of means, m, and standard deviations, σ, attainable on portfolios formed from the n assets has the shape illustrated in Figure 9-1. Formally, this feasible set is defined as

$$F \equiv \Big\{ <m, \sigma> \mid \text{for some } \alpha \text{ with } \alpha'e = 1, \, m = \alpha'E, \, \sigma^2 = \alpha'V\alpha \Big\}, \tag{9.2}$$

and its efficient boundary is defined as the southeast boundary of F.[3] In the definition the vector α denotes a portfolio whose i^{th} component, α_i, is the proportion of wealth placed in the ith asset. If a riskless asset with a sure return, ρ, is introduced, the efficient frontier including portfolios formed with this asset is the line tangent to F as shown.

By assumption, agents possess risk averse non-Neumann Morgenstern utility functions and will, therefore, choose efficient points. Figure 9-1 illustrates the familiar separation property (see Markowitz or Tobin) in the presence of a riskless asset. Since the efficient frontier is a line, the market line in $<m, \sigma>$ space, all investors will choose their portfolios as simple combinations of investment (or borrowing) in the riskless asset and a single portfolio of risky assets. In equilibrium, then, this efficient portfolio must consist of risky assets held in proportion to their total dollar value, i.e., it must be the market portfolio obtained by purchasing all variable risky assets.[4] Conversely, the market portfolio must be efficient, it is the minimum variance portfolio of risky assets that attains the market return, E_m.

Let $\tilde{x} = (\tilde{x}_1, \ldots, \tilde{x}_n)$ denote the vector of random returns on the n risky assets (represented as the columns of the state space tableau). In market equilibrium the famous security line equation takes the form

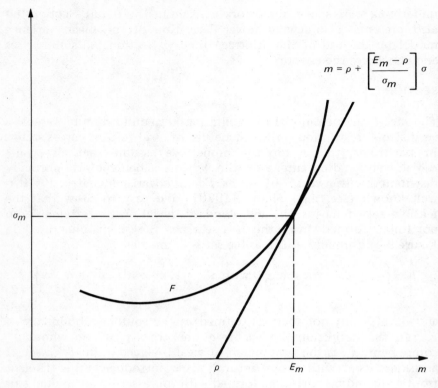

$$m = \rho + \left[\frac{E_m - \rho}{\sigma_m} \right] \sigma$$

Figure 9-1.

$$E_i = \rho + \lambda b_i; \quad i = 1, \ldots n, \tag{9.3}$$

where

$$b_i \equiv \frac{\mathrm{cov}\left\{ \tilde{x}_i, \tilde{x}_m \right\}}{\sigma_m^2} = (V\alpha_m)_i \tag{9.4}$$

and

$$\lambda \equiv E_m - \rho, \tag{9.5}$$

with α_m denoting the market portfolio, $E_m = \alpha'_m E$ and $\sigma^2_m = \alpha'_m V \alpha_m$ being, respectively, the mean and variance of the random market return, $\tilde{x}_m$. Equation (9.3) is simply the first order condition for the mean variance efficiency of the market portfolio. Once we identify the market portfolio as efficient the security line Equation (9.3) follows immediately—nothing further is required. This observation provides a clue to weakening the underlying assumptions. It is not difficult to show, for example, that since the market portfolio will still be efficient, the security line Equation (9.3), will hold in the absence of a riskless asset. The constant, ρ, is now interpreted as the zero-beta return; it is the return on all assets or portfolios uncorrelated with the market portfolio.

The simple and intuitive equilibrium linear relation between return, E_i, and the beta coefficient, b_i, accounts for much of the popularity of the mean variance model. The risk on an asset is completely described by its covariance with the market portfolio, or by the ratio of its covariance to the variance of the market, the beta coefficient, b_i; the risk premium is simply proportional to the beta coefficient. As asset's risk is priced away in individual portfolios except for that component of risk that is market dependent. As asset that is positively correlated must earn a risk premium, one that is negatively correlated is so valuable as a hedge that it will be priced at a discount from the riskless rate and, perhaps most strikingly, an asset with a zero beta coefficient—despite its uncertainty as measured, for example, by its variance—will be priced at the riskless rate of return.

The exact meaning of the security relation is not always made clear in the literature. It is not important that (9.3) is linear, what is important is that the market portfolio is an observable economic variable, the totality of wealth held at risk, and that it plays a pivotal role in the theory. The linearity of (9.3) is only of interest when it is understood that correlation with the market portfolio is the proper measure of risk in equilibrium. In fact, it is easy to show that unless arbitrage is possible there always exists some portfolio α such that:

$$E_i = \rho + \lambda (V\alpha)_i, \tag{9.6}$$

where λ is a constant chosen so that $\alpha'e = 1$.[5]

However appealing the linear relation (9.6) may appear, then, it is nearly devoid of economic content. In fact, given any collection of random variables with a nonsingular V, (9.6) will be satisfied for some portfolio, α, whether we are in equilibrium or not. As such, (9.6) is empty of any empirical content as well. The result (9.6) only becomes meaningful when something can be said about the nature of α.[6]

When we add the assumption that returns are jointly normal, or that utility functions are quadratic, the portfolio α can be shown to be the market portfolio, and the security line Equation (9.3) constitutes an empirically significant restriction on asset returns.[7] To put the matter somewhat differently, with given expectations, E, and a given covariance matrix, V (or given dependence of E and V on prices) then (9.6) can be solved for the market portfolio and, therefore, relative prices. This is a simultaneous equilibrium system and it would, for example, be antithetical to its spirit to impute to it any directional causality as in a statement such as, "the risk premium is *determined* by covariance with the market."

SECTION 9.2

There have been an enormous number of empirical studies directed either at testing the security line Equation (9.3) or applying it. The commonest approach is to assume that ex post returns are generated by some stochastic relation, most simply chosen as

$$\tilde{x}_i = E_i + \beta_i \tilde{\delta} + \tilde{\epsilon}_i; \quad i = 1, \ldots, n, \tag{9.7}$$

where $\tilde{\epsilon} = <\tilde{\epsilon}_1, \ldots, \tilde{\epsilon}_n>$ is a mean zero noise vector, E_i is a constant term representing the ex ante expected return, β_i is the ex ante beta coefficient and δ is a mean zero common factor representing the deviations of the market return from its trend. Equation (9.7) is a simple linear regression and is illustrated in Figure 9-2. If a time series (multiple) regression is run on (9.7) the resulting coefficients $<\hat{E}_i>$ and $<\hat{\beta}_i>$ will be estimates of the ex ante expected return and the beta coefficient respectively. It can be shown that $\tilde{\delta}$ will approximate the market portfolio and the ex ante beta coefficient, β_i, will approximate the ex ante coefficient, $b_i \equiv \sigma_{im}^2/\sigma_m^2$, in the security market line (9.3). Ignoring some basic and subtle statistical difficulties, it is now possible to consider a test of the linearity of the relation between $\hat{E}_i$ and $\hat{\beta}_i$ as a test of the mean variance capital model.[8] The consequences of such a test, performed by Blume and Friend on NYSE data, is illustrated in Figure 9-3. The relationship is roughly linear at least for low values of $\hat{\beta}_i$, but the intercept term is considerably higher than that of the prevailing riskless rate in the period. According to the mean variance model the intercept should be at the riskless rate. The discrepancy can be explained in a qualitative sense by noting that borrowing rates exceed lending rates

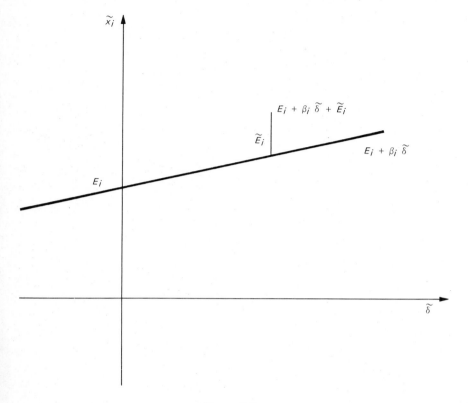

Figure 9-2.

(which, as Black shows, implies an intercept above the riskless lending rate). Alternative forms of the generating function have also been suggested and these seem to offer greater promise, but tests of the mean variance theory become much more difficult and, we shall argue, unnecessary.

In fact, the relation (9.7) of and by itself constitutes a far more satisfactory basis for a capital market theory without the additional baggage of mean variance theory. We will develop such a theory and for reasons that will become apparent refer to it as the arbitrage theory.[9] Throughout we will assume that the number of assets, n, is sufficiently large to permit our arguments to hold. We will, also, assume that the noise vector, $\tilde{\epsilon}$, is sufficiently independent to permit the law of large numbers to work. (Notice that in the generating model of (9.7) this would allow for independent industry effects if there were enough industries.)

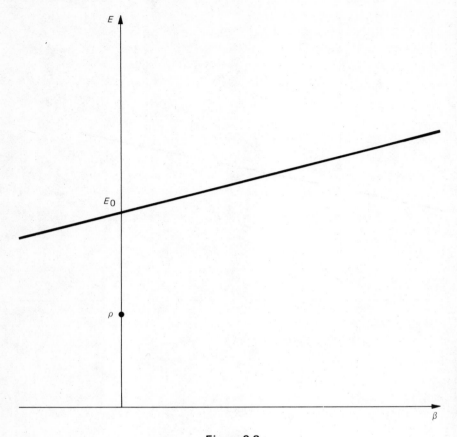

Figure 9-3.

Suppose, first, that we form an arbitrage portfolio, η, of the n assets. As an arbitrage portfolio, η uses no wealth, and

$$\eta' e = 0. \tag{9.8}$$

In other words, the wealth invested long in assets is exactly balanced by the amount borrowed from short sales and, net, the portfolio uses no wealth. Denoting the vector of mean returns by E and the vector of beta coefficients by β, the return on the arbitrage portfolio will be given by

$$\tilde{R} \equiv \eta' \tilde{x} = (\eta' E) + (\eta' \beta) \tilde{\delta} + \eta' \tilde{\epsilon}$$

$$\approx (\eta' E) + (\eta' \beta) \tilde{\delta}, \tag{9.9}$$

where we have, secondly, assumed that the arbitrage portfolio is sufficiently well diversified to permit us to use the law of large numbers to approximately eliminate the noise term, $\eta'\tilde{\epsilon}$.[10] In effect, by using a well diversified portfolio we have been able to eliminate the independent risk from the portfolio return.

Lastly, we can always choose the arbitrage portfolio in such a fashion that it eliminates systematic risk as well, i.e.,

$$\eta'\beta = 0. \tag{9.10}$$

(If an inadequate number of β_i coefficients are negative we will have to engage in short sales to accomplish (9.10) while maintaining a well diversified portfolio.) Having eliminated both components of risk, the portfolio return,

$$\tilde{R} = (\eta'E) + (\eta'\beta)\,\tilde{\delta} = \eta'E, \tag{9.11}$$

risklessly. By choosing the portfolio to be well diversified, to be an arbitrage portfolio satisfying (9.8) and to satisfy (9.10) we have been able to eliminate all risk and realize the return $\eta'E$. Since an arbitrage portfolio uses no wealth, it must now follow that its return,

$$\eta'E = 0. \tag{9.12}$$

If (9.12) did not hold, then by using no wealth we will have been able to obtain a riskless return. Furthermore, we would be able to obtain arbitrarily large returns by simply scaling up the arbitrage portfolio. This is incompatible with the absence of arbitrage, let alone equilibrium, and (9.12) must hold.

In summary, then, any portfolio satisfying (9.8) and (9.10), must also satisfy (9.12).[11] This is simply the algebraic statement that all vectors, η, orthogonal to e and β are orthogonal to E, and it follows that E must be a linear combination of e and β. Hence, there are constants E_0 and a such that for all i

$$E_i = E_0 + a\beta_i.[12] \tag{9.13}$$

Figure 9-4 illustrates this argument with just three assets. Suppose the assets in Figure 9-4 actually represent clusters (accumulation points) of assets sufficiently dense so that by forming portfolios one can obtain the three return-β points shown without any nonsystematic (ϵ) risk. The algebraic arbitrage argument simply says that the three points must lie on the line given by (9.13). In Figure 9-4, the

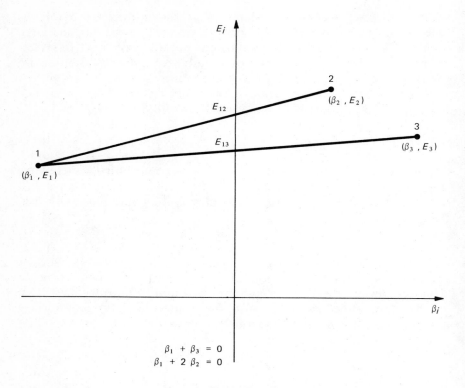

Figure 9-4.

three points illustrated do not lie on a security line. By taking a portfolio that splits wealth evenly between the first and third assets we obtain a return of E_{13} with no systematic, β risk. However, by combining the first and second assets with investments of 1/3 and 2/3 of wealth respectively we obtain the riskless return E_{12} which exceeds E_{13}. Now, by shorting (borrowing against) the E_{13} portfolio to go long in the E_{12} portfolio we can receive arbitrarily high returns without risk. To prevent this we must have $E_{12} = E_{13}$ which means that points 1, 2 and 3 must lie on a line such as (9.13).

If there is a riskless asset with a rate of return, ρ, then the same argument would reveal that $E_0 = \rho$. Alternatively, consider any well-diversified, nonarbitrage zero beta portfolio, i.e., a portfolio satisfying (9.10), and such that $\alpha' e = 1$. From (9.13) the return on such a portfolio will be E_0 and since we have eliminated all risk, we must have $E_0 = \rho$, the riskless rate, to prevent arbitrage. (If all well-diversified portfolios of risky assets have systematic risk then β

will be close to a constant vector and we can again take $E_0 = \rho$ in
(9.13)). In the absence of such riskless opportunities, though, E_0 can
still be identified as the expected return on all zero beta portfolios.
Finally, considering a portfolio of special interest such as the market
portfolio (of risky assets), α_m, we can normalize $\tilde{\delta}$ so that $\alpha_m \beta = 1$
and (9.13) becomes

$$E_i = E_0 + (E_m - E_0) \beta_i , \qquad (9.14)$$

where E_m is the expected return on the market portfolio.[13]
Equation (9.14) is the arbitrage equivalent of the mean variance
security line equation.

Notice that we did not have to assume that the market was in
equilibrium to derive our basic arbitrage condition (9.14). It is a
stronger result and depends essentially on the absence of arbitrage
possibilities rather than on the much more restrictive condition that
the market be in equilibrium as is required in the mean variance
theory.

The basic arbitrage condition generalizes easily to the l-factor case,
as well, provided only that the number of common factors is
significantly less than the number of assets.[14] By considering
alternative arbitrage portfolios it is possible to show that when the
generating model has the form

$$\tilde{x}_i = E_i + \beta_{il}\tilde{\delta}_1 + \ldots + \beta_{ik}\tilde{\delta}_k + \tilde{\epsilon}_i , \qquad (9.15)$$

the basic arbitrage condition takes the form

$$E_i = E_0 + (E_m - E_0) [\gamma_1 \beta_{il} + \ldots + \gamma_k \beta_{ik}] , \qquad (9.16)$$

where the γ_l are nonnegative constants normalized so that

$$\Sigma \gamma_l = 1.[15] \qquad (9.17)$$

In other words, the risk premium on the ith asset, $E_i - E_0$, is a
convex combination of its beta weights times the risk premium on
the market portfolio.

There is no need, however, for the market portfolio to play any
special role in this theory and, in fact, the basic arbitrage condition
can be written in a more appealing form than (9.16). The constants
in (9.16) arise from the algebraic arbitrage argument and our task is
to interpret them. Defining $\theta_l = (E_m - E_0) \gamma_l$ permits us to write
(9.16) as

$$E_i - E_0 = \theta_1 \beta_{il} + \ldots + \theta_k \beta_{ik} \ . \tag{9.18}$$

Consider a portfolio, α, which is zero beta on all factors except the lth. Formally,

$$\alpha' \beta_j = 0 \text{ if } j \neq l \ , \tag{9.19a}$$

$$\alpha' \beta = 1$$

and

$$\alpha' e = 1 \ , \tag{9.19b}$$

where β_i denotes the vector of ith factor weights, $<\beta_{1i}, \ldots, \beta_{ni}>$. (If such portfolios cannot be formed, then factors can be linearly combined simplifying the generating model.) Using (9.19) the risk premium on such a portfolio, $E_l - E_0$, is simply

$$E - E_0 = \alpha'(E - E_0) = \theta_l. \tag{9.20}$$

(E^l is not to be confused with the return on the lth asset; E^l denotes the return on the lth factor portfolio.) It follows that θ_l is the market risk premium on the lth market factor. Thus, all such portfolios offer the same risk premium, $E^l - E_0$, and we can rewrite the basic arbitrage condition as

$$E_i - E_0 = (E^1 - E_0)\beta_{i1} + \ldots + (E^k - E_0)\beta_{ik} \ . \tag{9.21}$$

In other words, the risk premium on any asset is given by the weighted sum of the factor risk premiums with weights equal to the beta coefficients of the asset. If one of the factors is chosen as the market portfolio, then its risk premium is treated like that for any other factor.

As an example, let us consider the form the basic arbitrage condition (9.21) takes with the following generating model

$$\tilde{x}_i = E_i + (1 - \beta_i)\tilde{\delta}_1 + \beta_i \tilde{\delta}_2 + \tilde{\epsilon}_i \ . \tag{9.22}$$

This model has been used in a number of recent empirical studies. The first factor, $\tilde{\delta}_1$, represents a zero beta factor chosen to be uncorrelated with the second factor, $\tilde{\delta}_2$, the market factor. From the basic arbitrage condition (9.21) we have

$$E_i = E_0 + (E^1 - E_0)(1 - \beta_i) + (E^2 - E_0)\beta_i \qquad (9.23)$$

$$= E^1 + (E^2 - E^1)\beta_i.$$

The model may now possess an ex ante expected return for a zero beta portfolio, E^1, in excess of the riskless rate, ρ (if such an asset exists). As with the single factor generating model (9.7), if $\tilde{\delta}_1$ is uncorrelated with the market factor, the mean variance theory will predict ρ as the intercept in (9.23) when estimated values are used (in large samples). In the absence of a riskless asset, though, mean variance theory will also imply that (9.23) is satisfied.

To empirically distinguish the arbitrage theory from mean variance analysis, then, by the use of the pricing relations alone and with this two factor model requires a demonstration that $E^1 \neq \rho$ if a riskless asset exists. With no riskless asset, however, it is difficult to distinguish between the two theories by such tests. Moving to an independent two factor model or to a three factor model would permit such a test. It must be understood, though, that the mean variance theory has a number of strong implications beyond simply the form of the pricing relation (9.3). As emphasized in Section 9.1, the pivotal role played by the market portfolio is central to mean variance theory and β_i must be the covariance term (divided by the market portfolio's variance) of the ith asset with the market portfolio and not any other. The observation that many well diversified portfolios behave like the market portfolio is a statement in support of a simple factor generating model and *not* in support of mean variance theory. In general, tests of the linear relation (9.13) are better interpreted as studies of the arbitrage theory rather than of mean variance theory.

In the next sections we will explore the theoretical and empirical relations among the arbitrage theory, mean variance theory, and the general state space framework.

SECTION 9.3

The simplest state space framework describes a world with n assets and m discrete, exclusive states, $<\theta_1, \ldots, \theta_m>$, that the world could be in. (Implicitly we will deal with a two-period world—where uncertainty is resolved in the second period—to avoid the problem of intertemporal allocation, but many of the results extend to the multiperiod context in an obvious fashion.) The matrix

$$
X \equiv \text{States} \quad
\begin{array}{c}
\theta_1 \\
\cdot \\
\cdot \\
\cdot \\
\theta_m
\end{array}
\overset{\displaystyle \text{Assets}}{\overset{\displaystyle X^1 \ldots X^n}{\left[\begin{array}{c} x_{ij} \end{array} \right]}} , \qquad (9.24)
$$

will denote the commonly agreed upon array of per-dollar (accounting unit) returns, where we define x_{ij} to be the gross return per dollar invested in asset j if state i occurs.[16]

Individuals choose their portfolios as combinations of the n assets so as to maximize the utility of their wealth and the only assumption on preferences is that all utility functions are monotone functions of the form $v(w_1, \ldots, w_m)$, where w_θ is wealth in state θ and for each θ there is some individual who exhibits no satiation in w_θ.[17]

Suppose, now, that the capital market is in equilibrium. It follows that there cannot exist any successful arbitrage strategies. To be specific, it must not be possible to insure a nonnegative return in all states and a positive return in at least one state with no net investment, i.e., without taking a position. Mathematically, if

$$
y = X\eta \qquad (9.25)
$$

where η is an arbitrage portfolio using no wealth, i.e.,

$$
\eta' e = 0 \ (e' \equiv <1, \ldots, 1>) , \qquad (9.26)
$$

then we cannot have $y \geqslant 0$.[18] If we did find such a solution, then without risk or cost, the portfolio $\lambda\eta$ would yield arbitrarily high returns in at least one state with no losses in any other states as λ, the scale of operation, diverged. As is shown in a footnote, by applying the duality results of linear programming this is equivalent to requiring the existence of a vector, p, such that

$$
p'X = e' \qquad (9.27)
$$

and

$$
p_\theta > 0 \qquad (9.28)
$$
[19]

The vector, p, is the vector of state space prices, p_θ, representing the current cost of a pure state space or contingent claim asset yielding one dollar if state θ occurs and nothing if θ does not occur.

Since $x_{\theta i}$ is the dollar return per dollar invested in asset i if state θ occurs, $p'X^i = \sum_\theta p_\theta x_{\theta i}$ simply values asset i up across states and, in equilibrium, this must equal its one dollar cost. Of course, if X is of less than full row rank, e.g., if the number of assets, n, is less than the number of states, m, then it will be impossible to form portfolios of the n assets equivalent to pure state space securities for all states and the above interpretation of p_θ is somewhat strained. In fact, it is easy to show that under such circumstances p will not even be unique and will, in general, lie in a subspace of dimension $m - n$. Now, p_θ is properly interpreted as an implicit price and the exact price system, with the property that the same allocation of wealth among the assets would occur if investors faced a market with prices, p_θ for pure state space assets, will depend upon both the subjective state space probabilities and the preferences of the investors. In general, though, no single price system will simultaneously allocate all agents as in the original situation since if not all contingencies are covered the equilibrium is not efficient relative to complete Arrow-Debreu equilibrium. As a consequence not all individual marginal rates of substitution across wealth in different states will be equal.

In the special case explored by Cass and Stiglitz where X is of full row rank a number of interesting results can be obtained. Now, $p' = e'X^{-1}$ is uniquely defined and $p'e = e'X^{-1}e$ is the aggregate cost of obtaining a sure dollar return in all states, or $(e'X^{-1}e)^{-1}$ is the riskless interest factor. In general, though, the existence of a nonnegative state price vector is all that can be ascertained from the assertion that the market is in equilibrium.

To verify this we must show that for any tableau of return, X, with an associated positive price vector, p, for which $p'X = e'$, there exists some structure of preferences such that the market is in equilibrium. To construct such a market consider a single individual who seeks to maximize his expected utility of wealth,

$$E\left\{u(\tilde{w})\right\} = \sum_\theta \pi_\theta u(wx'_\theta \alpha) \tag{9.29}$$

over portfolios α subject to $e'\alpha = 1$, where π_θ is the subjective probability assigned to state θ and is assumed positive, and where X_θ denotes the θth row of X. The first-order conditions take the form

$$\sum_\theta \pi_\theta \, u'(wx'_\theta \alpha) \, x_{\theta i} = \lambda; \, i = 1, \ldots, n , \tag{9.30}$$

where λ is a Langrange multiplier. Since $p'X = e'$, set

$$\pi_\theta \frac{1}{\lambda} u'(wx'_\theta \alpha) = p_\theta \tag{9.31}$$

or

$$u'(wx'_\theta \alpha) = \lambda p_\theta / \pi_\theta > 0. \tag{9.32}$$

Letting u be a concave utility function with everywhere positive marginal utility and α any portfolio, it is clear that λ and a vector of probabilities, π_θ, can be chosen to satisfy (9.32) and that, by concavity, this will be sufficient for an optimum. Notice, too, that information about the market portfolio, α, by itself, provides no further information about X, the equilibrium returns.

We can summarize our findings with the following assertion:

If we impose no a priori restrictions on individual preference structures beyond monotonicity (or, for that matter, on individual subjectively held anticipations) then the assertion that the market is in equilibrium implies the absence of arbitrage possibilities.[20] Conversely, if there are no arbitrage possibilities in a market, then there always exists a structure of preferences such that the market would be in equilibrium.

It follows that to obtain an empirically refutable capital market theory will require the imposition of further assumptions on the structure of the market. This is not to deny that information external to the capital market, savings rates, for example, might provide the required observable inferences on preference structures or distributions.

SECTION 9.4

Explicitly then, an empirically meaningful theory of the pricing of risky assets can be obtained only by placing some restrictions on preference structures or on the underlying subjectively perceived generating mechanism. The easiest way to understand the sense in which the arbitrage theory is based on a restriction of the latter sort is to delete the $\tilde{\epsilon}$ noise term in (9.15). In vector notation, (9.15) now asserts that the random vector of gross returns on the ith asset (across states), the ith column of the state space tableau, is a linear combination of a constant vector, e, and k vectors, $(\delta_1, \ldots, \delta_k)$. This is the same as requiring that the state space tableau be of rank less than or equal to $k + 1$ where the constant vector is in the basis. Equivalently, it implies that all assets when considered as points in an underlying state space lie in a subspace of dimension $k + 1$ spanned by the constant vector and the factor vectors. In this framework the arbitrage condition (9.21) must hold exactly to prevent a pure arbitrage situation from arising. One way to see this, without constructing arbitrage portfolios, is to use the result in Section 9.1 that assures that in the absence of arbitrage a state price vector, p, exists. As shown in a footnote, Equation (9.27) is identical to (9.21) with $E^l - E_0 = -p'\delta_l/p'e$.[2 1]

Mean variance theory can be thought of as representing a restriction either on preference structures or on distributions. In either case, though, the mean variance analysis can be considered as a special case of arbitrage theory in which the arguments hold exactly, rather than as approximations, despite the fact that all of the randomness has not been removed. To see what we mean, suppose that random returns are governed by the factor model (9.7) where $\tilde{\delta}$ is precisely the market portfolio's excess return, $(\tilde{R}_m - E_m)$ and the $\tilde{\epsilon}_i$ are mean zero and uncorrelated with $\tilde{R}_m$, but are not necessarily independent across assets, i. In fact, such a representation is always possible with any collection of random variables and represents no restriction at all (if second moments exist). Furthermore,

$$
\begin{aligned}
R_m &= \alpha'_m \tilde{x} \\
&= E_m + \tilde{\delta} + \alpha_m \tilde{\epsilon} \qquad (9.33) \\
&= \tilde{R}_m + \alpha'_m \tilde{\epsilon};
\end{aligned}
$$

and we must have $\alpha'_m \epsilon \equiv 0$.[2 2]

By the separation theorem given identical subjective anticipations every investor holds the same risky portfolio, α_m. In addition, when only means and variances matter, if any investor is given the opportunity to engage in an arbitrage operation, using no wealth, that offers a return uncorrelated with his own risky portfolio, α_m, he will do so unless its expected return is zero. In other words, the marginal contribution to risk by such an operation is zero.[2 3] This permits us to use (9.7) and the basic arbitrage argument to derive the mean variance capital pricing relation in a very direct fashion. Let η be an arbitrage portfolio, with $\eta'e = 0$, and chosen to be orthogonal to the market, $\eta'\beta = 0$. From (9.7) its random return is

$$
\eta'\tilde{x} = \eta'E + \eta'\tilde{\epsilon}, \qquad (9.34)
$$

and since $\eta'\tilde{\epsilon}$ is orthogonal to the market, the expected return

$$
\eta'E = 0. \qquad (9.12)
$$

This is precisely the arbitrage argument used in Section 9.2 and we conclude that

$$E_i = E_0 + (E_m - E_0)\beta_i,\qquad(9.14)$$

must hold with $E_0 = \rho$ in the presence of a riskless asset. The difference between this derivation and the original arbitrage argument came at the stage where we concluded that because $\eta'\tilde{\epsilon}$ was uncorrelated with $\tilde{R}_m$ the expected return, $\eta'E = 0$. In the absence of assumptions which justify focusing only on means and (co)variances this conclusion would be unwarranted. This is the sense in which the mean variance model or, at least, its analysis may be considered a special case of arbitrage theory, but it should be emphasized that in a strict sense the underlying assumptions of arbitrage theory and mean variance theory are distinct.

On purely theoretical grounds, then, it cannot be asserted that mean variance theory is a special case of arbitrage theory. In evaluating the theories on such grounds the argument must turn on the a priori appeal of their respective major assumptions. The assumptions that underly mean variance theory have been exhaustively studied in the literature and are outlined above and we will not repeat them. The primary assumption underlying the arbitrage theory is that only a small number of factors is significant.[24] Without presenting a formal argument for why this should be so we can, at least, argue that it is quite plausible.

Essentially, the question turns on whether substitution or income effects in both consumption and production are more important in the short run. Abstracting from capital gains, for the moment, suppose that the returns on investment are the returns on productive activities. In the short run, ideally in a differential time, productive activities will be fixed (as in a putty-clay model) and the returns to capital will be composed of ordinary returns plus (disequilibrium) profits. When the level of aggregate demand changes, sectors will accommodate in a Leontief-like fashion, but the output and profit response of each will be a linear function of the change. If capital receives the residual, after payments to other productive agents, then there will be a specific aggregate demand factor. Of course, if the change in aggregate demand is accompanied by important systematic shifts in demand across sectors and, consequently, in prices then this will not be the case.[25] To the extent to which such secular demand shifts take place and are significant they must be represented by factors in the generating model. In the short run, though, models of habit formation would suggest that price shifts would be of a second order and could be ignored. Finally, to the extent that anticipations of capital gains are extrapolative and based on learning from past experience, the number of factors would be further limited if the slow shift responses postulated on both the consumption and production sides were valid. These should prove to be important areas of future research. The precise determination of what the relevant factors are is crucial to fully understanding the theory and should be the subject of econometric study. While the above arguments suggest the importance of an aggregate demand or GNP or market factor, it will probably be necessary to break such a factor into its real and price components. In addition, other factors that affect long term trends and lead to secular shifts can also be expected to have an impact on returns. Increasing substitution of capital (human and machine) for labor is one example.

Before leaving the theoretical side of the comparison it should also be stressed that the arbitrage theory makes considerably less stringent requirements on the homogeneity of investors' ex ante anticipations than does the mean variance theory. Although, some weakening is possible, to obtain an empirically meaningful form of the pricing relation (9.6) mean variance theory essentially requires that all investors agree about both the expected returns and the covariance matrix.[26] Given agreement on the factor model of (9.15), however, the arbitrage theory is unaltered if agents hold differing subjective views on the distribution either of the market factors, $\tilde{\delta}$, or of the noise terms, $\tilde{\epsilon}$. As noted in Ross [1972] it is, at least in theory, possible to permit disagreement on the expectations, E, and the beta coefficients of the generating model as well without substantively altering the theory. Suppose, for example, that the wealth weighted sum of ex ante expected risky returns of agents was bounded above as the number of assets is increased. This is like requiring a surrogate ex ante market return to be bounded above. It will follow that each agent's expected return is bounded above and (9.21) will hold for the ex ante values adopted by each agent. If agents agree on factor risk premiums and if the ex post generating model is now a linear combination of the individual ex ante models (e.g., if it was some sort of average), then the basic arbitrage relation will hold ex post and will be testable as it stands. It is only necessary that agents agree on *what* the factors are, not on their impact on asset returns.[27]

In sum, on theoretical grounds we would argue that the arbitrage model may be expected to be quite robust, perhaps more so than the mean variance theory. The empirical implications of the two theories and the interpretation of the available data, however, is equivocal since, as we shall see, appropriately discriminating tests have yet to be attempted.

There are at least two ways to empirically test a theory; we may examine its assumptions or its implications. Neither of the dual assumptions of the mean variance theory, normality of returns or quadratic preferences, have fared well in testing, but there is still considerable room for doubt and no clear refutation is yet available. Blume, for example, finds no clear reason to discard the hypothesis of symmetric Paretian stability for monthly relatives of stock market prices (although this is quite different from accepting normality) and, although quadratic preferences seem at odds with casual observation (e.g., they exhibit increasing absolute risk aversion and, consequently, risky assets are inferior goods (see Arrow)), locally quadratic preferences will be acceptable if returns follow a simple diffusion process and this hypothesis, unfortunately, is untestable.[28] On the other hand, there is considerable evidence to support the basic arbitrage assumption that only a small number of factors matter. Farrar found by performing a factor analysis on New York Stock Exchange data that three factors were sufficient to explain over 93 percent of the covariance matrix in a factor analytic sense.[29] When oblique or nonorthogonal factors are permitted, as in the arbitrage theory itself, Farrar claims that no more than three can be found by any empirical method.

The most intensive effort to empirically test the mean variance theory, however, has focused on the implications of theory and, in particular, on the basic pricing relation. Unfortunately, though, as a test of mean variance theory such analysis is inappropriate and as a means of discriminating between mean variance theory and arbitrage theory, with simple models, it is useless.

All current tests assume that asset returns are generated by a model of the form of (9.15). Given a one or a dependent two-factor model, though, both mean variance theory and arbitrage theory lend to the simple pricing relation of (9.14). It is only with the assumption that the generating model is more complex that the arbitrage theory is distinguishable from mean variance theory on the basis of the pricing relation. The verification of a second factor in the cross section studies of return on the beta coefficient, for example, rather than destroying all of our capital market theory would instead constitute a significant piece of evidence in support of the arbitrage theory as against mean variance theory.

This raises the question of whether in the absence of a second significant factor (with independent beta coefficients not simply equal to one minus the market betas) it is possible to test the arbitrage theory as against mean variance theory. Surely not from the pricing relation, but what then?

In fact, if the number of assets is large such a test will be very difficult. As we have shown in Ross [1971:2], with a one factor generating model and a large number of assets, mean variance theory will be approximately correct, to the same order of approximation as arbitrage theory, irrespective of the underlying distributions (provided that second moments exist) or preference structure. In effect, then, there will be no empirical basis on which to distinguish the two theories in such a world, and any test in support of one will support the other. Of course, it is still open to reject the mean variance theory on the basis of its underlying assumptions.

With an independent two factor model it is at least conceivable that mean variance theory can be rejected while accepting the arbitrage theory. Suppose, that one of the factors is the market factor with beta coefficients $<\beta_i>$ and the other factor has coefficients $<\gamma_i>$. (Both $\tilde{\epsilon}$ and the second factor are uncorrelated with the market factor.) The basic pricing relation given by arbitrage theory asserts that

$$E_i - E_0 = \gamma_i[E_1 - E_0] + \beta_i[E_m - E_0] .\qquad(9.35)$$

If the factor term, $\gamma_i[E^1 - E_0]$ proves significant with γ_i different from $1 - \beta_i$ this will constitute a rejection of the mean variance theory in favor of the arbitrage theory.

Alternatively, suppose that neither factor is chosen to be the market factor. Now, the pricing relation becomes

$$E_i - E_0 = \beta_{i1}(E^1 - E_0) + \beta_{i2}(E^2 - E_0)$$

$$= [\beta_{i1}[\frac{E^1 - E_0}{E_m - E_0}] + \beta_{i2}[\frac{E^2 - E_0}{E_m - E_0}]](E_m - E_0).\qquad(9.36)$$

Mean variance theory would predict that

$$E_i - E_0 = \frac{\text{Cov } \tilde{x}_i, \tilde{x}_m}{\sigma_m^2} (E_m - E_0)$$

$$= [\frac{\sigma_1^2}{\sigma_m^2}\beta_{i1} + \frac{\sigma_2^2}{\sigma_m^2}\beta_{i2}](E_m - E_0),\qquad(9.37)$$

where, for simplicity, we have chosen the factors to be uncorrelated so that $\sigma_m^2 = \sigma_1^2 + \sigma_2^2$ and have normalized so that the market portfolio has $\beta_{m1} = \beta_{m2} = 1$. With the normalization we also have

$$E_m - E_0 = (E^1 - E_0) + (E^2 - E_0). \qquad (9.38)$$

In both theories, then, the market coefficient is a convex combination of the two beta coefficients. It follows that mean variance theory will be rejected if the estimated premium ratio

$$\frac{E^1 - E_0}{E^2 - E_0} \neq \frac{\sigma_1^2}{\sigma_2^2}, \qquad (9.39)$$

the ratio of the factor variances. It should be clear that similar tests can be constructed when the factors are not orthogonal.

Is it possible to reject the arbitrage theory while accepting mean variance theory? As we have seen, not on the basis of the pricing relation itself. However, if simple factor models were rejected as generating mechanisms while an ex ante covariance matrix and expectations vector could be estimated and the market portfolio efficiency relation (9.3) were accepted (i.e., not rejected), then this would lead us to reject arbitrage theory in favor of mean variance theory while not directly testing the underlying distributional or preference assumptions of mean variance theory. Given the success of factor analytic techniques, however, such a result seems unlikely.

SECTION 9.5

In the above sections we have developed a new theory of the pricing of risky assets. The arbitrage theory was built on the solid foundation of the state space framework and both the theoretical and empirical implications of the theory in contrast to mean variance capital market theory were discussed. It was argued, in particular, that the arbitrage theory follows directly from the generating models that are commonly used to test the mean variance theory and that, as a consequence, in this context the additional assumptions of mean variance theory are not necessary. Furthermore, the arbitrage theory permitted a significant weakening of the assumption that markets were in equilibrium.

Much work, however, remains. The arbitrage theory is constructed in the tradition of Popper and a number of empirical tests have been suggested. On the theoretical side, as footnotes have indicated, it is not difficult to extend the arbitrage theory to an intertemporal context. More pressing is the need to expand, both on the theoretical and empirical fronts, the argument outlined in Section 9.4 supporting the limited dependence of asset returns. For example, if the degree of interdependence in returns is high, it will be very difficult to develop a meaningful theory of competitive (or "small") firm behavior short of assuming that firms can fully assess the complex market valuations of risky assets in the absence of complete price signals. As a final point, neither the arbitrage theory nor any other theory has made a serious attempt to describe the disequilibrium dynamic adjustment of ex post observations to ex ante assumptions. Understanding the impact of information on market adjustment will be a prerequisite for such an analysis and of great interest in its own right.

NOTES TO SECTION NINE

1. The recent work on expanding the number of moments considered seems particularly unsatisfactory; there are an infinity of orthogonal expansions which may be used to split utilities and the Taylor expansion is only one of these.

2. For the full development of the mean variance theory the reader is referred to the work of Treynor, Sharpe and Lintner and to extensions by Black. The assumption of normality rather than quadratic utility functions is in the spirit of the paper, the results are the same in either case. In continuous time, though, utility functions are locally quadratic if returns are governed by a simple diffusion process and this probably constitutes the strongest possible argument for the mean variance model. See Ross [1971:3] or Merton [in this vol.] for development of this model. However, as Merton shows, in a dynamic diffusion model, with an intertemporally stochastic environment even the diffusion assumption will be inadequate to restore the traditional capital market theory. In particular, the presence of intertemporal dynamic programming state dependencies require the incorporation of terms involving covariances with state terms in the basic pricing relation. This necessitates further restrictions of, for example, the arbitrage sort of this paper to obtain empirically interesting results.

3. Notice that here we have imposed no short sales restrictions; such restrictions on all assets, for example, would restrict α to the unit simplex.

4. There are many exceptions to the above argument; e.g., ρ could be too great to allow tangency (although not in equilibrium (see Merton [1972:1])), or F could contain a straight line segment coincident with the market line and the market portfolio would be on that segment but ambiguous (see Fama)).

5. In the absence of arbitrage opportunities, e.g., in equilibrium, all arbitrage portfolios with no net expenditure,

$$\alpha'e = 0,$$

and no risk

$$\alpha'V\alpha = 0 ,$$

must have no return,

$$\alpha'E = 0.$$

Since V, the covariance matrix of $\tilde{x}$, is positive semidefinite, there exists C such that $V = CC'$, and $\alpha'V\alpha = 0$ is equivalent to $\alpha'C = 0$. If the matrix composed of the columns of C and e, $[C\!:\!e]$, is of full rank, then (9.6) always possesses a solution. On the other hand, if $[C\!:\!e]$ is of less than full rank then there will exist nontrivial arbitrage portfolios and to insure that such portfolios have no return, E must be a linear combination of e and the columns of C. Since C and $V = CC'$ span the same linear space there is, again, some α for which (9.6) holds. (This is easy to see since $\gamma'C = 0$ if and only if $\gamma'V = \gamma'CC' = 0$. The ranges of C and V are, thus, polar to the same space and since E_n is reflexive they are identical.)

6. This is in contrast to the work of Beja who derives (9.6) assuming complete contingent markets and somehow feels that it is a deep result.

7. The fact that a surrogate for the market portfolio is nearly always used in empirical work might suggest that the exact choice of α is unimportant. Nothing could be further from the truth, and the theoretical justification for the use of surrogates is found in Section 9.2 and not in the mean variance model. The empirical significance of these results is taken up in Section 9.4.

8. An alternative approach is to substitute (9.3) into (9.7) and directly test the mean variance capital market theory with a regression on returns. It is also possible for $\tilde{\delta}$ to exactly be the market portfolio, insuring that $\tilde{\epsilon}_i$ is uncorrelated with $\tilde{\delta}$ and $\beta_i = b_i$ exactly. This is done at the sacrifice of making $\tilde{\epsilon}$ singular (see Equation (9.33)).

9. What follows is not intended to be a truly rigorous exposition of arbitrage theory. Rather, our intent is to develop fully the consequences of this theoretical approach and the intuition behind it. A rigorous study of the argument together with the necessary qualifying assumptions can be found in Ross [1972] with some bounds on the approximation errors available in Ross [1971:2]. In Ross [1972] the key assumptions are that agents have a sufficient homogeneity of anticipations and that expected market return must be bounded above as the number of assets is increased. One further assumption is required. There must be at least one agent with bounded (relative) risk aversion. If not, then as assets are added and agents grow wealthier they might become increasingly risk averse at a rate that just offsets the diminishing unsystematic risk. Put simply, although the unsystematic risk is declining we must assure that at least one agent does not become increasingly concerned about it.

10. The sense of approximation can be taken as in quadratic mean or in some similar L_p metric on distribution functions. More subtly, approximation can be in the sense of any of the large number laws such as the Prohorov metric.

11. We've eliminated the condition that the portfolio be well diversified since the argument is algebraic and if the implication follows for all portfolios in some open neighborhood of a point of the order of $(\pm\frac{1}{n}, \ldots, \pm\frac{1}{n})$ it will hold on the whole space.

12. Of course, the result holds as an approximation with a finite number of assets, but we will not worry about this. See Ross [1971:2] and [1972] for a fuller discussion of the exact nature of the approximation.

13. This normalization is possible whenever $\alpha'_m\beta \neq 0$, and this will always be

true for the market portfolio if agents are risk averse. From (9.7) the return on the risky portfolio held by the νth agent is given by

$$\tilde{R}^\nu = \alpha^\nu \tilde{x}$$

$$= \alpha^\nu E + (\alpha^\nu \beta)\tilde{\delta} + \alpha^\nu \tilde{\epsilon}$$

$$= E_0 + (\alpha^\nu \beta)[a + \tilde{\delta}] + \alpha^\nu \tilde{\epsilon}$$

$$= E_0 + (\alpha^\nu \beta)[a + \tilde{\delta}],$$

and if the νth agent is risk averse he will insist on a compensation for bearing risk (more formally it follows from the concavity of his utility function), and, therefore

$$a(\alpha^\nu \beta) \geqslant 0,$$

with strict inequality in general (except where the utility function is improper at the certain wealth level of wE_0). If ω^ν denotes the proportion of wealth held by the νth agent, then

$$E_m - \rho = a(\alpha_m \beta)$$

$$= a\Sigma_\nu \omega^\nu (\alpha^\nu \beta)$$

$$> 0,$$

verifying that the normalization is permitted and that the market portfolio earns a premium.

14. In an intertemporal model if E_i or β_i are stochastic it may be necessary to make limited dependence factor assumptions about their movement as well to obtain a useful theory. More generally we can assume that all of the stochastic parameters are governed by a generating model of the form of (9.15).

15. There is also no need to impose any restrictions on the multivariate distribution of the factors.

16. The assumption of agreement on X when states, per se, are unobservable and subjective distributions can differ is not a restriction in any meaningful sense.

17. This is formally more general than the expected utility hypothesis, but not much different in most problems. If $v(\cdot)$ is to be in the form of an expected utility we may assume in a market context that the von-Neuman Morgenstern utility function is concave. As Raiffa has pointed out this is not very restrictive since, if the noncavities of individual utility functions are bounded, individuals could "fill them in" with fair side bets, and the nonconvexities would then be irrelevant for market equilibrium. Finally, with von-Neumann Morgenstern

utilities, individuals may differ in their subjective appraisal of the probabilities that various states will occur, but we will assume that for each state there exists some individual (with positive wealth) who assigns a positive probability to its occurrence.

18. We employ the following vector notation: $x \geqslant y$ if $x_i \geqslant y_i$, $x \gneqq y$ if $x \geqslant y$ and for some $i, x_i > y_i$; and $x > y$ if for all $i, x_i > y_i$. If x and y are vectors $x'y \equiv \Sigma_i x_i y_i$, the inner product. In addition, throughout the paper we will impose no restrictions on short sales.

19. Formally, we require that

$$
\begin{bmatrix} X & -I \\ e' & 0 \end{bmatrix} \begin{bmatrix} \alpha \\ y \end{bmatrix} = \begin{bmatrix} 0 \\ 0 \end{bmatrix} ,
$$

not possess a solution with y semipositive. This is equivalent to requiring that

$$
\begin{bmatrix} X & -X & -I \\ e' & -e' & 0 \\ 0 & 0 & e' \end{bmatrix} \begin{bmatrix} \alpha_1 \\ \alpha_2 \\ y \end{bmatrix} = \begin{bmatrix} 0 \\ 0 \\ 1 \end{bmatrix}
$$

not possess a nonnegative solution, $(\alpha_1, \alpha_2, y) \geqslant 0$. (We have simply set $\alpha = \alpha_1 - \alpha_2$ and without loss of generality required that $(\alpha_1, \alpha_2) \geqslant 0$. In addition, $e'y = 1$ insures that y is semipositive if it is nonnegative.)

By Farkas' Lemma, see, e.g., Gale, the above system will not have a solution only if its dual

$$
q'X + ve' = 0,
$$

$$
-q' + ze' \geqslant 0,
$$

$$
z < 0,
$$

possesses a solution $\qquad (q, v, z)$.

To obtain (9.27) and (9.28) we define $p' \equiv \frac{1}{v}q'$. Equation (9.27) follows directly from the definition of p' and the dual equations, and since

$$
-q' \geqslant -ze' > 0 ,
$$

it only remains to show that $v > 0$. Noting that X is a semipositive matrix, $-q'X$ is also semipositive and this implies that $v > 0$.

Notice that even if the subjective probability of a state θ occurring is zero, we still have $p_\theta > 0$. If the expected utility hypothesis governs preferences, though, we would be indifferent to wealth in state θ, violating nonsatiation. In this case we can modify the analysis to eliminate states for which all agree there is no probability of occurrence. However, even if the probability is zero, the possibility, as with picking a rational with the uniform measure on the unit interval, remains. In the absence of transactions costs even the most ardent believer in expected utility would demand infinite wealth in state θ if it was free. The lack of upper semicontinuity for the demand correspondence can pose difficulties for the existence of equilibrium in more complex models.

20. Of course, this leaves open the possibility that restrictions on investor risk aversion may have further implications. These results are similar to the more general work of Sonnenschein on the implications of agent optimization for aggregate excess demand functions.

21. A typical column (asset) in (9.27) takes the form

$$E_i(p'e) + \beta_{i1}(p'\delta_1) + \ldots + \beta_{ik}(p'\delta_k) = 1 \ .$$

Rearranging terms yields (9.21) or the expression in the text. Notice, too, that if there is a riskless asset its rate of return,

$$\rho = 1/p'e \ .$$

22. We have normalized $\alpha'_m \beta = 1$.

23. It is quite easy to show this formally. Suppose, for simplicity, that there is a riskless asset and that an investor holds a portfolio with returns $(1 - \alpha_0)\rho + \alpha_0 \tilde{R}_m$ where α_0 is the proportion of wealth, w, placed at risk. If $\Delta \tilde{z}$ is uncorrelated with $\tilde{R}_m$ its marginal contribution to his expected utility will be given by

$$E\left\{U'[w[(1-\alpha_0)\rho + \alpha_0 \tilde{R}_m]]\,\Delta \tilde{z}\right\}$$

$$= E\left\{U'[w[(1-\alpha_0)\rho + \alpha_0 \tilde{R}_m]]\,E\left\{\Delta \tilde{z}\right\}\right\}$$

if $(\tilde{R}_m, \Delta \tilde{z})$ are jointly normal or if $U(\cdot)$ is quadratic.

24. See Footnote (9) and Ross [1972] for a detailed study of the assumptions on which arbitrage theory is based.

25. If the shifts were random and independent then it would not matter, i.e., they would be part of the $\tilde{\epsilon}_i$ terms. It should also be noted that to the extent that the ex ante distributions held by agents differ from the ex post distributions a systematic factor similar to an errors in variable argument can enter. I am indebted to Ferdinand Vaandrager for help on this point.

26. See Lintner [1969] or Ross [1971:1] for some examples.

27. To make this point algebraically, let agents be indexed by "ν" and suppose the νth agent believes ex ante returns are generated by the model

$$x_i^\nu = E_i^\nu + \beta_i^\nu \delta^\nu + \epsilon_i^\nu \ , \tag{F1}$$

where the assumptions (9.15) are assumed to hold. Under the conditions described in the text (see Ross [1972]) the boundedness of a market return surrogate will imply that for each ν, the arbitrage condition will hold,

$$E_i^\nu = \rho + \lambda^\nu \beta_i^\nu; \quad \lambda^\nu = E_m^{\ \nu} - \rho, \tag{F2}$$

where we have assumed a riskless asset and ignored the approximation. If the true ex post model can be obtained from (F1) by aggregating with weights γ_ν, then true ex post

$$\tilde{x}_i = \sum_\nu \gamma_\nu \tilde{x}_i^\nu$$

$$= \sum_\nu \gamma_\nu E_i^\nu + \sum_\nu \gamma_\nu \beta_i^\nu \tilde{\delta}^\nu + \sum_\nu \gamma_\nu \tilde{\epsilon}_i^\nu$$

$$\equiv E_i + \beta_i \tilde{\delta} + \tilde{\epsilon}_i,$$

assuming that $\tilde{\delta}_\theta^\nu = \tilde{\delta}_\theta$. If the risk premiums, $\lambda^\nu = \lambda$ agree then (F2) aggregates to

$$E_i = \rho + \lambda \beta_i$$

which is now directly testable. To generalize the result, we can scale the $\tilde{\delta}^\nu$ factors, rescaling the β_i^ν variates accordingly, so that $\lambda^\nu = \lambda$ trivially. The requirement that $\tilde{\delta}_\theta^{\ \nu} = \tilde{\delta}_\theta$ is far more subtle, but if the subjectively perceived factor random variables have the same range it will be possible to define them on an underlying state space domain such that $\tilde{\delta}_\theta^{\ \nu} = \tilde{\delta}_\theta$ for all ν; disagreement is entirely captured by the subjective distribution over states. If the state space itself has economic content and is observable this will not be possible.

In all fairness to mean variance theory much the same sort of aggregation is also possible there, but if, as is the spirit of the theory, covariance matrices are specified a priori and not merely covariances with the market, considerably more agreement is required to permit the argument to go through.

28. Although even this is insufficient to derive (9.3). See Footnote 2. In an important work Clark, using cotten futures data, has rejected the hypothesis that these option prices are stable Paretian in favor of a subordinated normal. Such results are not, however, inconsistent with the arbitrage theory.

29. Farrar actually worked with 47 industrial equity groupings prepared by Standard and Poor. We have not, however, performed significance tests on the factor analytic results and, perhaps, by assuming that the covariance matrix follows a Wishart distribution it would be possible to test the simple factor models. In particular, one could see how much of the variance the one, two and so forth best factors could be expected to remove.

REFERENCES

Arrow, Kenneth. "The Role of Securities in the Optimal Allocation of Risk-Bearing." *Review of Economic Studies*, April (1964), pp. 91-96.

Beja, Avraham. "The Structure of the Cost of Capital under Uncertainty." *Review of Economic Studies*, July (1971), pp. 359-369.

Black, Fischer. "Capital Market Equilibrium with Restricted Borrowing." *Journal of Business*, March (1973).

Blume, Marshall. "Portfolio Theory: A Step Towards its Practical Application." *Journal of Business*, April (1970), pp. 152-173.

Blume, Marshall and Friend, Irwin. "A New Look at the Capital Asset Pricing Model." *Journal of Finance*, March (1973), pp. 19-33.

Clark, Peter. "A Subordinated Stochastic Process Model with Finite Variance for Speculative Prices." *Econometrica* (forthcoming).

Debreu, Gerard. *Theory of Value*. John Wiley, New York, 1959.

Diamond, Peter. "The Role of a Stock Market in a General Equilibrium Model with Technological Uncertainty." *American Economic Review*, September (1967), pp. 759-776.

Fama, Eugene. "Multiperiod Consumption-Investment Decisions." *American Economic Review*, March (1970), pp. 163-174.

Farrar, Donald. *The Investment Decision under Uncertainty*. Prentice-Hall, Inc., Englewood Cliffs, N.J., 1962.

Gale, David. *The Theory of Linear Economic Models*. McGraw-Hill, Inc., New York, 1960.

Hirschleifer, Jack. "Investment Decision under Uncertainty: Choice-Theoretic Approaches." *Quarterly Journal of Economics*, November (1965), pp. 509-536.

Lintner, John. "The Valuation of Risk Assets and the Selection of Risky Investments in Stock Portfolios and Capital Budgets." *Review of Economics and Statistics*, February (1965), pp. 13-37.

Lintner, John. "The Aggregation of Investors' Diverse Judgements and Preferences in Perfectly Competitive Security Markets." *Journal of Financial and Quantitative Analysis*, December (1969), pp. 347-400.

Merton, Robert. "An Analytic Derivation of the Efficient Portfolio Frontier." *Journal of Financial and Quantitative Analysis*, September (1972).

Merton, Robert. "An Intertemporal Capital Asset Pricing Model." *Econometrica*, Sept. (1973), pp. 867-87; also reprinted in this volume.

Popper, Karl. *The Logic of Scientific Discovery*. Hutchinson and Company, London, 1959.

Raiffa, Howard. *Decision Analysis: Introductory Lectures on Choices under Uncertainty*. Addison-Wesley Publishing Company, Inc., Reading, Massachusetts (1968).

Ross, Stephen. "On Homogeneous Anticipations in Capital Market Theory." Unpublished Manuscript (1971).

Ross, Stephen. "The General Validity of the Mean Variance Approach in Large Markets." Discussion Paper No. 12-72, Rodney L. White Center for Financial Research, University of Pennsylvania (1971).

Ross, Stephen. "Uncertainty and the Heterogeneous Capital Good Model," 1971. *Review of Economic Studies* (forthcoming).

Ross, Stephen. "The Arbitrage Theory of Capital Asset Pricing." Discussion Paper No. 2-73, Rodney L. White Center for Financial Research, University of Pennsylvania (1972).

Sharpe, William. "Capital Asset Prices: A Theory of Market Equilibrium under Conditions of Risk." *Journal of Finance*, September (1964), pp. 425-442.

Sharpe, William. *Portfolio Theory and Capital Markets.* McGraw-Hill, Inc., New York, 1970.

Sonnenschein, Hugo. "Market Excess Demand Functions." *Econometrica*, May (1974).

Treynor, Jack. "Toward a Theory of Market Value of Risky Assets." Unpublished Manuscript (1961).

Westerfield, Randolph. "Price Change and Volume Relationships and the Distribution of Common Stock Price Changes." Working Paper No. 6-73, Rodney L. White Center for Financial Research, University of Pennsylvania (1973).

❋ *Section Ten*

Investment for the Long Run[1]

Harry M. Markowitz

10.1 SUMMARY

Kelly (1956) and others, e.g., Latané (1957) (1959), Markowitz (1959, Chapter 6) and Brieman (1960) (1961), have asserted that in selecting among probability distributions of return this period, the investor who continually reinvests for the long run should maximize the expected value of the logarithm of increase in wealth. Mossin (1968) and Samuelson (1963) (1969), on the other hand, have presented examples of games in which the investor reinvests continually for the long run, has any of a wide range of apparently plausible utility functions, yet definitely should not follow the aforementioned "expected log" rule.

The argument of Kelly et al. is that, under the conditions considered, the investor who follows the expected log rule is almost sure to have a greater wealth in the long run than an investor who follows a distinctly different policy. We illustrate this argument in Section 10.3. On the other hand, Mossin and Samuelson argue that, for a wide range of plausible utility functions, the expected utility of the game as a whole provided by the expected log rule does not approach the expected utility provided by the optimum strategy, no matter how long the game is played. This argument is also illustrated in Section 10.3.

Given my beliefs concerning expected utility, which remain as in Markowitz (1959) Chapters 10 through 13, if it were in fact the case that the expected log rule did not provide asymptotically almost optimal expected utility for a wide range of utility functions, then I would have to reject the expected log rule as a general solution to the problem of reinvesting for the long run. The conclusion of this chapter, however, is that utility analysis does not refute the expected log rule. Rather it confirms the rule, and provides a more satisfactory theoretical justification for it than has been available heretofore.

As discussed in Section 10.4, for a given game with a fixed length T, we can define the outcome of the game in terms of either the ending wealth, W_T, or the rate of return, g, achieved during the game. It makes no difference, for fixed T, whether we express utility as a function $U(W_T)$ or as $V(g)$. But as T increases it is not equivalent to assume that $T(W_T)$ remains the same for all T as to assume that $V(g)$ remains the same for all T. Mossin and Samuelson in effect assumed that $U(W_T)$ remained the same for all T. We argue that it is a more plausible interpretation of "investment for the long run" to assume that $V(g)$ remains constant.

Theorem 1 of this study shows that, under very general conditions, if $V(g)$ is continuous then the expected log rule is asymptotically optimal; whereas if $V(g)$ is discontinuous then the expected log rule asymptotically provides an expected utility that is within $\gamma^{\max}$ of the optimal expected utility, where $\gamma^{\max}$ is the largest jump in $V(g)$.

Comparing theorem 1 with the Mossin-Samuelson argument, one might be tempted to conclude that the expected log rule is asymptotically desirable if constant $V(g)$ is assumed, but generally not asymptotically desirable if constant $U(W_T)$ is assumed. But theorems 2 and 3 show, under fairly general conditions, that the expected log rule is asymptotically optimal even when constant $U(W_T)$ is assumed, provided that $U(W_T)$ is bounded from above and below. I.e., the expected log rule is asymptotically optimal, under the conditions of theorems 2 and 3, provided that U does not approach $+\infty$ as W_T approaches ∞, and does not approach $-\infty$ as W_T approaches 0. Essential to the Mossin-Samuelson result, then, was the fact that every utility function, in the class considered by them, was unbounded either from above or below.

Given any $U(W_T)$ which is unbounded (either above or below) a St. Petersburg type of game can be constructed which shows that the particular unbounded $U(W_T)$ is absurd. From this it is argued that $U(W_T)$ should be assumed to be bounded, hence theorems 2 and 3 are applicable.

We rule out that

$$U(W_T) = \log(W_T)$$

as a reasonable utility function of final wealth. Thus a word is needed as to how the expected log rule can be asymptotically optimal for every bounded $U(W_T)$.

In short, this study argues that:

it is much more plausible to analyze behavior for the long run by assuming constant $V(g)$ than constant $U(W_T)$ as T increases. In this case theorem 1 applies; but

even if constant $U(W_T)$ were assumed, it must be bounded. In this case theorems 2 and 3 apply.

Theorems 1, 2, and 3 show general conditions under which the expected log rule provides asymptotically optimum, or almost asymptotically optimum expected utility.

It is not the position of Markowitz (1959), nor is it the position of this study, that all investors should invest for the long run. The risk averting investor may prefer to sacrifice some return in the long run for some additional stability in the short run. One value of the results for the long run, nevertheless, is to help us narrow the range of E, V efficient portfolios which need be considered for final portfolio selection. This view of the usefulness of the long run analysis is discussed in Section 10.6.

10.2 PREREQUISITES

Since portfolio theory has become of interest to theorists and practitioners with mathematical backgrounds ranging from none to much, we should specify the mathematical background assumed of the reader.

Sections 10.3 through 10.6 assume that the reader has had an introduction to probability and portfolio theory equivalent to the first six chapters of Markowitz (1959). The principal prerequisite assumed here that is not discussed in these six chapters is the use of the summation sign (Σ). The latter is discussed on pages 155-6 of Markowitz (1959) if the reader is not already familiar with it.

Section 10.7 onward in this chapter requires a greater familiarity with college mathematics, particularly analysis and probability. The earlier Sections, 10.3 through 10.6, are intended to illustrate the discussion. The later sections are intended to provide rigor and generality.

10.3 A PARADOX

Rather than relating who said what when, we shall describe the controversy by analyzing a simple special case. We first analyze the case in a manner which makes the expected log rule appear desirable; and then we analyze it in a manner which makes the expected log rule appear undesirable. Having thus illustrated the problem we show, for the simplified case, how the theorems presented later in the chapter resolve the apparent paradox.

This section makes assumptions, such as unchanging probability distributions of returns over time, not made in later sections. The purpose of this section is to illustrate the problem rather than seek generality.

Imagine a player who bets on a wheel such as that in Figure 10-1.

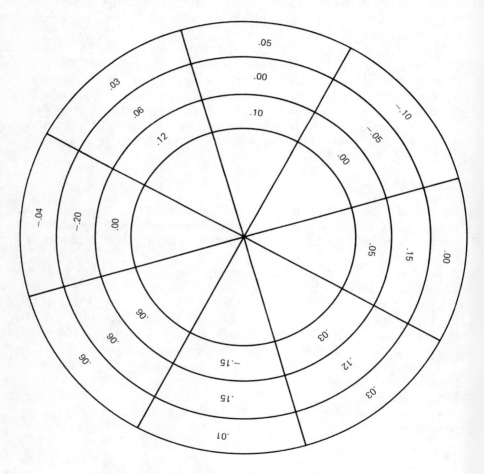

Figure 10-1.   Wheel of Fortune Illustrating Simplified Game

The wheel is marked with two or more concentric rings referred to as ring 1, ring 2, . . . , ring N. The wheel is also marked into M stopping points. Numbers, r_{ij}, written on the wheel for each combination of ring i and stopping point j, indicate the return per dollar bet on the ith ring if the wheel stops at the jth stopping point. Thus if the wheel stops as in Figure 10-1 the return per dollar invested in ring 1 is .05, the return per dollar invested in ring 2 is .00, and the return per dollar invested in ring 3 is .10.

We will sometimes refer to the rings as securities, and the r_{ij} as returns on securities. Cash, or a security with a fixed return, is represented by a ring with the same r_{ij} for all j.

The investor begins with an initial wealth $W_0 > 0$. He chooses an allocation of resources $X_1, X_2, \ldots, X_N$ such that $\sum_{i=1}^{N} X_i = 1$. The wheel is spun, stops at j_1 and his wealth then equals

$$W_1 = W_0 \cdot \sum_{i=1}^{N} X_i \cdot (1 + r_{ij_1})$$

$$= W_0 \cdot (1 + r_1)$$

where

$$r_1 = \sum_{i=1}^{N} X_i r_{ij_1} .$$

Here r_1 is the return in the first period on the portfolio as a whole.

Throughout the chapter we assume that the player bets his entire accumulated wealth on each spin of the wheel. Thus for the second spin the player bets $W_1 = W_0(1 + r_1)$ in total.

In this simplified case we will also assume that both the wheel and the investor's proportions X_i remain the same throughout the game. Thus the wheel is spun a second time, stops at j_2, and the investor's wealth becomes

$$W_2 = W_1 \cdot \sum_{i=1}^{N} X_i \cdot (1 + r_{ij_2})$$

$$= W_1 \cdot (1 + r_2)$$

$$= W_0 \cdot (1 + r_1) \cdot (1 + r_2).$$

After T spins the player's wealth equals the product

$$W_T = W_0 \cdot (1 + r_1) \cdot (1 + r_2) \cdot (1 + r_3) \ldots (1 + r_T) \tag{10.1}$$

where

$$r_t = \sum_{i=1}^{N} X_i r_{ij_t}, \text{ for } t = 1 \text{ to } T,$$

j_t being the stopping point of the wheel on the jth spin. Or, using the product sign π—which is to multiplication as Σ is to summation—we may write (10.1) as

$$W_T = W_0 \cdot \prod_{t=1}^{T} (1 + r_t). \tag{10.1a}$$

In this simplified case we will assume that the portfolio chosen must have

$$X_i \geqslant 0 \text{ for } i = 1 \text{ to } N$$

and that the wheel is such that

$$r_{ij} > -1 \text{ for all } i,j.$$

It follows that the investor cannot be completely wiped out in a single spin of the wheel.

Now let us consider whether the investor would be better advised to select portfolio (a) with proportions

$$X_1^a, X_2^a, X_3^a, \ldots, X_N^a$$

or portfolio (b) with proportions

$$X_1^b, X_2^b, X_3^b, \ldots, X_N^b.$$

The wealth, W_T^a, provided by portfolio (a) after T spins will be larger than the wealth, W_T^b, provided by portfolio (b), if and only if

$$W_T^a/W_0 > W_T^b/W_0$$

therefore if and only if

$$\log(W_T^a/W_0) > \log(W_T^b/W_0)$$

and therefore if and only if

$$(1/T)\log(W_T^a/W_0) > (1/T)\log(W_T^b/W_0).$$

Equation (10.1), and the basic property of logarithms that

$$\log(\prod_{t=1}^{T} (1 + r_t)) = \sum_{t=1}^{T} \log(1 + r_t),$$

imply that for any portfolio

$$(1/T)\log(W_T/W_0) = (1/T) \sum_{t=1}^{T} \log(1 + r_t);$$

hence the expected value of $(1/T)\log(W_T/W_0)$ is

$$(1/T) \cdot E \log (W_T/W_0) = (1/T) \cdot E \left\{ \sum_{t=1}^{T} \log (1 + r_t) \right\}$$

$$= (1/T) \sum_{t=1}^{T} E \log (1 + r_t).$$

But since, for a given player, r_1 has the same probability distribution as r_2, which has the same probability distribution as r_3, etc., we may write

$$(1/T) \cdot E \log(W_T/W_0) = E \log(1 + r) . \qquad (10.2)$$

This is unchanged as T increases.

Since the spins of the wheel are independent, the variance of $(1/T)\log(W_T/W_0)$ equals

$$(1/T^2) \cdot \text{var} \left\{ \sum_{t=1}^{T} \log (1 + r_t) \right\} = (1/T) \cdot \text{var} (\log (1 + r)). \qquad (10.3)$$

This approaches 0 as T approaches ∞.

Therefore as T increases, the expected value of $(1/T)\log(W_T/W_0)$ remains constant while its variance approaches 0. It follows that if $E \log(1 + r)$ is larger for portfolio (a) than portfolio (b), then as $T \to \infty$ the investor who always reinvests in the former is "almost sure" to do better than the investor who always reinvests in the latter. To be precise:

> suppose that p is some probability less than 1.0 (e.g., $p = .999999$). Suppose that a player investing in portfolio (a) would like to be this sure that he will beat a player investing in portfolio (b). He can be this sure by choosing T large enough; since (10.2) and (10.3) and the Tchebychev inequality[2] imply that there exists a T^* such that for a game of length T^* or longer the probability is at least p that player (a) will beat player (b).

The player who chooses the portfolio with greater $E \log(1 + r)$ can be as sure as he pleases (short of absolute certainty) that he will do better than a player who chooses a portfolio with lesser $E \log(1 + r)$. He only has to insist that T be large enough.

It would seem then that, in this simple case at least, the way to invest for the long run is to maximize $E \log(1 + r)$, i.e., to follow the expected log rule. But let us analyze the same game from another point of view.

Suppose that the investor is to play for a fixed number of periods, T, and then "cash in" his final portfolio wealth W_T. Let us also suppose, with Mossin and Samuelson, that the investor has a utility function of the form

$$U = \alpha(W_T)^\alpha$$

for some $\alpha \neq 0$. For example, perhaps his utility function equals $\frac{1}{2}(W_T)^{\frac{1}{2}}$ or $-\frac{1}{2}(W_T)^{-\frac{1}{2}}$. Any such function says utility increases with wealth. For functions with $\alpha < 1$ the rate of increase decreases as wealth increases. The investor's utility at the end of the T periods is

$$
\begin{aligned}
U &= \alpha(W_T)^\alpha \\
&= \alpha \cdot W_0^\alpha \cdot \left\{ \prod_{t=1}^{T} (1 + r_T) \right\}^\alpha \\
&= \alpha W_0^\alpha \cdot \prod_{t=1}^{T} (1 + r_t)^\alpha.
\end{aligned}
$$

Since the spins of the wheel are independent, the expected utility associated with reinvesting in a given portfolio is

$$EU = E \left\{ \alpha W_0^{\alpha} \cdot \prod_{t=1}^{T} (1 + r_t)^{\alpha} \right\}$$

$$= \alpha W_0^{\alpha} \prod_{t=1}^{T} E(1 + r_t)^{\alpha}$$

$$= \alpha W_0^{\alpha} \left\{ E(1 + r)^{\alpha} \right\}^T .$$

This is maximized by choosing the portfolio with greatest $E(1 + r)^{\alpha}$. As a rule this will not be the portfolio which maximizes $E \log(1 + r)$.

Suppose portfolio (a) maximizes $E \log(1 + r)$ while portfolio (b) maximizes $E(1 + r)^{\alpha}$ for the investor's particular α. Suppose that the value of $E(1 + r)^{\alpha}$ for portfolio (b) is k times as great as that provided by portfolio (a), where $k > 1$. The ratio between expected utility from portfolio (a) and that from (b) for the game as a whole is k^T. As $T \to \infty$, $k^T \to \infty$. Hence as T increases, the superiority of portfolio (b) over portfolio (a) increases without limit.

According to our previous argument, for sufficiently large T portfolio (a) is almost sure to beat portfolio (b). In fact, for any $p < 1$ there is a T^* such that for $T \geqslant T^*$ the probability that (a) beats (b) is at least p. Yet, when $U = \alpha(W_T)^{\alpha}$ the ratio of the expected utility provided by (b) to that provided by (a) can increase without bounds as T increases.

10.4 THE CATCH

The theorems presented later in this chapter address themselves to the apparent paradox illustrated in the preceding section. The theorems are proved under substantially more general assumptions than those of our previous discussion. For the time being, however, we will continue the simplified analysis, stating here without proof the implications of the theorems for the present special case, and how this reveals "the catch" in the apparent paradox. We begin by presenting some basic notions used in the theorems.

The theorems consider sequences of games $G_{T_1}, G_{T_2}, G_{T_3}, \dots$ The first game in the sequence may have $T_1 = 100$; i.e., it is to be played for 100 periods. The next game in the sequence may have $T_2 = 101$ or $T_2 = 200$, or any other number greater than 100; and in general

$$T_{j+1} > T_j$$

for $j = 1,2,3,\ldots$ A special case of such a sequence would be, for example

$$G_{100},\ G_{200},\ G_{300},\ldots$$

where G_{300} is a game consisting of 300 spins of the same wheel such as described in the preceding section.

As in the Mossin-Samuelson analysis we shall assume that, in some sense, the same utility function is used in each game in the sequence. We shall consider sequences of games, however, in which the utility function is assumed to stay the same in one of two different senses.

We may define the rate of growth g as

$$g = (W_T/W_0)^{1/T} - 1.$$

It follows immediately that

$$W_T = W_0 \cdot (1 + g)^T.$$

Thus if the investor had put all of his wealth in a savings account that paid (g) per period he would have ended the game with the same terminal wealth.

For a fixed T we can express utility equivalently as a function of W_T or as a function of g. E.g., if

$$U = U(W_T)$$

then

$$U = U(W_0 \cdot (1 + g)^T) = V(g)$$

by definition of $V(g)$. Either U or V can be used equivalently to evaluate a probability distribution of W_T or the implied probability distribution of g.

Any one game, then, may be described equivalently with a $U(W_T)$ function or a $V(g)$ function. On the other hand, we have a different sequence of utility functions associated with G_{T_1}, G_{T_2}, G_{T_3}, ... if we assume $U(W_T)$ is the same for all games G_T, or assume $V(g)$ is the same for all G_T.

If we think of a period as some fixed interval of time, such as a month, then the assumption that $U(W_T)$ is constant among games assumes, for example, that the investor has the same rankings among probability distributions involving terminal wealth = $500,000 *vs.* $1,000,000 *vs.* $2,000,000 whether the game is for 100 months, 200 months or 500 months. The assumption that $V(g)$ remains the same, on the other hand, asserts that the investor has the same preference rankings among probability distributions of say a ½, 1, or 1½ percent rate of return per month for the game as a whole whether the game is for 100 months, 200 months or 500 months.

While results are presented below for both constant $U(W_T)$ and for constant $V(g)$, it seems to be that assuming a constant $V(g)$ is the more plausible interpretation of "investing for the long run." Suppose that the management company of a mutual fund, or the trustee organization of a large private estate, takes as its goal "return" or "increase in wealth" over the long run. Suppose indeed that they are not willing to give up anything in the long run for a second goal of reducing short run fluctuations in wealth. In this case it seems to me more plausible that their utility function is expressible in terms of a 3 vs. a 6 vs. a 9 percent rate of return per annum over an indefinitely long period of time, rather than in terms of a 40 fold increase in wealth vs. a 60 fold increase in wealth vs. an 80 fold increase in wealth over an indefinitely long period of time.

Let G_{T_1}, G_{T_2}, G_{T_3}, . . . be a sequence of alternate possible games in which the same wheel is spun respectively T_1 times, T_2 times, T_3 times, etc. Theorem 1 implies that if $V(g)$ is the same for all games in the sequence, if utility does not decrease when g increases, and if $r_{ij} > -1$ for all i,j then:

> if $V(g)$ is continuous, the expected value of $V(g)$ provided by the expected log rule approaches the maximum obtainable expected $V(g)$ as $T \to \infty$.

> If $V(g)$ is not continuous, then the expected value of $V(g)$ provided by the expected log rule is within $\epsilon + \gamma^{max}$ of the maximum obtainable expected $V(g)$, where γ^{max} is the largest jump in the $V(g)$ function, and $\epsilon \to 0$ as $T \to \infty$.

In other words, the expected log rule provides asymptotically optimal expected utility if $V(g)$ is continuous, and at least asymptotically "nearly" optimal expected utility if $V(g)$ has only "small" jumps. This result is true even if the "maximum obtainable expected $V(g)$" is that provided by a strategy which allows the choice of portfolios to change from period to period.

Contrasting the results just quoted with those for the Mossin-Samuelson $U(W_T)$ function, one might conjecture that the expected log rule does well for constant $V(g)$ and poorly for constant $U(W_T)$.

Theorems 2 and 3, on the contrary, show that under certain conditions the expected log rule is also asymptotically optimal if $U(W_T)$ is bounded both from above and from below. Specifically, in the simple case of unchanging probabilities if U does not decrease with an increase in W_T, if U is bounded from above and below, if $r_{ij} > -1$ for all i,j and if the maximum obtainable $E \log(1 + r)$ is not equal to 0, then the expected value of $U(W_T)$ provided by the expected log rule is within ϵ of that provided by the optimum strategy—where ϵ approaches 0 as T increases. Thus the persistent difference between the expected utility provided by the expected log rule and that of the optimum strategy in the Mossin-Samuelson analysis is due to the fact that (W_T) is unbounded above if $\alpha > 0$, and unbounded below if $\alpha < 0$.

The question of bounded versus unbounded utility functions is not original to the analysis of the asymptotic optimality of the expected log rule.

10.5 AN EXAMPLE

Before we proceed to the general discussion, let us illustrate our introductory remarks with a numerical example.

Suppose, for this example, that a "wheel" has two outcomes: heads and tails. Suppose further for this example that only two choices are allowed the game player: He can either: (a) always receive a one percent increase; or (b) have a 75 percent increase in case of heads, and a 50 percent decrease in the case of tails. Alternative (a) provides $r = .01$ with certainty; alternative (b) provides a 50-50 chance of $r = -.5$ or $r = +.75$. In this example let us require that the player either always bet all of his wealth on (a), or always bet all of his wealth on (b).

Consider the choice of (a) or (b) by three investors. The first investor wants to maximize the expected value of terminal wealth W_T. This is actually the special case of maximizing the expected value of $\alpha(W_T)^\alpha$ in which $\alpha = 1$. We will refer to this player as the Mossin ($\alpha = 1$) Player. The second investor wants to maximize the expected value of the square root of W_T. He is a Mossin ($\alpha = \frac{1}{2}$) Player, since the utility functions $(W_T)^{\frac{1}{2}}$ and $\frac{1}{2}(W_T)^{\frac{1}{2}}$ are equivalent in their choices among alternative strategies. The third player follows the expected log rule. We call him our Kelly Player.

As seen in Section 10.3, in this game the Mossin ($\alpha = 1$) Player will pick the bet with the highest expected value of $(1 + r)$. This will be the same bet that maximizes expected r. Since alternative (b) provides an expected return of

$$\tfrac{1}{2}(-.5) + \tfrac{1}{2}(.75) = .125$$

while alternative (a) provides an expected value of

$$\tfrac{1}{2}(.01) + \tfrac{1}{2}(.01) = .01$$

the Mossin ($\alpha = 1$) Player will prefer (b).

Section 10.3 also implies that the Mossin ($\alpha = \tfrac{1}{2}$) Player will, in this game, choose the alternative which maximizes the expected value of $(1 + r)^{\tfrac{1}{2}}$ on a single spin (or flip). For alternative (a) this is

$$\tfrac{1}{2}(1.01)^{\tfrac{1}{2}} + \tfrac{1}{2}(1.01)^{\tfrac{1}{2}} = 1.005$$

For (b) the expected value of $(1 + r)^{\tfrac{1}{2}}$ is

$$\tfrac{1}{2}(.5)^{\tfrac{1}{2}} + \tfrac{1}{2}(1.75)^{\tfrac{1}{2}} = 1.015$$

Thus he too, in this particular example, will prefer (b).

The Kelly Player chooses the larger of

$$\tfrac{1}{2}\log_{10}(1.01) + \tfrac{1}{2}\log_{10}(1.01) = .0043$$

versus

$$\tfrac{1}{2}\log_{10}(.5) + \tfrac{1}{2}\log_{10}(1.75) = -.1505 + .1215$$

$$= -.0190$$

and selects (a) instead.

After, e.g., 2,000 flips of the coin the Kelly Player will have increased his wealth by a factor of $(1.01)^{2000}$ or over 400 million-fold. The fate of the two Mossin Players depends on the number of heads in the 2000 flips. If perchance there were exactly 1000 heads and 1000 tails, the ratio of their ending wealth to starting wealth would equal

$$(.5)^{1000} \cdot (1.75)^{1000} = (.875)^{1000}$$

$$\cong 10^{-58}$$

$$= \quad .000\ 000\ 000\ 000\ 000\ 000\ 000$$
$$000\ 000\ 000\ 000\ 000\ 000\ 000$$
$$000\ 000\ 000\ 000\ 001.$$

There is a 50-50 chance that the Mossin Players will do worse than this. If instead of $T = 2000$ we choose a larger value of T the story would be the same—only more so.

It would seem that alternative (b) is a miserable way to bet for the long run. Yet it does maximize expected W_T. If you added the probability of 2000 straight heads times $(1.75)^{2000}$ plus the probability of 1999 heads out of 2000 times $(.5) \cdot (1.75)^{1999}$ plus the sum of each other possible outcome times its probability you would find that the "expected value" of W_{2000} provided by (b) was $W_0 \cdot (1.125)^{2000}$ as compared to the mere $W_0 \cdot (1.01)^{2000}$ provided by (a).

This implies that if you would rather have your money ride on (a) than (b), your criteria cannot be to maximize the expected value of W_T; nor can it be to maximize the expected value of $\sqrt{W_T}$. You may still act according to the expected utility maxim. But neither $U = W_T$ nor $U = \sqrt{W_T}$ is your utility function.

We have argued that since T is of indefinite size in this discussion, utility should be expressed in terms of the rate of return g rather than terminal wealth W_T. It can be shown that for large T alternative (a) provides a larger value of expected $V(g)$ than does (b) in this example for any continuous everywhere increasing $V(g)$, even for $V(g) = \alpha g^\alpha (\alpha \neq 0)$.

The main result of this study is theorem 1. It is not the purpose of theorem 1 to compare the expected log rule with the rule which always maximizes expected $\alpha(1 + r_t)^\alpha$ each period. Rather the purpose of theorem 1 is to compare the expected log rule with whatever strategy maximizes expected $V(g)$ for a given game G_T as a whole. The latter, precisely optimal, strategy may involve varying the portfolio from period to period even if the same wheel is spun each time. The finding of optimal strategies for realistically complex games may be beyond the optimization capabilities of our largest computers. Yet, according to theorem 1, for sufficiently large T the precisely optimum strategy can do very little better than the simple expected log rule.

10.6 THE MORAL

We conclude from theorem 1 that if you were interested only in reinvesting for the long run, in the manner assumed here, you need not bother to solve for an optimum strategy. Such an optimum solution would require you to estimate your actual $V(g)$ function; estimate how future distributions of returns depend on time and preceding events; and perhaps may require untold calculations to determine. Instead just follow the expected log rule. For sufficiently large T there will be virtually no difference in the expected utility provided for the game as a whole.

Under conditions explored elsewhere [Markowitz (1959, pp. 121-125), and Young and Trent (1969)] the policy of maximizing expected logarithm for the current period may itself be approximated by a portfolio selected from the set of E, V efficient portfolios. In this case both the estimation problem and the computation problem are reduced to quite reasonable proportions, especially if some simplified model of covariance [as in Sharpe (1963), Cohen and Pogue (1967), or Markowitz (1959, pp. 96-101)] may be assumed.

Note that the advice to maximize $E \log(1 + r)$ applies to the portfolio as a whole rather than to some subset of the portfolio. Suppose, for example, that an analyst is asked to advise whether an investor who plans to continually reinvest for the long run should buy the common stock, the preferred stock, or some of each, of a given corporation. Unless it was in fact the investor's entire portfolio, it would not as a rule be even approximately correct to choose the combination of common and preferred which maximizes $E \log(+ r)$.

To see the error of trying to maximize $E \log(1 + r)$ for the portfolio as a whole by maximizing it for components of the portfolio, consider again securities (a) and (b) of the preceding section. We saw that security (a), providing $r = .01$ with certainty, had a greater $E \log(1 + r)$ than security (b) with a 50-50 chance of $r = -.50$ or $+.75$. But if a sufficiently large number of securities like (b) were available, and if their returns were uncorrelated, then a portfolio consisting of many such securities would provide $r = .125$ with near certainty, and would have a higher $E \log(1 + r)$ than a portfolio consisting of (a) only. Many securities with a lessor $E \log(1 + r)$ thus may (or may not) combine to provide a greater $E \log(1 + r)$ for the portfolio as a whole. We should make the individual decisions for their effect on the portfolio as a whole.

Theorem 1 is relevant to the user of E, V efficient set analysis, even if he is not dedicated exclusively to investment for the long run. Suppose that a portfolio analyst has computed an E, V efficient set for an investor or investment manager, and is about to graph the probability distribution of returns for several possibly desirable efficient portfolios. In accord with Baumol's (1963) observations, the analyst would presumably not draw plots for any efficient portfolio with standard deviation σ below the point with maximum $E - k\sigma$, for k equal to about 2 or 3. Below some such point, efficient portfolios may be viewed as less variable but not safer. Similarly, the analyst would presumably not draw plots for efficient portfolios with E and σ greater than one with approximately maximum $E \log(1 + r)$; for efficient portfolios with greater E and σ are more variable in the short run without presumably[3] providing additional return in the long run.

Thus the analyst may reasonably discard from further attention efficient portfolios below a "Baumol point" and above a "Kelly-Latané point."

10.7 THE GAME G_T

We now present our general model. We consider a game G_T played for T periods. At the beginning of each period, t, the player chooses portfolio proportions

$$X_{1t}, X_{2t}, X_{3t}, \ldots, X_{Nt}$$

such that $\sum\limits_{i=1}^{N} X_{it} = 1$. This choice may depend on the history which precedes period t. We now may imagine that the return per dollar invested is generated by the spin of a wheel as in Figure 10-2. The wheel in Figure 10-2 differs from that in Figure 10-1 in that:

it has a "wheel number," and

each stopping point on the wheel indicates the wheel number of the wheel to be spun next.

Thus if the current wheel stops as in Figure 10-2, the returns per dollar bet on rings 1, 2, and 3 respectively are .05, .00, and .10 and the wheel to be spun for the next period is 381. In this manner both the returns this period and the opportunities of subsequent periods are generated by the spin of the wheel. The number of stopping points and securities may vary from wheel to wheel.

In our earlier simplified analysis we assumed that the wheel had a finite number of stopping points. The variety of objects (giraffes, oceans, skyscrapers) fashioned by nature and man from the finite number of atoms of the earth suggests that the assumption is not a practical limitation. It is worth noting, however, that the theorems and their proofs apply if there are either a finite or a countably infinite number of stopping points on any wheel.

In the simplified analysis the player chose a portfolio from the constraint set described by

$$X_i > 0, \text{ for all } i$$

(in addition to $\Sigma X_i = 1$). The three theorems allow the portfolio $(X_{1t}, X_{2t}, \ldots, X_{Nt})$ to be selected from a constraint set S such that:

S is not empty;

S may depend on the current wheel but not on the prior choice of portfolio;

$\Sigma X_{it} = 1$ for all $(X_1, X_2, \ldots, X_N) \in S$.

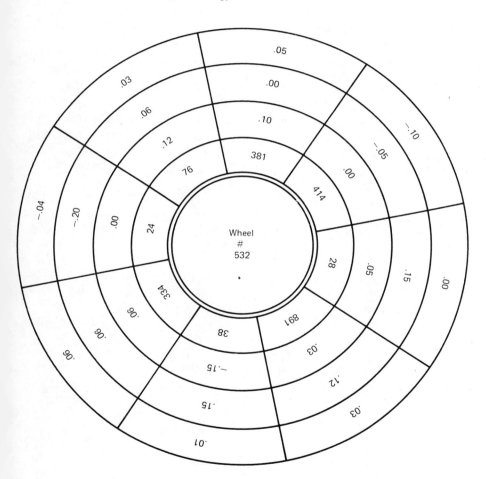

Figure 10-2. Wheel of Fortune Illustrating General Game

Later we present an additional restriction on the r_{ij} and the set S associated with any wheel in any G_T. We will not assume there, however, as we have not assumed here, that S is necessarily (for example) closed, or convex, or that $E \log(1 + r)$ necessarily achieves a maximum in S.

A strategy s is a rule specifying:

initial proportions invested, chosen from the set S of the first wheel; and

proportions to be invested at time t as a function of the history to date:

$$X_{it} = X_{it}(j_1, j_2, \ldots, j_{t-1})$$

where the portfolio $(X_{1t}, \ldots, X_{Nt})$ is contained in the set S associated with the wheel to be spun at time t.

For a given game G_T and a given strategy s, the history of a particular play is given by the sequence of stopping points. The stopping point of the first spin, j_1 implies: the returns r_{ij_1}; the return r_1 on the portfolio as a whole associated with strategy s; the next wheel to be spun; and the portfolio to be selected for the next spin according to strategy s. The pair of stopping points (j_1, j_2) implies in addition: the returns r_{ij_2}; the portfolio return r_2 associated with s; the third wheel to be spun, and so on.

There are a finite or countably infinite number of possible sequences of stopping points, or "histories," $(j_1, j_2, j_3, \ldots, j_T)$. In principle we can assign numbers $1, 2, 3, \ldots$ to each possible history. This assignment may be made completely arbitrarily as long as each possible sequence is assigned a number.

Thus the history of a particular play of the game G_T may be represented by a single positive integer, h_T. The structure of a game, as described in terms of wheels, implies a probability for each h_T. The returns in each period $r_1, r_2, \ldots, r_T$ obtained from following a given strategy s in a play of G_T is also implied by the integer h_T.

For each time period t there are a finite or countably infinite number of possible "partial histories" $(j_1, j_2, \ldots, j_t)$. Each such partial history can, in principle, be assigned a number h_t. The assignment of an integer to each possible partial history at time t may be made arbitrarily—without regard to the numbers assigned to the partial histories at time t', or to the numbers assigned to the total histories.

Any history h_T implies $T - 1$ partial histories:

$$h_1, h_2, h_3, \ldots, h_{T-1}.$$

Any partial history has a conditional probability distribution of the total history,

$$\text{prob}(h_t \mid h_t)$$

or for any later partial history

$$\text{prob}(h_{t'} \mid h_t)$$

for $T \geqslant t' > t$. By convention we will let $h_0 = 1$ be the "partial history" before the game begins. Thus $\text{prob}(h_t \mid h_0) = \text{prob}(h_t)$.

While there are a finite or countably infinite number of possible histories, there may be a continuum of possible strategies. This will cause us no difficulty since we will be either examining the properties of one strategy or comparing two of them.

10.8 THE SEQUENCE OF GAMES

We postulate a sequence of games G_T for $T = T_1, T_2, T_3, \ldots$ where $T_1 < T_2 < T_3 \ldots$. It may or may not be true that the first T_1 periods of G_{T_2} are "like" the game G_{T_1}. *The sequence of games* $G_{T_1}, G_{T_2}, \ldots$ can be quite loosely related.

For example, the game G_{T_1} may consist of 100 spins of a single wheel, call it wheel 1. The game G_{T_2} may consist of 200 spins of a different wheel, wheel 2. The game G_{T_3} may consist of 300 spins of wheel 1 again; G_{T_4} may consist of 400 spins of wheel 2 again; etc. We have already noted that the game $G_{T_{i+1}}$ is longer than the game G_{T_i}, and that they both have the same utility function either in the sense of $V(g)$ or $U(W_T)$. An additional major assumption concerning the sequence of games is presented later in this section.

We shall be concerned with two sequences of strategies: $s_{T_1}^k, s_{T_2}^k, s_{T_3}^k, \ldots$ being one sequence of strategies and $s_{T_1}^m, s_{T_2}^m, s_{T_3}^m, \ldots$ being the other. $s_{T_1}^k$ and $s_{T_1}^m$ are two out of perhaps countless ways of playing the game G_{T_1}; $s_{T_2}^k$ and $s_{T_2}^m$ are two ways of playing G_{T_2}; etc. The relationship we assume between $s_{T_j}^k$ and $s_{T_j}^m$ is that $s_{T_j}^k$ always selects an allocation with at least as high an $E \log(1 + r)$ as supplied by $s_{T_j}^m$. In other words for every game G_T, and for every partial history h_{t-1} where $1 \leqslant t \leqslant T$ we assume that the

$$E\left\{\log(1 + r_t) \mid h_{t-1}\right\}$$

provided by s_T^k is at least as great as that provided by s_T^m. On the other hand s_T^m may provide greater $EV(g)$ or $EU(W_T)$. The theorems analyze the extent to which the expected utility provided by s_T^m can exceed that provided by s_T^k as $T \to \infty$.

A basic assumption used in the proofs of the theorems is the following:

There exist $r^{low} > -1$ and r^{hi} such that for all games G_T in the sequence $G_{T_1}, G_{T_2}, G_{T_3}, \ldots$, and for either strategy s_T^k or s_T^m we always have

$$r^{low} \leqslant r_t \leqslant r^{hi}.$$

For example, if $r^{low} = 10^{-8}$ and $r^{hi} = 10^9$ then our assumption says that (by law or by investment practice) the returns and constraints in all the games $G_{T_1}, G_{T_2}, G_{T_3}, \ldots$ are such that

the investor cannot be wiped out in a single spin of the wheel; in fact he must retain at least one penny per million dollars bet on any one spin of the wheel; and he cannot win more than $1,000,000,000 per dollar bet on a single spin.

While r^{low} and r^{hi} are lower and upper bounds on r_t, they are not necessarily the greatest lower bound or least upper bound. Thus for either s_T^k or s_T^m or both, and for any or all of the games, $G_{T_1}, G_{T_2}, \ldots$ we may have r_t always "much greater" than r^{low}, or r_t "much less" than r^{hi}.

Another way of stating this basic assumption used in proving the theorems is that $\log(1 + r)$ is bounded from above and below for both of the strategies analyzed.

In addition to the explicit assumptions of the analysis, there are the implicit assumptions suggested by asking, for example, what kind of game would have

$$W_T = W_0 \cdot \pi(1 + r_t)$$

or would permit

$$E\left\{ \log(1 + r_t) \mid h_{t-1} \right\}$$

to always be greater for one strategy, s_T^k, than for another, s_T^m. A partial list of answers include:

commissions and other costs of transactions are ignored (hence for semi-"realism" the period should not be thought of as "too short"; but the investment decision can only be made once per period, hence the period should not be thought of as "too long");

there is no "round lot" consideration since the dollar amount invested, $W_{t-1} \cdot X_{it}$, may be very small; (the limitations in S are on the proportions X_{it} not on the amounts $W_{t-1} \cdot X_{it}$);

and so on. The world we are analyzing is clearly an abstraction; hence part of the need for some disclaimer, as in the footnote at the end of Section 10.6, concerning the precise interpretation of the Kelly-Latané point in the EV efficient set.

10.9 THE THEOREMS

The first theorem deals with the case in which utility is a function of g.

Theorem 1: if $V(g)$ is a monitonically increasing function; $G_{T_1}, G_{T_2}, \ldots$ is a sequence of games as described in the last two sections; and s_T^k and s_T^m are strategies associated with game G_T such that

$$E \left\{ \log(1 + r_t) \mid h_{t-1} \right\}$$

is always at least as great for s_T^k as for s_T^m then there exists a T^* such that for all $T \geqslant T^*$ the expected value of $V(g)$ provided by s_T^m is at most $\epsilon + \gamma^{max}$ greater than that provided by s_T^k, where γ^{max} is the largest jump of $V(g)$, and $\epsilon \to 0$ as $T \to \infty$.

Our assumptions concerning the constraint sets are too general for us to conclude that for every game G_T there exists a strategy which always maximizes

$$E \left\{ \log(1 + r_t) \mid h_{t-1} \right\}$$

and a strategy which maximizes $EV(g)$ or $EU(W_T)$. In such cases as these strategies do exist, however, we may let s_T^k be the strategy which always maximizes

$$E \left\{ \log(1 + r_t) \mid h_{t-1} \right\}$$

and let s_T^m be the strategy which maximizes $EV(g)$ or $EU(W_T)$. In this case we may think of s_T^k as the Kelly-Latané strategy and s_T^m as the maximizing strategy for the game G_T. If $V(g)$ is continuous then s_T^k is asymptotically optimal since the maximum advantage of s_T^m over s_T^k approaches 0 as T approaches ∞.

In theorems 2 and 3 we consider utility to be a bounded function $U(W_T)$. We do not derive results for this case in general, but for certain subclasses depending on

$$\overline{L}_T^k = (1/T) \sum_{t=1}^{T} E \left\{ \log (1 + r_t) \mid h_{t-1} \right\}$$

as provided by the strategy s_T^k.

Theorem 2: If, for a sequence of games as described in the preceding section, we have

$$\text{prob} \left\{ \overline{L}_t^k \geqslant \alpha > 0 \right\} \to 1 \text{ as } T \to \infty$$

then the expected value $U(W_T)$ provided by s_T^k approaches U^{hi}, the least upper bound of $U(W_T)$.

The assumption of theorem 2 is met if there is a riskless security whose yield, while perhaps varying with time, is always at least $\beta > 0$, where $\alpha = \log(1 + \beta)$.

Theorem 3: If, for a sequence of games as described in the preceding section, we have

$$\text{prob} \left\{ \overline{L}_T^k \leqslant \alpha < 0 \right\} \to 1 \text{ as } T \to \infty$$

then the expected utility provided by either s_T^k or s_T^m approaches U^{low}, the greatest lower bound of $U(W_T)$ for $W_T > 0$.

Under either the assumption in theorem 2 or that in theorem 3 the expected value of $U(W_T)$ provided by s_T^m cannot exceed that provided by s_T^k by more than ϵ, where $\epsilon \to 0$ as $T \to \infty$. This result for $U(W_T)$ is not true for assumptions as general as those for $V(g)$ in theorem 1.

10.10 PROPERTIES OF $V(g)$ AND $U(W_T)$

Section 10.10 establishes some properties needed to prove the three theorems.

Since $r^{\text{low}} \leqslant g \leqslant r^{\text{hi}}$, the expected utility of any strategy is unchanged if we replace $V(g)$ by a function which equals $V(g)$ for $r^{\text{low}} \leqslant g \leqslant r^{\text{hi}}$, equals $V(r^{\text{low}})$ for $g < r^{\text{low}}$ and equals $V(r^{\text{hi}})$ for $g > r^{\text{hi}}$. Thus we may assume that $V(g)$ in theorem 1, like $U(W_T)$ in theorems 2 and 3, is bounded. Since $W_T > 0$ in any game G_T, we may arbitrarily let $U(W_T) = U^{\text{low}}$ for $W_T \leqslant 0$ without changing the expected utility of any strategy. $U(W_T)$ thus extended, like $V(g)$ as just defined, is a bounded, monitonically increasing function

$$y = f(x)$$

defined for $-\infty < x < +\infty$. In this section we review some general properties of any such function.

Texts on mathematical statistics analyze the bounded, monotonic function

$$y = P(x)$$

= the probability that a random variable is less than or equal to x.

They show that $P(x)$ may be expressed as the sum of a continuous function and a step function, where the step function has at most a countable number of jumps. Either, but not both, functions may be identically zero. The difference between $P(x)$ and the general bounded, monotonically increasing function $f(x)$, is that:

$P(x)$ has 0 and 1 specifically as its greatest lower bound (GLB) and its least upper bound (LUB); while $f(x)$ may have any two numbers $y^{\text{low}} \leqslant y^{\text{hi}}$ as its GLB and LUB; and

$P(x)$ is continuous from the right, while $f(x)$ may be continuous from the right, from the left or neither at any point of discontinuity.

A slight modification of the argument which establishes the character of $P(x)$ shows that any bounded monotonically increasing $f(x)$ has the following properties:

$$f(x) = C(x) + \sum_{\substack{d_i \in D \\ d_i < x}} \gamma(d_i) + \theta(x)$$

where C is a bounded, continuous, monotonically increasing function (perhaps identically zero); D is an empty, finite or countably infinite set of real values $x = d_i$; $\gamma(d_i) > 0$ for each $d_i \in D$; $\theta(x) = 0$ for x not in D and $0 \leqslant \theta(x) \leqslant \gamma(x)$ for $x = d_i \in D$. $f(x)$ is continuous from the left, from the right or neither at a point $x = d_i$, depending on whether $\theta = 0$, $\theta = \gamma(x)$ or neither at the point. Since $C(x)$ is continuous, bounded, and monotonic, it is uniformly continuous;[4] i.e., for any $\epsilon > 0$ there exists $\delta > 0$ such that if $0 \leqslant x_2 - x_1 \leqslant \delta$ then $f(x_2) - f(x_1) \leqslant \epsilon$.

Since $\gamma(d_i) > 0$ for $d_i \in D$ and $\Sigma \gamma(d_i) \leqslant y^{\text{hi}} - y^{\text{low}}$, the sum of any subset of the $\gamma(d_i)$ is absolutely convergent. If D is not empty, $d_1, d_2, d_3, \ldots$ is an arbitrarily chosen sequence of all of the values of x at which f is discontinuous. Given any number $\gamma > 0$ there are at most a finite number of d_i with a larger value of $\gamma(d_i)$; e.g., only a finite number of d_i have $\gamma(d_i) > \gamma(d_1)$. Otherwise the sum of the $\gamma(d_i)$ would not be finite. Hence there exists a d_i with maximum $\gamma(d_i)$. We write γ^{max} for this maximum $\gamma(d_i)$.

The following property of $f(x)$ is particularly useful in the subsequent discussion:

Lemma 1. For every $\epsilon > 0$ there is a $\delta > 0$ such that if $\leqslant x_2 - x_1 \leqslant \delta$ then $0 \leqslant f(x_2) - f(x_1) \leqslant \epsilon + \gamma^{max}$.

Proof. The uniform continuity of the monotonically increasing, continuous function $C(X)$ implies that there is a value $\delta_1 > 0$ such that $0 \leqslant C(x_2) - C(x_1) \leqslant \epsilon/2$ provided $0 \leqslant x_2 - x_1 \leqslant \delta_1$. The convergence of the sum of the $\gamma(d_i)$ implies that there is an integer N such that $\sum\limits_{i=N+1}^{\infty} \gamma(d_i) \leqslant \epsilon/2$. Let $\delta_2 > 0$ be such that at most one $d_i \epsilon D$ with $i \leqslant N$ appears in any interval $a \leqslant x \leqslant a + \delta_2$. Let δ equal the smaller of δ_1 and δ_2. Then for any x_1, x_2 with $0 \leqslant x_2 - x_1 \leqslant \delta$ we have

$$f(x_2) - f(x_1) = C(x_2) + \sum_{\substack{d_i < x_2 \\ d_i \epsilon D \\ i \leqslant N}} \gamma(d_i) + \sum_{\substack{d_i < x_2 \\ d_i \epsilon D \\ i > N}} \gamma(d_i) + \theta(x_2)$$

$$- [C(x_1) + \sum_{\substack{d_i < x_1 \\ d_i \epsilon D \\ i \leqslant N}} \gamma(d_i) + \sum_{\substack{d_i < x_1 \\ d_i \epsilon D \\ i > N}} \gamma(d_i) + \theta(x_1)]$$

$$= [C(x_2) - C(x_1)] + [\sum_{\substack{x_1 \leqslant d_i < x_2 \\ d_i \epsilon D \\ i \leqslant N}} \gamma(d_i)] + \theta(x_2)$$

$$- \theta(x_1) + [\sum_{\substack{x_1 \leqslant d_i < x_2 \\ d_i \epsilon D \\ i > N}} \gamma(d_i)]$$

$$\leqslant \epsilon/2 + \gamma^{max} + \epsilon/2$$

(since $\theta(x_2)$ may be included in the first or second sum of $\gamma(d_i)$ as appropriate). Therefore

$$f(x_2) - f(x_1) \leqslant \epsilon + \gamma^{max}.$$

NOTES TO SECTION TEN

1. This article owes much to Paul A. Samuelson and to my wife Barbara. After several discussions with Professor Samuelson on the subject of this study, I found myself neither convinced by his position nor happy with the rigor of my own. This chapter was written so that I could see the argument myself, show it to Professor Samuelson, and share it with whomever else was interested. Dr. Barbara Markowitz read, typed, and critiqued several drafts.

2. Tchebychev's inequality says that the probability that a random variable will deviate from its expected value by more than k times its standard deviation is never greater than $1/k^2$. Therefore as variance and standard deviation approach 0 the probability of a given size deviation approaches 0. For example, let d be the difference between the $E \log(1 + r)$ provided by portfolio (a) and that provided by portfolio (b) in the text above. By hypothesis, d, is greater than 0 and does not depend on T. The probability that the actual value of $(1/T)\log(W_T/W_0)$ provided by portfolio (a) will deviate from its expected value by as much as one-half d, or that the actual $(1/T)\log(W_t/W_0)$ provided by portfolio (b) will deviate from its expected value by as much as one-half d, approaches 0 as their two variances approach 0.

3. We say "presumably" since (1) the asymptotic optimality of the expected log rule is shown here under certain simplified assumptions, such as no costs of transactions, as discussed in Section 10.8; and (2) while Trent and Young show that the historical average $\log(1 + r)$ of various portfolios is closely approximated by formulae depending only on historical E and V, nevertheless E, V approximations can be quite inaccurate in the case of highly speculative portfolios. For example, if a game player were allowed to borrow and bet to such an extent that $r \leqslant -1.0$ could occur, then $E \log(1 + r)$ would equal $-\infty$ while the various Trent and Young approximations might even be positive. Hopefully, future research will provide broader guidelines as to when E, V approximations may be trusted than the guidelines of Markowitz (1959) pages 121-2.

4. Uniform continuity may be shown as follows: Let $x_a < x_b$ be such that

$$f(x) - y^{\text{low}} < \epsilon$$

for $x < x_a$, and

$$y^{\text{hi}} - f(x) < \epsilon$$

for $x > x_b$, where y^{low} and y^{hi} are the GLB and LUB of $f(x)$. Let $X_A = x_a - 1$; let $x_B = x_b + 1$. Within the interval $X_A \leqslant x \leqslant x_B$, $f(x)$ is uniformly continuous because it is here continuous on a closed interval. Hence for any $\epsilon > 0$ there is a

$$\delta' > 0 \text{ such that } 0 \leqslant f(x_2) - f(x_1) \leqslant \epsilon$$

provided

$$0 \leqslant x_2 - x_1 \leqslant \delta' \text{ and } x_A \leqslant x_1 \leqslant x_2 \leqslant x_B.$$

Let δ equal the minimum of δ' or 1. For

$$0 \leqslant x_2 - x_1 \leqslant \delta, \text{ if } x_1 \leqslant x_A \text{ then } x_2 \leqslant x_1 + \delta \leqslant x_a;$$

hence

$$0 \leqslant f(x_2) - f(x_1) \leqslant (y^{\text{low}} + \epsilon) - y^{\text{low}} = \epsilon;$$

whereas if

$$x_2 \geqslant x_B \text{ then } x_1 \geqslant x_2 - \delta \geqslant x_b \text{ and } 0 \leqslant f(x_2) - f(x_1) \leqslant y^{\text{hi}} - (y^{\text{hi}} - \epsilon) = \epsilon.$$

Thus the same δ "works" throughout. I.e., for every $\epsilon > 0$ there exists $\delta > 0$, where δ depends on ϵ but not on x_1 or x_2, such that $0 \leqslant x_2 - x_1 \leqslant \delta$ implies

$$f(x_2) - f(x_1) \leqslant \epsilon.$$

※ *Section Eleven*

The Capital Asset Pricing Model: Some Open and Closed Ends*

Nils H. Hakansson[†]

11.1 INTRODUCTION

Portfolio analysis, in the modern sense, has barely been with us 20 years—its beginning is usually attributed to Markowitz's 1952 paper and to Tobin (1958). Over this brief span, it has thoroughly pervaded every aspect of finance, gained a strong foothold in economics, and is even beginning to make its presence felt in accounting. Portfolio theory has not only become a field of study in its own right but is an indispensable part of the foundations of corporation finance, the study of financial intermediation, and the modern analysis of money and capital markets.

At least four distinct models of portfolio choice have been "put on the market": the expected utility model, the mean-variance approach (in many versions), the long-run growth model, and the chance-constrained programming approach. Based on the market acceptance test, there is clearly one winner at this point. The mean-variance model of portfolio choice is so dominant that to many business school graduates portfolio theory is synonymous with mean-variance theory.

Why does the mean-variance (MV) model occupy such a dominant position? The usual explanation for the prominence, at any particular time, of a given theory in science is that a theory prevails until it

*This research was supported by Grant No. GS-35700 from the National Science Foundation.

†The author wishes to thank Mark Rubenstein for stimulating discussions on topics related to this chapter and Robert Grauer for computational assistance.

is replaced by a better one. Thus, we might expect—and this will indeed be borne out—that the answer to our question lies as much in the problems associated with the other models as in the net strength of the MV approach.

The chance-constrained programming (CCP) model of portfolio choice [see, e.g., Naslund and Whinston (1962), Agnew, Agnew, Rasmussen, and Smith (1969)] came into being in conjunction with the evolution of chance-constrained programming as a branch of linear programming. Typically, the objective is to maximize expected return subject to the return not falling below some specified rate with a minimum probability (such as .95). This feature, which reveals an intimate association with classical statistics, clearly offers some intuitive appeal. But CCP suffers from nontractability except in the case of normal distributions, and never attracted much following.[1] A fatal shortcoming in the view of many is the model's lack of consistency with the von Neumann-Morgenstern postulates [Borch (1968, pp. 41-42)].

The expected utility approach, sometimes referred to as *the* decision theoretic approach in situations involving risks, offers its converts a "completely" rational and general decision framework. Yet, most investors, as Roy (1952, p. 433) pointed out, are not grateful for the advice that they maximize expected utility (subject to environmental and other constraints). The model is widely viewed as rather nonoperational and many investors, after taking into account the work involved in employing it, are not sure they still want to be (completely) rational in the prescribed sense. However, the expected utility model is still gaining supporters and numerous individuals employ it as the primary criterion for judging the soundness of other portfolio models.

The long-run growth model,[2] which calls for maximizing the geometric mean of principal plus return in each period, is consistent with logarithmic utility (only). Even though the optimal policy of this model almost surely leads to more capital (though generally not expected utility) under reinvestment in the long run than competing policies do, it is rather nonintuitive and somewhat cumbersome computationally. While still not widely understood, the long-run growth model appears to be gaining in absolute terms.

In contrast, the MV model is highly intuitive—the very concepts mean and variance have almost become synonyms for risk and return. It also possesses a near-perfect balance between richness and simplicity: the separation property permits certain differences in risk tolerance among investors, yet results in linear relationships between "risk" and "return" for optimal portfolios as well as individual securities in equilibrium. This, in turn, provides an ideal setting for empirical tests—linear relations based on the most commonly used statistical measures. As a result, a great deal of empirical evidence has been gathered, much of it supportive of the model. Add to this the goodwill generated by familiarity and understandability, and the social dominance of the MV model no longer seems a mystery.

It is not the intent of this study to review the (mean-variance) capital asset-pricing model [Sharpe (1964) and Lintner (1965a, 1965b)] and the empirical tests, both supportive and nonsupportive, which have been performed in attempts to determine its explanatory power. An excellent summary of the literature on this subject has already been prepared by Jensen (1972). Rather, I shall attempt to explain some questions touching the larger context of capital asset pricing. In particular, I will point out why, in view of the fact that the essential equilibrium structure of the (present) capital asset-pricing model fits a richer structure than the mean-variance framework, the MV concept has been granted such an eminent position. Among other issues I will also attempt to give some insight into why the standard MV model was so slow in being extended to an intertemporal framework and why, when it was, this extension took on a very special form.

11.2 IS THE MARKET PORTFOLIO EFFICIENT?

Let us turn first to the standard (single-period) capital asset pricing model when the limited liability of financial assets is recognized. If all investors are rational in the von Neumann-Morgenstern sense, the MV assumptions now imply that preferences must be quadratic, i.e., investor k's utility of wealth function is of the form

$$u_k(w) = a_k w - w^2 \sim -(b_k - w)^2 \qquad a_k \text{ large,} \qquad (11.1)$$

where $\sim$ means equivalent and the $a_k (= 2b_k)$ are constants. Under homogeneous probability beliefs and unlimited borrowing and lending at the same rate, all investors hold the market portfolio (M) in conjunction with borrowing, lending, or neither, in equilibrium. This implies that the means (μ_{p2}) and standard deviations (σ_{p2}) of return of the optimal portfolios of all investors form a linear (upward-sloping) plot, usually called the capital market line (CML). Its equation may be written

$$\mu_{p2} = r_2 + m_2 \sigma_{p2} , \qquad (11.2)$$

where the parameters r_2 and m_2 represent the (equilibrium) interest rate and the (equilibrium) market price of risk. (The subscript 2 refers to the fact that we have assumed quadratic utility.) In this case we also obtain a linear relationship between μ_{i2} and β_{i2}, the equilibrium means and betas of returns (r_i) of all securities (and portfolios), where

$$\beta_{i2} \equiv \frac{\text{cov}(r_{i2}, r_{M2})}{\sigma_{M2}^2} ; \qquad (11.3)$$

the equation of the security market line may be written

$$\mu_{i2} = r_2 + (\mu_{M2} - r_2)\beta_{i2} . \qquad (11.4)$$

Equations (11.2) and (11.4), of course, are the foundations of virtually all empirical tests of the capital asset-pricing model.

Observe that the sole basis for the linearity of the mean-standard deviation plot of optimal portfolios is the fact that in equilibrium all investors hold portfolios combining the risk-free asset with the market portfolio of risky assets. This, in turn, is due to the separation property of the preference class (11.1). But the separation property holds for a considerably wider class of risk-averse functions than (11.1), namely, [Hakansson (1969), Cass and Stiglitz (1970)].

$$u_k(w) = \frac{1}{\gamma}(w + a_k)^\gamma \qquad \gamma < 1 \text{ and fixed} \qquad (11.5)$$

$$u_k(w) = -(a_k - w)^\gamma \qquad a_k \text{ large, } \gamma > 1 \text{ and fixed} \qquad (11.6)$$

and

$$u_k(w) = -\exp(a_k w) \qquad a_k < 0. \qquad (11.7)$$

(In (11.5), $\gamma = 0$ represents $\log(w + a_k)$.) Clearly, (11.1) is but one member of (11.6), with $\gamma = 2$. Thus, whenever investor preferences are described either by (11.5), (11.6) (with γ fixed), or (11.7), all investors, under our previous assumptions, choose the same mix of risky assets, which in equilibrium can only be that of the market portfolio. Thus, in mean-standard deviation space of return (or ending wealth), the plot of the optimal portfolios p is linear (and upward-sloping) and can be represented by the line

$$\mu_{p\gamma} = r_\gamma + m_\gamma \, \sigma_{p\gamma} . \qquad (11.8)$$

In general, we would, of course, expect the parameters r_γ (the equilibrium interest rate) and m_γ (the market price of risk) to depend on the risk tolerance parameter γ, as do the mean and standard deviation of the market portfolio,[3] $\mu_{M\gamma}$ and $\sigma_{M\gamma}$. But perhaps more important, the optimal portfolios need not be efficient in a mean-variance sense unless $\gamma = 2$ as in (11.1). Figure 11-1 shows the capital market line[4] when $\gamma = 2$ (line *AML*) and Figure 11-2 when $\gamma \neq 2$ (or (11.7) holds) (line $A'M'L'$). As Figure 11-2 indicates there will in general exist portfolios, under the equilibrium return structure (for any $\gamma \neq 2$ or (11.7)), which dominate the optimal portfolios in a mean-variance sense, yet no one will seek such portfolios simply because they are less desirable. In other words, when $\gamma \neq 2$ (or (11.7) holds), every investor will prefer *some* portfolio on line $A'M'L'$ to *every* portfolio on the (MV)-efficient frontier $A'B'$. And the market portfolio M' is clearly not (MV) efficient.

It is not difficult to construct examples for which the distance between $A'M'L'$ and $A'B'$ is substantial. However, when returns are "compact," Samuelson (1970) has shown that the optimal portfolios will be close to those derived from a quadratic function; thus, in this case we would expect $A'M'L'$ to lie close to $A'B'$. The same is true, under certain conditions, when the number of securities is large [Ross (1972)].

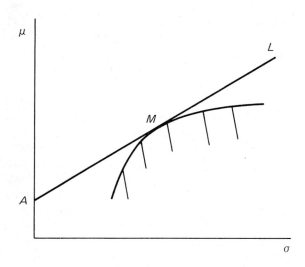

Figure 11-1.

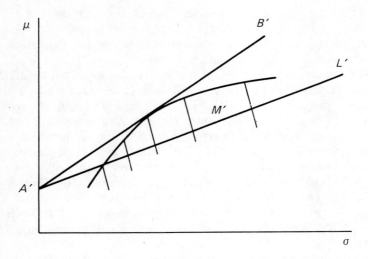

Figure 11-2.

In the single-period limited liability case, our examination of the capital market line has revealed that only the a priori insistence on MV efficiency favors (11.1) over (11.7) and over the members of (11.5) and (11.6) for fixed γ. We should also note that the class $(w + a_k)^{1/2}$, or $\log(w + a_k)$ (both belonging to (11.5)), say, is just as "rich" in preference patterns as (11.1) (it is actually "richer" since there are no constraints on the parameters a_k as in (11.1)). It is readily verified that all utility functions in (11.5) exhibit decreasing [Arrow-Pratt (1963, 1964)] absolute risk aversion, while the members of (11.6) possess increasing absolute risk aversion and the class (11.7) constant absolute risk aversion. In this case, the significance of these properties is that only with respect to the class (11.5) are risky assets normal goods. No one, to my knowledge, has ever argued, or purported to have given evidence, in favor of the proposition that risky assets such as securities are not normal goods. In sum, then, the contest (in the single-period limited liability case) between the capital market line in Figure 11-1 and that in Figure 11-2 $(A'M'L')$ is a contest as to which of two notions reigns supreme: MV efficiency or the normal goods nature of securities.

Upon further examination, however, there are at least two considerations which complicate the issue. First, if one chooses in favor of Figure 11-2, which γ in (11.5) is the "correct" one? This is, of course, an empirical matter, but on the basis of suggestions by

Samuelson and Merton (1974) and evidence by Friend and Blume (1974), a somewhat negative γ may have the best "fit." Second, only (11.1) of all the functions in (11.5), (11.6), and (11.7) generally yields a linear relationship between $\mu_{i\gamma}$ and $\beta_{i\gamma}$, the means and betas of securities in equilibrium.[5] With this in mind, and remembering the important role that the security market line has come to play in the capital asset-pricing model, it is perhaps easier to understand why the MV-efficiency concept has not been challenged despite its lack of normal goods ammunition (in the single-period limited liability case).

When $\gamma \neq 2$, a plot of the points $(\mu_{i\gamma}, \beta_{i\gamma})$ produces a scatter which may contain negative or flat "relationships." Such relationships have also been obtained from real data [see, e.g., Douglas (1969), Miller and Scholes (1972), Black, Jensen, and Scholes (1972), Blume and Friend (1972)]. The open question, then, is whether the data already collected, which has only been related to the MV-based capital asset-pricing model, gives any support to an alternative capital asset-pricing model based on one of the (normal goods) classes (i.e., γ) in (11.5), which, as noted, yields a capital market line as in Figure 11-2, a security market "scatter" in lieu of a "line," and for which the market portfolio is likely to be (MV) inefficient.[6]

11.3 INTERTEMPORAL MEAN-VARIANCE ANALYSIS

Few, of course, have based their defense for using the capital asset pricing model on the quadratic utility assumption. The majority rely, rather, on the normal distribution of return assumption when they wish to achieve consistency with the von Neumann-Morgenstern postulates. The general comfort most writers on the subject seem to feel in the presence of this assumption appears to stem from the near normality of empirical distributions of the log of price relatives [see, e.g., Fama (1965)], coupled with the closeness of the functions r and $\log(1 + r)$ for r near 0 (there are, of course, exceptions). Those who are most disturbed about the normal return assumption seem to object on the following grounds:

1. It clashes with the undisputed empirical fact known as limited liability.
2. It seems difficult to reconcile with the opportunity (generally present) to borrow at a riskless rate, given that the probability of repayment then is less than 1.
3. The normal distribution cannot be integrated with "most" utility functions exhibiting decreasing absolute risk aversion; in particular, normal distributions cannot be integrated with any member of

the class (11.5), the class of decreasing absolute risk aversion utility functions for which the separation property holds.[7]

4. The normal distribution does not reproduce itself multiplicatively. Thus, the assumption can be valid for at most one time-period length in a random-walk model (of returns).

5. In an n-period (Fisherian) consumption-investment model with $n \geqslant 2$, the nonnegativity of consumption can only be satisfied if the investor avoids all risk-bearing.[8]

In sum, it is apparent that while the normality assumption can rescue the MV approach, and in particular the standard capital market and security market lines, it can only do so (1) in a single-period framework, (2) by assuming preferences, which, with the exception of a "small" class, possess nondecreasing absolute risk aversion, and (3) by disregarding some obvious empirical realities.

Having observed that the normal distribution assumption does not yield a viable mean-variance framework in the multiperiod case, the remaining possibility for justifying the MV model in a (discrete-time) sequential context rests on the assumption of quadratic utility. First, consider the case of simple reinvestment in which decisions are governed by the (quadratic) terminal utility-of-wealth function[9]

$$u_0(w) = -(a - w)^2 \qquad a \text{ large};$$

this gives

$$u_0(w) > 0 \qquad\qquad w < a \text{ only}, \qquad (11.9)$$

$$u_0''(w) < 0 \qquad\qquad \text{all } w. \qquad (11.10)$$

Let r_{n2} be the (known) interest rate with n periods to go and let the returns in any two periods be independent; then the induced utility of wealth functions with n periods remaining to the horizon (ignoring possible solvency requirements) are given by [Mossin (1968)]

$$u_n(w) = -k_1 \ldots k_n (a_n - w)^2 \sim -(a_n - w)^2 , \qquad (11.11)$$

since $k_1, \ldots, k_n$ are positive constants. But, while $u_n''(w) < 0$ for all w,

$$u_n'(w) > 0 \qquad w < a_n \equiv \frac{a}{(1 + r_{12}) \ldots (1 + r_{n2})} \text{ only}, \quad (11.12)$$

and if the interest rates are bounded away from zero,

$$a_n \to 0 \qquad \text{as } n \text{ increases.} \qquad (11.13)$$

This is clearly an awkward situation: the more distant the horizon, the closer to 0 is the upper end of the interval over which our (currently relevant) utility function is increasing.

As a second illustration, consider a (Fisherian) multiperiod consumption-investment model in which the utility of consumption is additive and quadratic. The separation property will now hold, in the next to last period, only for large wealth levels, since the nonnegative consumption constraint is always binding for low wealth levels, altering the optimal mix of risky assets in no particular pattern.[10] As we move backwards in time, the minimum wealth level for which the separation property holds increases, systematically destroying the common portfolio basis on which the capital asset pricing model in any particular period rests.[11]

While, as we have seen, the possibilities of extending the standard capital asset pricing model to a discrete-time intertemporal setting are barred, this is not the case if decisions are presumed to be made continuously by consumer/investors. As shown by Merton (1971), when asset returns are lognormally distributed in such a model, all investors will hold the same mix of risky assets regardless of their preferences.[12] Thus, the preconditions of the (standard) capital asset-pricing model are met within the assumption of limited liability and without having to rely on quadratic utility. The most crucial assumptions embedded in the continuous-time version of the capital asset-pricing model are those of (1) "compact" returns, i.e., essentially that for increasingly small time intervals the skewness of the return distribution becomes small compared to the first two moments,[13] (2) stationary opportunities, and (3) absence of transaction costs. The second of these is clearly unrealistic but can be relaxed, giving rise to a richer capital asset pricing structure involving more than two "mutual funds" in which optimal portfolios need not be (MV) efficient [Merton (1973)]. As to the third assumption, it is clearly correct, as Merton points out (1973), that the absence of transaction costs (assumed in all of the models cited) is an argument in favor of continuous-time decision-making and that explicit cognizance of such costs almost surely would affect the optimal time between decisions. But it is not at all certain that recognition of realistic transaction costs implies that frequent portfolio revision is optimal.[14] In any case, the assumption of zero transaction costs is clearly easier to justify when the (prespecified) time between decisions is fairly long.

11.4 A "NONSTANDARD" MEAN-VARIANCE MODEL

The weakness of the mean of a distribution as a measure of "wealth" was amply demonstrated by Bernoulli (1954 transl.). In a multiperiod setting, the shortcomings of expected return or expected wealth are further magnified. For example, consider a reinvestment setting with stationary, temporally independent returns, including a positive interest rate and at least one positive risk premium. Denote wealth at the end of period n by w_n and return on portfolio p in period n by $r_n(p)$. Then we may have

$$E[w_n] \to \infty,$$

$$\text{Mode}[w_n] < \$1 \qquad n \text{ large},$$

$$\text{Median}[w_n] < \$1 \qquad n \text{ large}, \tag{11.14}$$

$$\Pr\left\{w_n < \$1\right\} \to 1.$$

In fact, a sufficient condition for (11.14) to hold is

$$E[r_n(p)] > \epsilon > 0$$

$$E[\ln\left\{1 + r_n(p)\right\}] < -\epsilon \qquad \text{all } n \tag{11.15}$$

for some ϵ, a condition not nearly as difficult to satisfy as generally believed. For example, suppose that the (ex ante) return distribution of the market portfolio in each period (year) is constructed from the realized returns "on the market" for the period 1926-65 as reported by Fisher and Lorie (1968, Table 1A) and assume an interest rate of 8 percent.[15] Then the market portfolio, purchased on a margin of 54.4 percent or less, satisfies (11.15) and hence (11.14); i.e., such portfolios, many of which clearly are incapable of making the investor insolvent in any *one* year, will gradually ruin him.[16]

An expectation which alerts the investor to the last part of (11.15), when it holds, is that of average compound return, $C_n - 1$, given by

$$C_n \equiv \left[\prod_{j=1}^{n} (1 + r_j(p))\right]^{1/n}. \tag{11.16}$$

The reason for this is that the last part of (11.15) holds (under weak regularity conditions) if and only if

$$E[C_n] - 1 \to \text{a negative number.} \tag{11.17}$$

As noted in Hakansson (1971, Sec. IV), maximization of $E[C_n]$ induces the decreasingly risk averse (myopic decision rule) utility of wealth function $w^{1/n}$ in each period.

Now consider the mean *and* variance of $C_n - 1$, average compound return over (the first) n periods (ACRN). It should be noted that the portfolio sequences obtained by invoking the standard efficiency notion are not (exactly) consistent with those obtained by a utility of wealth function except in certain cases (such as when there are two assets, one of which is riskless, and returns are stationary). But the class of utility functions

$$\frac{1}{\gamma} x^\gamma \qquad\qquad \gamma \leqslant 1/n, \qquad\qquad (11.18)$$

with the same γ applied in each period, appears to yield good approximations to the exactly efficient sequences. Besides offering myopic policies, this class (as well as the exactly efficient (ACRN) portfolio sequences) avoids long-run "ruin" if n is sufficiently large (just how large depends on the return structure—for the empirical example based on the Fisher-Lorie data, n need only be greater than or equal to 2) [Hakansson and Miller (1973)]. But perhaps the strongest evidence in favor of the investment policies implied by the class (11.18) is the fact that the (first-period) optimal investment policies for a very large class of (fairly risk-averse) terminal utility functions converges to the set which is optimal for (11.18) as the horizon becomes more distant [Hakansson (1974)].

Unfortunately, the optimal mix of risky assets for one γ in (11.18) is not obtainable as a linear combination of the optimal mixes for two different γ's. As a consequence, the ACRN model does not yield a "simple" capital asset pricing model with a capital market line and a security market line.[17] The preference structure is too "rich" for the market portfolio, combined with the riskless asset, to be optimal for everyone. The central lesson of the second half of this chapter then is that, from all indications, the possibility of a meaningful extension of the standard capital asset pricing model to a discrete-time multiperiod setting is closed; the assumptions which make the extension to an intertemporal setting possible in continuous time are not relaxable.

NOTES TO SECTION ELEVEN

1. Some chance-constrained portfolio models, referred to as "safety-first" models [e.g., Roy (1952)], have, via Chebychev's Inequality, tended to become

classified in the mean-variance category [see, e.g., Lintner (1965a) and Pyle and Turnovsky (1970)].

2. Generally credited to Williams (1936), Kelley (1956), Latané (1959), and Breiman (1960).

3. The numbers r_γ, m_γ, $\mu_{M\gamma}$, and $\sigma_{M\gamma}$ clearly also depend on the individual investor parameters a_k (in (11.1), (11.5), (11.6), and (11.7).

4. Here we implicitly adopt the definition: CML is that function which relates μ_p to σ_p for optimal portfolios in equilibrium. The "efficiency" of CML under assumption (11.1) is then viewed as a property of CML, not as a part of its definition.

5. The linearity of this relationship holds more generally for (11.1) than under our present assumptions (which include limited liability), namely, in the absence of a risk-less asset [Black (1972)], in the absence of riskless borrowing [Vasicek (1971)], and in the presence of differential borrowing and lending rates [Brennan (1971)]; it also holds in a continuous trading intertemporal model with arbitrary preferences under the geometric Brownian motion hypothesis [Merton (1971, 1973)]. In the latter case the linearity holds only instantaneously, not over a discrete interval [see, e.g., Jensen (1972, p. 386) for the discretized equation].

6. A beginning in this direction has been made by Kraus and Litzenberger (1972); see also Roll (1973) and Rubinstein (1973, 1974).

7. As is well known, integrability is no problem with respect to (11.7).

8. With respect to this point, several comments are in order. While it is true, as Fama (1970) has shown, that risk aversion with respect to consumption streams implies risk aversion with respect to current investment under weak conditions, the "interpretations" which this result has been given are fallacious and misleading. First, it is correct that a consumer who lives only for two periods and faces symmetric stable return distributions (with finite means) will choose an (MV) efficient portfolio [Fama (1971)]—but only if his utility function is defined for negative consumption levels and he is willing to "tolerate" such consumption levels (if not, he will choose a riskless portfolio). If the investor will not be around for the second period (i.e., his holdings are bequeathed) the assumption is more palatable—but then we do not really have a two-period model. One can, of course, argue that the probability of negative second-period consumption is negligible, or equal to ϵ. But then, under the random-walk-of-returns assumption, the probability of avoiding negative consumption over t periods is "on the order of magnitude" of $(1 - \epsilon)^t$.

9. Tobin's (1965) multiperiod mean-variance analysis, which is based on nonnormal distributions and disregards consumption, belongs in this category.

10. The fact that this constraint is binding for "low" wealth levels is partly due to the inferior goods nature of securities in this model. In models in which investors are decreasingly risk averse and securities are normal goods the nonnegativity constraint on consumption is often not binding [e.g., Hakansson (1970); see also Sibley (1974)]. The quadratic model is one example for which the separation property holds only locally [Hakansson (1969)].

11. Let $-(a_k - c)^2$ be the single-period utility of consumption function

component for individual k, where c is the amount of consumption. Then the optimality of the market portfolio mix in equilibrium, under nonnegative consumption, is preserved only if current individual wealth levels w^k are such that the ratios w^k/a_k are small or approximately equal for all individuals. Small ratios imply that all individuals are nearly risk-neutral in the relevant decision region while near-equal (but not small) ratios clearly represent an exceedingly restrictive condition. Among other things, both cases virtually rule out secular mobility of individuals.

12. Mathematically, the crucial property at work is that portfolios of log-normal assets will also be lognormally distributed in the continuous-time model—but not in the discrete-time case—with parameters that are simple weighted averages of the individual asset parameters [see, also, Ohlson (1972)].

13. For a more precise description of a compactness, see Samuelson (1970) and Ohlson (1973).

14. For example, the fact that mutual funds as a group have performed worse than the "market" has in part been attributed to excessive portfolio turnover [see, e.g., Jensen (1969)].

15. The choice of interest rate, for the purpose at hand, matters very little.

16. For an intuitive exposition of the forces at work, consider the following simplified example. Suppose $r_n(p)$ is either −60 percent or 100 percent with equal probability in each period. Then expected return is 20 percent in each period, causing expected capital to grow at 20 percent per period. Thus, after 10 periods our expected capital is more than six times what we started with since $E[w_{10}] \approx 6.19w_0$. But $\text{Mode}(w_{10}) = \text{Median}(w_{10}) \approx .33w_0$ and $\Pr\{w_{10}\} < w_0 \approx .62$, i.e., there is roughly a 62 percent chance that after 10 periods of investment we will have less capital than we started out with.

17. The same situation arises when nonmarketable assets [Mayers (1972)] or nonhomogeneous beliefs are introduced into the standard capital asset pricing model.

REFERENCES

1. N.H. Agnew, R.A. Agnew, J. Rasmussen, and K.R. Smith, "An Application of Chance Constrained Portfolio Selection in a Casualty Insurance Firm," *Management Science*, June 1969.

2. Kenneth Arrow, "Comments on Duesenberry's 'The Portfolio Approach to the Demand for Money and Other Assets,'" *Review of Economics and Statistics*, Supplement, February 1963.

3. Daniel Bernoulli, "Exposition of a New Theory on the Measurement of Risk," (transl. Louis Sommer), *Econometrica*, January 1954.

4. Fisher Black, "Capital Market Equilibrium with Restricted Borrowing," *Journal of Business*, July 1972.

5. Fisher Black, Michael Jensen, and Myron Scholes, "The Capital Asset Pricing Model: Some Empirical Tests," in *Studies in the Theory of Capital Markets* (ed. Michael Jensen), Praeger, 1972.

6. Marshall Blume and Irwin Friend, "A New Look at the Capital Asset Pricing Model," in *Methodology in Finance-Investments* (ed. James Bicksler), Heath, 1972.

7. Karl Borch, *The Economics of Uncertainty*, Princeton University Press, 1968.

8. Leo Breiman, "Investment Policies for Expanding Businesses Optimal in a Long-Run Sense," *Naval Research Logistics Quarterly*, December 1960.

9. Michael Brennan, "Capital Market Equilibrium with Divergent Borrowing and Lending Rates," *Journal of Financial and Quantitative Analysis*, December 1971.

10. David Cass and Joseph Stiglitz, "The Structure of Investor Preferences and Asset Returns, and Separability in Portfolio Selection: A Contribution to the Pure Theory of Mutual Funds," *Journal of Economic Theory*, June 1970.

11. George Douglas, "Risk in the Equity Market: An Empirical Appraisal of Market Efficiency," *Yale Economic Essays*, Spring 1969.

12. Eugene Fama, "The Behavior of Stock Market Prices," *Journal of Business*, January 1965.

13. Eugene Fama, "Multi-period Consumption-Investment Decisions," *American Economic Review*, March 1970.

14. Eugene Fama, "Risk, Return, and Equilibrium," *Journal of Political Economy*, January/February 1971.

15. Lawrence Fisher and James Lorie, "Rates of Return on Investment in Common Stock: The Year-by-Year Record, 1926-65," *Journal of Business*, July 1968.

16. Irwin Friend and Marshall Blume, "Demand for Risky Assets," *American Economic Review*, December 1975; also reprinted in this volume.

17. Nils Hakansson, "Risk Disposition and the Separation Property in Portfolio Selection," *Journal of Financial and Quantitative Analysis*, December 1969.

18. Nils Hakansson, "Optimal Investment and Consumption Strategies Under Risk for a Class of Utility Functions," *Econometrica*, October 1970.

19. Nils Hakansson, "Multi-period Mean-Variance Analysis: Toward a General Theory of Portfolio Choice," *Journal of Finance*, September 1971.

20. Nils Hakansson, "Convergence to Isoelastic Utility and Policy in Multi-period Portfolio Choice," *Journal of Financial Economics*, September 1974.

21. Nils Hakansson and Bruce Miller, "Compound-Return Mean-Variance Efficient Portfolios Never Risk Ruin," *Management Science*, December 1975. University of California, Berkeley, May 1973; forthcoming in *Management Science: Theory*.

22. Michael Jensen, "Risk, the Pricing of Capital Assets, and the Evaluation of Investment Portfolios," *Journal of Business*, April 1969.

23. Michael Jensen, "Capital Markets: Theory and Evidence," The Bell *Journal of Economics and Management Science*, Autumn 1972.

24. J.L. Kelley, "A New Interpretation of Information Rate," *Bell System Technical Journal*, August 1956.

25. Alan Kraus and Robert Litzenberger, "Skewness Preference and Valuation of Risk Assets," Research Paper No. 130, Graduate School of Business, Stanford University, December 1972.

26. Henry Latané, "Criteria for Choice Among Risky Ventures," *Journal of Political Economy*, April 1959.

27. John Lintner, "The Valuation of Risk Assets and the Selection of Risk Investment in Stock Portfolios and Capital Budgets," *Review of Economics and Statistics*, February 1965.

28. John Lintner, "Security Prices, Risk and Maximal Gains from Diversification," *Journal of Finance*, December 1965.

29. Harry Markowitz, "Portfolio Selection," *Journal of Finance*, March 1952.

30. David Mayers, "Non-marketable Assets and Capital Market Equilibrium Under Uncertainty," in *Studies in the Theory of Capital Markets* (ed. Michael Jensen), Praeger, 1972.

31. Robert Merton, "Optimum Consumption and Portfolio Rules in a Continuous-Time Model," *Journal of Economic Theory*, December 1971.

32. Robert Merton, "An Intertemporal Capital Asset Pricing Model," *Econometrica*, September 1973; also reprinted in this volume.

33. Merton Miller and Myron Scholes, "Rates of Return in Relation to Risk: A Re-examination of Some Recent Findings," in *Studies in the Theory of Capital Markets* (ed. Michael Jensen), Praeger, 1972.

34. Jan Mossin, "Optimal Multiperiod Portfolio Policies," *Journal of Business*, April 1968.

35. Bertil Naslund and Andrew Whinston, "A Model of Multi-period Investment Under Uncertainty," *Management Science*, January 1962.

36. James Ohlson, "Portfolio Choice in a Lognormal Market as the Period Spacing Goes to Zero," unpublished manuscript, October 1972.

37. James Ohlson, "The Asymptotic Validity of Quadratic Utility as the Trading Interval Approaches Zero," in *Stochastic Optimization Models in Finance* (ed. W. Ziemba and R.G. Vickson), Academic Press, 1975. Press.

38. John Pratt, "Risk Aversion in the Small and in the Large," *Econometrica*, January-April, 1964.

39. David Pyle and Stephen Turnovsky, "Safety-First and Expected Utility Maximization in Mean-Standard Deviation Portfolio Analysis," *Review of Economics and Statistics*, February 1970.

40. Richard Roll, "Evidence on the 'Growth-Optimum' Model," *Journal of Finance*, June 1973.

41. Stephen Ross, "Portfolio and Capital Market Theory with Arbitrary Preferences and Distributions—The General Validity of the Mean-Variance Approach in Large Markets," Rodney L. White Center for Financial Research Working Paper No. 12-72, University of Pennsylvania.

42. A.D. Roy, "Safety First and the Holding of Assets," *Econometrica*, July 1952.

43. Mark Rubinstein, "The Fundamental Theorem of Parameter Preference Security Valuation," *Journal of Financial and Quantitative Analysis*, January 1973.

44. Mark Rubinstein, "An Aggregation Theorem of Securities Markets," *Journal of Financial Economics*, September 1974.

45. Paul Samuelson, "The Fundamental Approximation Theorem of Portfolio Analysis in Terms of Means, Variances, and Higher Moments," *Review of Economic Studies*, October 1970.

46. Paul Samuelson and Robert Merton, "Generalized Mean-Variance Trade-

offs for Best Perturbation Corrections to Approximate Portfolio Decisions," *Journal of Finance*, March 1974.

47. William Sharpe, "Capital Asset Prices: A Theory of Market Equilibrium Under Conditions of Risk," *Journal of Finance*, September 1964.

48. David Sibley, "Permanent and Transitory Income Effects in a Model of Optimal Consumption with Wage Income Uncertainty," Working Paper, Bell Laboratories, Holmdel, N.J., May 1974.

49. James Tobin, "Liquidity Preference as Behavior Toward Risk," *Review of Economic Studies*, February 1958.

50. James Tobin, "The Theory of Portfolio Selection," in *The Theory of Interest Rates* (eds. F.H. Hahn and F.P.R. Brechling), Macmillan, 1965.

51. Oldrich Vasicek, "Capital Asset Pricing Model with No Riskless Borrowing," Unpublished manuscript, Wells Fargo Bank, March 1971.

52. J.B. Williams, "Speculation and the Carryover," *Quarterly Journal of Economics*, May 1936.

Fallacy of the Log-Normal Approximation to Optimal Portfolio Decision-Making Over Many Periods*

Robert C. Merton and Paul A. Samuelson

12.1 INTRODUCTION

Thanks to the revival by von Neumann and Morgenstern, maximization of the expected value of a concave utility function of outcomes has for the last third of a century generally been accepted as the 'correct' criterion for optimal portfolio selection. Operational theorems for the general case were late in being recognized, and it was appropriate that the seminal breakthroughs of the 1950s be largely preoccupied with the special case of mean-variance analysis.[1] Not only could the fruitful Sharpe-Lintner-Mossin capital asset pricing model be based on it, but in addition, it gave rise to simple linear rules of portfolio optimizing. In the mean-variance model, the well-known Separation or Mutual-Fund Theorem holds; and with suitable additional assumptions, the model can be used to define a complete micro-economic framework for the capital market, and a number of empirically testable hypotheses can be derived. As a result, a majority of the literature on portfolio theory has been based on this criterion.[2]

Unfortunately, the mean-variance criterion is rigorously consistent with the general expected-utility approach only in the rather special cases of a quadratic utility function or of gaussian distributions on security prices—both involving dubious implications. Further, recent empirical work has shown that the simple form of the model does not seem to fit the data as well as had been previously believed,[3] and

---
*We thank M.B. Goldman for scientific assistance. Aid from the National Science Foundation is gratefully acknowledged.

recent dynamic simulations[4] have shown that the behavior over time
of some efficient mean-variance portfolios can be quite unreasonable.

Aside from its algebraic tractability, the mean-variance model is
interesting because of its separation property. Therefore, there was
great interest in the Cass-Stiglitz (1970) elucidation of the broader
conditions under which a more limited form of a 'separation
theorem' must hold regardless of the probability distribution of
returns. The special families of utility functions with constant-rela-
tive-risk aversions or constant-absolute-risk aversions further gained
in importance.[5] But it was realized that real-life utilities need not be
of so simple a form.

The desire for simplicity of analysis led naturally to a search for
approximation theorems, particularly of the asymptotic type. Thus,
even if mean-variance analysis were not exact, would the error in
using it become small? A defense of it was the demonstration that
mean-variance is asymptotically correct if the risks are 'small' (i.e.,
for 'compact' probabilities); closely related was the demonstration of
the same asymptotic equivalence when the trading interval becomes
small (i.e., continuous trading). More recently, it has been shown
that as the number of assets becomes large, under certain conditions,
the mean-variance solution is asymptotically optimal.[6] In another
study (1974) we have developed a generalized mean-variance approximation procedure that is somewhat described by its title. This
enables all those with utility functions that are near to a particular
utility function to develop close approximations to optimal portfolios along a mean-variance tradeoff frontier generated by a series
expansion around that base function; this not only generalizes the
standard Markowitz-Tobin mean-variance analysis of money outcomes, but can sometimes also validate the Hakansson efficiency
frontier of expected average compound return and of its variance.

A particularly tempting hunting ground for asymptotic theories
was thought to be provided by the case in which investors maximize
the expected utility of terminal wealth when the terminal date
(planning horizon) is very far in the future. Recourse to the Law of
Large Numbers, as applied to repeated multiplicative variates (cumulative sums of logarithms of portfolio value relatives), has independently tempted various writers, hoping that one can replace an
arbitrary utility function of terminal wealth with all its intractability,
by the function $U(W_T) = \log(W_T)$: maximizing the geometric mean
or the expected log of outcomes, they thought, would provide an
asymptotically exact criterion for rational action, implying as a
bonus the efficiency of a diversification-of-portfolio strategy constant through time (i.e., a 'myopic' rule, the same for every period,

even when probabilities of different periods were interdependent!). So powerful did the max-expected-log criterion appear to be, that it seemed even to supersede the general expected utility criterion in cases where the latter was shown to be inconsistent with the max-expected-log criterion. For some writers, it was a case of simple errors in reasoning: they mistakenly thought that the sure-thing principle sanctified the new criterion.[7] For others, an indefinitely large probability of doing better by Method A than by Method B was taken as conclusive evidence for the superiority of A.[8] Still others never realized that it could conflict with the plausible postulates of von Neumann maximizing; or, more sophisticatedly, they tried to save the approximation by appealing to bounded utility functions.[9]

Except to prepare the ground for a more subtle fallacy of the same asymptotic genus, this study will only review the simple max-expected-log fallacy. We concentrate instead on the asymptotic fallacy that involves, not primarily the Law of Large Numbers, but rather the Central-Limit Theorem. It is well known that portfolio strategies that are uniformly the same in every period give rise to a cumulative sum of logarithms of returns that do approach, when normalized under specified conditions easily met a gaussian distribution—suggesting heuristically a Log-Normal Surrogate, whose two parameters: each period's expected log of return, and variance of log of return—will become 'asymptotically sufficient parameters' for efficient portfolio managing, truly an enormous simplification in that all optimal portfolios will lie on a new efficiency frontier in which the first parameter is maximized for each different value of the second. This frontier can be generated solely, by the family $U(W_T) = (W_T)^\gamma/\gamma$, and for $\gamma \neq 0$, this leads away from the simple max-expected-log portfolio. So this new method (if only it were valid!) would avoid the crude fallacy that men with little tolerance for risk are to have the same long-run portfolio as men with much risk tolerance. Furthermore, since the mean and variance of average-return-per-period are asymptotic surrogates for the log normal's first two moments (in a sense that will be described), Hakansson (1971b) average-expected-return—which to many [e.g., our study in (1974)] has no interest as a criterion for its own sake—seems to be given a new legitimacy by the Central-Limit Theorem. Furthermore, suppose the Log-Normal Surrogate were valid, so that the true portfolio distribution could then be validly replaced by a log-normal with its $E\{\log W_T\}$ and var$\{\log W_T\}$. In that case, the criterion of expected average compound return (which has no interest for any thoughtful person whose utility function is far away from log W_T) could when supplemented by the variance of average compound return, be given for the first time a true legitimacy for all persons with $U = W^\gamma/\gamma$. Furthermore, this would hold whether $1 - \gamma$ is a small positive number or whether γ is a very large negative number. The reason for this is that mean and variance of average compound return can be shown to be 'asymptotic surrogates' for the Log-Normal Surrogate's two sufficient parameters, $TE\{\log W_1\}$ and $T\mathrm{var}\{\log W_1\}$, W_1 being any single period's portfolio outcome. But, as we shall show, it is a fallacy of double limits to try to use the (unnormalized) Log-Normal Surrogate. And for people with $U = W^\gamma/\gamma$ and γ far from zero, the result can be disasterously bad.[10] What about the argument that expected average compound return deserves analysis because such analysis may be relevant to those decision makers who do not have a max $E\{U(\ )\}$ criterion and who just happen to be interested in average-compound-return? After some reflection, we think an appropriate reaction would be as follows: It is a free country. One can use whatever criterion he wishes. However, the analyst who understands the implications of various criteria has the duty to help people clarify the goals they will, on reflection, really want. If, after the analyst has done his duty of explaining the arbitrariness of the usual arguments in favor of average compound return, and the decisionmaker still persists in being interested in average compound return, that is his privilege. In our experience, once understanding of the issues is realized, few decision-makers retain their interest in average compound return.

One purpose of this study is to show, by counterexamples and examination of illegitimate interchange of limits in double limits, the fallacies involved in the above-described asymptotic log-normal approximation. What holds for normalized variables is shown to be generally *not* applicable to *actual* terminal wealths. Then, constructively, we show that, as any fixed horizon planning interval is subdivided into a number of subinterval periods that goes to infinity (causing the underlying probabilities to belong to a gaussian infinitely-divisible continuous-time probability distribution), the mean-log and variance-log parameters are indeed asymptotically sufficient parameters for the decision; so that one can prepare a (μ, σ) efficiency frontier that is quite distinct from the Markowitz mean-variance frontier of actual returns and not their logarithms; this logarithmic (μ, σ) frontier now provides many of the same two-dimensional simplifications (such as separation properties). The limit process involving breakdown of a finite T into ever-more subperiods is, of course, quite different from a limit process in which the number of fixed-length periods T itself goes to infinity.

There is still another kind of asymptotic approximation that attempts, as $T \to \infty$, to develop in Leland's (1972) happy phrase a 'turnpike theorem' in which the optimal portfolio proportions are well approximated by a uniform strategy that is appropriate to one of the special family of utility functions, $U(W_T) = (W_T)^\gamma / \gamma$, where $\gamma - 1$ is the limiting value of the elasticity of marginal utility with respect to wealth as $W_T \to \infty$. Letting γ then run the gamut from 1 to $-\infty$ generates a new kind of efficiency frontier, distinct from that of ordinary mean-variance or of $[E \{\log W\}$, var $\{\log W\}]$, but which obviously generalizes the single-point criterion of the would-be expected-log maximizers. It generalizes that criterion in that we now rationally trade-off mean return against risk, depending on our own subjective risk tolerance parameter γ. There is some question[11] as to the robustness of the Leland theorem for utility functions 'much different' from members of the isoelastic family; but the main purpose of our study is to uncover the booby traps involved in log-normal and other asymptotic approximations, and we do not examine this question in depth.

12.2 EXACT SOLUTION

In any period, investors face n securities, $1, \ldots, n$. One dollar invested in the jth security results at the end of one period in a value that is $Z_j(1)$, a positive random variable. The joint distribution of these variables is specified as

$$\text{prob} \left\{ Z_1(1) \leqslant z_1, \ldots, Z_n(1) \leqslant Z_n \right\} = F[z_1, \ldots, z_n] = F[z], \quad (12.1)$$

where F has finite moments. Any portfolio decision in the first period is defined by the vector $[w_1(), \ldots, w_n(1)]$, $\Sigma_1^n w_j(1) = 1$; if the investor begins with initial wealth of W_0, his wealth at the end of one period is given by the random variable

$$W_1 = W_0 [w_1(1)Z_1(1) + \ldots + w_n(1)Z_n(1)]. \quad (12.2)$$

By the usual Stieltjes integration over $F[z_1, \ldots, z_n]$, the probability distribution of W_1 can be defined, namely

$$\text{prob} \left\{ \log(W_1/W_0) \leqslant x \right\} = P_1 [x; w_1(1), \ldots, w_n(1)]$$

$$= P_1 [x; w(1)]. \quad (12.3)$$

An investment program re-invested for T periods has terminal wealth, W_T, defined by iterating (12.2) to get the random variable

$$W_T = W_0 \left[\sum_1^n w_j(1)Z_j(1)\right]\left[\sum_1^n w_j(2)Z_j(2)\right] \ldots \left[\sum_1^n w_j(T)Z_j(T)\right]$$

$$\tag{12.4}$$

$$= W_T[w(1), \ldots, w(T)].$$

It is assumed that the vector of random variables $[Z(t)]$ is distributed independently of $Z(t \pm k)$, but subject to the same distribution as $Z(1)$ in Equation (12.1). Hence, the joint probability distribution of all securities over time is given by the product

$$\text{prob}\left\{Z(1) \leqslant z(1), \ldots, Z(T) \leqslant z(T)\right\}$$

$$= F[z_1(1), \ldots, z_n(1)] \ldots F[z_1(T), \ldots, z_n(T)] \quad (12.5)$$

$$= F[z(1)] \ldots F[z(T)].$$

Since W_T/W_0 consists of a product of independent variates, $\log(W_T/W_0)$ will consist of a sum of independent variates. Therefore, its probability distribution is, for each T, definable recursively by the following convolutions,

$$\text{prob}\left\{\log(W_T/W_0) \leqslant x\right\} = P_T[x;w(1), \ldots, w(T)] \tag{12.6}$$

$$P_2[x;w(1),w(2)] = \int_{-\infty}^{\infty} P_1[x-s;w(2)]P_1[ds;w(1)]$$

$$P_3[x;w(1),w(2),w(3)] = \int_{-\infty}^{\infty} P_1[x-s;w(3)]P_2[ds;w(2)]$$

$$\vdots \qquad\qquad\qquad\qquad\qquad \vdots$$

$$P_T[x;w(1), \ldots, w(T)]$$

$$= \int_{-\infty}^{\infty} P_1[x-s;w(T)]P_{T-1}[ds;w(1), \ldots, w(T-1)].$$

Here, as a matter of notation for Stieltjes integration, $\int_{-\infty}^{\infty} f(s)dg(s) = \int_{-\infty}^{\infty} f(s)g(ds)$.

The investor is postulated to act in order to maximize the expected value of (concave) terminal utility of wealth

$$\max_{\{w(t)\}} E\left\{U_T(W_T[w(1), \ldots, w(T)]\right\} \tag{12.7}$$

$$= \max_{\{w(t)\}} \int_{-\infty}^{\infty} U_T(W_0 e^x) P_T[dx;w(1), \ldots, w(T)]$$

$$\equiv \overline{U}_T[w^{**}(1), \ldots, w^{**}(T); W_0].$$

Here, $U_T(\ )$ is a concave function that can be arbitrarily specified, and $[w_j(t)]$, for each t, is understood to be constrained by $\Sigma_1^n w_j(t) = 1$.

For a general U_T, the optimal solution $[\ldots, w^{**}(t), \ldots]$ will not involve portfolio decisions constant through time, but rather optimally varying in accordance with the recursive relations of Bellman dynamic programming, as discussed by numerous authors, as for example in Samuelson (1969). But, here, we shall for the most part confine our attention to uniform strategies

$$[w_1(t), \ldots, w_n(t)] \equiv [w_1, \ldots, w_n]. \tag{12.8}$$

For each such uniform strategy, $\log(W_T/W_0)$ will consist of a sum of independent and identically distributed variates. We write the optimal uniform strategy as the vector $w(t) \equiv w_T^*$, and abbreviate

$$P_T[x;w] \equiv P_T[x;w, \ldots, w], \qquad T = 2, 3, \ldots, \tag{12.9}$$

$$W_T[w] \equiv W_T[w, \ldots, w],$$

$$\overline{U}_T[w^*;W_0] \equiv \overline{U}_T[w^*, \ldots, w^*;W_0].$$

Actually, for the special utility functions,

$$U_T(W) = W^\gamma/\gamma, \gamma < 1, \gamma \neq 0 \tag{12.10}$$

$$= \log W, \gamma = 0,$$

it is well known that $w^{**}(t) \equiv w^*$, independent of T, is a necessary result for full optimality.

12.3 MAX-EXPECTED-LOG (GEOMETRIC-MEAN) FALLACY

Suppose Z_n represents a 'safe security' with certain return

$$Z_n = e^r \equiv R \geqslant 1. \tag{12.11}$$

If the other risky securities are optimally held in positive amounts, together their uncertain return must have an expected value that exceeds R. Consider now the parameters

$$E\left\{\log(W_1/W_0)\right\} = E\left\{\log(\sum_1^n w_j Z_j)\right\} = \mu(w_1 \ldots, w_n) = \mu(w),$$

$$\text{var}\left\{\log(W_1/W_0)\right\} = E\left\{[\log(\sum_1^n w_j Z_j) - \mu(w)]^2\right\}$$

$$= \sigma^2(w_1, \ldots, w_n) = \sigma^2(w). \tag{12.12}$$

For $w = (w_1, \ldots, w_n) = (0, 0, \ldots, 0, 1)$, $\mu(w) = r \geqslant 0$. As w_n declines and the sum of all other w_j become positive, $\mu(w)$ must be positive. However, $\mu(w)$ will reach a maximum; call it $\mu(w^{\dagger\dagger})$, and recognize that $w^{\dagger\dagger}$ is the max-expected-log strategy.

As mentioned in Section 12.1 many authors fallaciously believe that $w^{\dagger\dagger}$ is a good approximation to w^* for T large, merely because

$$\lim_{T\to\infty} \text{prob}\left\{W_T[w^{\dagger\dagger}] > W_T[w]\right\} = 1, \quad w \neq w^{\dagger\dagger}. \tag{12.13}$$

A by now familiar counterexample occurs for any member of the isoelastic family, Equation (12.10), with $\gamma \neq 0$. For a given γ, $w^*(t) \equiv w^*$, the same strategy, independent of T; since each γ is easily seen to call for a different w^*, it must be that $w^* \neq w^{\dagger\dagger}$ for all T and $\gamma \neq 0$, inasmuch as $w^* = w^{\dagger\dagger}$ only when $\gamma = 0$ and $U_T(W) = \log W$. Hence, the vague and tacit conjecture that w^* converges to $w^{\dagger\dagger}$ asymptotically as $T \to \infty$, is false.

Others, e.g. Markowitz (1972, p. 3), who are aware of the simple fallacy have conjectured that the max-expected-log policy will be 'approximately' optimal for large T when $U_T(\ )$ is bounded (or bounded from above). I.e., if $U_T(\ )$ is bounded (or bounded from above), then the expected utility maximizer, it is argued, will be 'approximately indifferent' between the $\{w^*\}$ and $\{w^{\dagger\dagger}\}$ programs as T becomes large.

The exact meaning of 'approximate indifference' is open to interpretation. A trivial meaning would be

$$\lim_{T\to\infty} EU_T(W_0 Z_T[w^*]) = M = \lim_{T\to\infty} EU_T(W_0 Z_T[w^{\dagger\dagger}]), \tag{12.14}$$

where M is the upper bound of $U_T(\ )$. This definition merely reflects the fact, that even a suboptimal strategy (unless it is too absurd) will lead as $T \to \infty$ to the upper bound of utility. For example, just holding the riskless asset with positive return per period $R = e^r > 1$, will, for large enough T, get one arbitrarily close to the bliss level of utility. Hence, even if Equation (12.14)'s definition of indifference were to make the conjecture true, its implications have practically no content.

A meaningful interpretation would be indifference in terms of an 'initial wealth equivalent'. That is, let $\Pi_{ij} W_0$ be the initial wealth equivalent of a program $\{w^i\}$ relative to program $\{w^j\}$ defined such that, for each T,

$$EU_T(\Pi_{ij} W_0 Z_T[w^i]) \equiv EU_T Z_T[w^j]). \tag{12.15}$$

$(\Pi_{ij} - 1)W_0$ is the amount of additional initial wealth the investor would require to be indifferent to giving up the $\{w^j\}$ program for the $\{w^i\}$ program. Thus, we could use $\Pi_{12}(T; W_0)$ as a measure[12] of how 'close' in optimality terms the $\{w^1\} \equiv \{w^{\dagger\dagger}\}$ program is to the $\{w^2\} \equiv \{w*\}$ program. The conjecture that max-expected-log is asymptotically optimal in this modified sense would be true only if it could be shown that $\Pi_{12}(T; W_0)$ is a decreasing function of T and

$$\lim_{T \to \infty} \Pi_{12}(T; W_0) = 1,$$

or even if $\Pi_{12}(T; W_0)$ were simply a bounded function of T.

Consider the case when $U_T(\ ) = (\ )^\gamma / \gamma, \gamma < 1$. Then,

$$EU_T(W_0 Z_T[w^*]) = W_0^\gamma E[(Z_T[w^*])^\gamma]/\gamma \tag{12.16}$$

$$= W_0^\gamma \left\{ E[(Z_1[w^*])^\gamma] \right\}^T / \gamma,$$

by the independence and identical distribution of the portfolio return in each period. Similarly, we have that

$$EU_T(\Pi_{12} W_0 Z_T[w^{\dagger\dagger}]) = (\Pi_{12} W_0)^\gamma \left\{ E[(Z_1[w^{\dagger\dagger}])^\gamma)] \right\}^T / \gamma. \tag{12.17}$$

Now, $\{w*\}$ maximizes the expected utility of wealth over one period (i.e., for the isoelastic family $w** = w*$), and since $w* \neq w^{\dagger\dagger}$ for $\gamma \neq 0$, we have that

$$E[(Z_1[w^*])^\gamma) \gtrless E[(Z_1[w^{\dagger\dagger}])^\gamma] \text{ as } \gamma \gtrless 0. \tag{12.18}$$

From Equations (12.15), (12.16), and (12.17), we have that

$$\Pi_{12}(T; W_0) = [\lambda(\gamma)]^{T/\gamma} , \qquad (12.19)$$

where

$$\lambda(\gamma) \equiv E[(Z_1[w^*])^\gamma]/E[(Z_1[w^{\dagger\dagger}])^\gamma].$$

From Equation (12.18), $\lambda(\gamma) > 1$ and $T/\gamma > 0$, for $\gamma > 0$; $\lambda(\gamma) < 1$ and $T/\gamma < 0$, for $\gamma < 0$, and, since λ is independent of T and W_0, we have from (7.19) that, for $\gamma \neq 0$ and every $W_0 > 0$,

$$\partial\Pi_{12}(T;W_0)/\partial T > 0, \qquad (12.20)$$

$$\lim_{T\to\infty} \Pi_{12}(T;W_0) = \infty.$$

Hence, even for $U_T(\ )$ with an upper bound (as when $\gamma < 0$), an investor would require as $T \to \infty$, an ever-larger initial payment to give up his $\{w^*\}$ program. Similar results obtain for $U_T(\ )$ functions which are bounded from above and below.[13] Therefore, the $\{w^{\dagger\dagger}\}$ program is definitely not 'approximately' optimal for large T.

Further, the suboptimal $\{w^{\dagger\dagger}\}$ policy will, for every finite T however large, be in a clear sense 'behind' the best strategy, $\{w^*\}$. Indeed, let us apply the test used in the Eisenhower Administration to compare U.S. and U.S.S.R. growth. How many years after the U.S. reached each real GNP level did it take the U.S.S.R. to reach that level? This defines a function $\Delta T = f(\text{GNP}_t)$, and some Kremlinologists of that day took satisfaction that ΔT was not declining in time. In a new calculation similar to the initial wealth equivalent analysis above, let us for each level of $E[U_T(W_T)]$ define $\Delta T = T^{\dagger\dagger} - T^*$ as the difference in time periods needed to surpass that level of expected utility, calculated for the optimal strategy $\{w^*\}$ and for the max-expected-log strategy $\{w^{\dagger\dagger}\}$; then it is not hard to show that $\Delta T \to \infty$ as $T \to \infty$. Again the geometric-mean strategy proves to be fallacious.

Finally, we can use the initial wealth equivalent to demonstrate that for sufficiently risk-averse investors, the max-expected-log strategy is a 'bad' program; bad, in that the $\{w^{\dagger\dagger}\}$ program will not lead to 'approximate' optimality even in the trivial sense of (12.14) and hence, will be dominated by the program of holding nothing but the riskless asset.

Define $\{w^3\} \equiv [0, 0 \ 0, \ldots, 1]$ to be the program which holds nothing but the riskless asset with return per period, $R \geqslant 1$. Let $\{w^1\}$ be the max-expected-log program $\{w^{\dagger\dagger}\}$ as before. Then, for the isoelastic family, the initial wealth equivalent for the $\{w^1\}$ program relative to the $\{w^3\}$ program, $\Pi_{13} W_0$, is defined by

$$\frac{W_0^\gamma}{\gamma} \Pi_{13}^\gamma E[(Z_T[w^{\dagger\dagger}])^\gamma] \equiv \frac{W_0^\gamma}{\gamma} R^{\gamma T}, \qquad (12.21)$$

or

$$\Pi_{13} = [\phi(\gamma)]^{-T/\gamma}, \qquad (12.22)$$

where $\phi(\gamma) \equiv E[(Z_1[w^{\dagger\dagger}])^\gamma]/R^\gamma$.

To examine the properties of the $\phi(\gamma)$ function, we note that since $\{w^{\dagger\dagger}\} \equiv [w^{\dagger\dagger}, w^{\dagger\dagger}, \ldots, w^{\dagger\dagger}]$ does maximize $E \log(Z[w;1]) \equiv E \log(\Sigma^{n-1} w_j [Z_j (1) - R] + R)$, it must satisfy

$$E\left\{[Z_j(1) - R]/Z[w^{\dagger\dagger};1]\right\} = 0, \qquad j = 1, 2, \ldots, n. \quad (12.23)$$

Multiplying (12.23) by $w_{j\dagger\dagger}$ and summing over $j = 1, 2, \ldots, n$, we have that

$$E\left\{(Z[w^{\dagger\dagger};1] - R)/Z[w^{\dagger\dagger};1]\right\} = 0 \qquad (12.24)$$

or that

$$E\left\{(Z[w^{\dagger\dagger};1])^{-1}\right\} = R^{-1}. \qquad (12.25)$$

From Equations (12.22) and (12.25), we have that

$$\phi(\gamma) > 0; \quad \phi(0) = \phi(-1) = 1. \qquad (12.26)$$

Further, by differentiation,

$$\phi''(\gamma) = E\left\{(Z[w^{\dagger\dagger};1])^\gamma \log^2(Z[w^{\dagger\dagger};1])\right\} > 0, \qquad (12.27)$$

and so, ϕ is a strictly convex function with a unique interior minimum at $\gamma_{\min}$ From (12.26), $-1 < \gamma_{\min} < 0$, and therefore, $\phi'(\gamma) < 0$ for $\gamma < \gamma_{\min}$. Hence, since $\phi(-1) = 1, \phi(\gamma) > 1$ for $\gamma < -1$.

But, from (12.22), $\phi(\gamma) > 1$ for $\gamma < -1$ implies that for any R, $W_0 > 0$, and $\gamma < -1$,

$$\lim_{T \to \infty} \Pi_{13}(T) = \infty, \qquad (12.28)$$

and therefore, such risk-averse investors would require an indefinitely large initial payment to give up the riskless program for the max-expected-log one.

Further, in the case where $R = 1$ and the riskless asset is noninterest bearing cash, we have that for $\gamma < -1$, $E[Z_1[w^{\dagger\dagger}; 1])^\gamma] > 1$ which implies that

$$\lim_{T\to\infty} EU_T(W_0 Z[w^{\dagger\dagger};T]) = \lim_{T\to\infty} W_0 \left\{ E[(Z[w^{\dagger\dagger};1])^\gamma] \right\}^{T}/\gamma$$
$$= -\infty, \qquad (12.29)$$

so that such a risk-averse person's being forced into the allegedly desirable max-expected-log strategy is just as bad for infinitely large T as having all his initial wealth taken away! Few people will opt to ruin themselves voluntarily once they understand what they are doing.[14]

12.4 A FALSE LOG-NORMAL APPROXIMATION

A second more subtle, fallacy has grown out of the more recent literature on optimal portfolio selection for maximization of (distant time) expected terminal utility of wealth.

After giving arguments based on maximizing expected average-compound-return that imply myopic and uniform strategies, $w(t) \equiv w_T$, Hakansson (1971b, pp. 868-869) proceeds to use the Central-Limit Theorem to argue that for large T, the distribution of terminal wealth will be approximately log-normal. Then, he approximates the mean and variance of average-compound-return by the first two moments of the associated Log-Normal Surrogate. To obtain an approximation to the efficient set for the mean and variance of average-compound-return, he (p.871) substitutes the Log-Normal Surrogate for the true random variable portfolio return in an isoelastic utility function and computes its expected value *prior* to any maximization. This done, he is able to use the property that maximization of W^γ/γ under the log-normal distribution reduces to a simple linear tradeoff relationship between expected log of return and the variance of log return with γ being a measure of the investor's risk-return trade off. More generally, if a portfolio is known to have a log-normal distribution with parameters $[\mu, \sigma^2] \equiv [E\log(W_1/W_0), \text{var} \log(W_1/W_0)]$, then for all utilities, it will be optimal to have a maximum of the first parameter for any fixed value of the second. While it is not true that for a fixed value of μ, all concave utility maximizers would necessarily prefer the minimum σ^2, it is true that for a fixed value of $\alpha \equiv \log[E(W_1/W_0)] = \mu + \tfrac{1}{2}\sigma^2$, all concave utility maximizers would optimally choose the minimum σ^2.[15] Hence, the Hakansson derivation can suggest that there exists an asymptotic 'efficient frontier' in either of the two related parameter spaces $[\mu, \sigma^2]$ or $[\alpha, \sigma^2]$. In the special case of the W^γ/γ family, the γ determines the point on that frontier where a given investor's optimal portfolio lies. One of us, independently, fell into this same trap.[16]

Unfortunately, substitution of the associated log-normal for the true distribution leads to incorrect results, as will be demonstrated by counterexample. The error in the analysis leading to this false conjecture results from an improper interchange of limits, as we now demonstrate.

For each uniform portfolio strategy $\{w\}$, define as in Equation (12.2), the one-period portfolio return in period t by

$$Z[t;w] \equiv \sum_1^n w_i Z_i(t) = W_t[w]/W_{t-1}. \tag{12.30}$$

Given the distributional assumption about asset returns in Section 12.2, the $Z[t;w]$ will be independently and identically distributed through time with

$$\text{prob}\left\{\log(Z[t;w]) \leqslant x\right\}_t \equiv P_1(x;w). \tag{12.31}$$

The T-period return on the portfolio is defined, for any $T \geqslant 1$, by

$$Z_T[w] \equiv \prod_{t=1}^T Z[t;w] = W_T[w]/W_0, \tag{12.32}$$

with

$$\text{prob}\left\{\log(Z_T[w]) \leqslant x\right\} \equiv P_T(x;w) \tag{12.33}$$

as in Equation (12.6) with the w's independent of time.

Define $Z_T^\dagger[w]$ to be a log-normally distributed random variable with parameters μT and $\sigma^2 T$ chosen such that

$$\mu T \equiv E\left\{\log(Z_T^\dagger[w])\right\} = E\left\{\log(Z_T[w])\right\} = TE\left\{\log(Z_1[w])\right\} \tag{12.34}$$

$$\sigma^2 T \equiv \text{var}\left\{\log(Z_T^\dagger[w])\right\} = \text{var}\left\{\log(Z_T[w])\right\}$$

$$= T \, \text{var}\left\{\log(Z_1[w])\right\}$$

We call $Z_T^\dagger[w]$ the 'surrogate' log-normal to the random variable $Z_T[w]$; it is the log-normal approximation to $Z_T[w]$ fitted by equating the first two moments in the classical maximum-likelihood Pearsonian curve-fitting procedure. Note that by definition

$$\mu = \mu(w) = \int_{-\infty}^{\infty} x P_1(dx;w), \qquad (12.35)$$

$$\sigma^2 = \sigma^2(w) = \int_{-\infty}^{\infty} (x - \mu)^2 P_1(dx;w).$$

Since each $\log(Z[t; w])$ in $\Sigma_1^T \log(Z[t; w])$ is an identically distributed, independent variate with finite variance, the Central-Limit Theorem applies to give us the valid asymptotic relation.[17]

Central-Limit Theorem. As T gets large, the normalized variable, $Y_T \equiv [\log(Z_T[w] - \mu(w)T]/\sigma(w)\sqrt{T}$, approaches the normal distribution. I.e.,

$$\lim_{T \to \infty} \text{prob} \left\{ Y_T \leqslant y \right\} = \lim_{T \to \infty} P_T[\sigma(w)\sqrt{T}\, y + \mu(w)T;w] \qquad (12.36)$$

$$= N(y) \equiv (2\pi)^{-1/2} \int_{-\infty}^{y} e^{-\frac{1}{2}t^2} dt,$$

where $N(\ )$ is the cumulative distribution function for a standard normal variate.

Since $\log(Z_T[w]) = \log(W_T[w]/W_0)$, this is the valid formulation of the log-normal asymptotic approximation for the properly standardized distribution of terminal wealth.

In a more trivial sense, both $P_T(x; w)$ for $Z_T[w]$ and also its surrogate, $\eta(x; \mu T, \sigma^2 T) \equiv N[(x - \mu(w)T)/\sigma(w)\sqrt{T}]$ for $Z_T[w]$, approach the same common limit, namely

$$\lim_{T \to \infty} P_T(x;w) = L = \lim_{T \to \infty} \eta(x;\mu T, \sigma^2 T), \qquad (12.37)$$

where

$$L = 1,\ \mu(w) < 0, \qquad (12.38)$$

$$= 0,\ \mu(w) > 0,$$

$$= \tfrac{1}{2},\ \mu(w) = 0.$$

But it is not the case that

$$\lim_{T\to\infty} \left\{ [L - P_T(x;w)] / [L - \eta(x;\mu T,\sigma^2 T)] \right\} = 1. \qquad (12.39)$$

From the *terra firma* of the valid Central-Limit Theorem, a false corollary tempts the unwary.

False Corollary. If the returns on assets satisfy the distributional assumptions of Section 12.2; then, as $T \to \infty$, the optimal solution to

$$\max_{\{w\}} E[U_T(W_T[w])] = \max_{\{w\}} \int_{-\infty}^{\infty} U_T[W_0 e^x] P_T(dx;w),$$

over all[18] *uniform* strategies $\{w\}$, will be the same as the optimal solution to

$$\max_{\{w\}} E[U_T(W_0 Z_T[w])] = \max_{\{w\}} \int_{-\infty}^{\infty} U_T[W_0 e^x] \eta'(x;\mu T,\sigma^2 T) dx,$$

where $\eta'(x; \mu T, \sigma^2 T) = (2\pi\sigma^2 T)^{-1/2} \exp[-(x - \mu T)^2 /2\sigma^2 T] = N'[(x - \mu(w)T)/ \sigma(w)\sqrt{T}] / \dot\sigma(w)\sqrt{T}$. I.e., one can allegedly find the optimal portfolio policy for large T, by 'replacing' $Z_T[w]$ by its surrogate log-normal variate, $Z_T^\dagger[w]$.

Let us sketch the usual heuristic arguments that purport to deduce the false corollary. From Equations (12.36) and (12.37), one is tempted to reason heuristically, that since Y_T is approximately distributed standard normal, then $\log(Z_T[w]) = \sigma\sqrt{T}Y_T + \mu T \equiv X_T$ is approximately normally distributed[19] with mean μT and variance σ^2, for large T. Hence, if X_T has a density function $P_T'(x;w)$ then, for large T, one can write the approximation

$$P_T'(x; w) \approx \eta'(x; \mu T, \sigma^2 T), \qquad (12.40)$$

and substitute the right-hand expression for the left-hand expression whenever T is large. As an example, from Equation (12.40), one is led to the strong (and false!) conclusion that, for large T,

$$\int_{-\infty}^{\infty} U(W_0 e^x) P_T'(x;w) dx \approx \int_{-\infty}^{\infty} U(W_0 e^x) \eta'(x;\mu T,\sigma^2 T) dx, \qquad (12.41)$$

in the sense that

$$\lim_{T\to\infty} [\int_{-\infty}^{\infty} U(W_0 e^x)P_T'(x;w)dx - \int_{-\infty}^{\infty} U(W_0 e^x)\eta'(x;\mu T,\sigma^2 T)dx]$$

$$= \int_{-\infty}^{\infty} U(W_0 e^x) \lim_{} [P_T'(x;w) - \eta'(x;\mu T,\sigma^2 T)]\,dx = 0. \qquad (12.42)$$

But, actually Equation (12.42) is quite false as careful analysis of the Central-Limit Theorem will show.

A correct analysis immediately shows that the heuristic argument leading to (12.41)-(12.42) involves an incorrect limit interchange. From Equation (12.36), for each T, the random variable Y_T will be seen to have a probability function $F_T(y; w) = P_T(\sigma(w)\sqrt{T}\,y + \mu(w)T; w)$. By definition, we have that

$$\overline{U}_T = \int_{-\infty}^{\infty} U(W_0 e^x)P_T(dx;w)$$

$$= \int_{-\infty}^{\infty} U[W_0 \exp(\sigma\sqrt{T}y + \mu T)]\,F_T(dy;w), \qquad (12.43)$$

and, for the surrogate-function calculation,

$$\int_{-\infty}^{\infty} U(W_0 e^x)\eta'(x;\mu T,\sigma^2 T)dx \qquad (12.44)$$

$$= \int_{-\infty}^{\infty} U[W_0 \exp(\sigma\sqrt{T}y + \mu T)]\,N'(y)dy.$$

Further, from the Central-Limit Theorem, we also have that, in the case where $P_T(\ ;w)$ and $F_T(\ ;w)$ have densities, $\partial P_T/\partial x = P'_T(x; w)$ and $\partial F_T/\partial y = F'_T(y; w)$,

$$\lim_{T\to\infty} F_T'(y;w) = N'(y). \qquad (12.45)$$

However, to derive Equation (12.42) from (12.43)-(12.45), the following limit interchange would have to be valid for each y,

$$\lim_{T\to\infty} \{U[W_0 \exp(\sigma\sqrt{T}y + \mu T)]\,F_T'(y;w)\} \qquad (12.46)$$

$$= \{\lim_{T\to\infty} U[W_0 \exp(\sigma\sqrt{T}y + \mu T)]\} \{\lim_{T\to\infty} F_T'(y;w)\}.$$

In general, as is seen from easy counterexamples, such an interchange of limits will be illegitimate, and hence, the False Corollary is invalid. In those cases where the limit interchange in Equation (12.46) is valid (e.g., U is a bounded function), the False Corollary holds only in the trivial sense of (12.14) in Section 12.3. I.e., as already noted, in the limit as $T \to \infty$, there will exist an infinite number of portfolio programs (including holding one hundred percent of the portfolio in the positive-yielding, riskless asset) which will give expected utility levels equal to the upperbound of U. As we now show by counterexample, it is not true that portfolio proportions, w^*, chosen to maximize expected utility over the $P_T(\ ; w)$ distribution will be equal to the proportions, $w^\dagger$, chosen to maximize expected utility over the surrogate $\eta(\ ; \mu T, \sigma^2 T)$, even in the limit.

To demonstrate our counterexample to the False Corollary, first, note that for the isoelastic family, the expected utility level for the surrogate log-normal can be written as

$$E(W_0 Z_T^\dagger [w])^\gamma / \gamma = W_0^\gamma \exp[\gamma \mu(w) T + \tfrac{1}{2} \gamma^2 \sigma^2 (w) T] / \gamma. \quad (12.47)$$

As Hakansson (1971b) has shown, maximization of Equation (12.47) is equivalent to the maximization of

$$[\mu(w) + \tfrac{1}{2} \gamma \sigma^2 (w)]. \quad (12.48)$$

Hence, from Equation (12.48), the maximizing $w^\dagger$ for Equation (12.47) depend only on the mean and variance of the logarithm of one-period returns.

Second, note that because the portfolio returns for each period are independently and identically distributed, we can write the expected utility level for the true distribution as

$$E(W_0 Z_T [w])^\gamma / \gamma = W_0^\gamma \left\{ E(Z_1 [w]^\gamma) \right\}^T / \gamma. \quad (12.49)$$

Hence, maximization of Equation (12.49) is equivalent to the maximization of

$$E(Z_1 [w]^\gamma) / \gamma, \quad (12.50)$$

which also depends only on the one-period returns.[20]

Consider the simple two-asset case where $Z[t; w] \equiv w(y_t - R) + R$ and where the y_t are independent, Bernoulli-distributed random variables with prob $\{ y_t = \lambda \} = \text{prob} \{ y_t = \delta \} = 1/2$ and $\lambda > R > \delta > 0$. Substituting into Equation (12.50), we have that the optimal portfolio rule, w^*, will solve

$$\max_{\{w\}} \left\{ [w(\lambda - R) + R]^{\gamma} + [w(\delta - R) + R]^{\gamma} \right\} / 2\gamma, \qquad (12.51)$$

which by the usual calculus first-order condition implies that w^* will satisfy

$$0 = (\lambda - R)[w^*(\lambda - R) + R]^{\gamma - 1} + (\delta - R)[w^*(\delta - R) + R]^{\gamma - 1}. \qquad (12.52)$$

Rearranging terms in Equation (12.52), we have that

$$[(R - \delta)/(\lambda - R)] = [(w^*(\lambda - R) + R)/(w^*(\delta - R) + R)]^{\gamma - 1} \qquad (12.53)$$

or

$$w^* = w^*(\gamma) = (A - 1)R/[\lambda - R) + A(R - \delta)], \qquad (12.54)$$

where

$$A \equiv [(R - \delta)/(\lambda - R)]^{1/\gamma - 1}.$$

From Equation (12.35), the surrogate log-normal for $Z_T[w]$ will have parameters

$$\mu = \mu(w) \equiv 1/2 \left\{ \log[w(\lambda - R) + R] + \log[w(\delta - R) + R] \right\}, \qquad (12.55)$$

and

$$\sigma^2 = \sigma^2(w) \equiv 1/2 \left\{ \log^2[w(\lambda - R) + R] + \log^2[w(\delta - R) + R] \right\} - \mu^2. \qquad (12.56)$$

The optimal portfolio rule relative to Equation (12.48), $w^{\dagger}$, will be the solution to

$$0 = 1/2 \left\{ \frac{\lambda - R}{w^{\dagger}(\lambda - R) + R} + \frac{\delta - R}{w^{\dagger}(\delta - R) + R} \right\}$$

$$\left(1 - \frac{\gamma}{2} \log[(w^{\dagger}(\lambda - R) + R)(w^{\dagger}(\delta - R) + R)] \right)$$

$$+ \frac{\gamma}{2} \left\{ \log[w^{\dagger}(\lambda - R) + R] \left(\frac{\lambda - R}{w^{\dagger}(\lambda - R) + R} \right) \right.$$

$$\left. + \log[w^{\dagger}(\delta - R) + R] \left(\frac{\delta - R}{w^{\dagger}(\delta - R) + R} \right) \right\}, \qquad (12.57)$$

which can be rewritten as

$$0 = \left(\frac{\lambda - R}{R - \delta} \right) \left[1 + \frac{\gamma}{2} \log(B) \right] - B \left[1 - \frac{\gamma}{2} \log(B) \right], \quad (12.58)$$

where $B \equiv [w^\dagger(\lambda - R) + R]/[w^\dagger(\delta - R) + R]$. Note that since both w^* and $w^\dagger$ are independent of T, if the False Corollary had been valid, then $w^* = w^\dagger$. Suppose $w^* = w^\dagger$. From the definitions of A and B and from Equation (12.53), we have that $B = A$ and $(\lambda - R)/(R - \delta) = A^{1-\gamma}$. Substitute A for B in Equation (12.58) to get

$$H(\gamma) \equiv A^{1-\gamma} \left[1 + \frac{\gamma}{2} \log(A) \right] - A \left[1 - \frac{\gamma}{2} \log(A) \right]. \quad (12.59)$$

For arbitrary λ, δ, and R, $H(\gamma) = 0$ only if $\gamma = 0$ (i.e., if the original utility function is logarithmic). Hence, $w^* \neq w^\dagger$ for $\gamma \neq 0$, and the False Corollary is disproved. The reason that $w^* = w^\dagger$ for $\gamma = 0$ has nothing to do with the log-normal approximation or size of T since in that case, Equations (12.48) and (12.50) are identities.

This effectively dispenses with the false conjecture that for large T, the log-normal approximation provides a suitable surrogate for the true distribution of terminal wealth probabilities; and with any hope that the mean and variance of expected-average-compound-return can serve as asymptotically sufficient decision parameters.

12.5 A CHAMBER OF HORRORS OF IMPROPER LIMITS

It is worth exposing at some length the fallacy involved in replacing the true probability distribution, $P_T(x; w)$, by its surrogate log-normal or normal approximation, $\eta(x; \mu T, \sigma^2 T) = N[(x - \mu T)/\sigma\sqrt{T}]$. First as a salutary warning against the illegitimate handling of limits, note that by the definition of a probability density of $P_T(x; w)$, $\partial P_T(x; w)/\partial x$, where such a density exists

$$\int_{-\infty}^{\infty} P'_T(x;w)\, dx \equiv 1. \quad (12.60)$$

Also, as is well known when summing independent, identically-distributed, nonnormalized variates, the probabilities spread out and

$$\lim_{T \to \infty} P'_T(x;w)\, dx \underset{x}{\equiv} 0. \quad (12.61)$$

Combining Equations (12.60) and (12.61), we see the illegitimacy of interchanging limits in the following fashion:

$$1 = \lim_{T\to\infty} \int_{-\infty}^{\infty} P'_T(x;w)\,\mathrm{d}x = \int_{-\infty}^{\infty} \lim_{T\to\infty} P'_T(x;w)\,\mathrm{d}x \qquad (12.62)$$

$$= \int_{-\infty}^{\infty} 0\cdot\mathrm{d}x = 0.$$

Similarly, as was already indicated for a nondensity discrete-probability example in the previous section, from the following true relation,

$$\lim_{T\to\infty} [P'_T(x;w) - \eta'(x;\mu T,\sigma^2 T)] = 0, \qquad (12.63)$$

it is false to conclude that, for $0 < \gamma < 1$,

$$\lim_{T\to\infty} \int_{-\infty}^{\infty} e^{\gamma x}[P'_T(x;w) - \eta'(x;\mu T,\sigma^2 T)]\,\mathrm{d}x$$

$$= \int_{-\infty}^{\infty} e^{\gamma x} \lim_{T\to\infty} [P'_T(x;w) - \eta'(x;\mu T,\sigma^2 T)]\,\mathrm{d}x$$

$$= \int_{-\infty}^{\infty} e^{\gamma x} \cdot 0\ \mathrm{d}x = 0. \qquad (12.64)$$

Hence, trying to calculate the correct $\overline{U}_T[w]$, in Equation (12.7) even for very large T, by relying on its surrogate

$$\int_{-\infty}^{\infty} e^{\gamma x}\eta'(x;\mu T,\sigma^2 T)\,\mathrm{d}x = \exp\left\{[\gamma\mu(w) + 1/2\gamma^2\sigma^2(w)]T\right\} \qquad (12.65)$$

leads to the wrong portfolio rules, namely to $w^\dagger \neq w^* \equiv w^{**}(t)$.

Thus, we hope that the fallacy of the surrogate log-normal approximation with respect to optimal portfolio selection has been laid to rest.

In concluding this debunking of improper log-normal approximations, we should mention that this same fallacy pops up with monotonous regularity in all branches of stochastic investment analysis. Thus, one of us, Samuelson (1965), had to warn of its incorrect use in rational warrant pricing.

Suppose a common stock's future price compared to its present price, $V(t+T)/V(t) \equiv Z[T]$, is distributed like the product of T independent, uniform probabilities $P[Z]$. For T large, there is a log-normal surrogate for

$$\text{prob}\{\log(Z[T]) \leqslant x\} \equiv \Pi_T(x) . \tag{12.66}$$

Let the 'rational price of the warrant' be given, as in the cited 1965 study, by

$$F_T[V] = e^{-\alpha T} \int_{-\infty}^{\infty} \max[0, V e^x - C] \Pi_T'(x) dx, \tag{12.67}$$

where C is the warrant's exercise price and $e^\alpha \equiv E\ V(t+1)/V(t)$. Although the density of the normalized variate $y \equiv (\log(Z[T]) - \mu T)/\sigma\sqrt{T}$ approaches $N'(y)$, it is false to think that, even for large T,

$$e^{\alpha T} \doteq \int_{-\infty}^{\infty} e^x \eta'(x;\mu T,\sigma^2 T) dx = \exp\left\{[\mu + 1/2\sigma^2]T\right\}. \tag{12.68}$$

Nor, for finite T, will we in other than a trivial sense, observe the identity

$$F_T[V] \equiv F_T^\dagger[V] \tag{12.69}$$

$$= \exp\left\{[-\mu - 1/2\sigma^2]T\right\} \int_{-\infty}^{\infty} \max[0, V e^x - C]$$

$$\eta'(x;\mu T,\sigma^2 T) dx.$$

It is trivially true that $\lim_{T\to\infty}\{F_T[V] - F_T^\dagger[V]\} = V - V = 0$, but untrue that $\lim_{T\to\infty}\{(V - F_T[V])/(V - F_T^\dagger[V])\} = 1$. Of course, if $\Pi_1(x)$ is gaussian to begin with, as in infinitely-divisible continuous-time probabilities, there is no need for an asymptotic approximation and no surrogate concept is involved to betray one into error.

Similar remarks could be made about treacherous log-normal surrogates misapplied to the alternative 1969 warrant pricing theory of Samuelson and Merton.[21]

To bring these calculations concerning false limits to an end, we must stress that limiting inequalities can be as treacherous as limiting equalities. Thus, consider two alternative strategies that produce alternative random variables of utility (or of money), written as U_I and U_{II} respectively and satisfying probability distributions $P_I(U; T)$ and $P_{II}(U;T)$. Too often the false inference is made that

$$\lim_{T\to\infty} \text{prob}\{U_I > U_{II}\} = 1 \tag{12.70}$$

implies (or is implied by) the condition

$$\lim_{T \to \infty} \left\{ E[U_\mathrm{I}] - E[U_\mathrm{II}] \right\} > 0 \tag{12.71}$$

Indeed, as was shown in our refuting the fallacy of max-expected-log, yielding U_I rather than the correct optimal U_II that comes from use of $w^* \neq w^{\dagger\dagger}$, it is the case that Equation (12.70) is satisfied and yet it is also true that

$$E[U_\mathrm{I} - U_\mathrm{II}] < 0 \text{ for all } T \text{ however large.} \tag{12.72}$$

Or consider another property of the $w^{\dagger\dagger}$ strategy: Namely,

$$\mathrm{prob}\left\{ Z_T[w^{\dagger\dagger}] \leqslant x \right\} \leqslant \mathrm{prob}\left\{ Z_T[w] \leqslant x \right\} \tag{12.73}$$

$$\text{for all } x < M(T;w),$$

where $M(T; w)$ is an increasing function of T with $\lim_{T \to \infty} M(T; w) = \infty$. Yet Equation (12.73) does not imply Equation (12.71) nor does it imply asymptotic First Order Stochastic Dominance. I.e., it does not follow from Equation (12.73) that, as $T \to \infty$,

$$\mathrm{prob}\left\{ Z_T[w^{\dagger\dagger}] \leqslant x \right\} \leqslant \mathrm{prob}\left\{ Z_T[w] \leqslant x \right\} \tag{12.74}$$

$$\text{for } all \ x \text{ independently of } T.$$

The moral is this: Never confuse exact limits involving normalized variables with their naive formal extrapolations. Although $a = b$ and $b = c$ implies $a = c$; still $a \approx b$ and $b \approx c$ cannot reliably imply $a \approx c$ without careful restrictions put on the interpretation of '$\approx$'.

12.6 CONTINUOUS-TIME PORTFOLIO SELECTION

The enormous interest in the optimal portfolio selection problem for investors with distant time horizons was generated by the hope that an intertemporal portfolio theory could be developed which, at least asymptotically, would have the simplicity and richness of the static mean-variance theory without the well known objections to that model. While the analysis of previous sections demonstrates that such a theory does not validly obtain, we now derive an asymptotic theory involving limits of a different type which will produce the conjectured results.

We denote by T the time horizon of the investor. Now, we denote by N the number of portfolio revisions over that horizon, so that $h \equiv T/N$ will be the length of time between portfolio revisions. In the previous sections, we examined the asymptotic portfolio behavior as T and N tended to infinity, for a fixed $h(= 1)$. In this section, we consider the asymptotic portfolio behavior for a *fixed* T, as N tends to infinity and h tends to zero. The limiting behavior is interpreted as that of an investor who can continuously revise his portfolio. We leave for later the discussion of how realistic is this assumption and other assumptions as a description of actual asset market conditions, and for the moment, proceed formally to see what results obtain.

While the assumptions of previous sections about the distributions of asset returns are kept, we make explicit their dependence on the trading interval length, h. I.e., the per-dollar return on the jth asset between times $t - \tau$ and t when the trading interval is of length h, is $Z_j(t, \tau; h)$, where τ is integral in h.

Suppose, as is natural once time is continuous, that the individual $Z_j(\ )$ are distributed log-normally with constant parameters. I.e.,

$$\text{prob} \left\{ \log[Z_j(t, \tau; h)] \leqslant x \right\} = N(x; \mu_j \tau, \sigma_j^2 \tau), \qquad (12.75)$$

where

$$E \left\{ \log[Z_j(t, \tau; h)] \right\} = \mu_j \tau \qquad (12.76)$$

and

$$\text{var} \left\{ \log[Z_j(t, \tau; h)] \right\} = \sigma_j^2 \tau,$$

with μ_j and σ_j^2 independent of h. Further, define

$$\alpha_j \tau \equiv (\mu_j + 1/2\sigma_j^2)\tau \qquad (12.77)$$

$$= \log[E \left\{ Z_j(t, \tau; h) \right\}],$$

and

$$\sigma_{ij} \tau \equiv \text{cov} \left\{ \log[Z_i(t, \tau; h)], \log[Z_j(t, \tau; h)] \right\}. \qquad (12.78)$$

As in Equation (12.11), the nth asset is riskless with $\alpha_m = r$ and $\sigma_n^2 = 0$.

We denote by $[w*(t; h)]$ the vector of optimal portfolio proportions as time t when the trading interval is of length h, and its limit as $h \to 0$ by $w*(t; 0)$. Then the following separation (or 'mutual fund') theorem obtains:

Theorem: Given n assets whose returns are log-normally distributed and given continuous-trading opportunties (i.e., $h = 0$), then the $\{w^*(t;)\}$ are such that: (1) There exists a unique (up to a nonsingular transformation) pair of 'mutual funds' constructed from linear combinations of these asets such that independent of preferences, wealth distribution, or time horizon, investors will be indifferent between choosing from a linear combination of these two funds or a linear combination of the original n assets. (2) If Z_f is the return on either fund, then Z_f is log-normally distributed. (3) The fractional proportions of respective assets contained in either fund are solely a function of the α_i and σ_{ij} ($i,j = 1, 2, \ldots, n$) an 'efficiency' condition. Proof of the theorem can be found in Merton (1971, pp. 384-386). It obtains whether one of the assets is riskless or not. From the theorem, we can always work here with just two assets: the riskless asset and a (composite) risky asset which is log-normally distributed with parameters (α, σ^2).[22] Hence, we can reduce the vector $[w^*(t; 0)]$ to a scalar $w^*(t)$ equal to the fraction invested in the risky asset. If we denote by $\alpha^*(\equiv w^*(t)(\alpha-r) + r)$ and $\sigma_*^2(\equiv w^{*2}\sigma^2)$, the (instantaneous) mean gain and variance of a given investor's optimal portfolio, an efficiency frontier in terms of (α^*, σ_*) or (μ^*, σ_*) can be traced out as shown in either Figure 12-1a or 12-1b. The (α^*, σ_*)-frontier is exactly akin to the classical Markowitz single-period frontier where a 'period' is an instant. Although the frontier is the same in every period, a given investor will in general choose a different point on the frontier each period depending on his current wealth and $T - t$.

In the special case of isoelastic utility,[23] $U_T = W^\gamma/\gamma$, $\gamma < 1$, $w^*(t) = w^*$, a constant, and the entire portfolio selection problem can be presented graphically as in Figure 12-2. Further, for this special class of utility functions, the distribution of wealth under the optimal policy will be log-normal for all t.[24]

Hence, from the assumptions of log-normality and continuous trading, we have, even for T finite and not at all large, a complete asymptotic theory with all the simplicity of classical mean-variance, but without its objectionable assumptions. Further, these results still obtain even if one allows intermediate consumption evaluated at some concave utility function, $V(c)$.[25]

Having derived the theory, we now turn to the question of the reasonableness of the assumptions. Since trading continuously is not a reality, the answer will depend on 'how close' $w^*(t;0)$ is to $w^*(t; h)$. I.e., for every $\delta > 0$, does there exist an $h > 0$, such that $\|w^*(t; 0) - w^*(t; h)\| < \delta$ for some norm $\| \; \|$, and what is the nature of the $\delta = \delta(h)$ function? Further, since log-normality as the

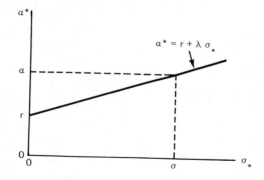

Figure 12-1a. (a^*, σ_*) — Efficiency Frontier

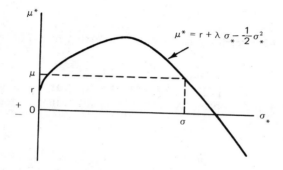

Figure 12-1b. (μ^*, σ_*) — Efficiency Frontier

distribution for returns is not a 'known fact', what are the conditions such that one can validly use the log-normal as a surrogate?

Since the answer to both questions will turn on the distributional assumptions for the returns, we now drop the assumption of log-normality for the $Z_j(\ ; h)$, but retain the assumptions (maintained throughout the study) that, for a *given* h,[26] the one-period returns, $Z_j(\ ,h; h)$ have joint distributions identical through time, and the vector $[Z(t, h; h)] \equiv [Z_1(t, h; h), Z_2(t, h; h), \ldots, Z_n(t, h; h)]$ is distributed independently of $[Z(t + s, h; h)]$ for $s > h$.

By definition, the return on the jth security over a time period of length T will be

$$Z_j(t, T; h) \equiv \prod_{k=1}^{T} Z_j(kh, h; h). \qquad (12.79)$$

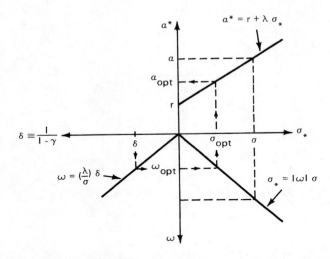

Figure 12-2. Portfolio Selection for Isoelastic Utility Functions

Let $X_j(k, h) \equiv \log[Z_j(kh, h; h)]$. Then, for a given h, the $X_j(k, h)$ are independently and identically distributed with non-central moments

$$m_j(i;h) \underset{k}{\equiv} E\left\{[\lambda X_j(k, h)]^i\right\}, \qquad i = 0, 1, 2, \ldots, \qquad (12.80)$$

and moment-generating function

$$\psi_j(\lambda; h) \underset{k}{\equiv} E\left\{\exp[\lambda X_j(k,h)]\right\} \qquad (12.81)$$

$$= E\left\{[Z_j(kh, h; h)]^\lambda\right\}.$$

Define the noncentral moments of the *rate of return* per period, $Z_j(kh, h; h) - 1$, by

$$M_j(1; h) = \alpha_j(h)h \underset{k}{\equiv} E\left\{Z_j(kh, h; h) - 1\right\}, \qquad (12.82)$$

$$M_j(2; h) = v_j^2(h)h + (\alpha_j(h)h)^2 \underset{k}{\equiv} E\left\{[Z_j(kh, h; h) - 1]^2\right\},$$

$$M_j(i; h) \underset{k}{\equiv} E\left\{[Z_j(kh, h; h) - 1]^i\right\}, \qquad i = 3, 4, \ldots,$$

where $\alpha_j(h)$ is the expected rate of return per unit time and $v_j^2(h)$ is the variance of the rate of return per unit time.

Samuelson (1970) has demonstrated that if the moments $M_j(\ ;h)$ satisfy

$$M_j(1; h) = 0(h), \tag{12.83}$$

$$M_j(2; h) = 0(h),$$

$$M_j(k; h) = o(h), k > 2,$$

then $\|w\ (t; 0) - w*(t; h)\| = 0(h)$ where '0' and 'o' are defined by

$$g(h) = 0(h), \text{ if } (g/h) \text{ is bounded for all } h \geqslant 0 \tag{12.84}$$

and

$$g(h) = o(h), \text{ if } \lim_{h \to 0}(g/h) = 0. \tag{12.85}$$

Thus, if the distributions of returns satisfy Equation (12.83), then, for every $\delta > 0$, there exists an $h > 0$ such that $\| w*(t; 0) - w*(t; h) \| < \delta$, and the continuous-time solution will be a valid asymptotic solution to the discrete-interval case. Note that if Equation (12.83) is satisfied, then $\alpha_j(h) = 0(1)$ and $v_j^2(h) = (1)$, and $\alpha_j \equiv \lim_{h \to o} \alpha_j(h)$ will be finite as will $v^2 \equiv \lim_{h \to o} v_j^{2j}(h)$

Given that $M_j(\ ;h)$ satisfies Equation (12.83), we can derive a similar relationship for $m_j(\ ;h)$. Namely, by Taylor series,[27]

$$m_j(1; h) = E\left\{\log(1 + [Z_j - 1])\right\} \tag{12.86}$$

$$= E\left\{ \sum_{i=1}^{\infty} (-1)^{i-1}[Z_j - 1]^i/i \right\}$$

$$= M_j(1; h) - 1/2 M_j(2; h) + o(h), \text{ from Equation (12.83)}$$

$$= 0(h),$$

and

$$m_j(2; h) = E\left\{\log^2(1 + [Z_j - 1)]\right\} \tag{12.87}$$

$$= E\left\{ \sum_{p=1}^{\infty} \sum_{i=1}^{\infty} (-1)^{i+p}[Z_j - 1]^{i+p}/ip \right\}$$

$$= M_j(2; h) + o(h)$$

$$= 0(h),$$

and, in a similar fashion,

$$m_j(k; h) = o(h), \text{ for } k > 2. \tag{12.88}$$

Thus, the $m_j(\ ;h)$ satisfy Equation (12.83) as well. If we define $\mu_j(h) \equiv m_j(1; h) / h$ as the mean logarithmic return per unit time and $\sigma^2(h) \equiv [m_j(2; h) - \mu^2(h)h^2] / h$ as the variance of the log return per unit time, then from Equations (12.82), (12.86) and (12.87), we have that

$$\alpha_j \equiv \lim_{h \to 0} \alpha_j(h) = \lim_{h \to 0} [\mu_j(h) + 1/2\sigma_j^2(h)] = \mu_j + 1/2\sigma_j^2 \tag{12.89}$$

and

$$v_j^2 \equiv \lim_{h \to 0} v_j^2(h) = \lim_{h \to 0} \sigma_j^2(h) = \sigma_j^2. \tag{12.90}$$

Equation (12.89) demonstrates that the true distribution will satisfy asymptotically the exact relationship satisfied for all h by the log-normal surrogate; from Equation (12.90), the variance of the arithmetic return will equal the variance of the logarithmic return in the limit. Hence, these important moment relationships match up exactly between the true distribution and its log-normal surrogate.

If we define $Y_j(T; h) \equiv \log[Z_j(T, T; h)]$, then from Equation (12.79), we have that

$$Y_j(T; h) \equiv \sum_{k=1}^{N} X_j(k, h), \text{ where } N \equiv T/h, \tag{12.91}$$

and from the independence and identical distribution of the $X_j(\ ; h)$, the moment-generating function of Y_j will satisfy

$$\phi_j(\lambda; h, T) \equiv E\left\{\exp[\lambda Y_j(T; h)]\right\} \tag{12.92}$$

$$= [\psi_j(\lambda; h)]^{T/h}.$$

Taking logs of both sides of Equation (12.92) and using Taylor series, we have that

$$\log[\phi_j(\lambda; h, T)] = (T/h)\log[\psi_j(\lambda; h)] \tag{12.93}$$

$$= (T/h)\log[\sum_{k=0}^{\infty} \psi_j^{(k)}(0; h)\lambda^k /k!]$$

$$= (T/h)\log[\sum_{k=1}^{\infty} m_j(k; h)\lambda^k/k!]$$

$$= (T/h)\log[1 + m_j(1; h)\lambda + 1/2m_j(2; h)\lambda^2 + o(h)]$$

$$= T[\lambda(m_j(1; h)/h) + (\lambda^2/2)(m_j(2; h)/h) + 0(h)].$$

Substituting $\mu_j(h)h$ for $m_j(1; h)$ and $\sigma_j^2(h)h + \mu_j^2(h)h^2$ for $m_j(2; h)$ and taking the limit as $h \to o$ in Equation (12.93), we have that

$$\log[\phi_j(\lambda; 0, T)] = \lim_{h \to 1} \log[\phi(\lambda; h, T)] \qquad (12.94)$$

$$= \lambda\mu_j T + 1/2\sigma_j^2 T\lambda^2,$$

and therefore, $\phi_j(\lambda; 0, T)$ is the moment-generating function for a normally-distributed random variable with mean $\mu_j T$ and variance $\sigma_j^2 T$.

Thus, in what is essentially a valid application of the Central-Limit Theorem, we have shown that the limit distribution for $Y_j(T, T; h)$ as h tends to zero, is under the posited assumptions gaussian, and hence, the limit distribution for $Z_j(T, T; h)$ will be log-normal for *all finite T*. Further from Equations (12.89)-(12.90), the surrogate log-normal, fitted in the Pearsonian fashion of earlier sections, will, for smaller and smaller h, be in the limit, the true limit distribution for $Z_j(T, T; 0)$.

It is straightforward to show that if the distribution for each of the $Z_j(\quad, h; h)$, $j = 1, 2, \ldots, n$, satisfy Equation (12.83), then for bounded $w_j(t; h)$, the 'single-period' *portfolio* returns, $Z[t; w(t), h]$, will for each t satisfy Equation (12.83). However, unless the portfolio weights are constant through time [i.e., $w_j(t) \equiv w_j$], the resulting limit distribution for the portfolio over finite time, will not be log-normal.

How reasonable is it to assume that Equation (12.83) will be satisfied? Essentially Equation (12.83) is a set of sufficient conditions for the limiting continuous-time stochastic process to have a continuous sample path (with probability one). It is closely related to the 'local Markov property' of discrete-time stochastic processes which allows only movements to neighboring states in one period (e.g., the simple random walk).

A somewhat weaker sufficient condition [implied by Equation (12.83); see also Feller (1966, p. 321)] is that for every $\delta > 0$,

$$\text{prob}\left\{-\delta \;\leqslant\; X_j(\;\;;h) \;\leqslant\; \delta\right\} = 1 - o(h), \tag{12.95}$$

which clearly rules out 'jump-type' processes such as the Poisson. It is easy to show for the Poisson that Equation (12.83) is not satisfied because $M_j(k;h) = 0(h)$ for all k and similarly, Equation (12.95) is not satisfied since prob $\left\{-\delta \leqslant X_j(\;\;\;;h) \leqslant \delta\right\} = 1 - 0(h)$.

In the general case when Equation (12.95) is satisfied but the distribution of returns are not completely independent nor identically distributed, the limit distribution will not be log-normal, but will be generated by a diffusion process. Although certain quadratic simplifications still occur, the strong theorems of the earlier part of this section will no longer obtain.

The accuracy of the continuous solution will depend on whether, for reasonable trading intervals, compact distributions are an accurate representation for asset returns and whether, for these intervals, the distributions can be taken to be independent. Examination of time series for common stock returns shows that skewness and higher-order moments tend to be negligible relative to the first two moments for daily or weekly observations, which is consistent with Equation (12.83)'s assumptions. However, daily data tend also to show some negative serial correlation, significant for about two weeks. While this finding is inconsistent with independence, the size of the correlation coefficient is not large and the short-duration of the correlation suggests a 'high-speed of adjustment' in the autocorrelation function. Hence, while we could modify the continuous analysis to include an Ornstein-Uhlenbeck type process to capture these effects,[28] the results may not differ much from the standard model when empirical estimates of the correlation are plugged in.

NOTES TO SECTION TWELVE

1. Notable exceptions that deal with the general case can be found in the works of Arrow (1965), Rothschild and Stiglitz (1970), and Samuelson (1967a). Along with mean-variance analysis, the theory of portfolio selection when the distributions are Pareto-Lévy has been developed by Fama (1965) and Samuelson (1967b).

2. The literature is so extensive that we refer the reader to the bibliography. Additional references can be found in the survey articles by Fama (1970) and Jensen (1972), and the book by Sharpe (1970).

3. See Black, Jensen and Scholes (1972) and Friend and Blume (1970).

4. See Hakansson (1971c).

5. Cass and Stiglitz (1970) showed that these utility functions were among the few which satisfied the separation property with respect to initial wealth for arbitrary distributions. Other authors [Hakansson (1970), Leland (1968),

Merton (1969, 1971) and Samuelson (1969)] have previously made extensive use of these functions.

6. For the first, see Samuelson (1970); for the second, see Merton (1969, 1971); for the last, see Ross (1972a).

7. See, for example, Aucamp (1971).

8. See Breiman (1960) and Latane (1959).

9. See Markowitz (1959, 1972).

10. In a spinoff study [Samuelson and Merton (1974)] to this one, we show that for $U = W^\epsilon/\epsilon$ and ϵ very small, a perturbation technique involving $E\left\{\log W_1\right\}$ and var $\left\{\log W_1\right\}$ can—quite independently of any log-normality—give a generalized mean-variance frontier for efficient local approximation. The two asymptotic moments of average compound return can, properly normalized, serve the same local-approximation purpose for $1/T$ small enough.

11. Ross (1972b) provides a rather simple example where the Leland result does not obtain.

12. $\Pi_{ij}(\ ;\ )$ could be used to rank portfolios because it provides a complete and transitive ordering. Note: If $\Pi_{ij}(\ ;\ ) > 1$ then $\Pi_{ji}(\ ;\ ) < 1$. However $\Pi_{ij}(\ ;\ ) \neq 1/\Pi_{ji}(\ ;\ )$.

13. See Goldman (1972) for some examples.

14. Goldman (1972) derives a similar result for a bounded utility function. Thus, Samuelson (1971, p. 2495) conceded too much in his criticism of the geometric-mean policy when he stated that such a policy would asymptotically outperform any other uniform policy for utility functions bounded from above and below.

15. See Merton (1973, appendix 2) for a proof.

16. The neatness of the heuristic arguments and the attractiveness of the results has led a number of authors to assert and/or conjecture their truth. See Samuelson (1971, p. 2496) where $\mu(w)$ and $\sigma^2(w)$ are misleadingly said to be 'asymptotically sufficient parameters', an assertion not correct for $T \to \infty$, but rather for increasing subdivisions of time periods leading to diffusion-type stochastic processes.

17. To apply the Central-Limit Theorem correctly, the choice for $\left\{w\right\}$ must be such that $Z[t; w]$ is a positive random variate with its logarithm well defined. Our later discussion of optimal policies is unaffected by this restriction since the class of utility functions considered will rule out $Z[t; w]$ with a positive probability of ruin. Cf. Hakansson (1971b, p. 868).

18. With reference to footnote 17, the corollary is false even if we restrict the set of uniform strategies considered to those such that prob $\left\{Z_T[w] = 0\right\} = 0$ for all finite T.

19. The argument is that a constant times a normal variate plus a constant, is a normal variate.

20. This is an important point because it implies that if the conjecture that $\left\{w^\dagger\right\} = \left\{w^*\right\}$ could hold for the isoelastic family for large T, then it would hold for T small or $T = 1$! I.e., $\mu(w)$ and $\sigma(w)$ would be sufficient parameters for the portfolio decision for any time horizon.

21. Samuelson and Merton (1969). Since Black-Scholes (1973) warrant pricing is based squarely on exact log-normal definitions, it is inexact for non-log-normal surrogate reasoning. See Merton (1973) for further discussion.

22. See Merton (1971, p. 388) for an explicit expression for α and σ^2 as a function of the α and σ_{ij}, $i, j = 1, 2, \ldots, n$.

23. See Merton (1969, p. 251 and 1971, pp. 388-394).

24. See Merton (1971, p. 392).

25. Further the log-normality assumption can be weakened and still some separation and efficiency conditions will obtain. See Merton (1973).

26. It is not required that the distribution of one-period returns with trading interval of length h_1 will be in the same family of distributions as the one-period returns with trading interval of length $h_2 (\neq h_1)$. I.e., the distributions need not be infinitely divisible in time. However, we do require sufficient regularity that the distribution of $X_j(T; h)$ is in the domain of attraction of the normal distribution, and hence, the limit distribution as $h \to 0$ will be infinitely divisible in time.

27. The series expansion is only valid for $0 < Z \leqslant 2$. Hence, a rigorous analysis would develop a second expansion for $Z > 2$. However, as is shown later in Equation (12.95), the probability that $Z > 2$ can be made arbitrarily small by picking h small enough. Thus, the contribution of the $Z > 2$ part to the moments $o(h)$.

28. Cf. Merton (1971, p. 401).

REFERENCES

Arrow, K.J., 1965, Aspects of the theory of risk-bearing (Yrjö Jahnssonin Säätiö, Helsinki).

Aucamp, D.C., 1971, A new theory of optimal investment, mimeo. (Southern Illinois University, Carbondal, Ill.).

Black, F., M. Jensen and M. Scholes, 1972, The capital asset pricing model: Some empirical tests, in: M. Jensen, ed., Studies in the theory of capital markets (Praeger Publishers, New York).

Black, F. and M. Scholes, 1973, The pricing of options and corporate liabilities, Journal of Political Economy 81, 637-654.

Borch, K., 1969, A note on uncertainty and indifference curves, Review of Economic Studies 36, 1-4.

Breiman, L., 1960, Investment policies for expanding business optimal in a long-run sense, Naval Research Logistics Quarterly 674-651.

Cass, D. and J. Stiglitz, 1970, The structure of investor preferences and asset returns, and separability in portfolio allocation: A contribution to the pure theory of mutual funds, Journal of Economic Theory 2, 122-160.

Fama, E., 1965, Portfolio analysis in a stable Paretian market, Management Science 11, 404-419.

Fama, E., 1970, Efficient capital markets: A review of theory and empirical work, Journal of Finance 25, 383-417.

Feldstein, M., 1969, Mean-variance analysis in the theory of liquidity preference and portfolio selection, Review of Economic Studies 36, 5-12.

Feller, W., 1966, An introduction to probability theory and its applications, vol. II (John Wiley, New York).

Friend, I. and M. Blume, 1970, Measurement of portfolio performance under uncertainty, American Economic Review LX, 561-575.

Goldman, M.B., 1974, A negative report on the 'near-optimality' of the max-expected-log policy as applied to bounded utilities for long-lived programs, Journal of Financial Economics 1, 97-103.

Hadar, J. and W. Russell, 1969, Rules for ordering uncertain prospects, American Economic Review 59, 25-34.

Hakansson, N., 1970, Optimal investment and consumption strategies under risk for a class of utility functions, Econometrica 38, 587-607.

Hakansson, N., 1971a, Capital growth and the mean-variance approach to portfolio selection, Journal of Financial and Quantitative Analysis 6, 517-558.

Hakansson, N., 1971b, Multi-period mean-variance analysis: Toward a general theory of portfolio choice, Journal of Finance 26.

Hakansson, N., 1971c, Mean-variance analysis of average compound returns, mimeo. (University of California, Berkeley).

Jen, F., 1971, Multi-period portfolio strategies, Working Paper no. 108 (State University of New York, Buffalo, N.Y.).

Jen, F., 1972, Criteria in multi-period portfolio decisions, Working Paper no. 131 (State University of New York, Buffalo, N.Y.).

Jensen, M., 1972, Capital markets: Theory and evidence, Bell Journal of Economics and Management Science 3, 357-398.

Latane, H., 1959, Criteria for choice among risky ventures, Journal of Political Economy 67, 144-155.

Leland, H., 1968, Dynamic portfolio theory, Ph.D. Thesis (Harvard University, Cambridge, Mass.).

Leland, H., 1972, On turnpike portfolios, in: G. Szegö and K. Shell, eds., Mathematical methods in investment and finance (North-Holland, Amsterdam).

Levy, H., 1973, Stochastic dominance among log-normal prospects, International Economic Review 14, 601-614.

Lintner, J., 1965, The valuation of risk assets and the selection of risky investments in stock portfolios and capital budgets, Review of Economics and Statistics XLVIII, 13-37.

Markowitz, H., 1959, Portfolio selection: Efficient diversification of investment (John Wiley, New York).

Markowitz, H., 1972, Investment for the long run, Rodney L. White Center for Financial Research Working Paper no. 20-72 (University of Pennsylvania, Philadelphia, Pa.); also reprinted in this volume.

Merton, R.C., 1969, Lifetime portfolio selection under uncertainty: The continuous-time case, Review of Economics and Statistics LI, 247-257.

Merton, R.C., 1971, Optimum consumption of portfolio rules in a continuous-time model, Journal of Economic Theory 3, 373-413.

Merton, R.C., 1972a, An analytical derivation of the efficient portfolio frontier, Journal of Financial and Quantitative Analysis 1851-1871.

Merton, R.C., ed., 1972b, The collected scientific papers of Paul A. Samuelson, vol. III (M.I.T. Press, Cambridge, 1972).

Merton, R.C., 1973, Theory of rational option pricing, Bell Journal of Economics and Management Science, 4, 141-183.

Merton, R.C., 1973, An intertemporal capital asset pricing model, Econometrica 41, 867-87; also reprinted in this volume.

Mossin, J., 1966, Equilibrium in a capital asset market, Econometrica 35, 768-783.

Ross, S., 1972a, Portfolio and capital market theory with arbitrary preferences and distributions—The general validity of the mean-variance approach in large markets, Wharton School of Finance Working Paper no. 12-72 (University of Pennsylvania, Philadelphia, Pa.).

Ross, S., 1972b, A counterexample taken from some portfolio turnpike theorems, mimeo. (University of Pennsylvania, Philadelphia, Pa.).

Rothschild, M. and J. Stiglitz, 1970, Increasing risk I, A definition, Journal of Economic Theory 2, 225-243.

Samuelson, P.A., 1965, Rational theory of warrant pricing, Industrial Management Review 6, 13-31; reprinted in Merton (1972b, ch. 199).

Samuelson, P.A., 1967a, General proof that diversification pays, Journal of Financial and Quantitative Analysis II, 1-13; reprinted in Merton (1972b, ch. 201).

Samuelson, P.A., 1967b, Efficient portfolio selection for Pareto Levy investments, Journal of Financial and Quantitative Analysis 107-122; reprinted in Merton (1972b, ch. 202).

Samuelson, P.A. 1969, Lifetime portfolio selection by dynamic stochastic programming, Review of Economics and Statistics LI, 239-246; reprinted in Merton (1972b, ch. 204).

Samuelson, P.A., 1970, The fundamental approximation theorem of portfolio analysis in terms of means, variances, and higher moments, Review of Economic Studies 37, 537-542; reprinted in Merton (1972b, ch. 203).

Samuelson, P.A., 1971, The 'fallacy' of maximizing the geometric mean in long sequences of investing or gambling, Proceedings of the National Academy of Sciences 68, 2493-2496; reprinted in Merton (1972b, ch. 200).

Samuelson, P.A. and R.C. Merton, 1969, A complete model of warrant pricing that maximizes utility, Industrial Management Review 10, 17-46; reprinted in Merton (1972b, ch. 200).

Samuelson, P.A. and R.C. Merton, 1974, Generalized mean-variance tradeoffs for best perturbation corrections to approximate portfolio decisions, Journal of Finance XXIX, 27-40.

Sharpe, W., 1964, Capital asset prices: A theory of market equilibrium under conditions of risk, Journal of Finance XIX, 425-442.

Sharpe, W., 1970, Portfolio theory and capital markets (McGraw-Hill, New York).

Tobin, J., 1958, Liquidity preference as behavior towards risk, Review of Economic Studies 25, 68-85.

Tobin, J., 1965, The theory of portfolio selection, in: F. Hahn and F. Brechling, The theory of interest rates (MacMillan, New York).

Section Thirteen

Comment on Merton and Samuelson

Nils H. Hakansson

Professors Merton and Samuelson have provided us with a skillful and detailed clarification of some of the important mathematical issues that arise in, and too often in the past have obscured, multiperiod portfolio choice situations. Personally, I am further indebted to them for pointing out an erroneous argument in my paper (1971, p. 871). But while their goal of elucidation has been admirably achieved on many points, this does not seem to be the case concerning the average-compound-return model (for which they show a pointed lack of adoration and) for which the reader may legitimately wonder about the role of the faulty argument [Hakansson (1971, p. 871)] described at the beginning of their Section 4. That argument, as he may of course already have discovered, can, like scaffolding, be removed from my paper without consequence to the central assertions made there. Since the corrected reasoning is available in Hakansson and Miller (1973, sec. III), it need not be reproduced here.

At the end of Section 4, Professors Merton and Samuelson write that there is no '. . . hope that the mean and variance of expected-average-compound-return (sic) can serve as asymptotically sufficient decision parameters' [note: no contrary assertion was made in my paper (1971)]. It is perhaps unfortunate that this conclusion is based on a stationary two-asset counterexample involving isoelastic utility, because in that case the set of exactly efficient N-period sequences is identical to that generated by the Merton-Samuelson Equation (50), all $\gamma \leqslant 1/N$. At any rate, the fact that their Equations (48) and (50), for $\gamma \neq 0$, give different solutions (the mainstay of the Merton-

Samuelson counterexample at the end of Section 4) was also posted in Hakansson (1971, bottom of p. 878) and illustrated by a three-asset example (e.g., points *W* and *Z* in Figure 4).

REFERENCES

Hakansson, N., 1971, Multi-Period Mean-Variance Analysis: Toward a General Theory of Portfolio Choice, *Journal of Finance* XXVI, 851-884.

Hakansson, N. and B. Miller, 1975, Compound-Return Mean-Variance Efficient Portfolios Never Risk Ruin, *Management Science*, 22, 391-400.

Merton, R. and P. Samuelson, Fallacy of the Log-Normal Approximation to Optimal Portfolio Decision-Making over Many Periods *Journal of Financial Economics* 1, 67-94; also reprinted in this volume.

✳ *Section Fourteen*

Tests of the Multiperiod Two-Parameter Model

Eugene F. Fama and James D. MacBeth*

14.1 INTRODUCTION

In the one-period two-parameter capital market equilibrium model of Black (1972), investors are assumed to be risk-averse [their utility functions $U(c_1, c_2)$ for consumption at time 1 and at time 2 are increasing, strictly concave functions of c_1 and c_2], the capital market is assumed to be perfect (there are no transactions costs or information costs, and all assets are infinitely divisible), and distributions of percent returns from time 1 to time 2 on all portfolios are assumed to be normal (equivalently, the joint distribution of asset returns is multivariate normal). Risk aversion, a perfect capital market, and normally distributed portfolio returns imply that investors choose efficient portfolios, where an efficient portfolio has the property that no other portfolio with the same or higher expected return has a lower variance of return.

The Black model also assumes that there is short-selling of all assets and complete agreement among investors about the parameters of portfolio return distributions. It then follows that in a market equilibrium one of the efficient portfolios is the market portfolio m, with return, expected return, and variance

$$\tilde{R}_m = \sum_{i=1}^{n} x_{im} \tilde{R}_i, \qquad (14.1a)$$

*This research is supported by the National Science Foundation. The comments of Michael Jensen and Nicholas Gonedes are gratefully acknowledged.

$$E(\tilde{R}_m) = \sum_{i=1}^{n} x_{im} E(\tilde{R}_i), \qquad (14.1b)$$

$$\sigma^2(\tilde{R}_m) = \sum_{i=1}^{n}\sum_{j=1}^{n} x_{im} x_{jm} \mathrm{cov}(\tilde{R}_i, \tilde{R}_j) = \sum_{i=1}^{n} x_{im} \, \mathrm{cov}(\tilde{R}_i, \tilde{R}_m), \quad (14.1c)$$

where tildes ($\sim$) are used to denote random variables; n is the number of assets in the market; and x_{im}, the proportion of portfolio funds invested in asset i in the market portfolio m, is the ratio at time 1 of the total value of all outstanding units of asset i to the total value of all assets.

A direct implication of the efficiency of the market portfolio m is the expected return-risk relationship

$$E(\tilde{R}_i) = E(\tilde{R}_0) + [E(\tilde{R}_m) - E(\tilde{R}_0)]\beta_i, \qquad (14.2)$$

where β_i, defined as,

$$\beta_i \equiv \frac{\mathrm{cov}(\tilde{R}_i, \tilde{R}_m)}{\sigma^2(\tilde{R}_m)} \qquad (14.3)$$

is $\mathrm{cov}(\tilde{R}_i, \tilde{R}_m)$, the risk of asset i in the market portfolio m, measured relative to $\sigma^2(\tilde{R}_m)$, the risk of m; and where $E(\tilde{R}_0)$ is the expected return on any zero-β asset or portfolio, that is, any asset or portfolio whose return is uncorrelated with the return on m. The assumption that investors are risk-averse implies a positive tradeoff of expected return for risk; that is,

$$E(\tilde{R}_m) - E(\tilde{R}_0) > 0. \qquad (14.4)$$

In the Sharpe (1964)—Lintner (1965) version of the model, there is also assumed to be indefinite borrowing and lending at a risk-free rate of interest, R_f, which implies that[1]

$$E(\tilde{R}_0) = R_f. \qquad (14.5)$$

There is much empirical work concerned with testing Equations (14.2), (14.4) and (14.5) and with testing the distributional assumption underlying the two-parameter model. Officer's (1971) evidence indicates that for monthly post-World War II percent returns on portfolios of New York Stock Exchange (NYSE) common stocks, the assumption of normality is a good working approximation. Fama and MacBeth (1973) test the implications of (14.2) that the expected return-risk relationship is linear in the risk measure β_i, that β_i is a complete measure of the risk of asset i in m, and that there is a positive tradeoff of expected return for risk. Using monthly data on NYSE common stocks, they are unable to reject any of these hypotheses. There is also much work, most notably by Black, Jensen and Scholes (1972), which indicates that in the post-World War II period, Equation (14.5) can be rejected. In this period, average returns on positive variance zero-β portfolios of NYSE common stocks seem systematically greater than riskless lending rates. Thus, the evidence at this point is that the Black model of Equation (14.2) seems to stand up well to the data, but Equation (14.5), the special implication of the Sharpe-Lintner version of the model, does not.

The Black model is a one-period model. Since empirical tests use data generated by a multiperiod world, the presumption is that the one-period model, in particular the expected return-risk Equation (14.2), applies on a period-by-period basis. In Fama (1970a), conditions are described under which the one-period model can be linked directly to a multiperiod world. The purpose of this study is to present some initial tests of whether these conditions are a valid approximation to real world capital markets. The first step is to discuss some extensions of the arguments of the Fama paper.

14.2 THE MULTIPERIOD MODEL: A REVIEW

In the one-period model, the problem of the risk-averse investor at time 1 is to divide his wealth w_1 between current consumption c_1 and an investment in some portfolio in such a way as to maximize the expected utility of consumption at time 1 and at time 2. Given a perfect capital market, the problem can be expressed formally as

$$\max_{c_1, h_1} E[U(c_1, \tilde{c}_2)] = \max_{c_1, h_1} \int_{R_2} U(c_1, \sum_{i=1}^{n} h_{i1}(1 + R_{i2})) dF(R_2),$$

$$\text{s.t. } 0 \leqslant c_1 \leqslant w_1, \sum_{i=1}^{n} h_{i1} = w_1 - c_1, \tag{14.6}$$

where $R_2 = (\tilde{R}_{12}, \ldots, \tilde{R}_{n2})$ is the vector of percent returns from time 1 to time 2 on the n available investment assets, $F(R_2)$ is the c.d.f. of $\tilde{R}_2$, and $h_1 = (h_{11}, \ldots, h_{n1})$ is the vector of dollar investments chosen at time 1. Wealth, consumption, and investments are stated at terms of the numeraire, 'dollars'. The two-parameter portfolio theory of Markowitz (1959) tells us that if the distribution of $\tilde{R}_2$ is multivariate normal, the optimal portfolio is efficient. Black's (1972) two-parameter theory of capital market equilibrium then says that with short-selling and complete agreement among investors with respect to the distribution of $\tilde{R}_2$, in a market equilibrium one of the efficient portfolios is the market portfolio m from which the expected return-risk relationship of Equation (14.2) follows directly.

In a multiperiod world, the individual faces a sequence of consumption-investment decisions, one for each of the decision times preceding his death, and in general the decision at any time t must take account of the fact that similar decisions must be made in the future. But if there are conditions under which the problem faced at each decision time t can be put in the form of (14.6), and if one assumes that at time t the joint distribution of one-period asset returns is multivariate normal, then at each decision time the individual chooses an efficient portfolio. Thus the first step toward understanding the conditions for period-by-period application of the results of the two-parameter model is to study the conditions under which, even though operating in a multiperiod context, the individual's problem at each decision time can be stated as in (14.6).

Let the individual's tastes for lifetime consumption be represented by the utility function $U_{\tau+1}(C_{\tau+1}|\phi_{\tau+1})$, where $\tau + 1$ is the time of the individual's death (taken to be known for certain in earlier periods), $\phi_{\tau+1}$ is the 'state-of-the-world' at time $\tau + 1$, and $C_{\tau+1} = (c_1, \ldots, c_{\tau+1})$ is the vector of period-by-period consumption, which is what we always refer to when we use the term 'lifetime consumption'. The state-of-the-world $\phi_{\tau+1}$ includes not only a description of the world (returns on assets, prices of consumption goods, etc.) as it is at $\tau + 1$ but also the descriptions that apply to earlier times; that is, for all $t \leqslant \tau + 1$, $\phi_t \subset \phi_{\tau+1}$. Given past consumption of $C_{t-1} \equiv (c_1, \ldots, c_{t-1})$, the problem facing the individual at time t is to choose feasible values for consumption c_t and investments $h_t = (h_{1t}, \ldots, h_{nt})$ in the n available assets that[2]

$$\max_{c_t, h_t} E[U_{\tau+1}(C_{t-1}, c_t, c_{t+1}, \ldots, \tilde{c}_{\tau+1} \mid \tilde{\phi}_{\tau+1})],$$

$$\text{s.t. } 0 \leqslant c_t \leqslant w_t, \ \sum_{i=1}^{n} h_{it} = w_t - c_t.$$

In words, at each decision time t the individual is assumed to behave as if he maximizes the expected utility of lifetime consumption—a task made formidable by the fact that the current decision depends on what will be done in the future and future decisions depend on the somewhat random evolution of the state-of-the-world.

The individual is assumed to proceed as if he solves this problem by the dynamic programming process of backward optimization. That is, to make his decision for time t, he first decides what he will do at the last decision point, time τ. The problem he will face at τ can be expressed as follows: Subject to the constraints

$$0 \leqslant c_\tau \leqslant w_\tau \text{ and } \sum_{i=1}^{n} h_{i\tau} = w_\tau - c_\tau,$$

$$\max_{c_\tau, h_\tau} E[U_{\tau+1}(C_{\tau-1}, c_\tau, \tilde{c}_{\tau+1} \mid \tilde{\phi}_{\tau+1})]$$

$$= \max_{c_\tau, h_\tau} \int_{\phi_{\tau+1}} U_{\tau+1}\left(C_{\tau-1}, c_\tau, \sum_{i=1}^{n} h_{i\tau}(1 + R_i(\phi_{\tau+1}))\right.$$

$$\left.\mid \phi_{\tau+1}\right) dF_{\phi_\tau}(\phi_{\tau+1}) \equiv U_\tau(C_{\tau-1}, w_\tau \mid \phi_\tau),$$

where $R_i(\phi_{\tau+1})$ is the percent return on asset i in state $\phi_{\tau+1}$, and $F_{\phi_\tau}(\phi_{\tau+1})$ is the c.d.f. of $\phi_{\tau+1}$, given state ϕ_τ at time τ. The derived function $U_\tau(C_{\tau-1}, w_\tau \mid \phi_\tau)$ shows the maximum expected utility of lifetime consumption if the individual arrives at time τ with wealth w_τ and past consumption $C_{\tau-1}$ and finds that the state-of-the-world is ϕ_τ.

Since U_τ provides a complete summary, in expected utility terms, of all the decisions the consumer might make at time τ, it can be used as an input—in formal terms, it is the objective function—for the next stage in the decision process. That is, when, at time t the individual now looks ahead to determine how he will behave at time $\tau - 1$, the problem he will face at $\tau - 1$ can be expressed as follows: Subject to the constraints

$$0 \leqslant c_{\tau-1} \leqslant w_{\tau-1} \text{ and } \sum_{i=1}^{n} h_{i,\tau-1} = w_{\tau-1} - c_{\tau-1},$$

$$\max_{c_{\tau-1}, h_{\tau-1}} E[U_{\tau+1}(C_{\tau-2}, c_{\tau-1}, \tilde{c}_\tau, \tilde{c}_{\tau+1} \mid \phi_{\tau+1})]$$

$$= \max_{c_{\tau-1}, h_{\tau-1}} \int_{\phi_\tau} U_\tau\left(C_{\tau-2}, c_{\tau-1}, \sum_{i=1}^{n} h_{i,\tau-1}(1 + R_i(\phi_\tau))\right.$$

$$\left.\mid \phi_\tau\right) dF_{\phi_{\tau-1}}(\phi_\tau) \equiv U_{\tau-1}(C_{\tau-2}, w_{\tau-1} \mid \phi_{\tau-1}).$$

The new derived function $U_{\tau-1}(C_{\tau-2}, w_{\tau-1}|\phi_{\tau-1})$ shows the maximum expected utility of lifetime consumption if the individual arrives at time $\tau - 1$ having consumed $C_{\tau-2}$ in the past, with wealth $w_{\tau-1}$ available, finds that the state-of-the-world is $\phi_{\tau-1}$, and makes optimal decisions both at time $\tau - 1$ and at time τ.

From the description of the first two steps, it is clear that the process of backward optimization induces a sequence of maximum expected utility functions, defined for any $t \leqslant \tau$ as

$$U_t(C_{t-1}, w_t \mid \phi_t) \equiv \max_{c_t, h_t} E[U_{\tau+1}(C_{t-1}, c_t, \tilde{c}_{t+1}, \ldots, \tilde{c}_{\tau+1}|\tilde{\phi}_{\tau+1})]$$

$$= \max_{c_t, h_t} \int_{\phi_{t+1}} U_{t+1}(C_{t-1}, c_t, \sum_{i=1}^{n} h_{it}(1 + R_i(\phi_{t+1}))$$

$$\mid \phi_{t+1}) dF_{\phi_\tau}(\phi_{t+1}),$$

$$\text{s.t. } 0 \leqslant c_t \leqslant w_t, \sum_{i=1}^{n} h_{it} = w_t - c_t. \tag{14.7}$$

In general, $U_t(C_{t-1}, w_t|\phi_t)$ is the expected utility of lifetime consumption if at time t the individual finds himself in state ϕ_t, his wealth is w_t, his past consumption was C_{t-1}, and he makes optimal consumption-investment decisions at time t and at all future decision points. Thus $U_t(C_{t-1}, w_t|\phi_t)$ summarizes the results, in terms of the expected utility of lifetime consumption, of optimal consumption-investment decisions at time t and at all future decision times as a function of ϕ_t, w_t and C_{t-1}.

A major result in Fama (1970a) is that if the individual is risk-averse, that is, if his utility function $U_{\tau+1}(c_1, \ldots, c_{\tau+1}|\phi_{\tau+1})$ is an increasing strictly concave function of $(c_1, \ldots, c_{\tau+1})$, then for any $t \leqslant \tau$, $U_t(C_{t-1}, w_t|\phi_t)$ is an increasing strictly concave function of (C_{t-1}, w_t). Thus each of the induced maximum expected utility functions has the properties of a risk-averter's utility function.

To see the implications of this result, let us examine the decision at time t, where the choice of t is arbitrary, in more detail. In the framework of (14.7), the decision now involves maximizing expected utility with respect to the derived function $U_{t+1}(C_t, w_{t+1}|\phi_{t+1})$. To emphasize that at time t past consumption C_{t-1} is known, this function might better be written as

$$U_{t+1}(C_t, w_{t+1}|\phi_{t+1}) = U_{t+1}(c_t, w_{t+1}|\phi_{t+1}, C_{t-1}). \quad (14.8)$$

Then the decision problem at t becomes

$$\max_{c_t, h_t} E[U_{t+1}(c_t, \tilde{w}_{t+1} \mid \tilde{\phi}_{t+1}, C_{t-1})]$$

$$= \max_{c_t, h_t} \int_{\phi_{t+1}} U_{t+1}(c_t, \sum_{i=1}^{n} h_{it}(1 + R(\phi_{t+1}))$$

$$\mid \phi_{t+1}, C_{t-1})dF_{\phi_T}(\phi_{t+1}),$$

$$\text{s.t. } 0 \leqslant c_t \leqslant w_t, \sum_{i=1}^{n} h_{it} = w_t - c_t. \quad (14.9)$$

Although U_{t+1} summarizes the results of optimal decisions for all periods subsequent to t, conditional on C_{t-1} it has the form of a utility function for consumption at time t and wealth at time $t + 1$. Moreover, the concavity of U_{t+1} in (C_t, w_{t+1}) implies concavity in (c_t, w_{t+1}) for any given C_{t-1}. Thus, at least in form, (14.9) represents the consumption-investment decision for time t as a one-period problem. Indeed the major difference between (14.9) and the one-period, two-parameter problem as represented in (14.6) is that the derived utility function U_{t+1} in (14.9) allows the utility of (c_t, w_{t+1}) to depend on past consumption C_{t-1} and on the state-of-the-world ϕ_{t+1}. But the appearance of C_{t-1} in the utility function is of no analytical consequence. It simply says that tastes for consumption at time t may depend on the standard of living, C_{t-1}, attained in the past. When time t arrives, however, C_{t-1} is known, and for any given C_{t-1}, U_{t+1} is characteristic of the utility function of a risk-averter with a one-period horizon. The role of ϕ_{t+1} in U_{t+1} is, however, more consequential.

In a consumption-investment model of the type presented here, the dependence of utility on the state-of-the-world has three major possible sources. First, as suggested by Hirshleifer (1965), tastes for consumption goods and thus for dollars of consumption may simply be state dependent. Second, utilities for given dollars of consumption depend on the available consumption goods and services and their prices, and these are elements of the state-of-the-world.[3] Finally, the investment opportunities (e.g., return distributions) to be available at any given future time may depend on events occurring in the past, and such uncertainty about investment prospects induces state dependent utilities. Thus, the most direct way to exclude state dependent utilities and so to establish a link between the multiperiod model and the one-period, two-parameter model is to assume that the consumer behaves as if the consumption opportunities (in terms of goods and services and their prices) and the investment opportunities (distributions of portfolio returns) that will be available at any future time can be taken as known and fixed at any earlier time, and that the consumer's tastes for given bundles of consumption goods and services are independent of the state-of-the-world.

But the major results of the one-period model can be obtained in a multiperiod framework without completely excluding state dependent utilities. To focus on the important aspects of the argument, for any t, let

$$\tilde{\phi}_{t+1} \equiv (\tilde{R}_{t+1}, \tilde{P}_{t+1}, \tilde{I}_{t+1}, \phi_t),$$

where $\tilde{R}_{t+1}$ is the vector of percent returns from t to $t + 1$ on assets available at t, $\tilde{I}_{t+1}$ indicates the characteristics of investment opportunities (e.g., distributions of portfolio returns) available at $t + 1$, $\tilde{P}_{t+1}$ represents the prices of consumption goods at $t + 1$, and ϕ_t is the past history of R, I, and P. The individual's utility function for lifetime consumption $U_{\tau+1}(C_{\tau+1} | P_{\tau+1}^H)$ is now assumed to depend on lifetime dollar consumption, $C_{\tau+1}$, and on $P_{\tau+1}^H$, the history of the prices of consumption goods up to and including time $\tau + 1$. Let us also define

$$S_{t+1} \equiv \phi_{t+1} - R_{t+1}^H;$$

that is, S_{t+1} includes all elements of the state-of-the-world at time $t + 1$, except for R_{t+1}^H, the history of returns on investment assets up to and including time $t + 1$. Equivalently, at time t

$$\tilde{S}_{t+1} \equiv (\tilde{P}_{t+1}^H, \tilde{I}_{t+1}^H) = (\tilde{P}_{t+1}, \tilde{I}_{t+1}, S_t),$$

where I_{t+1}^H is the history of the characteristics of investment opportunities up to and including time $t + 1$. Thus S_{t+1} is the history of consumption prices and investment opportunities at time $t + 1$.

The first step in the argument is to note that

$$F_{\phi_t}(\phi_{t+1}) = F_{\phi_t}(R_{t+1}, P_{t+1}, I_{t+1}).$$

In words, since the state-of-the-world ϕ_t is known, the uncertain elements of $\tilde{\phi}_{t+1}$ at time t are $\tilde{R}_{t+1}$, $\tilde{P}_{t+1}$, and $\tilde{I}_{t+1}$, returns on investment assets, prices of consumption goods, and investment opportunities at $t + 1$. Next come two critical assumptions: Returns on investment assets at $t + 1$ are assumed to be independent of the $t + 1$ prices of consumption goods and characteristics of investment opportunities; and $\tilde{R}_{t+1}$, $\tilde{P}_{t+1}$, and $\tilde{I}_{t+1}$ are assumed to be independent of the history of returns through time t R_t^H, so that

$$F_\phi(\phi_{t+1}) = F_{S_t}(R_{t+1})F_{S_t}(P_{t+1},I_{t+1}). \qquad (14.10)$$

Thus although distributions of returns on investment assets need not be the same from period to period, returns are nevertheless serially independent. Moreover, the prices of consumption goods and the characteristics of investment opportunities at any time $t + 1$ are independent of current and past returns on investment assets, although, of course, returns on investment assets from $t + 1$ to $t + 2$ do indeed depend on $\tilde{I}_{t+1}$.

In the present framework, when the individual looks ahead to the decision he will face at time τ, the expected utility consequences of optimal decisions are summarized by the function

$$U_\tau(C_{\tau-1}, w_\tau \mid S_\tau) \equiv \max_{c_\tau, h_\tau} E[U_{\tau+1}(C_{\tau-1}, c_\tau, \tilde{c}_{\tau+1} \mid \tilde{P}_{\tau+1}, P_\tau^H)]$$

$$= \max_{c_\tau, h_\tau} \int_{\phi_{\tau+1}} U_{\tau+1}(C_{\tau-1}, c_\tau, \sum_{i=1}^{n} h_{it}(1 + R_{i,\tau+1})$$

$$\mid P_{\tau+1}, P_t^H)dF_{\phi t}(\phi_{\tau+1})$$

$$= \max_{c_\tau, h_\tau} \int_{R_{\tau+1}} V_{\tau+1}(c_\tau, \sum_{i=1}^{n} h_{i\tau}(1 + R_{i,\tau+1})$$

$$\mid C_{\tau-1}, S_\tau)dF_{S_\tau}(R_{\tau+1}),$$

$$\text{s.t. } 0 \leqslant c_\tau \leqslant w_\tau, \sum_{i=1}^{n} h_{i\tau} = w_\tau - c_\tau,$$

where

$$V_{\tau+1}(c_\tau, w_{\tau+1} \mid C_{\tau-1}, S_\tau)$$

$$= \int_{P_{\tau+1}, I_{\tau+1}} U_{\tau+1}(C_{\tau+1} \mid P_{\tau+1}, P_\tau^H)dF_{S_\tau}(P_{\tau+1}, I_{\tau+1}).$$

Thus, at time τ the maximum expected utility of lifetime consumption, as given by U_τ, is a function of past consumption $C_{\tau-1}$, current wealth w_τ and $S_\tau \equiv \phi_\tau - R_\tau^H$, all elements of the state-of-the-world except R_τ^H. Note that $S_\tau \equiv (P_\tau^H, I_\tau^H)$ appears in U_τ even though only $P_{\tau+1}^H$ appears in $U_{\tau+1}$. Although *tastes* for consumption do not depend on investment opportunities, as one would expect, the *maximum expected utility* of lifetime consumption at τ is determined in part by the history of investment opportunities.

At any time t, $t \leqslant \tau$, the expected utility consequences of optimal decisions at t and at all future decision times can be summarized by the function

$$U_t(C_{t-1}, w_t \mid S_t) \equiv \max_{c_t, h_t} E[U_{\tau+1}(C_{t-1}, c_t, \tilde{c}_{t+1}, \ldots, \tilde{c}_{\tau+1}^H \mid \tilde{P}_{\tau+1})]$$

$$= \max_{c_t, h_t} \int_{\phi_{t+1}} U_{t+1}(C_{t-1}, c_t, \sum_{i=1}^{n} h_{it}(1 + R_{i,t+1})$$

$$\mid S_{t+1}) \mathrm{d}F_{\phi t}(\phi_{t+1}) \tag{14.11}$$

$$= \max_{c_t, h_t} \int_{R_{t+1}} V_{t+1}(c_t, \sum_{i=1}^{n} h_{it}(1 + R_{i,t+1})$$

$$\mid C_{t-1}, S_t) \mathrm{d}F_{S_t}(R_{t+1}) \tag{14.12}$$

$$\text{s.t. } 0 \leqslant c_t \leqslant w_t, \sum_{i=1}^{n} h_{it} = w_t - c_t,$$

where

$$V_{t+1}(c_t, w_{t+1} \mid C_{t-1}, S_t)$$

$$= \int_{P_{t+1}, I_{t+1}} U_{t+1}(C_t, w_{t+1} \mid S_{t+1}) \mathrm{d}F_{S_t}(P_{t+1}, I_{t+1}). \tag{14.13}$$

Thus, at time t, the maximum expected utility of lifetime consumption, as given by U_t, is a function of past consumption C_{t-1}, current wealth w_t, and $S_t = (P_t^H, I_t^H)$, the history of consumption prices and investment opportunities.

But although his fate depends on the evolution through time of the elements of S, because $\tilde{R}_{t+1}$ and $(\tilde{P}_{t+1}, \tilde{I}_{t+1})$ are independent, the consumption-investment decision at any time t can be based on the derived function V_{t+1} of Equation (4.13), which is not explicitly a function of (P_{t+1}, I_{t+1}). Intuitively, since the returns on investment assets at $t + 1$ are independent of both the prices of consumption goods and the characteristics of investment opportunities at $t + 1$, the individual cannot use the portfolio decision at time t to hedge against the uncertainty in $\tilde{P}_{t+1}$ and $\tilde{I}_{t+1}$. Thus the consumption-investment decision at time t can be based on the derived utility function V_{t+1}, which is not explicitly a function of P_{t+1} and I_{t+1}, but which appropriately takes account of the effects of uncertainty about $\tilde{P}_{t+1}$ and $\tilde{I}_{t+1}$ on expected utility.

Moreover, although C_{t-1} and $S_t \equiv (P_t^H, I_t^H)$ appear in V_{t+1}, their only role is to indicate the starting point for the consumption-investment decision at time t. That is, at time t the expected utility of lifetime consumption indeed depends on past dollar consumption, current and past prices of consumption goods and the characteristics of current and past investment opportunities. But at time t, C_{t-1}, P_t^H and I_t^H are known, so that the only variables in V_{t+1} that are affected by the consumption-investment decision at t are current consumption, c_t, and wealth at $t + 1$, w_{t+1}.

With this perspective it is then easy to see that (14.12) expresses the consumption-investment decision problem for time t in exactly the same form as the statement of the one-period problem in (14.6). Moreover, the results of Fama (1970a) imply that if $U_{\tau+1}$ is concave in $C_{\tau+1}$, V_{t+1} is concave in (c_t, w_{t+1}), so that the individual is risk-averse with respect to current consumption and wealth at $t + 1$. Thus if the distribution of $\tilde{R}_{t+1}$ is multivariate normal, the results of the one-period, two-parameter portfolio model of Markowitz (1959) apply, and the optimal portfolio at any time t is efficient. If in addition there is short-selling of all assets and complete agreement among investors with respect to the return distributions available at any time t, then the results of the one-period, two-parameter Black (1972) model of capital market equilibrium apply. That is, at any time t, in a market equilibrium the market portfolio m is efficient so that the expected return-risk relationship of Equation (14.2), with time subscripts added to each of its components, applies to each period. Thus the link between the one-period and the multiperiod models is established.

The story, however, hinges on the nontrivial assumptions, summarized in Equation (14.10), that at any time t, $\tilde{R}_{t+1}$ is independent of R_t^H, and $\tilde{P}_{t+1}$ and $\tilde{I}_{t+1}$ are independent of both $\tilde{R}_{t+1}$ and R_t^H. At least for common stocks, there is already substantial evidence in support of the assumption that returns on investment assets are serially independent.[4] But the assumption that consumption good prices and the characteristics of investment opportunities at time t are independent of current and past returns on investment assets is untested. And this assumption rules out many reasonable kinds of relationships. For example, if $\tilde{P}_{t+1}$ is independent of $\tilde{R}_{t+1}$ and of R_t^H, then the returns on the securities of retail food chains at any time $t + 1$ must be independent of current and past food prices.[5] Likewise, if I_{t+1} is independent of $\tilde{R}_{t+1}$ and R_t^H, this rules out a situation where the level of interest rates shifts somewhat randomly from one period to the next (e.g., the level of interest rates follows a random walk) since this implies a negative relationship between returns on long-term bonds at $t+1$ and the level of interest rates at $t + 1$, and interest rates are elements of $\tilde{I}_{t+1}$.[6]

Finally, if the independence assumptions summarized in Equation (14.10) are not valid, it does not follow that the results of the one-period, two-parameter model are invalid in a multiperiod world. Merton (1972) presents an elegant continuous time model in which the other assumptions of the two-parameter model are assumed to hold, but (14.10) does not hold. He shows that in a market equilibrium, expected returns are related to risk in the manner of Equation (14.2), but that expected returns are also determined in part by the extent to which an asset provides a hedge against uncertainty in prices of consumption goods, a hedge against uncertainty in the characteristics of investment opportunities, or more generally, a hedge against any sources of uncertainty that affect both returns on investment assets and induced tastes for wealth.

But although Merton's work is a fundamental extension of the theory, the value of the extension depends on the extent to which it improves on the empirical description of average returns provided by the basic two-parameter model. And such improvement requires that Equation (14.10), or some similar independence condition, is an inadequate description of the world. The rest of this chapter is meant to be a short initial step toward the resolution of this empirical matter.

We must note, however, that violation of the independence assumptions summarized in Equation (14.10) is necessary if Merton's model is to improve on the description of average returns provided by the basic two-parameter model but it is not sufficient. For example, if returns on some investment assets are related to prices of some consumption goods or to characterisitcs of investment opportunities, then these assets provide a vehicle with which investors, if they so desire, can hedge against uncertainty in future consumption goods prices or investment opportunities. But this will affect the expected returns on these assets only if on balance investors have substantial risk aversion or risk preference with respect to these sources of uncertainty. If induced tastes for these sources of uncertainty do not run strong, that is, if they have a negligible effect on investment decisions, or if there is not a substantial dominance of risk averters over risk preferrers (or vice versa),[7] then Merton's model will not noticeably improve on the description of average returns provided by the simple two-parameter model. In short, substantial violation of the independence conditions summarized in Equation (14.10) is a necessary ingredient to the empirical success of the Merton model, but the value of the model ultimately depends on its success in describing differences in average returns.

14.3 EMPIRICAL TESTS

In the tests of the independence assumption of Equation (14.10), we concentrate on the search for interdependence between returns on investment assets from t to $t + 1$ and uncertainty about the characteristics of investment opportunities. The only allowance for uncertainty in the prices of consumption goods is to work with real rather than nominal returns. We deal with a world where there are two goods—a consumption good and a payoff good called money or dollars. Returns on investment assets are in money, but investors desire money only for its value in consumption. Thus in examining the behavior of returns and investment opportunities, it is appropriate to work in units of the consumption good, that is, in real terms, rather than in units of money.

In looking for relationships between returns and investment opportunities, we further concentrate on the quantities that define the investment opportunity sets in the Black (1972) and Sharpe (1964)-Lintner (1965) versions of the two-parameter model. In the Black model, all minimum variance portfolios—portfolios that minimize variance at different levels of expected return—can be described as combinations of the market portfolio m and the minimum variance portfolio whose return is uncorrelated with the return on m. Formally, returns on minimum-variance portfolios are given by

$$\tilde{R}_{et} = \tilde{R}_{zt}(1 - \beta_e) + \beta_e \tilde{R}_{mt}$$

$$= \tilde{R}_{zt} + (\tilde{R}_{mt} - \tilde{R}_{zt})\beta_e, \tag{14.14}$$

where z is the minimum variance zero-β portfolio, and where β_e is the proportion of portfolio funds invested in m, with $1 - \beta_e$ invested in z. Since $\tilde{R}_{zt}$ and $\tilde{R}_{mt}$ are uncorrelated, β_e is also the 'beta-risk' of portfolio e in the sense of Equation (14.3). It is clear that the behavior through time of the returns on all minimum variance portfolios can be determined from the behavior of the two portfolio returns, $\tilde{R}_{zt}$ and $\tilde{R}_{mt}$, and in the Black model efficient portfolios are a subset of the minimum-variance portfolios.[8]

Similarly, in the Sharpe-Lintner model, all efficient portfolios are combinations of riskless lending or borrowing (which does not exist in the Black model) with the market portfolio and can be described by

$$\tilde{R}_{et} = R_{ft}(1 - \beta_e) + \beta_e \tilde{R}_{mt}, \qquad \beta_e \geqslant 0. \qquad (14.15)$$

Thus it is clear that in this model the time series behavior of the relevant investment opportunity set is completely described by the time series behavior of R_{ft} and $\tilde{R}_{mt}$.

14.3.1 The Data

If π_t is the purchasing power of money (the value of a dollar in terms of the consumption good) and v_{it} is the money value of asset i at time t, then the percent real return on the asset from $t-1$ to t is

$$R_{it} = \frac{v_{it}\pi_t - v_{i,t-1}\pi_{t-1}}{v_{i,t-1}\pi_{t-1}} = (1 + R_{it}^*)(1 + \Delta_t) - 1$$

$$= R_{it}^* + \Delta_t + R_{it}^*\Delta_t, \qquad (14.16)$$

where R_{it}^* is the nominal percent return and

$$\Delta_t = (\pi_t - \pi_{t-1})/\pi_{t-1}$$

is the percent change in the purchasing power of a dollar from $t-1$ to t.

This study uses monthly data, and the proxy for 'the consumption good' is the bundle of goods of the Consumer Price Index (CPI). The Index gives the price of consumption in terms of money so that its reciprocal is the purchasing power of a dollar. Depending on data availability, we work with the period 1953-1971 or 1953-1972. The CPI was upgraded substantially at the beginning of 1953. Both the number of items priced and the number of items prices monthly were increased. Thus we choose to concentrate on a period of clean data.

The proxy for a one-month riskfree real rate of interest, R_{ft}, is the percent real return on a Treasury Bill with a one-month maturity. The proxy for R_{mt}, the return on the market portfolio, is the one-month percent real return on a value weighted portfolio of all NYSE common stocks. Thus, like those of others, our tests are deficient in that our market portfolio does not cover bonds, preferred stock, real estate, etc. But common stocks are important in their own right. What we learn from them is important in understanding the behavior of the investment opportunity set.

Finally, the proxy for R_{zt}, the real return on the minimum variance zero-β portfolio, is obtained in a rather complicated manner, discussed in detail in Fama and MacBeth (1973, 1974). In brief, the approach involves forming (and periodically revising) twenty common stock portfolios on the basis of ranked values of estimates of β for individual securities. Then each month a regression of the twenty portfolio returns on estimates of their β's is fit, and the time series of R_{zt} is the time series of the estimated regression intercepts. The procedure is identical to that in Fama and MacBeth (1973, 1974), except that here all calculations, including estimation of the β's, are carried out with real returns.[9] The properties of the estimated regression intercepts and the sense in which they can be interpreted as the returns on the minimum variance zero-β portfolio are discussed in detail in Fama and MacBeth (1974).

The data for Δ_t and R_{ft} cover the period 1953-1972, but data on R_{mt} and R_{zt} are only through 1971.

14.3.2 Changes in Equilibrium Expected Returns: ANOVA

The independence conditions summarized in Equation (14.10) can hold if the investment opportunity set is constant through time or if uncertainty about the opportunity set to be available at time t is independent of returns on investment assets from $t-1$ to t. The first step, then, is to test for changes in the investment opportunity set of the two-parameter model. If changes are observed, then we can ask whether they are related to investment returns in ways that violate Equation (14.10).

From the discussion of Equation (14.14) we know that the returns on all efficient portfolios in the Black version of the one-period, two-parameter model can be determined from the returns on the minimum-variance zero-β portfolio z and the return on the market portfolio m. Moreover, since the Black model is a two-parameter model, we need only be concerned with the means and variances of the returns on efficient portfolios, and these can be described in terms of the means and variances of $\tilde{R}_{zt}$ and $\tilde{R}_{mt}$. Likewise, in the Sharpe-Lintner version of the two-parameter model, we are concerned with $\tilde{R}_{ft}$ and the mean and variance of $\tilde{R}_{mt}$.[10]

But tests for changes in variance are sensitive to departures from normality. And although, from the work of Officer (1971), normality seems to be a good working approximation for monthly returns, inspection of the frequency distributions of $\tilde{R}_{zt}$, $\tilde{R}_{mt}$ and $\tilde{R}_{ft}$ shows the slight tendency toward leptokurtosis which is typical of returns on investment assets, and which is precisely the sort of departure from normality likely to cause false rejection in tests for changes in variance. Thus we feel that formal tests for changes in variance are not useful for our purposes, and we concentrate on tests for changes in expected returns.

The first set of tests is based on simple one-way analysis of variance. For the variables Δ_t and R_{ft} we divide the twenty-year period 1953-1972 into four five-year subperiods, while for R_{zt} and R_{mt} we use three five-year periods and a final four-year period. Table 14-1 shows overall and subsample means and standard deviations for each of the variables, along with the analysis of variance F-statistics and their cumulative probabilities. An analysis of variance tests the hypothesis that all of the subsample means for any given variable come from the same population. Large F-statistics and cumulative probabilities cause rejection of the hypothesis.

The analysis of variance tests are quite consistent with the hypothesis that $E(\tilde{R}_{mt})$, the expected return on our proxy for the market portfolio, is constant during the 1953-1972 period. Indeed, the low F statistic and visual inspection indicate that the subperiod means of R_{mt} are rather strikingly close to one another. And a cumulative probability slightly in excess of 0.9 is not strong evidence against the hypothesis that the expected real rate of interest $E(\tilde{R}_{ft})$ is constant during the 1953-1972 period. In short, on the basis of the evidence in Table 14-1 we cannot reject the hypothesis that the expected returns on the portfolios that define the investment opportunity set of the Sharpe-Lintner version of the two-parameter model are constant during the sample period covered by our data.

The same conclusion does not hold for the Black model. There is strong evidence in Table 14-1 that $E(\tilde{R}_{zt})$, the expected return on our proxy for the minimum-variance zero-β portfolio, is not constant during the 1953-1971 period.

But the conclusion that $E(\tilde{R}_{mt})$ and $E(\tilde{R}_{ft})$ are stationary while $E(\tilde{R}_{zt})$ is not seems strange. For example, if shifts in $E(\tilde{R}_{zt})$ reflect

Table 14-1. Tests for Stationarity of Expected Returns: ANOVA

Variable	R_{mt}	R_{zt}
F statistic	0.28	5.70
Fractile	0.15	>0.99

Degrees of freedom = 3,224

Variable	Δ_t	R_{ft}
F statistic	24.00	2.40
Fractile	>0.99	0.92

Degrees of freedom = 3,236

	$\bar{R}_m$	$s(R_m)$	$\bar{R}_z$	$s(R_z)$
1953-71	0.0101	0.0372	0.0056	0.0314
1953-57	0.0101	0.0349	0.0113	0.0208
1958-62	0.0117	0.0371	0.0121	0.0286
1963-67	0.0118	0.0293	-0.0081	0.0303
1968-71	0.0059	0.0483	0.0076	0.0413

	$\bar{\Delta}$	$s(\Delta)$	$\bar{R}_f$	$s(R_f)$
1953-72	-0.0019	0.0023	0.0008	0.0019
1953-57	-0.0010	0.0026	0.0005	0.0024
1958-62	-0.0011	0.0019	0.0008	0.0020
1963-67	-0.0018	0.0017	0.0014	0.0016
1968-72	-0.0038	0.0016	0.0007	0.0015

shifts in expected returns on low risk assets, we should also observe shifts in $E(\tilde{R}_{ft})$, and this is not the case.

It is our suspicion that the difference between the analysis of variance results for R_{zt} and those for R_{mt} and R_{ft} reflects the deficiency of our proxy for the minimum variance zero-β portfolio. Thus, comparison of $s(R_m)$ and $s(R_f)$ in Table 14-1 leaves no doubt that, for a *one-month* investment horizon, a one-month Treasury Bill is a very low risk portfolio, at least relative to the risk of our proxy for the market portfolio. And our proxy for R_{mt}, though far from perfect, is at least representative of the investment experience of common stocks; and common stocks are certainly a large part of the true market portfolio. On the other hand, a proxy for R_{zt}, like ours, which is a portfolio of common stocks only, may be so far from the minimum-variance zero-β portfolio called for by the Black model that tests based on the proxy portfolio do not carry much information about the quantity of interest. For example, it is quite likely that the 'true' minimum-variance zero-β portfolio, z, of the Black model is composed primarily of default-free bonds of different maturities with common stocks weighted very little or at least very differently than in our all common stock proxy for z. But since we have no direct evidence on this question, we take the results in Table 14-1 at face value and proceed under the assumption that we have detected changes in $E(\tilde{R}_{zt})$.

Finally, there is strong evidence in Table 14-1 that the expected percent change in purchasing power $E(\tilde{\Delta}_t)$ changes during the 1953-1972 period. Since the expected real rate of interest $(E(\tilde{R}_{ft})$ seems to be constant or nearly so, and since[1][2]

$$\tilde{R}_{ft} \cong \tilde{\Delta}_t + R_{ft}^*,$$

the inference is that the *one*-month nominal rate R_{ft}^*, quoted in the market at time $t-1$, varies in such a way as to offset changes in $E(\tilde{\Delta}_t)$. And this inference is further supported by the finding in Table 14-1 that the standard deviation of the real rate, $s(R_f)$, is less than $s(\Delta)$. But this topic is discussed in more detail later.

14.3.3 Short-Term Changes in Expected Returns

The analysis of variance is a convenient technique for testing for changes in means that persist for some time—in the case of Table 14-1, for five- or four-year subperiods. But there may be changes in expected returns that are more transient in nature. For example, R_{mt} may be generated by a stationary autoregressive or moving average process so that $E(\tilde{R}_{mt}|R_{m,t-1}, R_{m,t-1}, \ldots)$ depends on the historical sequence of returns—which is a violation of the independence condition of Equation (14.10). Nevertheless, if the process (and thus its unconditional mean) is stationary, an analysis of variance test like that in Table 14-1 will generally yield the correct conclusion that the unconditional mean of the process is the same in different long subperiods.

Evidence that a variable is generated by some stationary autoregressive-moving average process is to be found in its estimated autocorrelation function. Table 14-2 shows the first three sample autocorrelations for the monthly values of R_{ft}, R_{zt}, R_{mt}, and Δ_t for the period beginning in 1953 and ending in 1971 (R_{zt} and R_{mt}) or 1972 (R_{ft} and Δ_t). The table also shows

$$s(\hat{\rho}) = \sqrt{1/N},$$

where N is the number of months in the period (228 or 240) and $s(\hat{\rho})$ is an estimate of the standard error of the sample autocorrelation under the assumption that the true autocorrelation is zero.

From a purely statistical viewpoint, the first-order autocorrelation of R_{zt} in Table 14-2 is large relative to its standard error and in this sense is 'significant'. On the other hand, the square of the sample autocorrelation coefficient for lag τ is an estimate of the proportion of the variance of the variable that can be attributed to a linear relationship between values of the variable τ periods apart. In these terms—and from the practical viewpoint of the effects of autocorrelation on the individual's portfolio decision, these are the relevant terms—the sample autocorrelations of the three return variables, R_{mt}, R_{zt}, and R_{ft}, in Table 14-2, all of which are less than 0.2 in absolute value, are small.

Moreover, there is good reason to suspect that the measured

Table 14-2. Estimated Autocorrelation Functions of Δ_t, R_{ft}, R_{mt} and R_{st}

	1953-71		1953-72	
	R_{mt}	R_{zt}	Δ_t	R_{ft}
$\hat{\rho}_1$	0.11	0.18	0.35	0.10
$\hat{\rho}_2$	0.02	-0.05	0.37	-0.13
$\hat{\rho}_3$	0.01	0.10	0.26	-0.04
$s(\hat{\rho})$	0.06	0.06	0.06	0.06

first-order autocorrelations of the return variables, small as they are, are upward biased. Thus, although R_{mt} is called the return on the market portfolio from the end of month $t-1$ to the end of month t, for many stocks the last trade of month t does not come at the end of the month. The reported return for month $t+1$ for these stocks then reflects the implicit movement in the price of the stock from the last trade of month t to the end of month t. Since there is much positive comovement in the returns on individual stocks, the result is that the reported market return for $t+1$ in part reflects the market return for t. Thus part of the measured positive serial correlation of R_{mt} is a consequence of measurement error—the fact that the individual common stock returns used to compete R_{mt} do not cover the same time period.

As direct evidence on the existence and extent of this effect, we note that the measured first-order autocorrelation of the returns on an equally weighted portfolio of NYSE common stocks for the 1953-1971 period is 0.19, as compared to 0.11 for the value weighted portfolio in Table 14-2. This difference is to be expected since the smaller less actively traded stocks—the stocks most responsible for the spurious measured autocorrelations in the portfolio returns—receive less weight in the value weighted portfolio than in the equally weighted portfolio. By the same token, the effect is also likely to be larger for R_{zt} than for R_{mt}. In constructing the portfolio z, the largest weights are assigned to stocks with measured β's much different from 1.0, and the smaller, less actively traded stocks tend to be heavily represented in that category.

In R_{ft}, the real rate of interest, a similar problem arises from spurious autocorrelation in Δ_t. Although beginning in 1953 all major items in the CPI are sampled on a monthly basis, some items are still sampled less frequently, and even those sampled monthly are not priced at the same time during the month. If the money prices of consumption goods have some positive comovement, the result is some amount of spurious positive autocorrelation in measured percent changes in purchasing power.

In short, from both the practical and the statistical viewpoints the measured autocorrelations of R_{ft} and R_{mt} are not large. From the practical viewpoint the measured first order autocorrelation of R_{zt} is also small, and the apparent statistical significance of the first order coefficient is attenuated by the fact that a large amount of the measured autocorrelation is probably spurious. We conclude that the autocorrelations provide no evidence of short-term changes in expected returns, substantial enough to cause rejection of the independence condition of Equation (14.10).

Although, when looked at individually, the short-term variation of each of the return variables seems random, there is still a chance that there are lead or lag relationships among the three returns which would also be a violation of the independence condition of Equation (14.10). To check this, we examined regressions between pairs of the three return variables for various leads and lags, but no meaningful relationships were identified.

Finally, it is of some interest to note that the behavior of the autocorrelations of $\triangle_t$ is substantially different from the behavior of the autocorrelations of the return variables. After lag 1, the autocorrelations of the return variables are close to zero and they stay close to zero for higher order lags (which we do not report in Table 14-2). On the other hand, the autocorrelation function of $\triangle_t$ is quite flat; the first three coefficients are close in magnitude and only one of the first twelve coefficients is as small as 0.25. Such behavior is consistent with the representation of $\triangle_t$ as the sum of a mean, $E(\tilde{\triangle}_t)$, which itself conforms to some nonstationary process (e.g., a random walk) plus transient noise.[13] And recall that the analysis of variance tests also produce clear evidence of changes in $E(\tilde{\triangle}_t)$.

Moreover, for the 1953-1972 period, the estimated autocorrelations of the nominal rate of interest R_{ft}^* are very close to 1.0 for at least 24 lags, which is strong evidence of a nonstationary process and consistent with the representation of R_{ft}^* as a random walk. But although there is clear-cut evidence that $E(\tilde{\triangle}_t)$ and R_{ft}^* wander through time, neither the analysis of variance tests nor the autocorrelations produce much evidence that $E(\tilde{R}_{ft})$, the expected value of real rate, changes through time. Since $R_{ft} \cong \triangle_t + R_{ft}^*$, the inference is that the wandering of R_{ft}^* offsets the wandering of $E(\tilde{\triangle}_t)$—that is, the variation in the nominal rate of interest is just a reflection of variation in the expected value of the percent change in purchasing power—an idea that we now consider in some detail.

14.3.4 The Nominal Rate of Interest, the Real Rate and the Inflation Rate

The evidence from the analysis of variance tests implies that there are shifts in $E(\tilde{R}_{zt})$ which persist for fairly long periods. We have suggested, however, that since similar results are not observed for R_{mt} and R_{ft}, perhaps the results for R_{zt} are due to the fact that our all common stock version of z is a poor proxy for the minimum-variance zero-β portfolio called for by Black's model. But even if our version of z is a good proxy for the minimum-variance zero-β portfolio, the fact that $E(R_{zt})$ shifts through time is not in itself evidence against the independence conditions summarized in Equation (14.10). To violate (14.10), for $\tau > 0$ there must be a relationship between $E(\tilde{R}_{zt})$ and $R_{z,t-\tau}$, or $R_{m,t-\tau}$, or $R_{f,t-\tau}$ or the current or past return on any other asset or portfolio. The autocorrelations and pairwise regressions discussed in the previous section yield no strong evidence of such relationships. They also yield no important evidence of short-term changes in expected returns of the sort that would imply a violation of (14.10).

But autocorrelations and the analysis of variance are rather general procedures for testing for changes in means. With more specific hypotheses about the way expected returns change through time, perhaps we can devise more powerful tests. In formulating such specific hypotheses, we concentrate on R_{ft}, primarily because hypotheses about the behavior of $E(\tilde{R}_{ft})$ are relatively easy to develop and test.

Ignoring the cross-product term in (14.16), which in monthly data is always trivial, for any month t, the realized real interest rate

$$R_{ft} = R_{ft}^* + \Delta_t .\tag{14.17}$$

On the other hand, it is also true that the nominal rate R_{ft}^*, which is observed at time $t-1$, can be interpreted as the market's expectation at time $t-1$ of the real rate for month t minus its expectation of the percent change in purchasing power:

$$R_{ft}^* = E(\tilde{R}_{ft}) - E(\tilde{\Delta}_t).\tag{14.18}$$

Our general hypothesis is that if there is variation through time in the expected real rate $E(\tilde{R}_{ft})$, this will generally be reflected in the variation of the nominal rate R_{ft}^*. To test this hypothesis, however, we must, more or less arbitrarily, specify some functional relationship between $E(\tilde{R}_{ft})$ and R_{ft}^*. Thus suppose that the relationship between the expected real rate of interest for month t and the nominal rate observed at time $t-1$ is linear:

$$E(R_{ft}|R_{ft}^*) = \gamma_0 + \gamma_1 R_{ft}^*.\tag{14.19}$$

From Equation (14.18), we can then see that (14.19) implies a linear relationship between the expected percent change in purchasing power from $t-1$ to t and R_{ft}^*:

$$\begin{aligned} E(\tilde{\Delta}_t \mid R_{ft}^*) &= \gamma_0 + (\gamma_1 - 1.0)R_{ft}^* \\ &= \gamma_0 - \gamma_2 R_{ft}^*, \qquad\qquad \gamma_2 \equiv 1.0 - \gamma_1. \end{aligned}\tag{14.20}$$

The coefficient γ_0 can be interpreted either as the expected real rate or as the expected percent change in purchasing power, conditional on a zero value of the nominal interest rate. The coefficient γ_1 is the fraction of the nominal rate R_{ft}^* which is added to γ_0 to get the expected real rate for period t, with the remaining fraction $\gamma_2 = 1.0 - \gamma_1$ of R_{ft}^* subtracted from γ_0 to get the expected percent change in purchasing power. Alternatively, differencing (14.19) and (14.20) we find that γ_1 can be interpreted as the fraction of any change in the nominal rate that can be attributed to a change in the expected real rate, while $\gamma_2 = 1.0 - \gamma_1$ is the fraction of any change in R_{ft}^* that reflects a change in the expected percent change in purchasing power.

Since the model postulates linear relationships between the expected real rate for month t and the nominal rate observed at $t-1$ and between the expected percent change in purchasing power and the nominal rate, estimates of the coefficients γ_0, γ_1, and γ_2 of these relationships can be obtained from regressions of R_{ft} on R_{ft}^* and of Δ_t on R_{ft}^*. The results of such regressions for the periods 1953-1972 and 1960-1972 are shown in Table 14-3. The t statistics shown are the usual ratios of parameter estimates to their standard errors, while $\hat{\rho}_\tau$ is the residual serial correlation for lag τ.[14]

The regressions in Table 14-3 provide no clear-cut evidence that the expected real rate of interest changes during the 1953-1972 period. For the 1960-1972 period, the estimate of γ_1 in (14.19) is 0.01 so that almost all of the variation in the nominal rate of interest is a reflection of variation in the expected percent change in purchasing power. For the 1953-1972 period, the point estimate provided by the regressions is that ninety percent of the variation of R_{ft}^* reflects variation in the expected percent change in purchasing power while only ten percent reflects variation in the expected real rate of interest. But in statistical terms, since $t(\gamma_1) = 1.03$, the point estimate $\gamma_1 = 0.10$ does not allow us to say with much confidence that γ_1 is different from zero even for the 1953-1972 period. Thus the regressions do not allow us to reject the hypothesis that the expected real rate of interest is constant during the 1953-1972 period.

Substituting Equation (14.18) into (14.17), we easily determine that the variation through time in the realized real rate of interest R_{ft} has only two sources: variation in the expected real rate $E(\tilde{R}_{ft})$ and deviations of the percent change in purchasing power from its expected value. In contrast, variation in the return on a portfolio of equity investments, like R_{mt}, is also and most likely primarily determined by other sources of uncertainty. (Some indirect evidence

Table 14.3.

$$R_{ft} = \hat{\gamma}_0 + \hat{\gamma}_1 R_{ft}{}^* + \hat{\epsilon}_t$$

1953-72

$$R_{ft} = 0.0006 + 0.10 R_{ft}{}^* + \hat{\epsilon}_t$$

$t(\hat{\gamma}_0) = 2.03 \quad t(\hat{\gamma}_1) = 1.03 \quad \hat{\rho}_1(\hat{\epsilon}) = 0.09, \quad \hat{\rho}_2(\hat{\epsilon}) = 0.13, \quad \hat{\rho}_3(\hat{\epsilon}) = -0.04$

Coeff. of det. = 0.00

1960-72

$$R_{ft} = 0.0010 + 0.01 R_{ft}{}^* + \hat{\epsilon}_t$$

$t(\hat{\gamma}_0) = 2.54 \quad t(\hat{\gamma}_1) = 0.06 \quad \hat{\rho}_1(\hat{\epsilon}) = 0.04, \quad \hat{\rho}_2(\hat{\epsilon}) = 0.08, \quad \hat{\rho}_3(\hat{\epsilon}) = -0.12$

Coeff. of det. = −0.01

$$\Delta_t = \hat{\gamma}_1 - \hat{\gamma}_2 R_{ft}{}^* + \hat{\eta}_t$$

1953-72

$$\Delta_t = 0.0006 - 0.90 R_{ft}{}^* + \hat{\eta}_t$$

$t(\hat{\gamma}_0) = 2.01 \quad t(-\hat{\gamma}_2) = -9.82 \quad \hat{\rho}_1(\hat{\eta}) = 0.09, \quad \hat{\rho}_2(\hat{\eta}) = 0.13, \quad \hat{\rho}_3(\hat{\eta}) = -0.04$

Coeff. of det. = 0.29

1960-72

$$\Delta_t = 0.0010 - 0.99 R_{ft}{}^* + \hat{\eta}_t$$

$t(\hat{\gamma}_0) = 2.52 \quad t(\hat{\gamma}_2) = -8.98 \quad \hat{\rho}_1(\hat{\eta}) = 0.04, \quad \hat{\rho}_2(\hat{\eta}) = 0.08, \quad \hat{\rho}_3(\hat{\eta}) = -0.12$

Coeff. of det. = 0.34

on this is the fact that the standard deviations of R_{ft} in Table 14-1 are trivial relative to the standard deviations of R_{mt}.) Thus if there are general shifts in the level of expected returns on investment assets, they should be most easily identified from the behavior of R_{ft}. This would seem to give added importance to the fact that none of our tests allow us to reject the hypothesis that $E(\tilde{R}_{ft})$ is constant during the 1953-1972 period.

14.4 SHORT-TERM BONDS AND COMMON STOCKS AS HEDGES AGAINST INFLATION

The estimated regressions of Δ_t on R_{ft}^* reported in Table 14-3 do, however, provide strong evidence that the nominal rate of interest, R_{ft}^*, observed in the market at $t-1$, includes a good assessment of the expected percent change in purchasing power from $t-1$ to t. Thus for the 1953-1972 period, about 29 percent of the variance of the percent change in purchasing power, Δ_t, can be attributed to the regression relationship between Δ_t and R_{ft}^*, that is, to variation in $E(\Delta_t | R_{ft}^*)$. For the 1960-1972 period the coefficient of determination is 0.34.

But the best evidence for the conclusion that in setting the nominal interest rate, the market makes a rather good assessment of the expected percent change in purchasing power is in the autocorrelations of the residuals from the regressions of Δ_t on R_{ft}^* in Table 14-3. In Table 14-2, the autocorrelations of Δ_t for the 1953-1972 and 1960-1972 periods are on the order of 0.3 to 0.4. These autocorrelations provide a measure of the extent to which one can improve one's estimate of the expected percent change in purchasing power for month t from knowledge of the time series of past values of Δ_t. The autocorrelations of the residuals from the regressions of Δ_t on R_{ft}^* are, however, close to zero. The implication is that the nominal interest rate observed at $t-1$ captures at least all the information about the percent change in purchasing power from $t-1$ to t, that is in the time series of past values of Δ_t.[15]

In short, the evidence in Table 14-3 is that a one-month Treasury Bill is somewhat of a hedge against one-month changes in the purchasing power of money. The accepted dogma, of course, is that common stocks are the appropriate investment instrument for hedging against inflation. Thus we now examine the extent to which common stocks provide a hedge against one-month changes in the purchasing power of money.

The evidence from the analysis of variance tests and autocorrelations does not allow us to reject the hypothesis that the expected real return on our proxy for the market portfolio is constant during the 1953-1971 period. In addition, all of the tests (analysis of variance, autocorrelations, and the regressions of Table 14-3) indicate that $E(\tilde{\Delta}_t)$ does indeed change through time. But these two conclusions do not in themselves imply that the expected nominal return on m, $E(\tilde{R}_{mt}^*)$, adjusts to reflect the variation of $E(\tilde{\Delta}_t)$. In fact, analysis of variance tests and autocorrelations on R_{mt}^* yield numbers and thus conclusions almost identical to those for R_{mt}.[16] Thus we also cannot reject the hypothesis that $E(\tilde{R}_{mt}^*)$ is constant through time. And more 'sophisticated' tests also support this conclusion. Specifically, if all or most of the variation in the nominal rate R_{ft}^* is a reflection of variation in $E(\tilde{\Delta}_t)$, then if $E(\tilde{R}_{mt}^*)$ also adjusts the changes in the expected inflation rate, there should be a positive relationship between $E(\tilde{R}_{mt})$ and R_{ft}^*; that is, $E(\tilde{R}_{mt}^* | R_{ft}^*)$ should be a positive function of R_{ft}^*. Estimated regressions of R_{mt}^* on R_{ft}^* yield no evidence of such a relationship. The estimated slope coefficients in such regressions are always close to zero and are negative at least as often as they are positive.

If $E(\tilde{\triangle}_t)$ changes through time, it is not possible for both the expected nominal and the expected real return on the market portfolio m to be literally constant through time. And the empirical evidence should not be interpreted in this way. Rather it says that any variation in the expected values is so small relative to other sources of variation in $\tilde{R}_{mt}$ and $\tilde{R}_{mt}^*$ that any changes in the expected values cannot be identified reliably.

We think that a reasonable way to interpret the combined results is as follows. The regressions in Table 14-3 indicate that R_{ft}^*, the one-month nominal interest rate observed at $t-1$, contains a rather good estimate of $E(\tilde{\triangle}_t)$, the expected value of the percent change in purchasing power from $t-1$ to t. Thus the market shows some competence in predicting inflation. Moreover, it seems unreasonable that this competence is only exercised in the market for one-month bonds. More likely, whatever assessment of $E(\tilde{\triangle}_t)$ is included in R_{ft}^* is also included when the market sets the prices of all other assets at $t-1$. Thus the fact that we cannot identify changes in $E(\tilde{R}_{mt}^*)$ in response to changes in $E(\tilde{\triangle}_t)$ does not mean that the response mechanism does not exist. Rather, other sources of variation in $\tilde{R}_{mt}^*$ are so large relative to changes in $E(\tilde{R}_{mt}^*)$ in response to $E(\tilde{\triangle}_t)$ that such changes are not statistically observable.

But even if one-month expected nominal returns on common stocks contain the same assessment of the expected percent change in purchasing power as the one-month nominal interest rate, the one-month bond is still better as a specific hedge against the one-month change in purchasing power. Once the nominal interest rate is set, the only uncertainty in the real return on the one-month bond is in the deviation of the percent change in purchasing power from its expected value, whereas this is a trivial fraction of the uncertainty in the real return on common stock.

14.5 CONCLUSIONS

Although investors face multiperiod decisions problems, there are conditions under which the results of the one-period, two-parameter model apply period by period—that is, at each decision point it is optimal for investors to choose portfolios that are efficient in the mean-variance sense, and each period the relationship between risk and expected one-period return is the familiar Equation (14.2). In addition to the assumptions made in the development of the two-parameter model itself (a perfect capital market, investor risk aversion, and normal distributions of one-period portfolio returns), the critical assumption in a multiperiod context is that, for any t, returns on portfolio assets from $t-1$ to t are independent of stochastic elements of the state-of-the-world at time t that affect investor tastes for given levels of wealth to be obtained at t. This 'independence condition' is stated formally in Equation (14.10).

One such element of the state-of-the-world is the nature of investment opportunities to be available at time t. For example, if the level of expected returns on investment portfolios to be available at time t is to some extent uncertain at time $t-1$, and if the returns from $t-1$ to t on some investment assets are more strongly related to the level of expected returns at t than returns on other assets, then the former assets are better vehicles for hedging against the level of expected returns at t. As shown by Merton (1972), this can affect the demands for assets and their prices in such a way that the simple results of the one-period, two-parameter model no longer hold.

In the empirical tests of this study, however, there is no evidence of measurable relationships between returns on investment assets from $t-1$ to t and the level of expected returns to be available at t. Indeed, in our opinion there is no reliable evidence that the level of expected returns changed during the 1953-1972 period.

But our tests of the independence condition of Equation (14.10) are only a short step toward establishing the relevance of the results of the two-parameter model in a multiperiod world. We look at the implications of (14.10) for relationships between returns on investment assets and characteristics of investment opportunities. We ignore, for example, the important question of whether there are any relationships between returns on particular sets of investment assets and prices of given consumption goods of the sort that would represent a violation of (14.10). Moreover, in concentrating on the characteristics of investment opportunities, we further limit attention to one parameter, the expected return, and we look only at proxies for those portfolios that determine the investment opportunity set in the Black (1972) and Sharpe (1964)-Lintner (1965) two-parameter models of capital market equilibrium. Obviously, much remains to be done.

NOTES TO SECTION FOURTEEN

1. A complete development of expressions (14.2), (14.4) and (14.5) is given by Black. The Black model is an extension of the Sharpe-Lintner model, which

in turn is an extension of the two-parameter portfolio model of Markowitz (1959). For a discussion of the history of the two-parameter model and related empirical work, see Jensen (1972). For a discussion of the interpretation of Equation (14.2) as a direct implication of the efficiency of the market portfolio, see Fama and Miller (1972, ch. 7), and for a discussion of the interpretation of β_j of Equation (14.3) as a measure of relative risk, see Fama and MacBeth (1973).

2. At the expense of complications that are merely notational, n can be made to depend on t or on ϕ_t. As shown in Fama (1970), the model is also easily extended to allow the time of death to be stochastic.

3. For detailed discussions of the relationships between utility functions for dollars of consumption and utility functions for consumption goods, see Fama (1972), or Fama and Miller (1972, chs. 1 and 8).

4. For a review of the literature on this question, see Fama (1970b).

5. It is well to note, however, that when the one-period problem is stated in (14.6) in terms of a utility function $U(c_1, c_2)$ that includes only dollars of consumption as arguments, the implicit assumption is either that prices of consumption goods at time 2 are perfectly predictable at time 1 or that they are statistically independent of returns on investment assets from time 1 to time 2. Thus the assumption that $\tilde{P}_{t+1}$ and $\tilde{R}_{t+1}$ are independent is also implicit in the one-period model.

6. A similar statement does not necessarily apply to common stocks. Considered alone, a permanent shift in the level of equilibrium expected percent returns on common stocks implies a negative relationship between returns observed at $t+1$ and the characteristics of investment opportunities at $t+1$. But such a relationship need not exist (or be substantial enough to be observed), if the shifts in expected returns are positively correlated with permanent shifts in the expected cash payoffs on common stocks.

7. Merton himself recognizes and discusses cases where, although investors are risk-averse with respect to lifetime consumption, they can be risk averters or risk preferrers with respect to specific sources of uncertainty.

8. From the facts that $E(\tilde{R}_{mt}) > E(\tilde{R}_{zt})$ and $\tilde{R}_{mt}$ and $\tilde{R}_{zt}$ are uncorrelated, Black shows that there is a positive value of β_e, call it β_e^*, which separates efficient minimum-variance portfolios ($\beta_e \geq \beta_e^*$) from inefficient minimum-variance portfolios ($\beta_e < \beta_e^*$). Thus the zero-β portfolio z is itself inefficient. For a geometric discussion see Jensen (1972) or Fama and MacBeth (1974).

9. This purity in the use of real returns turns out to be unnecessary. In every case, the estimates of portfolio β's computed from real returns are trivially different from the estimates computed from nominal returns. And in the regression of real portfolio returns for month t on estimates of β's from real returns, the slope coefficient is the same as in the nominal regression, and the intercept (our proxy for R_{zt}) is the intercept from the nominal regression plus the percent change in purchasing power for month t.

10. At time $t-1$, the one-month nominal interest rate R_{ft}^* is known, but prior to $t-1$, R_{ft}^* is not known and must be treated as a random variable. In addition, the real return on a one-month Bill, $\tilde{R}_{ft}$, is also a random variable because of uncertainty about $\tilde{\Delta}_t$.

11. See Scheffé (1959, ch. 10).

12. For returns on one-month Treasury Bills the cross-product term $R_{ft}^* \triangle_t$ in Equation (14.16) is always trivial relative to R_{ft}^* and $\triangle_t$. See Fama (1973).

13. This is discussed in some detail in Fama (1973).

14. Since R_{ft} is computed from the exact expression (14.16), the fact that the estimates of γ_0 obtained from the regressions of R_{ft} on R_{ft}^* are the same as those obtained from the regressions of $\triangle_t$ on R_{ft}^* is testimony to the adequacy of the approximation given by (14.17) and thus to the development of Equations (14.17) through (14.20). Indeed the only hint in the regressions that (14.17) is an approximation is in the slight differences between the t statistics of $\hat{\gamma}_0$ in the two sets of regressions.

15. This line of reasoning is developed in detail in Fama (1973) where it is argued that the nominal rate actually captures much more information than is in past values of $\triangle_t$.

16. In fact, the time series variation of the real returns on the portfolios m and z is not much different from the time series variation of the nominal returns. For example, for the 1953-1971 period, the standard deviations of the nominal returns on m and z are the same up to four decimal places as the standard deviations of the real returns. The primary reason for the very similar behavior of the real and nominal returns on these portfolios is clear from Table 14-1. Variation in the percent change in purchasing power $\triangle_t$ is trivial relative to the variation of R_{zt} and R_{mt}. Specifically, the standard deviations of R_{zt} and R_{mt} are about 15 and 20 times larger than the standard deviations of $\triangle_t$, so that the variances of R_{zt} and R_{mt} are, respectively, over 200 and over 400 times larger than that of $\triangle_t$.

REFERENCES

Black, F., 1972, Capital Market Equilibrium with Restricted Borrowing, *Journal of Business* XLV, 444-455.

Black, F., M. Jensen and M. Scholes, 1972, The Capital Asset Pricing Model: Some Empirical Results, in: M. Jensen, ed., Studies in the theory of capital markets (Praeger, New York).

Fama, E.F., 1970a, Multiperiod Consumption-Investment Decisions, *American Economic Review* LX, 1963-174.

Fama, E.F., 1970b, Efficient Capital Markets: A Review of Theory and Empirical Work, *Journal of Finance* XXV, 383-417.

Fama, E.F., 1972, Ordinal and Measurable Utility, in: M. Jensen, ed., Studies in the Theory of Capital Markets (Praeger, New York).

Fama, E.F., 1973, Short-Term Interest Rates as Predictors of Inflation, unpublished.

Fama, E.F. and J.D. MacBeth, 1973, Risk, Return and Equilibrium: Empirical Tests, *Journal of Political Economy* LXXXI, 607-636.

Fama, E.F. and J.D. MacBeth, 1974, Long-Term Growth in a Short-Term Market, *Journal of Finance* XXIX, 857-885.

Fama, E.F. and M.H. Miller, 1972, The Theory of Finance (Holt, Rinehart and Winston, New York).

Hirshleifer, J., 1965, Investment Decision under Uncertainty: Choice Theoretic Approaches, *Quarterly Journal of Economics* LXXIX, 509-536.

Jensen, M.C., 1972, Capital Markets: Theory and Evidence, *Bell Journal of Economics and Management Science* III, 357-398.

Lintner, J., 1965, The Valuation of Risk Assets and the Selection of Risky Investments in Stock Portfolios and Capital Budgets, *Review of Economics and Statistics* XLVII, 13-37.

Markowitz, H., 1959, Portfolio Selection: Efficient Diversification of Investment (Wiley, New York).

Merton, R., 1972, An Intertemporal Capital Asset Pricing Model, *Econometrica* 41, 867-87; also reprinted in this volume.

Officer, R.R., 1971, A Time Series Examination of the Market Factor of the New York Stock Exchange, Ph.D. Dissertation (University of Chicago, Chicago).

Scheffé, H., 1964, The Analysis of Variance (Wiley, New York).

Sharpe, W.F., 1964, Capital Asset Prices: A Theory of Market Equilibrium under Conditions of Risk, *Journal of Finance* XIX, 425-442.

About the Editors

Irwin Friend is Richard K. Mellon Professor of Finance and Economics at The Wharton School, University of Pennsylvania, and Director of its Rodney L. White Center for Financial Research. He is a past president of the American Finance Association.

James L. Bicksler is Director of Research, Graduate School of Business Administration, Rutgers University.

AUTHOR AFFILIATIONS

James L. Bicksler, Graduate School of Business Administration, Rutgers University.

Marshall E. Blume, The Wharton School, University of Pennsylvania.

Marcus C. Bogue, Graduate School of Industrial Administration, Carnegie-Mellon University.

Eugene F. Fama, Graduate School of Business, University of Chicago.

Irwin Friend, The Wharton School, University of Pennsylvania.

Nils H. Hakansson, Graduate School of Business Administration, University of California, Berkeley.

Yoram Landskroner, The Jerusalem School of Business Administration, The Hebrew University of Jerusalem.

John Lintner, Graduate School of Business Administration, Harvard University.

James D. Macbeth, Graduate School of Business, University of Chicago.

Harry M. Markowtiz, IBM.

Robert C. Merton, Alfred P. Sloan School of Management, Massachusetts Institute of Technology.

Steward C. Myers, Alfred P. Sloan School of Management, Massachusetts Institute of Technology.

Richard Roll, Graduate School of Industrial Administration, Carnegie-Mellon University.

Stephen A. Ross, The Wharton School, University of Pennsylvania.

Paul A. Samuelson, Alfred P. Sloan School of Management, Massachusetts Institute of Technology.